JAPAN'S FOREIGN AID

POLITICS IN ASIA AND THE PACIFIC
Interdisciplinary Perspectives

Haruhiro Fukui
Series Editor

Japan's Foreign Aid: Power and Policy in a New Era,
edited by Bruce M. Koppel and Robert M. Orr, Jr.

Popular Protest and Political Culture in Modern China: Learning from 1989,
edited by Jeffrey N. Wasserstrom and Elizabeth J. Perry

Southeast Asia in the New International Era, Clark D. Neher

FORTHCOMING

China Under Reform: A Preliminary Reassessment, Lowell Dittmer

Japan's Land Policy and Its Global Impact, Shigeko N. Fukai

Mass Politics in the PRC: State and Society in Contemporary China,
Alan P.L. Liu

Nationalism in Contemporary Japan, Bruce Stronach

Global Television and the Politics of the Seoul Olympics,
James F. Larson and Park Heung-Soo

Comparative Politics of Asia, Sue Ellen M. Charlton

JAPAN'S FOREIGN AID

Power and Policy in a New Era

EDITED BY

Bruce M. Koppel
and Robert M. Orr, Jr.

Westview Press
BOULDER • SAN FRANCISCO • OXFORD

Politics in Asia and the Pacific: Interdisciplinary Perspectives

---

This Westview softcover edition is printed on acid-free paper and bound in library-quality, coated covers that carry the highest rating of the National Association of State Textbook Administrators, in consultation with the Association of American Publishers and the Book Manufacturers' Institute.

Published in 1993 in the United States of America by Westview Press, Inc., 5500 Central Avenue, Boulder, Colorado 80301-2877, and in the United Kingdom by Westview Press, 36 Lonsdale Road, Summertown, Oxford OX2 7EW

Library of Congress Cataloging-in-Publication Data
Japan's foreign aid : power and policy in a new era / edited by Bruce M. Koppel and Robert M. Orr.
p. cm.
Includes bibliographical references and index.
ISBN 0-8133-8643-8
1. Economic assistance, Japanese. I. Koppel, Bruce M.
II. Orr, Robert M.
HC60.J375 1993
338.9'152—dc20 92-38896
CIP

Printed and bound in the United States of America

The paper used in this publication meets the requirements of the American National Standard for Permanence of Paper for Printed Library Materials Z39.48-1984.

10 9 8 7 6 5 4 3 2 1

Contents

Acknowledgments

Putting together a collection of this scope required the cooperation of many people and institutions. Indeed, we are especially proud of the international collaboration that characterizes this volume.

We first thank the contributing authors, most of whom came together with us in June, 1990 at the East-West Center to discuss the concept of this book and the issues that needed to be addressed. As Japanese aid system officials became aware of what we were doing, they offered cooperation in many ways, and for that we and the contributing authors are grateful. As the papers came in and the editing rounds began, we want to thank Jeni Miyasaki and Cynthia Nakachi for their help in typing, formatting, and pursuing various queries. Finally, we want to acknowledge four individuals who played especially important roles as the project progressed: Ambassador Julia Chang Bloch, formerly head of the Asia Bureau in USAID, and a prime mover in the United States-Japan aid dialogue; Lori Foreman, currently with the Nature Conservancy but formerly an assistant to Ambassador Bloch at USAID and a source of much insight on the American and Japanese foreign aid systems; Masaji Takahashi, a long-time senior official in JICA and consul-general in Honolulu during the time we were putting the book together; and Shinsuke Horiuchi, the executive director of the Foundation for Advanced Studies in International Development in Tokyo and an individual with an extremely fresh perspective on the past and future of Japan's ODA.

Bruce M. Koppel
Robert M. Orr, Jr.

1

A DONOR OF CONSEQUENCE: JAPAN AS A FOREIGN AID POWER

Robert M. Orr, Jr., and Bruce M. Koppel

Introduction

This book offers the first examination of Japan's foreign aid policies based on a comparative assessment of the evolution of those policies in specific countries and regions. During the last three decades, few developments in the international community have been as striking and rapid as Japan's rise to the pinnacle of world influence. In the late 1970s, it became apparent to many that Japan had arrived as a global trade power. By 1985, following the Plaza accords and the significant appreciation of the yen, Japan also gained recognition as a global financial superpower.

Almost unnoticed were Tokyo's earlier decisions to dramatically increase foreign aid expenditures, starting with the doubling plans announced by Prime Minister Takeo Fukuda in 1977. By 1978, Japan was already the leading bilateral[1] donor of foreign aid to Asia. By 1989, Japan's global aid disbursements had surpassed all other donors and while the leadership in aid expenditures is likely to shift back and forth between Japan and the United States, this achievement represents a real landmark for Japan as a global economic power.

Turning Points

It was not long ago that Japan was a major recipient of foreign aid. As late as 1964, the year that the Tokyo Olympics took place, the vaunted bullet train was built with World Bank funds. Just three years before, the government had created the first of several institutions designed to implement its own infant foreign aid program. The stated goal of Japan's economic cooperation program, as it was called, was the explicit promotion of Japanese exports. Prime Minister Hayato Ikeda had announced his plans to promote the doubling of national income in 1961 and Japan's aid policy dovetailed nicely with efforts to build the domestic economy. As Alan Rix[2] has shown, this became a fairly constant theme in Japanese aid policy, namely using assistance to address Japan's own vulnerabilities.

Export promotion remained the raison d'etre of the Japanese aid program throughout the 1960s. A turning point in the evolution of Japan's aid policy was the imposition of the Arab oil embargo on industrialized nations viewed as sympathetic to Israel following the Yom Kippur War in 1973. Japan moved rapidly to downgrade the tenuous ties which she maintained with Israel and attempted to appease OPEC Arab states with gifts of foreign aid. Japan hoped that the oil spigots would be turned on again to relieve the fuel shortages that were beleaguering the Japanese archipelago. This policy succeeded in having the oil embargo lifted for Japan, but inadvertently it was also the first step in the true globalization of Japan's aid program. Eventually Japan began to rationalize providing aid in terms of resource diplomacy.

By the late 1970s, Japan faced other vulnerabilities. Washington began to take a tougher look at Tokyo's trade policies as the bilateral balance of payments deficits burgeoned for the United States. As Japan's dependence on America as a trading partner and export market continued to increase, many in Tokyo viewed the potential of U.S. protectionism as yet another threat. Calls for burden sharing and greater participation by Japan in financially supporting collective security arrangements in Asia as well as the global security objectives of the Western alliance were more frequently and openly heard. In response, Japanese officials began to define aid as a component of "comprehensive security," defined at home as related to Japan's security but described to American negotiators and legislators as part of Japan's contribution to Western security. American pressure on Japan helped Japanese Ministry officials make the case for ever larger aid budgets throughout the 1980s. Consequently, during the 1980s, a consensus in support of aid as a foreign policy tool, not simply as an international economic tool, began to emerge.

The Instruments of Economic Cooperation

Forms

Japan possesses a variety of international economic cooperation instruments. The term Official Development Assistance (ODA) is used to describe grants, technical aid, and concessional yen loans extended by the Government of Japan. These, along with non-concessional lending usually coming from the Export-Import Bank of Japan, fall under the rubric of economic cooperation, frequently used by outsiders to describe the full range of Japan's economic relations with developing nations. However, among Japanese aid planners, private investment as well is characterized as economic cooperation. Occasionally Japanese aid planners use ODA and economic cooperation interchangeably. This causes confusion in Western capitals, especially when Japan makes major aid pledges at the annual Group of Seven summits, since other industrialized donors more strictly adhere to the Development Assistance Committee (DAC) definition of ODA.[3]

In providing almost half of its ODA in the form of concessional lending, Japan extends more loans than any other donor. This policy is often criticized in the DAC. Japanese aid policy planners usually rationalize the comparatively low concessionality of their assistance by arguing that it instills discipline in recipients.[4] While it is undoubtedly true that many aid policymakers in Japan adhere to this approach, the two track budgetary system Japan uses to finance ODA must also be regarded as a contributing factor. All of Japanese grant aid is funded by the General Account which is accrued through revenues such as custom's duties and personal income tax. Yen loans, however, are half financed though the General Account while the other half comes from the Fiscal Investment and Loan Program (FILP). The FILP consists largely of the postal savings of Japanese citizens whose loaned funds must be repaid with interest. While reliance upon the FILP as a source for ODA funding has diminished since the 1970s, it is still a significant factor in budgeting for foreign aid and helps to explain why it is so important that the loans extended must be paid back in full.[5]

Purposes

Japanese assistance is characterized by large scale infrastructure such as bridges, dams, highways, airports and port facilities. This approach is quite compatible with "economic cooperation" because it means that often a division of labor exists between the Japanese private sector and the government's efforts. Frequently, the extension of Japanese ODA acts as a seal of approval for private investors who feel that government confidence in a recipient's ability to repay loans means a safer haven for investment.

Another indicator of this "division of labor" is the Japanese approach to graduating aid recipients to the ranks of non-recipients. In the American aid system, when a recipient country attains a certain gross national product (GNP) per capita and/or loses political or security significance, the country graduates. This means it loses eligibility to receive aid. Japan's approach to graduation is gradual. Rather than completely terminating assistance to countries that have comparatively higher GNPs, Japan adjusts the degree of concessionality by changing the mix of grants, concessional yen-loans, and commercial credits. The poorest nations receive largely grants, middle income countries receive concessional loans, and newly industrializing economies see principally non-concessional lending.

Regional Distribution

There have been profound changes in Japan's regional distribution of aid since the early 1970s. Until that time, Japan's ODA was concentrated in the Asia-Pacific region, indeed, peaking at 98 percent in 1972. The oil crisis the following year turned out to be a seed of change, not only in terms of creating a new rationale linking assistance to resource diplomacy, but also in helping policymakers justify a globalization of the program. For the first time, during the administration of Prime Minister Masayoshi Ohira, the Japanese government announced its intention to provide 70 percent of its ODA to Asia, 10 percent to Africa, 10 percent to the Middle East, and 10 percent to Latin America. By 1990, the ratio of Japanese assistance extended to Asia had dropped to 59 percent with increasingly higher percentages to other regions, notably sub-Saharan Africa and eastern Europe.

The Aid Policy-Making System

Japan's aid policy-making system involves representatives from various segments of society. While the day-to-day management of policy is generally led by the bureaucracy, the system is subject to lobbying by the private sector as well as pressure and influence from the public and the National Diet.

Bureaucracy

The Japanese aid program was born from the post-World War II reparations which Tokyo extended to the nations of Southeast Asia. These reparations came primarily in the form of goods rather than funding and laid the basis for the export oriented-aid program which first emerged in the early 1960s.[6]

Initially, non-concessional economic cooperation policy was largely formulated in the Ministry of International Trade and Industry (MITI). By 1960, the Economic Cooperation Bureau in the Ministry of Foreign Affairs was established in order to place more of a foreign policy stamp on economic cooperation. Two agencies were later created to implement policy. In 1961, the Overseas Economic Cooperation Fund (OECF) came into being with the mandate to discharge concessional loans. The following year the government formed the Overseas Technical Cooperation Agency (OTCA) with responsibility for disbursing technical assistance.

Right from the beginning, jurisdictional rivalries within the bureaucracy over control of ODA policy were apparent. The Ministries of Finance (MOF), Foreign Affairs (MOFA), and MITI all claimed that the OECF, the emerging backbone of the system, should be placed under their respective ministries. Finally it was decided to put the OECF under a neutral and much smaller agency, the Economic Planning Agency (EPA). The OTCA was placed under the jurisdiction of the Ministry of Foreign Affairs. In 1974, the OTCA was replaced by the Japan International Cooperation Agency (JICA), an organization with only a slightly different mandate than it's forerunner.

Particularly for yen loans, a four ministry deliberation committee (*Yon Shocho Kyogi Taisei*) was mandated with authority over each and every loan to be extended. Over the years, this system has seen considerable bureaucratic squabbling. This has contributed the seemingly opaque nature of Japanese foreign aid policy. However, as export promotion as an explicit objective of the state waned, the locus of ODA policy-making shifted away from MITI and to MOF and MOFA and it is between these ministries where compromise and conflict carry the most weight in the creation and management of ODA policy today.

Conflict among the ministries revolves around institutional "constituencies." MITI tends to consider Japanese commercial interests a priority in policy-making. MOF focuses on the fiscal responsibility of potential recipients and tends to favor loans. The Finance Ministry is also generally the strongest supporter of providing funds to Multilateral Development Banks (MDBs). This is because MOF retains more influence on MDB policy. MOF is the source for most Japanese government representatives to the multilateral banks. The Economic Planning Agency, weakest of the four within the bureaucracy, tends to side with MOF on many issues. MOFA sees aid policy more in the context of Japan's overall foreign policy interests. This often means strategic considerations including the effect ODA policy decisions might have on the all-important U.S.-Japan relationship.[7] In essence, the four ministry system operates not unlike the Security Council of the United Nations in which each of the permanent members retains a veto power. Even if the veto is not exercised, the possibility of exercising (or foregoing) a veto remains a means of influencing the shape of decisions.

The National Diet

In the United States, the Foreign Assistance Act is the legislative vehicle by which the Congress retains considerable influence over the formation and management of American aid policy. Unlike the Congress, the Japanese Diet has little influence and, in fact, no comparable laws governing foreign aid exist. Japan's aid bureaucracy submits budget requests to the Diet based upon the needs of each of the aid policy formulating and implementing institutions. This contrasts sharply with the American approach, in which Congress reviews appropriations requests country by country and plays additional major roles by legislatively earmarking aid funds for specific nations and functions.

The Diet's interest in Japanese aid has increased in recent years, however, particularly after revelations about a yen-loan kickback scandal which took place in the Philippines during the Marcos regime. The Diet's interest is demonstrated in several ways. For example, in November 1988, a cabinet committee on ODA was created to keep a closer eye on aid. The Liberal Democratic Party's (LDP) Special Committee on External Economic Assistance has increased it's activities requiring top ranking aid bureaucrats to explain policy in much greater detail than in the past. Finally a cadre of both LDP and opposition party members have increasingly sought reform in the aid program. Several Japan Socialist Democratic Party members (JSDP) have even proposed a Japanese version of the Foreign Assistance Act.[8]

Since the Executive Branch in Japan is not as strong as in the United States, Prime Ministerial influence on the aid process is not comparable with the influence the President of the United States can have on U.S. aid policy. If the Prime Minister is particularly interested, as in the case of Yasuhiro Nakasone, his voice on aid policy can be heard. The Prime Minister can also have influence on aid policy simply by what countries are chosen for state visits. As Rix shows us in his chapter on Japanese aid to ASEAN, Prime Ministerial politics in Southeast Asia can have considerable impact on the distribution of ODA funds. Contemporary Japanese diplomatic custom dictates that aid packages be presented with almost all of these visits.

Public Opinion

Until recently the Japanese public could be counted on for firm support for the ODA program. For example, in a survey taken by the Prime Minister's office in 1988, over 80 percent of the respondents supported ODA commitments at current or even higher levels. Despite what appears to be strong support for the program, however, many in the Foreign Ministry are concerned that it may indeed be soft. These concerns are not entirely misplaced.

The Japanese press has increasingly focused on Japanese aid, exposing projects that have been mismanaged and projects with negative social and environmental impacts. Some newspapers have also criticized the Japanese aid program for being too closely connected to American strategic interests. Many in the Ministry worry that these reports will undermine public support for ODA. In an effort to combat the negative press, the Foreign Ministry announced in December 1989 that a survey they undertook showed that 90 percent of Japan's aid was effective. In several cases, the Foreign Ministry has asked journalists to participate in evaluation missions for selected projects. These steps suggest just how sensitive the bureaucracy is to potential downturns in public support. A dramatic drop in support would make it more difficult for the Foreign Ministry to rationalize more aid spending with the Ministry of Finance.

Non-Governmental Organizations

Another source of criticism of Japan's ODA policies has been the non-government organization (NGO) community in Japan. Japan has not had a strong NGO tradition, but as the NGO movement in Japan has gained strength, it has been recognized as both a strong critic of Japan's ODA and as a potentially strong asset for Japan's ODA if appropriate relationships between the NGOs and the aid bureaucracy can be developed.

In the 1980s, most other major bilateral and multilateral donors recognized the special strengths of NGOs, particularly for work on rural development and poverty, and increasing discussions on how best to involve NGOs in aid design and implementation became a common concern. Japan's aid system came to this recognition comparatively slowly, as much for the growing domestic political impact of the Japanese NGOs as for their potential utility in ODA program design and implementation.

In 1985, recommendations that the Japanese ODA system should work more closely with Japanese NGOs succeeded in changing the attitudes of many officials in Tokyo.[9] These recommendations and the positive reaction to them were the results of NGO criticism of Japan's ODA along with deep concern over the dearth of personnel involved in the management of the aid program. Japanese NGOs have been especially concerned about international environmental and humanitarian issues. From this perspective, they have been very critical of Japan's aid program, which they tend to see as beholden to the interests of Japan's big companies. At the same time, there are many who believe that NGOs, along with the private sector, could help take up the slack in the ODA personnel system.

The Private Sector

The private sector has had an important role in the creation and implementation of Japanese foreign aid policy from the initiation of the program. This is partly related to the close relationship between the state and the private sector which is in evidence throughout the Japanese political economy as well as a traditional dearth of governmental personnel in the aid program. The aid system in Japan has simply not kept up with the dramatic budget increases. Japan currently has roughly the same number of aid personnel as Great Britain, which has a program only 1/5 the size of Tokyo's. This means aid planners and implementors are frequently overworked or are unable to carry out proper oversight functions. In addition the Japanese private sector, through it's world-wide network of trading companies and construction firms, is deeply involved in many developing nations, particularly in Asia. In Tokyo, these companies have their own networks through business related associations. These associations often lobby members of the Diet as well as the bureaucracy in an effort to mold policies which favor their interests.

A basic tenet of Japanese foreign aid is the so-called "request basis" (*yosei shugi*) which means that aid must be requested by the recipient rather than the donor proactively offering assistance. This allows Japanese companies to advise the recipient government as to which kind of funding, grants, concessional or non-concessional loans, Tokyo would be most willing to provide. This has also left Japanese firms open to charges of manipulating requests more conducive to corporate rather than recipient interests.

Foreign Aid Modes

The "modes" of foreign aid refer to how foreign aid is actually made available. Every donor establishes regulations which indicate the conditions under which aid can be disbursed. In the 1980s, two issues in particular received wide attention among all donors. The first issue is that of "tying." This refers to requirements set by the donor that goods and services to be purchased with aid funds must come from particular sources or countries. The major criticisms have been directed at donors who establish tying provisions which require that only their own goods and services be utilized. The problem is that such goods and services may neither be the most appropriate nor the most economic. The second issue is that of "policy conditionality." This refers to requirements set by the donor for policy changes to be undertaken by the recipient government. Aid disbursement is linked to the acceptance and implementation of these policy conditionalities by recipient governments.[10] The major criticism has been that the policy conditionalities may favor the economic interests of the donor country, e.g. by making recipient country markets more accessible. The problem is that adoption of such policies as the result of donor conditionalities may not be feasible in social or political terms and does little, in some views, to build an internal constituency for maintaining the policies.

Criticisms of Japan from other donors, particularly the United States, on these two issues have been particularly strong, namely for having too much tied aid and too little policy conditionality.

Tied vs. Untied Aid

In the mid 1980s, Japan embarked upon a major aid untying campaign. According to figures the Japanese government submitted the DAC in 1988, only 12.8 percent of all Japanese ODA was tied, lower than any other member country.[11] Nonetheless, because of the "buddy-system" of Japanese firms, this still begs the question: How much business do Japanese companies actually receive? Under grant assistance, like most donors, including the United States, aid remains strongly tied and Japanese companies win almost all bids. The only exception is through grant aid disbursed directly from the Foreign Ministry and where contract bidding is administered by the British Crown Agents or the United Nations Development Program. This procedure is common for Japanese aid to SubSaharan Africa and is becoming more common in the Indonesia and the Philippines. In general, however, untying grant assistance has proved to be more difficult to rationalize, not least because it comes straight from the taxpayer. In addition, because grant assistance is linked to the annual budget cycle, the funds must be spent within the fiscal year. The government feels it is easier to place pressure on Japanese firms rather than foreign firms to spent the funds within that deadline.

Most of the progress in bona fide untying has come in the area of yen loan procurement. In 1989, only 25 percent of all contracts in the category were won by Japanese firms with most awards going to developing country contractors.

Another long term bone of contention, particularly with the United States, has been the tying that takes place as a result of the engineering specifications of projects. These specifications often result from the fact that Japanese engineering and construction firms are usually engaged to prepare project designs and are not prohibited from subsequently bidding on their own specifications. In some cases, these firms prepare these designs to back up the recipient country's request for aid, a point that can lead to the kinds of conflict discussed in Dr. Prasert's chapter on Thailand. In response to considerable pressure, the OECF began the process of untying this category in 1989 by permitting non-Japanese firms to engage in project design. Japanese firms have not taken the untying process passively and the process itself, e.g. with regard to project design and specifications, is moving slower than some would like.

Japan has made considerable progress in relaxing official tying provisions in Japanese ODA. For example, an increasing proportion of Japanese ODA is under the "general untied" category rather than the more restrictive "LDC untied" category.[12] However, the real issue is not official tying, but rather the intricate web of relationships among Japan's engineering and construction firms and the government aid policy system.

Policy Conditionalities

A major difference between the American and Japanese aid programs has been the Japanese emphasis on economic/commercial concerns while the American aid program has focused more on political/strategic rationales for aid-giving. The United States has also been more willing to link economic and sometimes political policy conditionality to it's assistance in an effort to get recipients to adopt more free market economic and more democratic political principles. By comparison, the Japanese government has been reluctant to place greater explicit pressure on recipients to pursue specific policies. This is particularly true in Asia where Japan is sensitive to Asian concerns about Japan's World War II activities as well as what Japan's international intentions in the region are.[13] The exception to this rule has been in Africa where Japan often has camouflaged conditionality admonishments by saying they were simply being consistent with regional IMF policy.

The end of the cold war, the Gulf War, and the strong criticism directed at Japan for what some saw as a sluggish response to global environmental problems have prompted many politicians and policymakers in Tokyo to reconsider the use of their increasing international political and economic voices. Japanese aid planners now speak of the need to suggest environmental caution to major recipients. The Gulf War showed the dangers of arms exports to volatile leaders in political hotbeds. Thus following the war, Japanese planners have increasingly discussed how to use aid as a means of discouraging arms exports. Prime Minister Toshiki Kaifu proposed collective action in this regard at the London G-7 summit in 1991. Nonetheless, there are practical difficulties in implementing such a policy. For example, Japan's largest recipient of ODA in the 1980s was China, which also happens to be a major arms exporter.

Assessing Japan's Aid Policy

In 1978, Japan became the leading bilateral donor of official development assistance (ODA) in Asia. In 1989, Japan became the leading bilateral donor globally. Japan's ascendance as an ODA power has closely paralleled Japan's rise as an economic power. The association is not accidental. Japan has used ODA as an instrument, along with other instruments, to build international economic relationships and to encourage domestic economic expansion. Other objectives and motives have also been present, ranging from pressure by the U.S. on Japan to growing concerns about political stability and security in Asia to issues of debt relief in Latin America and famine relief in Africa.

However, there is general agreement that Japan's aid has, from the outset, been more closely tied to economic objectives in Japan that would be the case, for example, for American aid. The relationships between Japan's aid and Japan's economic interests have been the focus of several important studies of Japan's aid undertaken during the 1980s. Rix published a landmark volume in 1980 which analyzed the decision-making process and has published several additional articles on this theme. Dennis Yasutomo wrote about the political aspects of Japan's aid strategy in 1986 and has continued an interest in understanding Japan's motivations for aid. Robert M. Orr, Jr. has looked at aid policy-making and the U.S.-Japan relationship in his writings. Shafiq Islam's edited collection of essays on Japan's aid and the edited collection by Ippei Yamazawa and Akira Hirata covered various aspects of all these approaches.[14]

The focus of these studies has primarily been on the formation of Japan's aid policies on a global level. There have been very few studies of Japan's aid policies in the context of specific recipient country settings.[15]There have been no comprehensive nor comparative examinations of the practice of Japan's aid in the context of specific evolving bilateral relations with recipient countries, especially with less developed and middle-income countries. This book addresses these gaps by providing the first collection of studies to comparatively examine Japan's aid policies in the context of evolving international relations, with specific recipient countries and regions.

In addition to the face value of analyzing Japan's interactions with a variety of countries, the studies that follow contribute to strengthened understanding of how Japan makes, manages, and evaluates foreign policy. To ensure this, common terms of reference were developed and agreed to by all the authors. The relevant objectives of those terms were that taken together, the studies would contribute to:

1. improving conceptualization of Japan's ODA policy in the context of Japan's evolving bilateral and regional foreign economic and political policies;

2. assessing how ODA policy and management have been influenced by changing relationships among Japan's international economic and political policies; and
3. evaluating how and why Japan's ODA policies vary between regions and among countries within regions.

For this purpose, each chapter examines Japan's aid relationships with attention to these three central issues:

1. how to best conceptualize Japan's aid policies in the context of an evolving bilateral and regional relationship;
2. how to understand the linkages among Japan's aid policies and other economic and political instruments of Japan's international relationships, and;
3. how to evaluate the utilization of specific modes and levels of ODA.

Improving Conceptualization of Japan's ODA Policy

In terms of how Japan's foreign policy and economic policy systems are interpreted conceptually, understanding has been built principally on the basis of analyses of Japan's economic, political, and security relationships with the U.S. and assessment of relationships between Japan's changing global and regional (primarily economic) roles and Japan's broad foreign policy and economic policy objectives. Debates about how these policies are formed, managed, and evaluated revolve around propositions about characteristics of government-economy relationships, attributes of inter-organizational politics within Japan's bureaucracy, and the roles of external pressure from other Countries (especially the U.S.).

To test the robustness of these conceptions and to assess how policy and administrative systems are changing, what is needed are in-depth country-focused analyses that examine the aid relationship with Japan in the context of an evolving bilateral economic and political relationship. From this perspective, it becomes possible to assess Japan's policies in terms of the balance between the imperatives of global and regional policy preferences and strategies and the specific requirements and opportunities of a given bilateral relationship.

Linkages Among Japan's Economic and Political Policies

In terms of the evolving world economy and Japan's crucial role in it, there are numerous questions about how Japan recognizes, evaluates, and manages economic and political differentiation in the world economy. For example, it is not surprising that the majority of Japan's ODA stays within Asia, but for the same reason it is less clear why the international allocation of Japan's ODA is changing. It is less clear what and who governs levels and terms of ODA within and between regions as well as relationships in specific cases between ODA and trade, investment, and other political, social, and security matters.

Current understandings of Japan's international economic policies revolve around the issues of whether, to what degree, under what circumstances, at what rate, and how Japan manages trade, aid, and investment together. However, to date, the debate has been too narrow. Hypotheses about linkages in Japan's international economic cooperation policies have not been adequately evaluated through comparative analyses of Japan's economic and political relationships with specific countries. Such analyses are necessary to assess how much elasticity there is in Japan's economic cooperation policies, what accounts for this elasticity (or lack of it), and how the elasticity is distributed across policy, programming, and implementation functions as well as among different economic, political, and administrative actors in any bilateral relationship involving Japan as a donor.

Variation in ODA Policies

In what directions, if at all, are Japan's economic cooperation policies--in terms of formation, management, and evaluation--changing, how fast are they changing, and if there is variation by region and country, what is determining this variation now, what will determine the scope of this variation in the future, and who are and will be the major actors and beneficiaries? These questions reference a wide range of points including:

1. Japan's objectives for ODA policies in specific cases, the relationship of these objectives to other political and economic arenas in Japan, as well as associations (and disassociations) with the economic, political, and security objectives of other donors;
2. Assessments of the changing international economic and political environment, how these changes are defined and evaluated by

Japan; and how ODA policies are revised or reinforced as a result in specific countries;

3. Changing modes of cooperation and competition with other donors on both a regional and third country basis;
4. the roles of regionalism and bilateralism as principles in Japanese foreign policy;
5. implementation capabilities and orientations of Japan's aid system, including the status of self-help and request-based assistance as guidelines for aid policy; and
6. the evolution of recipient country donor management capabilities and strategies, especially in a multipolar donor and investment environment, and the relationships of these capabilities and strategies to wider recipient country economic and political decision-making capabilities.

Cases Covered

The studies of specific countries in this book all reference Asia. Five of the countries studied—Indonesia, China, Thailand, the Philippines, and Bangladesh—were the five largest recipients of Japanese aid respectively in 1990.[16] In another, Burma, Japan has been by far the largest donor since the 1950s, and was the site of Tokyo's first post-war reparations. The Republic of Korea is where Japan initiated government to government loans in 1965 and while no longer a recipient of concessional assistance, shows a Japanese approach to graduation policy. Vietnam is where Japan is expected to play a lead role.

This book also offers several broader regional analyses. ASEAN is taken as a separate case study since it represents 35 percent of all Japanese aid annually. The Pacific Island states, Latin America, Africa, and the Middle East each constitute different kinds of problems for Japan's aid policy given changing international demands and domestic impulses for Japan to shoulder more global economic and political responsibilities. Japan's leading role in the Asian Development Bank is explored as an instrument of Tokyo's evolving international economic cooperation strategy and as a case study of Japan's approach to multilateral banks. In our closing chapter, we assess what the studies tell us about the past and future of Japan's ODA, particularly as an indicator of Japan's changing conceptions of its international roles and responsibilities.

Endnotes

1. Foreign aid comes from two types of sources (usually called donors)—bilateral and multilateral. A "bilateral" donor refers to an individual country, e.g., Japan or the United States, that provides the foreign aid. A multilateral donor refers to some form of intergovernmental organization, e.g., the World Bank or the International Monetary Fund, that provides the foreign aid.

2. See Alan Rix, "The Social Basis and Philosophy of Japanese Aid," paper presented at conference-workshop sponsored by the Maureen and Mike Mansfield Foundation, Missoula, Montana, May 14-17, 1987.

3. The DAC is based in Paris and is an organ of the Organization for Economic Cooperation and Development. The Committee consists of all the European donors, plus Australia, Canada, Japan, and the United States. According to the DAC, the following criteria must be met if aid is to qualify as ODA. First, it must be provided by an official agency of the donor. Second, the objectives of the assistance must be mainly to promote the economic development and welfare of the recipient country. Third, the aid must be sufficiently concessional to avoid becoming a severe burden on the developing country and must convey a grant element of at least 25 percent. ODA can consist of capital grant assistance, technical cooperation, capital subscriptions, government loans, or contributions to United Nations agencies and international financial institutions.

4. Susan J. Pharr has suggested that in this sense Japanese foreign aid policy resembles aspects of a Republican administration's domestic policy in the United States. See Susan J. Pharr's statement before the Subcommittee on Asian and Pacific Affairs, Committee on Foreign Affairs, House of Representatives, September 28, 1988., p.11.

5. Jun Nishikawa, "Japan's Economic Cooperation: New Visions Wanted," *Japan Quarterly*," (October-December 1989), p. 394.

6. Masaya Shiraishi, *Japan's Relations with Vietnam: 1951-1988* (Ithaca: Cornell Southeast Asia Program, 1990), p. 22.

7. For further discussion of the aid policy process in Japan, see Alan Rix, *Japan's Economic Aid* (New York: St. Martin's Press, 1980) and Robert M. Orr, Jr., *The Emergence of Japan's Foreign Aid Power* (New York: Columbia University Press, 1990).

8. Toshiaki Takatsuka, "Kokkai kara Mita Seifu Kaihatsu Enjo," (The Diet Looks at ODA) *Gaiho Jiho* (Revue Diplomatique), No. 1266 (March 1990): p. 35. The JSDP was formerly known as the Japan Socialist Party (JSP).

9. See the paper: ODA Jisshi ni Koritsuka Kenkyukai (Research Group to Improve the Implementation of ODA), "Seifu Kaihatsu Enjo no Kokateki Koritsuteki Jisshi ni Tsuite" (About Efficient and Effective Implementation of ODA), Tokyo, December 1985.

10. In practice, conditionalities can be "hard" and "soft." Hard conditionalities mean that unless a recipient government agrees to certain policy changes, the aid will not come. IMF standby programs typically involve hard conditionalities that are summarized in the agreements. Soft conditionalities do not have an explicit "do it or else" linkage, but rather there is a more implicit link. In such cases, the aid project description might not state that the aid required the policy change, but rather might indicate that since a government was undertaking a policy change, aid was needed to help support it. In the 1980s, most bilateral donors engaged in some form of soft conditionality for non-socialist economies and something closer to hard conditionality for many of the transforming socialist economies in Europe and Asia.

11. Ministry of Foreign Affairs, *Wagakuni no Seifu Kaihatsu Enjo* (Our Country's Official Development Assistance), vol. 1 (Tokyo: Association for the Promotion of International Cooperation, 1990), p. 29. (Hereafter cited as *Wagakuni*).

12. "General untied" means that procurement of goods and services can be from any source. "LDC untied" means that procurement of goods and services can come from any country classified as an LDC or from Japan.

13. See: Bruce Koppel and Michael Plummer, "Japan's Ascendancy as a Foreign-Aid Power: Asian Perspectives," *Asian Survey* (November, 1989)29.11: pp 1043-1056.

14. See: Shafiq Islam, ed., *A Yen for Development* (New York: Council on Foreign Relations, 1991); Ippei Yamazawa and Akira Hirata, ed., *Development Cooperation Policies of Japan, the United States, and Europe* (Tokyo: Institute of Developing Economies, 1992). Publications by Alan Rix include: *Japan's Economic Aid: Policy-Making and Politics* (London: Croom Helm, 1980); *Japan's Aid Program: Quantity and Quality* (Canberra: Australian International Development Assistance Bureau, 1987); and *Japan's Aid Program: A New Global Agenda* (Canberra: Australian International Development Assistance Bureau, 1990.) Publications by Dennis T. Yasutomo include: *The Manner of Giving: Strategic Aid and Japanese Foreign Policy* (Lexington, MA: Lexington

Books, 1986); "Why Aid? Japan as an Aid Great Power?" *Pacific Affairs* (Winter, 1990), vol. 62., pp. 1-40. Publications by Robert Orr include: *The Emergence of Japan's Foreign Aid Power* (New York: Columbia University Press, 1990); and "The Aid Factor in U.S.-Japan Relations," *Asian Survey* (July, 1988), Vol. 28, pp. 740-56.

15. An exception that actually helped motivate this book was: Bruce Koppel with the assistance of Hirohisa Kohama, Akira Takahashi, and Toru Yanagihara, *Japan-U.S. ODA Cooperation: Perspectives from India, Indonesia, and the Philippines*. Background paper for the Conference on ODA Management and Asia's Economic Development, Honolulu, Hawaii: East-West Center, 1988. See also: Koppel and Plummer, "Japan's Ascendency as a Foreign Aid Power."

16. *Wagakuni* (1991), p.87.

2

MANAGING JAPAN'S AID: ASEAN

Alan Rix

Introduction

The Association of South-East Asian Nations (ASEAN)[1] has always posed a problem for Japanese aid: how to acknowledge and support ASEAN as a viable and effective grouping, while satisfying the varied and often conflicting needs of each of the member countries. The Japanese Ministry of Foreign Affairs does not greatly emphasize ASEAN as a separate category in its aid figures, but individually and collectively the ASEAN countries are (with China) the top priority in Japan's bilateral ODA. Successive Japanese prime ministers in recent years have all supported the ASEAN relationship. Former Prime Minister Nakasone associated himself closely with improving ASEAN relations (notably in science and technology assistance, technical training, and trade promotion). The former Foreign Minister, Mr. Abe, reaffirmed Japan's commitment to economic cooperation with ASEAN in an important speech in Manila in June 1986, and included a range of promises on local cost financing, more diverse loans, technical cooperation, ASEAN export promotion, technology transfer and Japanese investment. Mr. Takeshita launched the ASEAN-Japan Development Fund at the ASEAN Summit in September 1988. Just before he left office in 1989, he visited ASEAN to reaffirm Japan's commitment to the Association, particularly in the areas of "human resource development" and industrial adjustment in ASEAN. Of special importance were government and private assistance to develop infrastructure for export-oriented industries.

ASEAN is undoubtedly of central importance to the Japanese aid effort. This chapter assesses what the Japanese say and do about ASEAN aid, how their approach has changed over recent years, and what has influenced these changes. ASEAN poses particular problems of aid management for Japan at both macro and micro levels.

Japan's ODA to ASEAN

Table 2.1 sets out Japanese bilateral ODA to each of the ASEAN countries in 1980, 1985 and 1990. The group's share of Japan's bilateral ODA is the largest identifiable segment of Japan's total ODA. From 1980-1990, it declined only a small amount (from 36% to 33%), although in 1978 it was 44.7 per cent of Japan's total bilateral ODA. Aid to ASEAN is now three times the share of ODA going to China. Within total ASEAN flows, there have been shifts in the balance of the separate recipients. Singapore and Brunei, as relatively wealthy countries, receive only small amounts of aid while Indonesia, the Philippines, and Thailand, traditionally the main recipients, continue to receive the largest flows. Indonesia remains the focus of Japan's Southeast Asian aid priorities, but Japan also supports Thailand as a key factor in mainland security, economic development, and Japanese investment flows. Japan also recognizes Malaysia's strategic location and resource reserves, and its policies of learning from Japan's experience. The large loans to Malaysia in the mid-80s were mainly for gas development, the Port Kelang power station, the ASEAN fertilizer project, and other infrastructure works.

Grants to ASEAN countries have not increased as rapidly as loans. ODA grants to ASEAN in 1980 were 28.1 per cent of total bilateral grants. By 1990 the share had fallen to 10.6 per cent. This reflects the diversification of capital grants towards poorer countries. Singapore and Malaysia attract loans rather than grants, but Thailand, the Philippines, and Indonesia still remain among the top recipients of Japan's grant aid. In loans, ASEAN has remained the leading aid recipient group, and actually increased its share of total bilateral loans during the 1980s (39.7 per cent in 1980 and 50.5 per cent in 1990).

Grants include capital grants and technical assistance. In the technical assistance field, ASEAN is again at the forefront among Japan's aid recipients. Training for ASEAN students is the main priority under the technical training program, as a result of the Japan-ASEAN Science and Technology Cooperation scheme. ASEAN was also

TABLE 2.1 Japan's ODA Disbursements to ASEAN Countries, 1980, 1985, and 1990 (disbursement basis, US$ millions)

	Grants	*Loans*	*Total*	*% of Japan's Bilateral ODA*
Indonesia				
1980	59	290	350	17.9
1985	76	84	161	6.3
1990	701	167	868	12.5
Philippines				
1980	35	59	94	4.8
1985	70	170	240	9.4
1990	494	153	647	9.3
Thailand				
1980	70	119	189	9.7
1985	117	147	264	10.3
1990	172	246	419	6.0
Malaysia				
1980	13	53	66	3.3
1985	24	102	126	4.9
1990	60	312	372	5.3
Singapore				
1980	6	-2	4	0.2
1985	12	-4	8	0.3
1990	14	-24	-10	--
Brunei[a]				
1985	1	-	1	0.04
1990	3	-	3	0.04

[a]Brunei received no aid in 1980.
Source: MOFA, MITI and DAC statistics.

the target for a program to invite young ASEAN farmers, workers, and teachers to visit Japan and meet their Japanese counterparts.[2] An emphasis on ASEAN is seen in other parts of the technical aid program—equipment, project-based technical aid, and development surveys.[3] Indeed in 1988, 33 per cent of all the development surveys were conducted in ASEAN countries. Likewise, there is an emphasis on

ASEAN in Japan's cultural relations assistance, notably in the provision of educational resources and Japanese language and studies programs.

What Determines the Aid Relationship?

The reasons for ASEAN's high aid profile are to be found in Japan's concerns about its long-term interests being endangered by events in the ASEAN region. Like many motives for foreign aid, Japan's aid to ASEAN is, at its crudest, an expensive insurance policy, and much more deliberately so than Japan's aid to other recipients. The Ministry of Foreign Affairs' 1989 aid report blandly states that:

> In regard to the distribution of aid to Asia, the allocation from hereon of a considerable portion of Japan's aid to that region is seen as appropriate, because of (1) our close relations within Asian countries, (2) the presence of low income countries with large populations and high development needs, (3) middle-income countries such as ASEAN having large demands for capital, particularly loans.[4]

While the Ministry of Foreign Affairs recognizes calls by the Development Assistance Committee and other international bodies to spread its aid more widely to poorer nations, and indicates a preparedness to do so, the central emphasis on Asia will not be changed. There will, however, be severe pressure on aid flows to ASEAN from greater Japanese commitments to other Asian nations, and Japanese support for economic development in Eastern Europe. The size of future aid budget increases will be one pointer to Japan's capacity to meet all these demands.[5]

The fundamental importance of ASEAN as a group of aid recipients to Japanese aid policy is nonetheless undiminished. The primary influence shaping Japan's aid policy towards ASEAN has been Japan's postwar approach to the Southeast Asian region based on a policy of risk management. A second element comprises the various bilateral relationships that have evolved with each of the ASEAN member countries, while a third element has been the Japanese political and administrative structures managing aid to ASEAN. Notable here is the heavy reliance on prime ministerial diplomacy in dealing with ASEAN. Furthermore, despite the excess of diplomatic rhetoric that envelops these relations, Japanese objectives have always been clear, and uppermost in driving the ASEAN aid program.

Japan's Historical Risk Management Approach to the Region

Japan's Southeast Asian diplomacy began before the Second World War, as policies of *nanshin* (southward advance) and the economic benefits to Japan of trade with the region became fully realized.[6] The economic rationale for military domination of the region from 1941 to 1945 was paramount and, in the postwar period, there have been several main features of Japan's Southeast Asian policy that can be disentangled.

First, there is an emphasis on trade and, later, investment relations. The initial thrust of Japan's postwar "economic cooperation" with Southeast Asia had this as its basis.[7] In the early postwar period, the trade promotion aspect dominated the aid program, bound up as it was both with reparations and the re-establishment of Japan's trade diplomacy.

Second, there is an emphasis on resources. While a part of trade, they nonetheless involve a separate set of actions and policies. Relations with all the countries of ASEAN have incorporated a "resources diplomacy" aspect involving energy, mineral and timber raw materials and food. The same thrust is seen today in the China aid relationship. ASEAN resource suppliers have also welcomed the market that Japan provides, although one of the early tensions in the Japan-ASEAN relationship concerned resource imports and supplies. It alerted Japan to the collective bargaining power of the Association and arose from 1973 criticism from ASEAN natural rubber producers about production and support of Japan's synthetic rubber that threatened the ASEAN industry.[8] Japan still relies on ASEAN as a supplier of vital resources and raw materials. This is likely to continue as demands increase for new types of resources (e.g. rare metals and rare earths for high tech industries). In its resources policy for the year 2000, MITI has signalled the closer linking of aid with resource exploration and exploitation.[9]

Third is the broader issue of Japan's national security. This involves both economic and military security. The Japanese Government has long held to the philosophy that Japan's security is premised on, amongst other things, the security and stability of Southeast Asia. This message has been translated into many facets of Japan's Southeast Asian diplomacy. While a special relationship with ASEAN was Japan's major priority after the end of the Vietnam War, it was still linked to a wider notion of Japanese security interests in the region, as well as U.S. security objectives.[10] These revolved around protection for the Straits of Malacca and the Lombok Strait, maintenance of stable political systems in the region (not necessarily democratic but not communist), the fostering of close relations with political elites in the region, and support for the economic bases of those regimes. The primacy of political stability was seen by Japan to rely on economic development as its mainstay, and to this priority Japan tailored its economic aid program. As Heishiro Ogawa, a former ambassador to China, puts it:

> As for the Asian region as a whole, we first need to look at ASEAN's formation and consolidation. This process is helpful to Asia's stability. We must properly assist, and cooperate in its future nurturing. If China, Indochina and ASEAN can each consolidate and stabilize, it will be beneficial in creating stability in Asia.[11]

Trade, resources, diplomacy, and security as components of the foundation to Japan's ASEAN aid was reinforced in the period following the Fukuda initiative of 1977. The emptiness of Japan's ASEAN policy and its unwillingness to take ASEAN cooperation seriously[12] was partly rectified by the Fukuda Doctrine. What Prime Minister Fukuda did was to accept the inevitability of ASEAN as a basis for realistic economic and political policies, the need for these policies to be stated frankly, and the need for consistent direction and purpose in Japan's approach.

ASEAN was therefore a new element in Japan's Southeast Asian policy after the mid-1970s, and has remained so because of continuing instability in Indochina, difficulties in the relationship with Burma, strong economic growth in some member countries, and the mutually beneficial nature of relations as they have developed with ASEAN since the enunciation of the Fukuda Doctrine in 1977. The principles set out in that Doctrine (rejection of a regional Japanese military role, close and friendly ties, and an equal partnership) encapsulated many existing policy objectives, but did inject a new element, the "equality of partnership." In setting an objective of close and friendly relations between ASEAN and Japan, the Fukuda Doctrine shaped the way policy was developed thereafter. For example, the centrality of ASEAN concerns to Japan's aid to China was stressed by Prime Minister Ohira in 1979.[13] As Elsbree and Hoong suggest, Japan's ASEAN policy is the mainstay of its Southeast Asian political policy, but an asymmetrical economic relationship will remain.[14] Japan is, however, attempting to address that imbalance, with its major push for industrial development in Asia.

Bilateral Relationships

The second element of Japan's approach to ASEAN has been its ongoing relationship with each of the five (now six) member nations. Each has its special features and own dynamics. Most of Japan's dealings with the region are at the bilateral level. Indeed, there is a strong view amongst some in Japan that ASEAN's strength could be a threat to Japan. This was undoubtedly a factor in Japan's initial reactions to ASEAN's establishment. It still lingers twenty years later. For example, a former ambassador to Thailand and South Korea, Torao Ushiroku, argues that

> It is clear that the ASEAN countries are important to Japan, but there are doubts about its solidarity as a group. Would it not be longer lasting if ASEAN were a loose grouping, without ambitious joint activities? It would be easier to construct a basis of economic co-operation with ASEAN and individual bilateral cooperation from this perspective.[15]

There are undoubtedly "ASEAN" features that are increasingly setting the broad parameters for bilateral aid ties with Japan, and into which some aspects of bilateral programs are fitted. For example, the Ministry of Foreign Affair's *Japan and ASEAN* publicity book celebrating ASEAN's twenty years of establishment, refers to the following formal meeting forums:[16] Japanese prime ministerial visits to ASEAN; ASEAN Foreign Ministers' meetings (and the post-ministerial conferences); Japan-ASEAN Economic Ministers' Conferences, and the Japan-ASEAN Forums. It also lists the following joint programs: ASEAN industrial projects; ASEAN human resources development; plant renovation; science and technology cooperation; ASEAN-Pacific human resources cooperation; ASEAN trade, investment and tourism promotions center; cultural cooperation; young people's visits programs; Japanese language education; ASEAN youth scholarships; and research cooperation. Alongside these broad joint programs, and the new ASEAN-Japan Development Fund, bilateral capital and technical cooperation is still vigorously pursued. This will be discussed in detail below.

Japan's ODA Decision-making Structures

A third influence on Japan-ASEAN relations has been the decision-making structure for aid. There is no doubt that, after 1976, Japan began a concerted policy push to cement its ties with ASEAN, and ASEAN has since enjoyed a special status in Japanese foreign policy. The regularity of prime ministerial diplomacy has helped maintain this favored status, but the wider aid system in Japan reflects mainly the entrenched bilateral aid machinery.

The Ministry of Foreign Affairs (MOFA) divides its Southeast Asian responsibilities into Indochina plus Thailand and Burma on the one hand, and the other ASEAN countries on the other. Both divisions lie within the Asian Affairs Bureau. Neither the Ministry's Economic Cooperation Bureau nor MITI's Economic Cooperation Department have specific regional divisions.

The Overseas Economic Cooperation Fund (OECF) has three loans divisions that involve ASEAN, Indochina, and Oceania, but not separately. The Japan International Cooperation Agency (JICA) has no geographical divisions, but does have representative offices in all ASEAN countries. OECF has offices in only four—Thailand, Malaysia, Indonesia, and the Philippines. There is, therefore, no simple process of "ASEAN" aid decision-making. It moves between bilateral, regional, and special decision-making processes, but the political input is naturally high.

How have these three elements come together to shape Japan's ASEAN aid policy? It is important to acknowledge Japan's consistency of purpose over a long period in its approach to aid for Southeast Asia—a desire to push economic growth, support regional priorities, maintain friendly ties, extract resources, and promote trade and investment. Familiarity and habit have been paramount in that policy, and once Japan began to take ASEAN seriously in the late 1970s, bilateral aid programs were couched in a vague regional philosophy. However, the persistence and strength of regularized bilateral decision-making processes meant that regional agenda-setting took place only at levels where the political sensitivities could be resolved. Aid implementation was not particularly influenced by the demands of leaders' rhetoric, and even the regional programs (such as the ASEAN-Japan Development Fund) are carried out through individual country projects (see below).

ASEAN Aid Programs: Continuity and Change

The old cliche "continuity and change" is highly appropriate in the case of Japan's aid to ASEAN. The continuities of bilateral project aid are overlaid with a plethora of innovative programs (such as those mentioned above) designed to suit a variety of political interests. The late 1980s saw the emergence of a number of new issues in Japan's aid ties with ASEAN. Foremost among these is the new push for industrial development in ASEAN, and the problems of debt relief for some ASEAN countries. Both issues raise the question of the nature of ODA management and the role of Japan's private sector in economic cooperation with the ASEAN region.

According to the former Director-General of the MOFA's Economic Cooperation Bureau, Koichiro Matsuura, the common problem affecting the ASEAN countries (except for Singapore) is that of debt, particularly yen-denominated debt, and including private sector debt.[17] On his visit in May 1989, Mr. Takeshita promised new softer loans to assist Malaysia's yen debt, while Japan pledged new funds to Indonesia at the meeting of the Intergovernmental Group on Indonesia (IGGI) in June 1989. The promise of $2000 million included yen loans ($1200 million), Export-Import Bank loans ($650 million) and $150 million in Japan-ASEAN Development Fund money. The OECF loans were down from the previous year, and project loans were only half of that pledged, the other half being fast-disbursement program aid. Japan was reported to be unhappy with Indonesia's heavy reliance on "special assistance" and would prefer to extend project aid because of its greater donor manageability.[18] Matsuura predicts growing project aid and a reduction in program loans for Indonesia.

Efforts to resolve the debt problems of the Philippines are extremely important to Japan, given the strategic location of the Philippines, the need to ensure the country's political stability, and Japan's position as its largest donor. Japan's contribution to the multilateral consultative group was about $1 billion of the US $3.5 billion committed for 1989, plus additional untied Eximbank funds over three to five years.[19]

Debt relief schemes remain, however, basically bilateral assistance programs. A wider cooperative mechanism is industrial development, into which Japan has been directing efforts since the early 1980s. The ASEAN joint projects begun with fanfare in 1977 under Mr. Fukuda have not been successful; the problems of intra-ASEAN agreement on industrial priorities were too great. Only urea plants in Indonesia and Malaysia have received funding so far.[20] Japan's Ministry of International Trade and Industry began arguing in its 1985 economic cooperation white paper for a major initiative to assist smaller industrial projects in ASEAN. MITI's proposed approach was to respond to demands for industrial development in ASEAN in a three-fold way: enhancement of investment activities by Japan, using OECF, Eximbank, and other funds; stimulation of small and medium industry in ASEAN using OECF two-step loans, plus export promotion activities; and enhancement of technology transfer through various government and private technical cooperation bodies. In this way, MITI argued, a more effective international division of labor and industrial coordination could take place.[21]

TABLE 2.2 New Asian Industries Development Plan

- A plan to develop foreign exchange earning industries in Asian countries (January, 1987, Tamura, MITI Minister)
- Specifically to choose the appropriate method in each country from (a) export processing area development (regional development approach) or (b) selection of export potential industries (industry sector approach).

Stage 1	*Stage 2*	*Stage 3*
Main Master Plan Development	(a) Develop Industry Plans	Implementation of Plans
1986: Thailand, Malaysia	Thailand: textiles, furniture, ceramics, plastics, metals, toys	Industry development, yen loans
1987: Indonesia, Philippines		Investments
1988: India, Pakistan	Malasyia: metals, cermaics electronics	
1988: Pakistan	Indonesia: handmade rubber goods, electrical goods, ceramics, plastics, aluminum goods	Internal Finance
	Philippines: still under discussion	Human resource development
	(b) Develop Regional Plan	Export promotion
Discuss with LDC governments and choose development approach	Thailand, China Philippines under discussion	

Source: MITI documents.

By the following year, the MITI White Paper was proposing the new aid plan in the context of a new international division of labor in manufacturing, to occur through greater product and process differentiation between Japan and the developing Asian countries. This would involve less raw materials basic processing in Japan, Japanese finishing of low value-added products exported from Asian countries, and greater joint venturing for these purposes between Japanese and Asian corporations.[22]

Thus Japan intends to widen the pattern of its aid/trade/technology transfer links with ASEAN countries. The MITI White Papers identify as a target for official aid the nurturing of export-oriented industries, infrastructure for industrial development, and "soft infrastructure." In the area of joint government/private activity, it focuses on the promotion of investment, support for local small and medium industry, and active technology transfer. MITI expects the full range of official aid bodies to participate in these programs.[23]

The new Asian Industries Development Plan and the ASEAN-Japan Development Fund have been criticized as marking Japanese attempts to strengthen "control over an emerging Asian regional economy" and "integrating the Asian economies under Japanese leadership."[24] While the situation is far from being that easily explained, the AID plan is a major step forward by Japan in recognizing the benefits of closer industrial cooperation with the economies of Southeast Asia and China, and has several distinctive features. It is a joint public-private sector activity, which exploits the horizontal division of labor between Japan and Asia and targets industrial rather than resources or infrastructure development. It also involves the preparation of country plans and sector-specific policies. The plan is consistent with MITI objectives in enhancing that ministry's aid profile and the broad policy objective of Japan's economic restructuring, and reveals a clear Japanese intention to establish a central position in financing Asian industrial development. The AID plan involves South Asian as well as the ASEAN countries and China, as Table 2.2 indicates.[25]

The ASEAN-Japan Development Fund was first mooted publicly by Prime Minister Nakasone at the December, 1987 Manila ASEAN Summit and launched the following year by his successor. There were initially some doubts expressed about the potential interest cost and the strings to be attached to the new aid.[26] The Fund is a specific mechanism for assisting private sector development in the ASEAN countries. It involves at least $2 billion over three years, all of which is to be fully untied. The scheme is intended to be additional to ongoing aid programs. Two-thirds of the funds will come through the OECF as yen loans and the rest via the Eximbank. Most loans will be "two step loans" to financial institutions in each ASEAN country, which will then on-lend to private sector borrowers. Projects are supposed to involve intra-regional cooperative activities, and the Fund will be monitored by both

Japan and the governments of ASEAN member countries. An ASEAN-Japan Investment Company has also been established to assist in mobilizing private capital for investment in ASEAN countries. However, the regional flavor of the scheme is rather thin. Regional projects (Category A) will have access to only ten per cent of AJDF funds, while those for member country-based projects (Category B) will get 80 per cent of funds. The other ten per cent will go to supporting the Japan-ASEAN Investment Company.[27]

In fiscal 1988, the OECF provided Malaysia with the first of the AJDF loans, a two-step-loan of $37 million "to support Malaysia's policy of promoting development of the country's small and medium enterprises in the tourism sector."[28] $150 million was loaned to Indonesia from the Fund in 1989 for long-term low-interest loans to small-scale firms and private plantation projects.[29] Loans were also made to Thailand and the Philippines. Japanese Government sources indicate that implementation under the Fund is proceeding slowly.

Much has been said about the objectives that Japan has for its AID plan and the ASEAN-Japan Development Fund. There is no doubt that there is a strong element of a new "trinity" (*san-mi ittai*) for aid delivery woven into these programs. A MITI official describes this approach as a mix of ODA, private overseas investment, and import promotion. He explains that the ODA portion is for necessary public works, industrial infrastructure—such as roads, electricity, and water—and for developing local technical skills through JICA-operated projects.[30] It is a more integrated form of industrial development, combining several means of maximizing economic development objectives. While the AJDF is more likely to be government-led than the New AID plan, it is legitimate to ask whether projects funded under either scheme will be those of greatest priority in LDC development objectives. However, it is a little too early to be making dire predictions about the Japanese private sector controlling LDC export industry priorities.

MITI has certainly been prominent in establishing these new programs and has been able to lift its Asian aid to a regional level rather than just a country or project level. The Ministry of Foreign Affairs appears to accept the MITI approach as the basis of Japan's aid policy towards ASEAN, as official MOFA reports (such as the annual *Gaiko Seisho* or "Diplomatic Blue Book") make abundantly clear. Nevertheless, the aid implementation mechanisms for individual projects remain unchanged and in this sense, MITI is unable to exert control over the ASEAN aid process. Where MITI's influence has been important is in giving real substance to Japan's ASEAN policy, although this may well indicate a poverty of alternatives, despite reasonably active cultural cooperation.

A clearer picture of the direction of Japan's ASEAN policy can be gained from the Japanese prime minister's visit of May 1989. Mr. Takeshita was on his final overseas trip before leaving office—a type of "lame duck diplomacy," but still one rich in traditional fanfare, rhetoric, and *omiyage* (souvenirs). The Takeshita approach consisted of five main points: (1) stronger ASEAN-Japan relations marked by continuity, consistency, and reliability; (2) strengthening of Takeshita's "international cooperation concept;" (3) cooperation for peace and conflict resolution in Cambodia; (4) explanation of Japan's position on Asia-Pacific cooperation; and (5) a call for greater appreciation of Japan's efforts in supporting the global economic order.[31] On the aid front, he was reported as proposing an expansion of aid plus wider transport, communication, and cultural links.

The visit was a standard ASEAN tour: dropping in to all countries for a day or two, a round of golf, a keynote speech in one of the capitals (this time in Jakarta) and a series of promises to each of the leaders about economic cooperation. The ASEAN features of the visit were restricted to Takeshita's announcement of the several principles of Japan's policy and exhortations to closer cooperation, "continuity and consistency" being the watchwords. The Asian requests were all bilateral, the negotiations were all bilateral, and the aid promises were all bilateral. There was no multilateral gathering of the ASEAN and Japanese leaders, no specific ASEAN initiative from Takeshita. There was simply a repeat of the regular performance of juggling bilateral and group policy. Japanese newspapers referred to the visit as one to "the five ASEAN nations".

The Takeshita line was by no means new. It was designed to symbolize the consistency and continuity of Japan-ASEAN relations, and offered little in the way of change in Japan's approach. Japanese newspapers were rather negative, although they recognized the need for the trip to reassure ASEAN about continuity.[32] Foreign journalists were less kind, highlighting Takeshita's pending departure, the "begging act" on aid, and disappointment with the keynote speech.[33] Nevertheless, press comment in *The Indonesia Times*, for example, was mild in comparison to criticism of earlier Japanese prime ministerial visits.[34] The standard line was reaffirmed when Prime Minister Kaifu briefly visited Indonesia in April 1990, and re-stressed ASEAN's importance to Japan.[35]

Some of the main concerns of the ASEAN nations outside their own bilateral aid programs with Japan, relate to general trends in Japan's aid flows. There are fears that additional aid to Latin America, Eastern Europe, and China will reduce the relative share going to ASEAN.[36] As noted above, the MOFA sees the concentration of aid on

Asia as appropriate, although there may be limits to this. A more immediate issue for Japan is that of assistance to Vietnam, which would add a significant new recipient for large-scale economic infrastructure project aid in ASEAN's immediate neighborhood. ASEAN's fear of an effect on their own aid flows is real.

When he spoke in Jakarta, Mr. Takeshita pledged that there would be "positive consideration to extend financial cooperation, despatch personnel and provide necessary non-military materials to assist the introduction of an effective control mechanism to facilitate the peace process" in Indochina. As well as that, however, Takeshita said that "it is our intention, after a political settlement has been reached, to cooperate in the reconstruction and development of Indochina."[37] Indeed, 1988 saw an enormous jump in aid to Vietnam from only $300,000 in 1987 to $4.1 million (although most of this was channeled through multilateral agencies). The MOFA says that "visits by officials of both governments to enhance mutual understanding, and exchange of persons in the cultural and academic fields, is growing steadily."[38]

The MOFA stresses that aid to Vietnam at this stage is focussed on humanitarian assistance (disaster relief and medical aid) and cultural assistance.[39] The ministry was reported as asking for private funds to support meetings on preserving Vietnamese historical ruins.[40] At the same time, government officials recognize that Vietnam has bright prospects for economic development, and that Japan is in a good position to act as a donor, especially given Japan's traditional preference for economic infrastructure funding, and Vietnam's great needs in this area.[41] More Japanese businesses are preparing for renewed economic ties with Vietnam, and it is clear that a push towards resumption of official aid ties with Vietnam may not be too far distant. Even the Director-General of MOFA's Asian Affairs Bureau, Tanino Sakutaro, was quoted in an official MFA journal as follows: "With aid to Vietnam frozen, various forms of exchange cannot proceed. Trade is carried out very timidly. I'd like to return this situation to a rather more natural one in due course."[42]

Such a return could be in the offing as practical effect has been given to reviewing aid to Vietnam by the creation of a "Mekong Study Group" within the Ministry of Construction. Its task is to assess what sort of economic cooperation with Laos, Cambodia, and Vietnam is possible, so that aid can be implemented once diplomatic solutions are reached.[43]

Conceptualizing Japan's Aid to ASEAN

Japan is by far the largest donor to each of the ASEAN countries. Japan's dominance of ASEAN aid is an outgrowth of a number of mutually reinforcing factors. First, Japan's policy since the 1950s has been to emphasize its "natural" role in assisting Southeast Asia. As discussed above, this view was based on concepts of Japan's cultural and racial affinities, its highly pragmatic economic strategy, and a carefully targeted resource diplomacy. Japan has felt most comfortable with an Asian-centered aid policy, and for reasons discussed above, has maintained that approach.

Second, with that basic policy and the maintenance of a high level of aid commitment to four of the six ASEAN countries, the accumulation of aid projects, experts, interests, and networks, represented a "cycle of predictable (and in any case safe) commitments."[44]

Thirdly, other structural factors have been important. Indonesian aid has been locked into the IGGI framework since 1967, Philippine aid was tied initially to commitments to the Marcos regime and, more recently, to resolution of the Philippine debt problem and support for the regime of Corazon Aquino. In Malaysia's case, that government's attempts to emulate Japan's economic performance (the Look East Policy) brought a favorable response in aid commitments.[45] Thailand's important political position vis-a-vis Indochina was also a special reason for close aid relations, supported by American policy towards Thailand.

Fourth, there is the factor of domestic Japanese aid politics. In the ASEAN case, prime ministerial politics have been paramount since 1977. The involvement of Japanese leaders in the ASEAN heads of government summits since the second meeting in 1977 has located ASEAN aid initiatives at the top of the political agenda in Japan. The ASEAN trip is the only major prime ministerial visit to a developing region that is now almost obligatory for Japanese leaders. It has placed the broad parameters of aid to ASEAN in the *omiyage gaiko* (souvenir diplomacy) category, removed from the strictly bureaucratic arena. There are few other aspects of Japan's aid where this separation and ritualization are possible. It reflects a broad consensus within Japanese government circles about the importance of the ASEAN countries to Japan's future and to the future of the Asia-Pacific region.

Although the major decisions about setting the ASEAN aid agenda fall largely to the political level, it is the bureaucratic commitment to maintaining aid to ASEAN that underlies the political process, and it is the ability of the Japanese aid system to implement the ASEAN aid program that ultimately determines its effectiveness. ASEAN aid is the mainstay of the day-to-day operation of the Japanese aid system, and prime ministerial announcements have tended to follow administrative settings in terms of content and size. Conversely, however, bureaucratic management of the ASEAN relationship is immeasurably strengthened by the political sensitivity of Japan's ASEAN policies. Prime ministerial diplomacy and bureaucratic management are mutually supportive. There is no doubt that aid to ASEAN is the centerpiece of Japan's aid program. It represents a lengthy aid relationship, it appears to justify the MOFA's emphasis on aid to enhance political stability, it bolsters a broad set of economic relationships between Japan and the economies of the region, and reflects a highly instrumentalist Japanese foreign policy towards Southeast Asia. As one Japanese commentator put it, "Southeast Asia is the indispensable geo-political partner for resources-poor Japan in order to survive."[46]

Appraisals of Japanese policy from within the region have not always been positive. There has been wariness of the impact of Japan's relations with China, and concern about the passivity of Japan towards ASEAN, but also fears about ASEAN's dependence on Japan for capital, technology, and expertise and Japan's inadequate understanding of Southeast Asian societies.[47] One writer calls the relationship "basically colonial in both political and economic terms; i.e., while Japan has penetrated their economies, it does not provide a reasonable access to their products in its own domestic markets."[48]

A major issue in understanding Japan's ASEAN aid policies is that of leadership. In 1963, James Morley foresaw that Japan had "an unquestionably greater capacity for Asian leadership than ever before," through an integrated regional cooperative process.[49] Japan's potential economic impact on Asia was becoming clear, and Japan's objectives of an "integrative" regional leadership role in Asia was discussed.[50] Sudo portrays the Fukuda Doctrine as a "vigorous attempt to deal confidently with this turbulent region ...with this attempt, and despite its limited success, Japan has moved one step further in attaining its role of a regional leader in Southeast Asia."[51] Rix argued in 1982 that "Japan's desire to act as a 'bridge' or interpreter of Asia to the West, however ill-defined, still appears strong, although Japan has not opted to use ASEAN as its exclusive channel to the region."[52] Elsbree and Hoong in 1984 put it thus:

> If Japan can be said to have a political policy toward Southeast Asia, it might be labelled "Support ASEAN" - within the confines of overall foreign policy and without assuming any risk. It is a policy without detailed commitment and, hence, does not arouse domestic opposition. It enables Japan to play a supportive role without

> assuming the initiative; it dovetails with resource diplomacy, and it is congruent with the U.S. relationship, the first priority in foreign policy.[53]

A number of factors have changed since this was written. Japan's aid-giving rationale is perhaps less obviously instrumental. The main emphases of the Fukuda Doctrine have been successively maintained and reaffirmed. ASEAN has preserved its position as the focal point of aid policy, despite greater commitments by Japan to China. Recent souring of relations with China, however, has reinforced the strength and stability of ASEAN ties with Japan. Furthermore, the ASEAN policy *does* now have detailed commitments attached to it. There are specific mechanisms in place to enhance Japan-ASEAN aid relations. Indeed, the range and variety of these programs, although conducted largely on a bilateral basis, tell of the seriousness with which Japan is attempting to satisfy ASEAN wishes for effective economic cooperation. Mr. Takeshita's approach highlighted less of the "equal partnership" first raised by Mr Fukuda in 1987. Instead he stressed the relationship's solidity.

> Japan and ASEAN are 'natural friends' bound geographically and historically, but at the same time, considering our common ideals based on freedom and individual creativity, we are 'eternal partners, thinking together and advancing together.'[54]

What do these commitments and aid flows add up to in terms of Japan's ability or determination to take a hand in setting, not only a development agenda, but a broader regional economic policy agenda? There are opposing trends. On the one hand, the new AID plan and the ASEAN-Japan Development Fund mask a Japanese desire to involve itself more directly in assigning and funding development priorities. On the other hand, bureaucratized decision-making processes in Tokyo, and the limited number of Japanese aid staff on the ground in the ASEAN countries, make fine-tuning of those mechanisms a difficult task. The government-private sector cooperative model that marks this form of economic cooperation is an attempt to make aid delivery more efficient. Japan is taking a positive stance in trying to integrate the industrial development of the ASEAN group, Japan, and other Asian countries. Success in this attempt will hinge on the effectiveness of country policy setting at the planning stages in Tokyo, obviously a crucial aspect of the AID program, as Table 2.2 indicates. While the domestic aid system is rapidly organizing country-specific policy facilities within the aid administration, there is considerable overlap and excessive proliferation of such capacity through the various ministries and agencies.

It may yet be too early to assess the effectiveness of the ASEAN aid initiatives in influencing Japan's industrial cooperation with Southeast Asia. When looked at in terms of Japan's total aid program, ASEAN policies certainly stand out. Naturally, general policy deals with the quantitative aspects of Japan's performance and with global agenda issues such as debt relief, the environment, and the LLDCs. But it is towards the ASEAN countries that bilateral policy attention is mainly focussed. This, as discussed earlier, is a matter of long-standing concentration on ASEAN aid and entrenched bureaucratic and political priority accorded to those countries. There is, however, no clear indication that Japan is using its ASEAN policies as either a forerunner for other bilateral or regional programs, or an example of innovative aid policies of relevance to the wider donor community.

The priority given to ASEAN countries, and the type of aid given, is the result of longstanding and close aid ties, not an innovation in aid thinking or an attempt to instil new directions in Japan's aid program. Leadership status in regional aid-giving has been conferred on Japan by virtue of the size, impact, and continuity of Japan's aid to ASEAN. For the several reasons cited in this chapter, Japan has achieved the capacity of a regional aid power. If its AID plan proceeds as it hopes, a new integration in Asian industry is possible. Yet Japan's leadership style is still couched in the passivity criticized by ASEAN observers in the past. It is not a moral leadership, nor a style given to grandstanding, despite political posturing by some prime ministers. Leadership is not a status greatly sought after by Japan, but is the outcome of the long-standing development of aid policies carefully designed to protect Japanese interests by the nurturing of economic growth and political stability in the ASEAN countries.

Conclusions

Japan's ASEAN aid policy is concerned with practical outcomes as well as symbolic achievements. Its dominance of the development priorities of the ASEAN member nations is a strong object lesson in the power of historical and cultural ties, however bitter though they may have been in the past. It also demonstrates the importance of security considerations for Japan, and the complexity of these security precautions. In addition, the potent mixture of political and administrative management of the Japan-ASEAN aid relationship is an obvious lesson in the variety of aid management processes. Although aid to ASEAN is the core of Japan's aid program, its management style is neither representative of, or common elsewhere in, Japan's aid program. Aid to ASEAN is singular in terms of priority and difficulty. No other recipient, even China, has the same status. No other donor but Japan is expected to maintain the same levels of generosity and initiative. No other donor is the object of so much caution on the part of its beneficiaries. But no other set of aid relationships has so vividly vindicated Japan's particular brand of aid policy.

Endnotes

1. Thanks are due to the following organizations for their support of this work: Australian Research Council, Ohira Memorial Foundation, The University of Queensland, and The East-West Center.

2. *Kokusai Kyoryoku Jigyodan Nenpo 1989* (Japan International Cooperation Agency, Annual Report, 1989), p.22

3. Development surveys are project identification surveys.

4. Gaimusho, *Wagakuni no Seifu Kaihatsu Enjo 1989*, (Ministry of Foreign Affairs, Japan's Official Development Assistance, 1989). (Hereafter referred to as *Wagakuni 1989*), Vol. 1, p.156.

5. Alan Rix, *Japan's Aid Program: A New Global Agenda* (Canberra, Australian Government Publishing Service, 1990).

6. Tessa Morris Suzuki, "The South Seas Empire of Ishihara Hiroichiro: A Case Study in Japan's Economic Relations with Southeast Asia 1914-41" in Alan Rix and Ross Mouer (eds). *Japan's Impact on the World* (Brisbane, JSAA, 1984), pp.151-69.

7. Sueo Sudo, "Nanshin, Superdomino, and the Fukuda Doctrine: Stages in Japan-Southeast Asian Relations", *Journal of Northeast Asian Studies*, Vol. V, 3, Fall, 1986, pp. 35-51; Alan Rix, "Japan and ASEAN: More than Economics", in A. Broinowski (ed.), *Understanding ASEAN* (London, Macmillan, 1982), pp.169-95.

8. Rix, "Japan and ASEAN," pp.179-81.

9. *Kokusai Kaihatsu Janaru* (International Development Journal), June 1990, pp. 38-9.

10. Sudo, "Nanshin, Superdomino and the Fukuda Doctrine". On US policy see Sheldon Simon, "United States Security Policy and ASEAN," *Current History*, Vol 89, No. 545, March 1990.

11. Gaimusho Sengo Gaikoshi Kenkyukai, *Nihon Gaiko 30-nen: Sengo no Kiseki to Tenbo, 1952-1982* (Ministry of Foreign Affairs Postwar Diplomacy Research Committee: Thirty Years of Japan's Diplomacy: Origins and Approaches in the Postwar Period, 1952-1982), Tokyo, 1982, p.233.

12. "Japan: the Missing Link in ASEAN's Blueprint," *Far Eastern Economic Review*, April 30, 1976, pp. 43-8.

13. This is well-covered in articles by Sueo Sudo, "From Fukuda to Takeshita: A Decade of Japan-ASEAN Relations," *Contemporary Southeast Asia*, 10, 1, September 1988, pp.119-143; "Japan's ASEAN Relations: New Dimensions in Japanese Foreign Policy," *Asian Survey*, Vol. XXVIII, 5, May 1988; pp. 509-25. See also the view of the former Japanese Foreign Minister, Sonoda Sunao in *Sekai Nihon-ai* (The world and Japan in friendship), (Tokyo, Daisansei Kenkyukai, 1981), pp.126-36. On ASEAN aid and China see Dennis Yasutomo, *The Manner of Giving: Strategic Aid and Japanese Foreign Policy* (Lexington, Lexington Books, 1986), p. 98.

14. Willard H. Eisbree and Khong Kim Hoong, 'Japan and ASEAN," in Robert S. Ozaki and Walter Arnold (eds.), *Japan's Foreign Relations: A Global Search for Economic Security* (Boulder, Westview Press, 1984,) pp.131-2.

15. *Nihon gaiko 30-nen*, p.232

16. Gaimusho, *Nihon to ASEAN* (Japan and ASEAN), 1987.

17. *Kokusai kaihatsu janaru*, July 1989, pp. 14-17

18. *Far Eastern Eonomic Review*, June 1, 1989, pp. 50-51.

19. *Japan Times Weekly*, July 22, 1989

20. *Nihon to ASEAN*, 1987, p. 18

21. Tsusho Sangyosho, *Keizai Kyoryoku no Genjo to Mondaiten 1985* (Ministry of International Trade and Industry, Present Situation and Problems of Economic Cooperation), Tokyo, 1986, pp.145-51.

22. *Keizai kyoryoku no genjo to mondaiten 1986*, pp. 179-83.

23. *Keizai kyoryoku no genjo to mondaiten 1985*, pp. 87-151

24. David Arase, "Japanese Objectives in Pacific Economic Cooperation," Honolulu, Hawaii: East West Center Resource Systems Institute, November 1988.

25. Recent issues of the MITI White Paper on Economic Cooperation have details of activities under the New AID plan.

26. *Far Eastern Economic Review*, July 2, 1987, pp.66-7.

27. *Kokusai kaihatsu janaru*, May 1990, p. 63.

28. Overseas Economic Cooperation Fund, *Annual Report 1989*, p. 35.

29. *Asahi Shimbun*, May 4 1989 and *Kokusai Kaihatsu Janaru*, May 1990, p. 77.

30. *Kokusai kaihatsu janaru*, July 1989 pp. 92-4. MITI's FY 1990 budget allocation of AID plan-related projects rose by 10 per cent to 3117 million yen, mostly for Thai and Malaysian projects (*Kokusai kaihatsu janaru*, March 1990, pp.59-60).

31. *Asahi Shimbun*, April 25 1989

32. *Yomiuri Shimbun*, May 7 1989.

33. *Far Eastern Economic Review*, May 18, 1989.

34. Survey of *The Indonesian Times*, 1977-1989.

35. *Kokusai kaihatsu janaru*, June 1990, p.35.

36. Interview with MITI economic cooperation official, December 13 1989.

37. See text of Takeshita's speech in Gaimusho hen, *Gaiko Seisho: Waga Gaiko no Kinkyo*, 33 (Ministry of Foreign Affairs, Diplomatic Blue Book: present situation of Japans' diplomacy), Tokyo, 1989, pp. 308-17. This quote is on pp. 312-13.

38. *Gaiko seisho* 33, p. 169. For an analysis of Japan's ODA relations with Vietnam, see the chapter in this book by Juichi Inada.

39. *Wagakuni 1989*, Vol. 2, p. 40.

40. *Japan Times*, December 12, 1989.

41. Interview with MITI economic cooperation official, December 13, 1989.

42. In the roundtable discussion, "Hendo suru tonan ajia shokoku to nihon no taio (The changing nature of Southeast Asia and Japan's response), *Gaiko Forum*, No. 14, November 1989, p. 29.

43. *Kokusai kaihatsu janaru*, May 1990, p. 39.

44. Alan Rix, *Japan's Economic Aid: Policymaking and Politics* (London, Croom Helm, 1980), pp. 263-5.

45. Lim Hua Sing, "Japanese Perspectives on Malaysia's 'Look East' Policy," *Southeast ASEAN Affairs*, 1984, pp. 231-45; Lee Poh Ping. "Malaysian perceptions of Japan before and during the 'Look East' Period," *Asia Pacific Community*, No. 29, Winter 1985, pp. 97-108.

46. Reijiro Toba, "Japan's Southeast Asia Policy in this last decade," *Asia Pacific Community*,No. 15, Winter 1982, p. 42.

47. Lau Teik Soon, "Uncertain Prospects for Japan-ASEAN Relations," *Asia Pacific Community*, No. 4, Spring/Summer 1979, pp. 9-20; Frances Lai Fung-wai, *Without a Vision: Japan's Relations with ASEAN (Singapore:* National University of Singapore, Occasional Paper, No. 40, 1981); David Chiang-Kau Lang, "Japan's ASEAN Gaiko: a Reassessment," *Asian Profile*, Vol. 11, No. 2. April 1983, pp. 153-65.

48. Radha Sinha, "Japan and ASEAN: A Special Relationship?" *The World Today*, Vol. 38, No. 12, December 1982, pp. 483-92.

49. James W. Morley, "Japan's Position in Asia," *Journal of International Affairs*, Vol. 17, 1963, pp. 142-54.

50. Yung-hwan Jo, "Regional Cooperation in Southeast Asia and Japan's Role," *Journal of Politics*, Vol. 30, No. 3, August 1968, pp. 780-97.

51. Sueo Sudo, "The Road to Becoming a Regional Leader: Japanese Attempts in Southeast Asia, 1975-1980," *Pacific Affairs*, Vol. 61, No. 1,Spring 1988, p. 50

52. Rix, "Japan and ASEAN," p. 195.

53. Eisbree and Hoong, "Japan and ASEAN," p. 131.

54. *Gaiko no seisho* 33, pp. 316-7.

3

BOLSTERING THE NEW ORDER: JAPAN'S ODA RELATIONSHIP WITH INDONESIA

Jeff Kingston

Introduction

By virtue of its massive aid program, Japan finds itself in the unfamiliar and uncomfortable position of being out in front on important measures of both international prestige and responsibility. In that position, Japan has become a target of building frustrations and high expectations from around the globe. It is a nation collectively groping for a new raison d'etre for its international economic cooperation activities, yet proud of its achievements, seeking to avoid miscues on the international stage while at the same time eager to flex economic muscles bulked up on the steroids of trade surpluses.

> The partly arrogant, partly gun-shy stance of the present reflects the difficulty of dealing with the dual legacy of Showa: Japan as an economic and nonmilitary big power, about which no history anywhere has very much to say. The related uneasiness has to do with the changes in the world stage on which Japan must play its new as yet unscripted role.[1]

Existing aid scripts have not played particularly well in the Third World where "inexorable" and "intractable" are familiar adjectives. To be fair, effective development assistance is a process only poorly understood. The art of giving is in flux, the only certainty being the desperate need for solutions. Resolving Third World indebtedness is one of the most critical problems on the development agenda, for it threatens to undo progress and further circumscribe opportunities. It is on this treacherous stage that Japan has chosen to take its first leading international role and the initial reviews have not been charitable.

In the case of Indonesia, Japan seems to be coming into its own, cooperating with western donors, taking initiatives and generating a development momentum based on unspectacular fundamentals: economic stability, structural adjustment, and trade promotion. Japan has assisted Indonesia in weathering adverse trends and external developments while promoting economic stabilization and structural adjustment. However, how do short-term financial "fixes" fit in with long term strategies of promoting trade oriented development? Since Japanese assistance is largely in the form of loans, how can Japan's assistance help Indonesia resolve its problems as Asia's largest debtor?

Indonesia has not yet turned the corner on many of its obstacles to development and Japan is stumbling through the challenges of improvisation, but both nations have emerged from the 1980s closer to their elusive objectives and further along in resolving their problems than most. While shortcomings merit continued scrutiny and vigorous countermeasures, it is also worth acknowledging how much has been accomplished under difficult conditions.[2]

Japan's ODA and Indonesia

This analysis focuses on Japanese economic cooperation broadly defined, including ODA, other official flows (OOF) and private flows (PF). ODA and OOF are seen as intermediate steps towards promoting PF and sustainable development in Indonesia. In order to realize Indonesia's proclaimed goal of achieving economic take-off, the Indonesian government also accords critical importance to foreign investments and enhancing the role of the private sector.[3] Indeed, the impressive array of economic reform measures unveiled in Indonesia since 1983 seek to pare back the regulatory impediments that have dampened private initiative and nurtured inefficiency.[4]

Indonesia is the largest recipient of Japanese economic assistance, both cumulatively and on an annual basis since 1987. In 1990, Japan's aid package totaled $1.81 billion, including $110 million in grants and technical assistance focusing on basic human needs and transfer of technology and know-how. About $1 billion consisted of project loans aimed at promoting infrastructure development while $700 million was committed in the form of "special assistance," quickly disbursed funds for alleviating balance of payments pressures and budget shortfalls. This special assistance, first extended in 1987, is a new wrinkle in Japan's aid program and is featured in the following analysis.

Why is Indonesia number one? Japan's economic ties with Indonesia are substantial. Indonesia is the second largest recipient in the world of Japanese direct foreign investment after the U.S. For example, Japan has a cumulative investment in Indonesia's non-oil sector between 1967-1990 of $7.9 billion.[5] By comparison, the U.S. cumulative investment in the non-oil sector totals $2 billion, ranking behind Hong Kong ($3.4 billion) and just ahead of West Germany ($1.85 billion), Taiwan ($1.6 billion) and the Netherlands ($1.5 billion).[6] Japan is Indonesia's largest trading partner in both exports and imports. Indonesia is the largest supplier to Japan of LNG (liquid natural gas) and also exports significant amounts of oil to Japan. The abundance of natural resources and cheap labor, combined with the market potential of nearly 180 million consumers, make Indonesia attractive to Japanese business.

Japan's geopolitical interests are also at stake, as Indonesia borders on both the Straits of Malacca and Lombok, Japan's shipping lifelines to Mideast oil. Indonesia is also the linchpin of the Association of Southeast Asian Nations (ASEAN) which by virtue of its market size, potential economic power, and natural endowments will play an increasingly important role in the Pacific Basin. Promoting Indonesia's economic development in particular is proposed as a means to strengthen Indonesian and regional political stability and to foster friendly relations between Japan and the region, thus serving critical economic and security interests of Japan.[7] The prominence accorded to Indonesia also reflects the ambivalent legacy of Japan's occupation of 1942-1945, when Indonesia was "liberated" from the Dutch only to be subjugated by the Japanese.

There is a strong community of interest between Indonesia and Japan. There are large numbers of Indonesian specialists[8] in Japan and they have high level access to both government and corporate decision-makers. This has been facilitated over the years by alumni associations, educational and cultural exchanges, business ventures, and the myriad contacts developed between officials as a result of extensive bilateral discussions. Likewise, several Indonesian officials and businesspeople have good access in Japan and know who, where, and when to lobby.

The Inter-Governmental Group on Indonesia (IGGI)

Until recently, the Inter-Governmental Group on Indonesia was the principal arena for donor relations with Indonesia. Japan's own aid relationship, like that of other major bilateral donors, has not been exclusively confined to that arena, but there is no question that the existence of the IGGI had a significant influence on the characteristics of Japan's aid relationships with Indonesia.

What was the IGGI? An abortive coup in 1965 signalled the beginning of the end of President Sukarno's reign. The government's economic ministers began adding up the bill from the profligacy that had been a hallmark of the Sukarno era. In 1966, inflation was running at over 600% and Indonesia's scheduled debt service payments of $530 million exceeded total foreign exchange earnings.[9] Most of the nation's debt of $2.4 billion was owed to communist bloc creditors, including nearly $1 billion to the Soviet Union, which had largely financed unproductive military procurements. Japan was owed $231 million while the top Western creditors were the U.S.($179 million), West Germany ($122 million), France ($115 million), and Italy (91 million). In addition, the IMF was owed $102 million.

Indonesia needed to arrange a debt rescheduling agreement and attract new aid. To this end a meeting was held in Tokyo during September, 1966 among twelve non-communist creditors, leading to the provision of new credit totaling $174 million. In a follow-up meeting in December of that same year, discussions among members of the Paris Club sought ways to lighten Indonesia's debt burden and to mount what would effectively be a bail-out. In February 1967, the IGGI emerged from a more formal meeting in Amsterdam attended by Australia, Belgium, France, West Germany, Italy, Japan, the Netherlands, the United Kingdom, and the U.S., with observers from Switzerland, Norway and New Zealand and representatives from the IMF, the World Bank (IBRD), the Asian Development Bank, the United Nations Development Program, and the Organization for Economic Cooperation and Development. The participants agreed to meet regularly to discuss Indonesia's economic problems and coordinate their aid packages.

From the beginning, Japan played a key role, hosting the first meeting of creditors and subsequently contributing one third of the original aid request, matching the U.S. share. Assistance began on an emergency basis and was aimed at stabilizing balance of payments problems in exchange for the government's commitment to adopt anti-inflationary austerity policies. From 1966-68 there was no project aid. The Indonesian Central Bank merely sold the foreign exchange within Indonesia, arguing the country needed to ease its domestic credit squeeze and that the government has only a small capacity to implement development projects. Eventually Indonesia's Sukarno era debts were rescheduled on favorable terms under the auspices of the IGGI.

Indeed, from its inception in 1967, the IGGI played a crucial role in managing the international financial community's response to Indonesia's recurrent financial crises. For example, in 1975, the IGGI mounted another massive bailout stemming from the huge accumulation of debts by the state petroleum company, Pertamina.[10] Western donors and banks took the lead in arranging a $2 billion bail-out with Japan contributing $200 million in emergency loans. In addition, IGGI members facilitated a rescheduling of much of Pertamina's $10 billion in debts.

The IGGI served as an international forum for an exchange of ideas, and for coordination of bilateral aid programs and the efforts of the international banks. Meetings were held every June shortly after the World Bank issued its annual review of the Indonesian economy. Levels of aid commitments were announced and Indonesia was generally praised by its creditors for pragmatic economic policies and, since 1983, for pushing ahead with an ambitious economic liberalization agenda.

Japanese officials appear unanimous in their preference for working through such an aid consortium, particularly since it carries the imprimatur of the multilateral development banks. Japan's leading role as a donor tends to be obscured, in keeping with Tokyo's preference for maintaining a low profile and working behind the scenes. Some Japanese officials privately express reservations about the dominance of World Bank/U.S. approaches and concerns within the consortium, but most Japanese officials I interviewed thought Japan's interests were well served by the IGGI, averting an appearance of unilateralism and self-interest. Indonesians also prefer an international forum where no single bilateral donor can dominate.

In the 1960s, Japan played a facilitating role in creating the IGGI, and committed a substantial amount of money for a country which itself had recently been a borrower of World Bank funds. This can be viewed as a form of reparations and also a desire to play a bigger international role. In the 1970s, Japan also contributed a relatively large proportion of the bail-out package, but did not take a leading role. Since this was in the aftermath of anti-Japanese riots during Prime Minister Tanaka's 1974 visit, it is understandable that Japan wanted to keep a low profile.[11]

In the 1980s, Japan took the lead in arranging and financing another bail-out, and indeed this seems to have been the expectation given

Japan's abundant financial resources and close economic ties with Indonesia.[12] Japan became first among equals in IGGI, contributing nearly half of the total IGGI commitments on a bilateral basis, supplemented by its contributions through international banks. Since 1988, Japan's total contributions even exceed those of the international banks and it translated this number one donor status into more clout within the IGGI. A recent report by a government-commissioned study group charged with setting Japan's basic strategy towards development assistance to Indonesia suggested that Japan must exercise leadership in the IGGI, particularly in terms of developing long term debt, trade, and fiscal strategies. While remaining committed to working within IGGI, the report recommends that, "Japan should not depend on the World Bank, the IMF or the U.S."[13]

From the IGGI to the CGI

In early 1992, a serious difference of opinion developed between the Dutch and Indonesian governments over the behavior of the Indonesian military in dealing with suppression of dissidence in East Timor,[14] a province in eastern Indonesia. Several donor countries expressed displeasure through private channels. Those so objecting included the Japanese, the Australians, and the Canadians. Their expressions were firm but were couched in a framework which saw the violations of human rights that occurred as aberrations rather than as the systematic results of objectionable policies. Dutch criticism was sharp and very public and went so far as to question the appropriateness of a continuing aid relationship with Indonesia. In effect, the Dutch publicly charged that the events in East Timor were not aberrations. The Indonesian government, never warm to outside public criticism of its politics, was particularly sensitive to criticism from the Dutch, who were both former colonial masters and, as the chair of the IGGI, a donor country with a role well beyond its means. In fact, the IGGI was the only major donor consortium not chaired by the World Bank.

In March, 1992 the Indonesian government decided that it did not need Dutch aid nor the Dutch in the IGGI. Consequently, the government decided it would be better to disband the IGGI as it was then constituted and formulate a new consortium, the Consultative Group for Indonesia (CGI) with the World Bank as chair. There was little objection from other members of the IGGI to these developments, most of whom, including the Japanese, were directly informed by the Indonesians of intentions to disband the IGGI before any public steps were taken. Japan and other donors, satisfied that private expressions had led to acceptable steps by the Indonesian government to investigate the incidents, did not object to the Indonesian proposal. Consequently the donor consortium, minus the Dutch, continues its relationship with Indonesia in the form of the CGI. For Japan, the episode reinforced two points in Japan's aid philosophy with Indonesia: (1) refrain from public criticisms of Indonesian politics, and (2) work through the consortium when that is useful and work outside it when that appears appropriate.

Differing Philosophies?

It is increasingly evident that Japan is not in complete accord with the approach of other OECD nations to resolving global debt problems and hence plans to play a more assertive role in countries such as Indonesia where Japanese interests and influence are paramount. Japan believes that it is in its own interest to promote development that will strengthen Indonesia's long term balance-of-payments prospects. Currently this translates into promoting non-oil export production capacity and supporting continued economic liberalization aimed at improving Indonesia's efficiency and competitiveness. Japanese suggest that an almost-Messianic belief in the market is overdone by the U.S. They point to numerous market failings, and prefer a more guided and targeted approach to harness market dynamism.

Based on its own experience, Japan favors loans over grants because it believes them to be more effective in nurturing responsible economic management and creating incentives for the recipient to make the project work. Japanese officials maintain that countries like Indonesia can afford to repay loans, and it is well to remember that much of the new lending to Indonesia amounts to debt rescheduling and balance-of-payments support. The Japanese government views public grants and loans as a means to bolster investors' confidence in the economy and encourage private sector flows.

Japan's ODA policy therefore moves on the premise that a major condition for sustainable development is encouraging flows of foreign direct investment.[15] Keeping the Japanese private sector involved in Indonesia's drive to develop a manufacturing export sector is seen as a better way to impart technology and efficiency while creating strong economic incentives on both sides to make the ventures viable. This long-term strategy calls for increasing Indonesia's export capacity to generate enough revenues to meet the large new debt obligations it is incurring and gradually lessen dependence on external assistance.[16]

Democracy and Aid?

The New Order government has an enviable record on economic development, but has slighted political development. President Suharto has ruled in an authoritarian manner since 1967 and moved resolutely to quell protests and opposition. Since the beginning of 1989 there has been speculation that Suharto would retire in 1993 when his current term expires, generating concerns about the potential for instability amidst jockeying over the succession. Over the years, Suharto has groomed no obvious successor and has wielded considerable power partly by playing rival groups off against one another and not permitting the rise of any potentially threatening successor candidate. The president has recently indicated that he will probably run for re-election, despite public criticism that he is an obstacle to overdue political reforms and greater democracy. In April, 1990, Prime Minister Toshiki Kaifu made the obligatory ASEAN pilgrimage, bearing the customary financial *omiyage* and uttering the usual diplomatic pleasantries, but startled observers by raising the nettlesome issue of political succession in talks with President Suharto. He expressed Japanese concerns about an orderly transition and continued political stability.

Prime Minister Kaifu's remarks suggest that Japan plans to play a more assertive role, reticent as it may seem by western standards. In an April 4, 1991 speech to the Diet by Prime Minister Kaifu entitled "On Japan's ODA in Relation to Military Expenditures and Other Matters of the Developing Countries" Japan's ODA is explicitly linked for the first time to supporting democracy. This reflects Tokyo's response to criticisms that it lacks an aid philosophy and has been too utilitarian and reactive to external pressures, namely from the U.S., in its patterns of assistance.[17] The speech and the White Paper it was based on do not indicate that Japan will start to twist arms and aggressively intervene on behalf of democracy, but rather convey a groping for a donor philosophy that will mollify its detractors while not tying it into rigid positions.

Indonesia hands in Tokyo suggest that Japan has no intention of leading a crusade for liberty, and the prime minister's remarks did not signal the advent of linkage. The lingering legacy of the war continues to influence diplomatic exchanges, imposing obligations and restrictions on Japan's relations with Asia which militate against any moves that smack of meddling in internal political affairs. In addition, the real and the choreographed "resentment and suspicion" also serve the Foreign Ministry's efforts to justify high levels of ODA to Asia in its continuing battles with the Finance Ministry and others. As one

Japanese banker confided in discussing the potential turmoil that may accompany political succession, "At the end of the day, we will still have enormous interests in Indonesia and will work with the government that the Indonesians choose."

Aid as an Economic Catalyst

Japan views its ODA and OOF as a means to enhance private sector investments and flows of financial resources to developing nations. By helping Indonesia deal with short-term balance of payments problems and averting a debt rescheduling, Japan has provided critical support to the IGGI's ongoing economic liberalization initiatives and bolstered international confidence.[18] Investors are increasingly attracted by the progressive opening of the economy through deregulation and are reassured by IGGI's and Japan's evident commitment.

Trends in Indonesia's non-oil sector are illuminating. Faced with the prospect of becoming a net oil importer in the early 21st century, Indonesia has placed great emphasis on economic diversification and a shift from import substitution oriented industrialization towards export-oriented manufacturing and processing of raw materials. To this end, the government has taken steps to facilitate foreign investments and provide a supportive regulatory framework for manufactured exports. The results are impressive. In 1986 and 1987, Japanese investors committed $160 million to 20 export oriented projects while in 1988 and 1989 the value of investments in export oriented projects rose to $1.4 billion in 63 projects.[19] Through the first five months of 1990, an additional $473 million was committed to 14 projects. Since 1988, there has also been a surge in investments from South Korea, Taiwan, and Hong Kong as they seek to relocate facilities where production costs are lower and as a means to tap GSP privileges and elude protectionist barriers.

Following the largely Japanese financed government bailout of late 1986, there has been a boom in overall foreign investment flows to Indonesia, exceeding $4 billion in 1988 and 1989 and nearly matching that level in the first six months of 1990.[20] Meanwhile, domestic investment levels are also growing rapidly, from $4.4 billion in 1986, to nearly $15 billion in 1988, partially reflecting the repatriation of ethnic Chinese capital in response to the more favorable operating environment secured by economic liberalization.

In a broader perspective, total financial flows to developing countries between 1979-1982 rose 35% over flows between 1976-78, while flows to Indonesia rose 43% during the same period.[21] Total financial flows to developing countries recorded between 1983-1987 declined 21% from the 1979-82 levels, but *rose* nearly 8% in the same period for Indonesia. Looking at private bilateral flows, the level recorded for all developing countries between 1979-82 rose 27% while private flows to Indonesia jumped 57%. In the 1983-87 period developing countries experienced a 51% drop in private bilateral flows while Indonesia recorded a slightly less unfavorable 39% decline. Pragmatic economic management, timely debt service, and high levels of official bilateral and multilateral flows maintained under the auspices of the IGGI enabled Indonesia to avoid the Latin American plight where the financial spigots have run dry.[22]

New Initiatives

Recent initiatives taken by the Japanese government are aimed at encouraging a higher flow of investments to Indonesia. These include investment seminars and assisting Japanese companies to locate prospective local partners as part of what is called the New AID Plan (NAP).[23] The Japan Export Trading Organization (JETRO) is aiming to stimulate investments by medium and small size Japanese firms, providing them with background information and identifying promising sectors. Based on Japan's experience, Japanese officials believe that small and medium scale enterprises can serve as engines of growth, job creation, and appropriate technology transfer.[24]

Another new organization, the Japan International Development Organization (JAIDO) was set up with funding from the OECF and the Keidanren. JAIDO aims to establish joint ventures between Japanese companies and developing country counterparts, providing small amounts of seed money but relying largely on private sector initiative and funding.[25] Perhaps to a greater degree than any other organization, JAIDO reflects a hybrid cooperative public/private sector approach to development and the importance attached to revenue generating ventures. Both the JAIDO and NAP programs belie Japan's image of not taking initiatives, and show a willingness to experiment and improvise.[26]

Trading Conundrum?

Canadian scholar Martin Rudner argues that Japan faces an embarrassing conundrum if its policy of promoting Indonesia's manufacturing export sector actually pans out. He says that "strategy that focuses ODA on export-oriented development must, in the last analysis, provide for reciprocity in terms of import development... [and] a greater openness of the Japanese economy to exports from that region."[27] Rudner concludes by noting the irony of a trade oriented development policy ultimately compelling Japan to reconsider its restrictive trading policies.

Japan has a reputation for importing raw materials and closing the door to manufactured goods. In the case of Indonesia, in 1989, 62.3 % of Indonesia's exports to Japan were fuels, while an additional 11.2% were raw materials and metal ores. This suggests that the Indonesian export profile fits the pattern. However, closer examination indicates that Japan is beginning to address the issues of trade adjustment raised by Rudner. The percentage of Japan's imports of manufactured goods from Indonesia out of total imports from Indonesia rose from 4.2% in 1985 to 20% in 1990.[28] In absolute terms, the value of manufactured imports rose from $426 million to $2 billion in the same five year period. Total imports from Indonesia rose 50% between 1986 and 1989 while manufactured imports rose four fold. Nonetheless, since Japan only imports about 18% of Indonesia's manufactured exports, clearly there is room for even greater progress. To a large extent, Japanese subsidiaries producing in Indonesia have concentrated on third country markets and have not yet made much headway in cracking the Japanese market.[29]

It is also a matter for concern that over 40 percent of Indonesia's manufactured exports to Japan consist of plywood and veneered panels.[30] Further sharp increases in Japan's imports of Indonesian manufactured products, and diversification of these imports (other than textiles, plywood, rubber and glass), are considered a priority by the Japanese government. "Japan, for its part, must import products from countries having large accumulated debts, such as Indonesia. Special preferential measures to achieve this would be beneficial."[31]

Such expressions of good intentions have been greeted with skepticism in the past, but recent trends suggest that the Japanese are making headway. In the Japanese view, promoting trade oriented development, and granting market access to boost that trade, is crucial to the long term strategy of helping Indonesia to service and ease its considerable debt burdens. And, in supporting expansion and diversification of labor intensive manufacturing, Japan is also assisting in addressing the critical problems of unemployment, as well as the medium-term transition to the post-oil era.

Indonesia's Debt Crisis and Japan's Responses

In 1985, the Paris Club agreed upon a sharp realignment in currency values that led to a near doubling in the value of the yen against the dollar by the end of 1987. The aim of weakening the dollar was to address the bilateral trade problems between the U.S. and Japan. However, the unintended consequences for Asian countries were enormous. By mid-1986, the Indonesian government was bitterly complaining that *endaka*, the dramatic appreciation of the yen, was ruining Indonesia, adding some several billion dollars to its annual debt service burden at the same time that oil revenues were plummeting due to low international oil prices. Indonesia was caught in a squeeze, since one third of its debts were denominated in appreciating yen, while most of its export revenues were denominated in depreciating dollars. There were suggestions that Indonesia might have to reschedule and there were proposals to permit Indonesia to pay back its yen denominated debts at the exchange rate prevailing when the debts were incurred, roughly 240 yen per dollar.

The silver lining of *endaka* was that it induced the relocation of Japanese productive facilities to lower cost countries such as Indonesia. There were fears about the hollowing out of Japanese industry and a potential boomerang effect, but currency realignment and labor shortages made a compelling case for Japan to shed its relatively labor intensive operations and move them where wages were lower. While the outflow was not nearly as large as many analysts predicted, *endaka* did get firms thinking about the virtues of lowering their production costs and many eventually did take the plunge.

In assessing Indonesia's successful diversification into manufactured exports, one long time observer argues that without *endaka* Indonesia would not have shifted as fast from its mainly import substitution industrialization strategy and made such significant progress in boosting the manufacturing export sector.[32] *Endaka* was a significant factor in forcing open the Japanese market for Indonesia's non-oil exports and inducing rapid increases in Japanese manufacturing sector investments in the late 1980s. Thus, Indonesia may have lost in terms of its debt portfolio, but it gained critical support for its industrialization and deregulation policies. In this sense, the unintended consequences of the Plaza Accords were largely positive for Indonesia.

As labor shortages intensify in Japan and if the yen appreciates further, Indonesia is likely to gain a larger share of Japanese investments. There is a perception that Thailand is relatively saturated and that the operating environment is deteriorating, the Philippines and China suffer from political instability, Malaysia has relatively high wage costs, and Vietnam is in both political and economic limbo.[33] Although the investment and regulatory environment in Indonesia is still flawed and there are mild concerns about the prospects for continued political stability after Suharto steps down, it is still a relatively attractive venue for a range of manufacturing ventures, particularly for products based on Indonesia's own abundant natural resources.

Bail-Out

The 1986 fall in oil prices severely battered the Indonesian economy and nearly precipitated a debt rescheduling. Oil prices fell below $10 per barrel, sharply cutting government revenues and more than doubling the current account deficit to -$4.1 billion in the 1986-87 fiscal year. At the same time, Indonesia was also coping with the impact of *endaka*, meaning that Indonesia had to devote a larger percentage of its dollar denominated oil revenues to service its yen denominated debts. In the 1985-86 fiscal year, oil and gas exports generated 58% of government revenues. This dropped to 39% in the 1986-87 fiscal year, plummeting from close to $7 billion to less than $4 billion in one year. This occurred at a time when debt service payments were rising from $4 billion in 1985 to $4.4 billion in 1986 and to $5.4 billion in 1987. Thus the drop in oil prices was catastrophic, threatening the nation's fiscal balance and its ability to honor its debt obligations. It is in this context that the Indonesian government proposed that the Japanese permit Indonesia to repay its yen denominated debts at the pre-Plaza Accord exchange rate.

Based on a series of interviews, it is possible to reconstruct the Japanese response to this crisis and in the process, gain insights on the making of foreign aid policy within the various participating bureaucracies. By the summer of 1986, following the June IGGI conference, Japanese officials were becoming increasingly concerned about Indonesia's deteriorating economy. One of the officials who played a key role in the bail-out suggested that Japan's response was most strongly influenced by the perception that Indonesia's troubles were caused by external forces beyond its control.[34] Having served in Indonesia as the head of the Ex-Im Bank office from 1981-1985, this gentleman was both intimately familiar with and favorable to Indonesia's program of economic reforms. He felt that the Japanese government should respond to Indonesia's problems by recognizing these efforts and as a means to encourage further deregulation and non-oil export promotion. Indonesia's record of sound economic management also made it easier to justify the bail-out to officials in the Ministry of Finance.

What ensued was an unprecedented Japanese government-sponsored debt rollover implemented with uncharacteristic dispatch and with great immediate benefits for the Indonesian government. The Ex-Im Bank played a key role in pushing the case for extending credits to Indonesia to help it cope with its severe balance-of-payments pressures and to finance rupiah costs of ongoing World Bank projects, which are normally borne by the recipient nation.

By the mid-1980s, Japan was blushing at its unprecedented trade surpluses, and the export-promoting Ex-Im Bank was an institution in need of a new calling. In carving out a new role for the Ex-Im Bank, proponents of the Indonesian bail-out seized the opportunity created by the Maekawa Report (April 1986) which "...announced that Japan should harmonize its economic structure with the international environment, correct the trade imbalance, and further expand economic cooperation with developing nations."[35] Later at the IMF/World Bank Annual Meetings, Finance Minister Miyazawa announced that the proposed recycling of Japan's capital surplus should focus on supporting the Baker Plan and relieving debt problems in the Third World.[36] The recycling would be implemented mainly through Ex-Im Bank and OECF untied loans, and was designed to include initiatives aimed at alleviating debt pressures on debt troubled developing countries like Indonesia which had not undergone debt rescheduling.

Indonesia's calamity was fortuitous both in terms of its timing, *and* because Japan has traditionally concentrated its aid efforts in Asia. Indonesia's strong track record on economic reforms and Japan's desire to begin an ambitious capital surplus recycling plan to appease its critics created a special set of circumstances that facilitated the Japanese Ex-Im Bank taking a lead role in arranging an Indonesian bailout. In addition, a community of interests came into play as there was a flurry of bilateral missions, formal and informal meetings and discussions that conveyed the urgency of the problem and laid the basis for concerted action. Prodding this along were high level political exchanges. For example, President Suharto's personal economic envoy, Widjojo Nitisusastro, visited Tokyo several times and called on the contacts he had built up over the years as Indonesia's senior economic statesman. He enlisted the assistance of his old friend, former prime minister Fukuda, who reportedly used his extensive political influence to ensure that Japan would respond quickly and generously to Indonesia's plight.

By March 1987, the Ex-Im Bank had arranged to extend $900 million in quick disbursing special assistance, outside the IGGI framework, averting a formal debt rescheduling, easing balance of payments pressures, and also helping Indonesia maintain its development momentum by funding the local costs of several World Bank projects. The loans played a catalytic role for commercial banks, mostly from Japan, who followed by supplying $300 million in syndicated loans. Without this decision to provide local cost financing, external funding in the aid pipeline would have been frozen and some ongoing projects would have been halted.

Since 1987, Japan has continued to provide high levels of special assistance amounting to $700 million in 1990 alone. Other IGGI donors contributed $300 million in special assistance in 1990. However, the nature of special assistance is changing. The Japanese are imposing stricter conditions and are earmarking allocations of special assistance more closely. In the FY 1990 package, for example, the OECF provides $500 million of the total special assistance in soft loans, divided between commodity and sector loans, aimed at supporting development in nine specific sectors. The remaining $200 million is provided by the Ex-Im Bank at stiffer lending terms more or less on a par with World Bank loans. These funds are designated for local financing associated with on-going World Bank and ADB projects. This process of tightening accountability and designating allocations has not been universally popular on the Indonesian side even though such flows do remain fungible and as such they free up government resources for other uses.

Who Decided?

Japan's quick response to Indonesia's plight and the unprecedented nature of that aid suggest that Japan's aid policymaking process is in flux. Several ministries and agencies have a piece of the aid action, but it is generally conceded that four predominate; the Ministry of Foreign Affairs (MOFA), the Economic Planning Agency (EPA), the Ministry of International Trade and Industry (MITI) and the Ministry of Finance (MOF). In the 1990s, the Ministry of Foreign Affairs, the Ministry of Finance, the Overseas Economic Cooperation Fund, and the Ex-Im Bank will dominate the aid process. In the case of the Indonesian bail-out, the Ex-Im Bank with the support of the other three institutions, took the initiative, signalling its shift from trade promotion to capital surplus recycling activities. This does not indicate a trend since the smaller staff of the Ex-Im and OECF limit their ability to manage aid policy while there is a lack of specialized staff in the MOF. The MOFA has trained some area specialists, but directly controls only a small share of the funds. Significantly, the absence of a centralized aid administration did not impede a timely response in the Indonesian case. Cumbersome as it may appear, Japan's aid system can be very adept at crisis management. It also helps that Indonesia is a recognized priority.

Gaiatsu

Robert Orr has examined the role of *gaiatsu* in Japan's overall aid policy decision-making.[37] The fundamental idea of *gaiatsu* is that Japan's ODA policy is a response to pressure of one kind or another from the United States. The pressure can be direct, as when the United States asks Japan to do something, or it can be indirect, relying strongly on Japanese interpretations of probable American positions.

In terms of Japan's aid to Indonesia, however, there is little to suggest that Japan's ODA is principally a response to U.S. pressure. Indeed, Japan is increasingly taking initiatives based on an interpretation of its own interests. Japan's own interests in Indonesia are so compelling and pervasive that there is no need for the U.S. to prod Japan. The bailout engineered in 1987 was Japan's initial foray into capital surplus recycling, a policy that was designed to respond to foreign pressures about Japan's massive trade surplus, but it does not appear that *gaiatsu* was either a decisive or direct factor influencing the Japanese response to Indonesia. At most, it helped create a favorable context for Ex-Im Bank attempts to lobby MOF to set a precedent on lending to Indonesia, permitting local cost financing of development projects and initiation of two-step loans through Indonesian banks.

Graduating?

The days of special assistance are numbered. One official says it is the first and last time such a bail-out will be arranged. The MOF is clearly worried about setting a precedent and finding other problem debtors lining up at the trough pointing to the Indonesian example. Officials are eager to graduate Indonesia from special assistance, arguing that it is dangerously addictive and encourages bad habits. Moreover, any sustained rise in oil prices would improve Indonesia's economic prospects and remove the rationale for balance-of-payments oriented relief. There seems to be a consensus on the Japanese side that it is time to end or substantially decrease special assistance. In 1991, the Ex-Im Bank is stopping its allocations while the OECF is sharply cutting its special assistance.

From Indonesia's perspective, however, continued special assistance is critical since debt service payments will exceed $6 billion in 1991 and remain at high levels through 1993. The fungibility of external funding permits Indonesia some leeway and by some unofficial estimates, about one half of the special assistance has been devoted to debt payments. In fact, high levels of IGGI assistance have been continuously exceeded by Indonesia's total debt service burden. Since 1987, IGGI aid packages have annually amounted to $4-5 billion while Indonesia's annual debt service has hovered near $7 billion. Debt repayments in 1987 and 1988 amounted to nearly 50% of government revenues. Thus, Japan and IGGI have stabilized the Indonesian economy, but a net outflow of funds due to a staggering debt service has sapped the economy and will continue to do so for the next few years.

Conclusion

At the behest of the IGGI, Indonesia embarked on an extensive and successful program of economic deregulation and fiscal austerity, stabilizing an economy battered by an array of adverse external developments. The government has embraced a trade-oriented development strategy, featuring the adoption of various reforms. These will ease the transition to the post-oil era during the early decades of the 21st century. Japan, and to a lesser extent other IGGI donors, have lent critical support to this ongoing process of economic liberalization, easing the financial crunch of the late 1980s with timely and generous infusions of fresh lending.

Indonesia has gained a reputation for being a model debtor, although its debt management strategy has relied on a donor managed rollover. Indonesia has borrowed some breathing room and along with IGGI donors is banking on manufactured exports and fiscal restructuring to ease looming debt service burdens. It seems a gamble well worth taking. Even if Indonesia falls well short of its goal of economic take-off by the turn of the century, its macro-economic prospects have improved as a result of structural adjustment. Translating this gain into tangible benefits for more Indonesians remains a priority.

In the 1990s, Japan's aid agenda in Indonesia will be dominated by project lending and two-step loans.[38] Project lending will concentrate on developing infrastructure and communications, helping to raise efficiency, lowering production costs, improving the investment climate and generally supporting private sector initiatives, foreign and domestic, to tap Indonesia's enormous potential. Two-step loans are favored as a means of targeting loans to promising export sectors. The World Bank argues that two-step loans amount to inefficient subsidies, but Japanese officials argue that stifling interest rates in excess of 20% inhibit development of otherwise promising small-and-medium size enterprises.

Despite an apparently viable long-term development strategy and adept tactical forays in resolving short-term crises, one senses a moderate degree of pessimism in Japanese circles about Indonesia's economic prospects, however. There are concerns about an orderly political succession and questions whether new leadership will back economic reforms with the same degree of authority as President Suharto. Moreover, Indonesia's agenda of reform remains daunting, requiring politically divisive initiatives involving privatization of state enterprises, dismantling of monopolies held by cronies and revamping a legal framework inadequate for the demands of modern business. Vulnerabilities and obstacles may well arise as the New Order tackles the problems of political reform and economic democracy. There are concerns that Japan will be drawn into the fray, a result of its high economic profile and strong links with ethnic Chinese businessmen.

From a policy perspective, Japan's avowed emphasis on private sector initiatives does not seem adequate to achieve all of the goals that Tokyo seems to have in mind. Sectoral loans and special assistance helped Indonesia over the hump, but this was not merely a case of recycling large amounts of yen and staving off the creditors. Japanese assistance helped sustain government services that directly benefitted the poor and such needs will remain even after the financial crisis has attenuated. Indeed, even if private sector initiatives are wildly successful, there will still be a need for substantial government to government assistance aimed at the large number of Indonesians who are unlikely to enjoy any tangible gains. With a proliferation of demands on Japanese development assistance and prospects for slower growth in the economic cooperation budget, there are clear pressures to favor private sector initiatives, but these can not adequately address the full range of Indonesia's development problems.

Endnotes

1. Carol Gluck, "The Idea of Showa," *Daedalus*, Summer 1990, p.22.

2. In doing so I pass over the somewhat checkered history of Japanese economic cooperation in Indonesia. Readers interested in exploring this record are directed to the following: "Japanese Official Destruction and Alienation (ODA), *AMPO:Japan Asia Quarterly Review*, vol.21, no.4, 1990; Y. Murai, *Musekinin Enjo Taikoku Nippon* (Japan:Irresponsible Aid Giant) (Tokyo:JICC Publishers, 1989); K. Suzuki, *Kokusaiha Guin to Riken no Uchimaku ODA Ni Muragaru Seijica Tachi* (Inside Story of Diet Members Vested Interests in ODA) (Tokyo: Yell Books, 1989); K. Sumi, *ODA Enjo No Genjitsu* (The Reality of the ODA Program), (Tokyo:Iwanami Shinso, 1990); *Kokusai Enjo Bijinesu:ODA wa do Tsuwakereteiruka* (International Aid Business: How Aid is Used, the True Colors of ODA) (Tokyo: Aki Shobo,1990).

3. This perspective is well articulated in the Commencement Address at the Institut Pengembangan Manajemen Indonesia by Drs. Radius Prawiro, Coordinating Minister for Finance, Economy, Industry and Development Supervision, Republic of Indonesia, December 1989.

4. For details on Indonesia's economic liberalization efforts see "Survey of Recent Developments," *Bulletin of Indonesian Economic Studies* (BIES), various issues since 1983; Moh. Arsjad Anwar, Iwan Aziz, Mari Pangetsu, and Hadi Soesastro, "The Indonesian Economy: Problems and Prospects" Paper Presented at the Second Convention, East Asian Economists Association, *East Asian Economies in the 1990s*, Bandung, August 1990. For a more critical view see, Anwar Nasution, "Managing External Balances Under Global Economic Adjustment: Case of Indonesia 1983-1988" University of Indonesia/ Kyoto University. Paper presented at the *Conference on the Future of Asia-Pacific Economies (FAPE III): Emerging Role of Asian NIES and ASEAN*, Bangkok, November, 1989.

5. Bank Indonesia. 1990 figure through the end of May. Panama has a higher level, most of which is paper investments.

6. U.S. investments overall are larger than total Japanese investments if oil sector investments are included. For a thorough comparison and assessment of foreign investment in Indonesia up through 1987, see Hal Hill, *Foreign Investment and Industrialization in Indonesia*.(Singapore:Oxford, 1988).

7. "Price of Security: Japan's Aid to Indonesia Reflects Strategic Concerns," *Far Eastern Economic Review*,September 27, 1990.

8.Most are not academics, but rather business-people and bureaucrats with significant Indonesian experience.

9. This discussion draws on Wayne Robinson, "Imperialism, dependency and peripheral industrialization: the Case of Japan and Indonesia," in R. Higgot and R. Robinson, eds., *Southeast Asia: Essays in the Political Economy of Structural Change* (London: Routledge and Keegan Paul, 1985); Hamish MacDonald, *Suharto's Indonesia*, Fontana, 1980; Qomarrozaman, "Foreign Aid," *Business News* July 10, 1990 (Part two of a four part series); G.A. Posthumus, *The Inter-Governmental Group on Indonesia* (Rotterdam: Rotterdam University Press, 1971).

10. H.W. Arndt,"Survey of Recent Developments," *Bulletin of Indonesian Economic Studies*, vol.X, no.2 (July) 1974. B. Glassburner, "In the Wake of General Ibnu: Crisis in the Indonesian Oil Industry," *Asian Survey*, (1976) vol. XVI, no.12, pp. 1099-1112; *Far Eastern Economic Review*, February 7, 1976, pp.62-63.

11. The violence of the riots was apparently directed at Japanese firms and Japanese products, leading many observers to assume that anti-Japanese sentiments motivated the rioters. Internal political rivalries in the Suharto government also played a role, as did close economic ties between high ranking officials and ethnic Chinese businessmen.

12. In 1986, Japan took the initiative in arranging another bail-out, providing emergency special assistance aimed at easing balance of payments deficits and fiscal problems caused by a drastic drop in oil prices. Since 1987 Japan has continued to provide large amounts of special assistance.

13. Country Study for Development Assistance to the Republic of Indonesia, "Basic Strategy for Development Assistance," January 1990. (Organized by the Japan International Cooperation Agency), p. 16. Hereafter cited as "Country Study".

14. At least 50 persons were killed when the military opened fire on a demonstration. Subsequent investigations exonerated the military.

15. This long held Japanese view has been embraced by the OECD, *Development Cooperation in the 1990s*. (Paris:OECD, 1989), pp.78-82.

16. For a detailed Japanese analysis of the Indonesian economy see, K. Okaido, "Indonesia-Country Sectoral Study," *The OECF Research Quarterly*, no.63 (August) 1989, pp.4-57 (in Japanese).

17. *Japan Times* Oct. 6, 1990, p.1,3.

18. Masaaki Horiguchi, "Transfer and Flow of Private Capital," Paper presented at the 13th Japanese-Indonesian Conference, June 6, 1988. For a bleaker view from the mid-1980s highlighting the need for reforms see, Toshihiko Kinoshita, "Japanese Investment in Indonesia: Problems and Prospects," *Bulletin of Indonesian Economic Studies*, vol.XXII, No.1, (April) 1986, pp.34-56.

19. Bank Indonesia statistics on an approval basis.

20. Capital Investment Coordinating Board figures on an approval basis. For comparison, 1986 foreign investment was $826 million.

21. Figures in this section are drawn from OECD, *Geographical Distribution of Financial Flows to Developing Countries*, 1976/1979 to 1984/87 issues.

22. "Indonesia: The Hottest Spot in Asia," *Business Week*, August 27, 1990, p.44-45.

23. Interview JETRO June 1990.

24. "Country Study," p.43.

25. Through April, 1990, Indonesia has attracted the greatest number of JAIDO projects, 3 of 9 representing joint ventures worth some 11 billion yen involving an industrial estate, and factories for metal forging, and knit weaving and dying. Interview at JAIDO July, 1990.

26. One can anticipate that critics will belittle these efforts as subterfuge and only aimed at promoting Japan's narrow commercial advantage, old wine in a new bottle, but it seems that the blending of public and private sector efforts holds promise and is in step with current thinking in the OECD. See: OECD, *Development Cooperation in the 1990s*, (Paris: OECD, 1989).

27. Martin Rudner, "Japanese Official Development Assistance to Southeast Asia," *Modern Asian Studies*, 23, I (1989), 73-116.

28. MITI, *White Paper on International Trade*, as cited in T. Kinoshita, "Deregulation Policy and Foreign Debt Management in Indonesia toward the 21st Century," Paper presented at the Indonesian Economists Association, Jakarta, Sept, 1990. Also see *Far Eastern Economic Review*, September 27, 1990, p.56.

29. This also seems to be the case with Japanese firms operating in Brazil, although the prospects for rising exports of manufactured goods from Indonesia to Japan appear reasonably good, especially as recent investment projects come on line. See Leon Hollerman, *Japan's Economic Strategy in Brazil*, (New York: Lexington, 1988).

30. JETRO, *Japan's Growing Manufactured Imports from East Asia*, 1989, p.20-21.

31. "Country Study," p.15.

32. Interviews, T. Kinoshita, Head of 1st Loan Division, Ex-Im Bank of Japan.

33. Many Japanese are positive about business prospects in Vietnam and praise the industriousness of its workforce.

34. Interview with T. Kinoshita, Ex-Im Bank, September, 1990.

35. Toshihiko Kinoshita, "Developments in the International Debt Strategy and Japan's Response" Revised English version (mimeo), August, 1990, p.9. Original Japanese version appeared in *Kokusai Mondai* (International Affairs), no. 356 (November),1989, pp.51-69.

36. The original $10 billion recycling package was increased to $30 billion in April, 1987.

37. Robert M. Orr, Jr., *The Emergence of Japan's Foreign Aid Power* (New York, Columbia University Press, 1990).

38. The OECF and EX-Im Bank lend funds to Indonesian banks which are then lent to Indonesian borrowers, usually small and medium sized enterprises, at rates which are lower than prevailing rates.

4

FROM REPARATIONS TO *KATAGAWARI*: JAPAN'S ODA TO THE PHILIPPINES

Akira Takahashi

Introduction

From the beginning, Japan has consistently claimed that her official development assistance to developing nations ought to contribute to building economic self-reliance on their part. In other words, in principle, the purpose of giving ODA was not to build continuing dependence on Japanese aid by recipient countries, but rather to enable recipient countries ultimately to become less reliant on ODA.

In practice, however, the allocation and impacts of Japan's ODA have not been restricted to nor entirely consistent with these lofty goals. Japan's ODA has often been allocated and utilized in ways linked plainly and primarily with the promotion of Japanese business interests. While such links were and are not now necessarily incompatible with reducing the needs that countries have for ODA nor with the strengthening of a country's economic self-reliance, concerns have grown that the objective of promoting economic self-reliance might be only incidental compared to the objective of promoting Japanese business interests. Pressure from both inside and outside Japan based on this concern is encouraging Japan to consider articulating a clearer ODA philosophy as well as considering needs to restructure its ODA system in directions indicated by a clarification of purposes.

Japan's ODA relationships with the Philippines have proven to be one of the prime justifications for reassessing the purposes and organization of Japan's ODA. From the beginning of Japan's ODA endeavors, the Philippines has been a major concern and has consistently presented a number of fundamental questions about the nature and purposes of Japan's ODA. One of the region's most advanced developing countries as recently as 1960, the Philippines has been left behind in terms of economic development by countries in Asia it once led-—including Korea, Taiwan, Thailand, and Malaysia. Despite three decades of support from bilateral and multilateral donors—and a close relationship with the United States—there are few prepared to seriously argue that the Philippine economy in the 1990s has any better prospects than it has had in three previous decades.[1] Significant levels of serious inequality, poverty, and corruption have persevered and have co-existed with significant commitments to at least the formal trappings of democracy.

In fact, it was assistance extended to the Philippines during the final years of the Marcos regime that ignited broad public debates within Japan about the basic purposes (and shortcomings) of Japan's ODA. There was evidence of projects that were poorly done and worse, projects that were never completed despite the absorption of large amounts of Japanese ODA funds. The Marcos scandals made the Japanese public aware of the possibilities that not all ODA programs were good for the people of the nations receiving the ODA and that in some cases, only the privileged groups in recipient countries, as well in the donor country, benefitted. These concerns did not subside with the fall of the Marcos regime and Japan's rise to become the leading bilateral donor to the Philippines. In fact, the expansion of Japan's ODA role in the Philippines has brought additional problems.

It is not surprising therefore that by the late 1980s, opinion surveys in Japan were indicating that Japanese taxpayers were growing skeptical of ODA in general and of ODA to the Philippines in particular. Several points of criticism have been repeated most often and their link to the Philippine case is clear. For example, does ODA reach those who really need it? Is it Japanese business groups and not those in recipient countries who are getting the maximum advantage out of ODA? Has Japan worsened the corruption and durability of dictatorial regimes by supporting them with the provision of ODA? The links from these questions to the Philippine case are clear, but the importance of the questions goes further. As Japan considers criteria for ODA allocation that include democratization and reduced proportions of domestic expenditures in developing countries on military matters, the Philippine case raises difficult issues of interpretation and application. What is democratization in form and substance? What are "appropriate" levels of military expenditures given insurgencies on one side and military participation in political life on the other?

From Reparations to Economic Cooperation

There were several reasons in the 1950s for Japan to give high priority to the Philippines. These included geographical closeness and the Philippine position astride major sea lanes, historical association in the pre-war period during which time Japanese business interests began to establish themselves in the Philippines, lingering and indeed festering resentments against the Japanese in the Philippines because of the harsh occupation experience, and the presence of natural resources crucial for Japan's growing industries.

The transfer of official capital resources to the Philippines was first initiated as reparations for war damages. Reparations programming was implemented from 1956 until 1976. During this period, the Philippines was allocated $550 million, the largest amount among countries which received Japanese reparations aid. Indonesia, which was the second largest, received $220 million, less than half the amount received by the Philippines. Overall use of the reparations funds provided to the Philippines in the forms of services and commodities is shown in Table 4.1. One third of the funds were used for public works such as water supply, airports, and school houses. A quarter of the funds went to transportation and communication projects such as railroad cars, freighters, ferry boats, and motor vehicles such as trucks and buses. Sixteen percent of the reparations funds were used to construct various industrial establishments such as cement and steel mills. During this period, additional yen loan credits of $14.2 million were provided in 1959 and 1961 using reparations claims as security. These credits were utilized for the construction of the Marikina Dam north of Manila, improvement of telecommunication networks, and improvement and extension of the railroads operated by the Philippine National Railways.

Of course, reparations are different from development assistance, even if the Japanese government has classified reparations as part of her historical ODA, in accordance with current guidelines of the OECD Development Assistance Committee (DAC). Reparations were provided to compensate a country for war damages caused by Japan. The Philippines was the recipient of substantial levels of external

TABLE 4.1 Sectoral Distribution of Reparations (net disbursement by %)

Public works	34.4	water supply, airport, school house
Transportation and communication	26.1	railrode coach, freighter, ferry boat, vehicle
Industry	15.8	cement mill, steel mill, machinery, equipment, materials
Agriculture and fishery	6.8	pump, tractor, fishing boat
Education, health, research	4.9	medical equipment
Electric power	0.8	generator, transmission
Mining	0.5	dump track, refinery
Consumer goods	3.5	rayon fabric, fertilizer
Service	3.0	expenses of the Reparation Mission
Credit on reparation	2.7	telecommunication, railroad
Salvage	1.5	
Total ($550 million)	100.0	

Source: Ministry of Foreign Affairs.

resources from Japan during early stages of Philippine efforts at economic development as an independent nation. However, it is difficult to conclude that reparations contributed effectively to broad-based capital formation in the Philippines during the 1950s and 1960s.

Certainly reparations were significant for the construction of infrastructure in the Philippines. However, in terms of capital goods such as equipment, vehicles, and boats, there were many cases of misallocation, misuse, and waste including several observed by this writer in the 1950s and 1960s. Considerable portions of these goods were distributed among established business groups, but resources were hardly used in ways that generated systematic industrial development and modernization. From the perspective of Philippine political and economic elites, reparations were literally a dole-out from heaven. On the other hand, the common *tao* of the Philippines had very limited access to the benefits of reparations, although they were supposed to be the beneficiaries as they suffered the most during the war. By contrast, in Japan, procurement of reparations goods contributed greatly to rehabilitation of war-damaged Japanese manufacturing and to the revival of Japan's trading corporations (*sogo shosha*). Reparations provided a sizable export market for products and the *shosha* served as brokers for all the procurement transactions.

Throughout the 1960s, Japan's development cooperation with the Philippines remained as reparations. Development assistance in a more genuine sense started toward the end of the 1960s. In 1969, Japan provided a $30 million loan to finance construction of the national trunk road now called the Maharlika Highway. The loan was secured, however, by expected future reparations. What soon followed were to become annual yen credit packages to finance the import of various commodities from Japan and the construction of various infrastructure projects. In recognition of Japan's established role, albeit principally through reparations, of providing concessional financing for developmental purposes to the Philippines, Japan became a member of the Consultative Group for the Philippines in 1971. The group was led then as now by the World Bank. Japanese grant aid started in 1972 with the installation of a flood forecast system in the Pampanga River Basin, and then continued to increase throughout the 1970s. Food assistance and technical cooperation also grew.

Consequently, by the time formal reparations programming ended in 1976, Japan had established a flow of both loans and grants to the Philippines for development financing purposes. It is important to recognize that the continuities involved were not limited to a flow of funds, goods, and services. Fundamental operating objectives and modalities established during the reparations period also carried over. There are four characteristics of the objectives and modalities from the reparations period that have carried over into the development assistance period.

The first was the strong roles of Japanese businesses as both the purveyors and beneficiaries of Japan's aid. The second was the strong tendency of Japan-Philippine aid programming to reflect the convergent interests of Japanese businesses and the Philippine political and economic elite in political stability and conservative socioeconomic reform in the Philippines. The third was that while this convergence did not necessarily exclude programming with broader developmental consequences, such consequences were not a primary concern. The fourth was that Japan's ODA policy was consistently secondary to the objectives and interests that the United States had in the Philippines. Japan accepted without challenge the U.S. economic and security stake in the Philippines and along with that, the U.S. interpretations of what protecting those stakes required. These continuities remained substantially in force until the late 1980s, when concerns about the Philippines among the Japanese public threatened to contaminate Japanese public support for ODA in general, did differences between Japanese interests and the U.S. stake begin to appear in any meaningful way. With the sequence of events in 1991 leading to the closure of Clark airbase, the decision to vacate Subic naval base by the end of 1992, and the continuing erosion of the U.S. ODA role in the Philippines, the transformation of U.S. interests in the Philippines present, or more accurately, challenge Japan with a potentially quite different agenda for ODA policy to the Philippines in the 1990s.

Significance of Japanese Aid

Through the 1970s and 1980s, Japan's share in the total ODA received by the Philippines was consistently in the 46-55% range.[2] In 1989, for example, the Philippines was one of 30 countries where Japan's share was the largest among all bilateral donors. As a recipient of Japanese ODA, the Philippines ranked between third (1975) and fifth (1970) in amounts received during the 1970s. This reflected the high position the Philippines held in Southeast Asia as a recipient of reparations payments, as noted earlier, and it reflected the importance as well of the Philippines for Japan's interests in the region generally and for Japan's business interests in particular. In the early 1980s, the Philippines ranking in Japan's ODA portfolio dropped due to the rise of Bangladesh, Thailand, and Burma as recipients, but the Philippines remained a major and increasingly visible recipient as the Philippine economy deteriorated and Japanese public opinion considered the increasing evidence that Japanese ODA was being significantly misused in the Philippines.

With the start of the Aquino government in February, 1986, the Philippines resumed a higher position, second only to China, as the Japanese government made a major effort, along with the U.S., to support the new regime and the redemocratization efforts underway. In 1987 and 1988, the Philippines maintained a position as the number

TABLE 4.2 Japan's ODA to the Philippines (net disbursement in US$ millions)

Year	*Grants*	*Loans*	*Total*
1970	15.7	3.4	19.2
1971	24.3	5.3	29.6
1972	38.2	65.2	103.4
1973	70.4	71.2	141.5
1974	33.0	40.3	73.3
1975	36.2	34.0	70.3
1976	3.0	78.6	81.6
1977	7.5	102.4	109.9
1978	16.5	187.7	204.2
1980	35.7	58.7	94.4
1981	45.0	165.1	210.1
1982	45.1	91.3	136.4
1983	62.0	85.1	147.0
1984	57.7	102.4	160.1
1985	69.7	170.3	240.0
1986	80.4	357.6	438.0
1987	111.8	267.6	379.4
1988	131.1	403.6	534.7
1989	176.1	227.7	403.8
1990	153.0	494.0	647.0

Remarks:
1) Years before 1978 are fiscal years.
2) Capital grants between 1970 and 1975 were calculated as balances of total grants and technical cooperation.

Source: Ministry of Foreign Affairs, *Wagakuni no Seifu kaihatsu enjo 1989* (ODA of Japan), 1989; Ministry of Foreign Affairs, *Japan's Official Development Assistance 1990* (Tokyo, 1991).

three recipient of aid from Japan behind Indonesia and China. In 1990, the Philippines was the second largest recipient of grant aid ($91 million) exceeded only by Bangladesh. Between 1957 and 1981, the Philippines received ¥260 billion and ranked as the sixth largest overall recipient of Japanese ODA. In the 1980s, a continuing high flow of ODA from Japan, especially after the political changes in 1986, made the Philippines the leading overall recipient of Japanese ODA (Table 4.2). Viewed from the receiving side, 28% of the cumulative amount (commitment) of ODA the Philippines received from 1978 to

1988 came from Japan (Table 4.3). Throughout the 1970's, Japan and the United States were the two principal donors of bilateral assistance to the Philippines. In the 1980's, over 80% of development assistance was provided by these two countries (Table 4.4).

TABLE 4.3 Cumulative Amount of ODA, 1978–1988 (commitment in US$ millions)

	Grant	*Loan*	*Total*
Multilateral	292.3	6,496.8	6,789.1
IBRD/IDA	192.4	4,169.0	4,171.0
ADB	91.3	2,245.7	2,257.3
UN	192.4		192.4
EC	81.3		81.3
OPEC		47.5	47.5
IFAD	5.0	34.6	39.6
Bilateral	2,514.1	4,074.5	6,588.6
Japan	628.8	3,123.1	3,749.9
United States	1,439.4	361.0	1,800.8
West Germany	92.2	170.0	262.3
Canada	129.1		129.1
Australia	127.4		127.4
Italy	33.3	60.0	93.3
Spain		91.0	91.0
Netherlands	19.5	43.2	62.7
Others	46.4	226.0	272.9

Source: Republic of the Philippines, National Economic and Development Authority.

During most of the period covered by the Marcos regime (1965-1986), Japanese ODA loans were used to support projects related to energy and infrastructure such as electric power, roads, and harbors. Since the economic collapse in October, 1983[3] and especially since 1986, ODA loans have been used for additional purposes such as financing essential commodity imports, addressing basic human needs concerns, regional development, and environmental programming. Examples include relief funds to offset international debts, electrification of low income

TABLE 4.4 Share of Japan and the United States in ODA to the Philippines, 1983–1988 (net disbursement in US$ millions)

	Bilateral				
Year	*Japan*	*United States*	*Others*	*Total*	*Multilateral*
1983	147.02 (41.6)	133.00 37.6)	73.66 (20.8)	353.71 (100.0)	57.93
1984	160.07 (45.0)	129.00 (36.3)	66.64 (18.7)	355.71 (100.0)	40.44
1985	240.00 (54.9)	135.00 (30.9)	62.55 (14.3)	437.55 (100.0)	49.25
1986	437.95 (49.4)	367.00 (41.4)	81.87 (9.2)	886.82 (100.0)	69.25
1987	379.37 (53.7)	230.00 (32.6)	96.47 (13.7)	705.85 (100.0)	69.38
1988	534.72 (67.7)	121.00 (15.3)	133.57 (16.9)	789.29 (100.0)	65.10

Source: Republic of the Philippines, National Economic and Development Authority.

districts of Manila, improving garbage collection in metropolitan regions, integrated development of Cebu City, and a number of reforestation projects. Capital grants traditionally were focused on education and manpower development and on agriculture and health. More recently, capital grants have been used to address poverty issues in rural areas. Strengthening soil research, extending upland irrigation, strengthening support services for agrarian reform, and improving access to safe drinking water are examples.

Japan's ODA is notable for having relatively high proportions of loan financing. This point has become a target of criticism by scholars of both receiving nations and fellow donors. This writer has reservations about assuming that grant aid is always better quality aid than loan aid. Certainly in some cases, such as the poorest of the developing countries, loan aid only adds to difficult repayment burdens and as such can contribute to deterioration of domestic economic and financial conditions in the recipient country. However, in middle income countries of Southeast Asia, such as the Philippines, grant aid is not necessarily a better form of assistance than loan aid in contributing to the achievement of economic self-reliance. Grant aid often strengthens tendencies of dependence and undermines domestic exertions to mobilize internal resources at both national and local levels. Even in rural development projects, the availability of external grant aid often brings about further dependence on foreign resources, exacerbates domestic political rivalries over which communities receive outside support of any kind, and in some cases serves as the currency for strengthening those political interests which can use grant aid to extract political support and other concessions.

By the 1980s, Japan's aid to the Philippines reached an important juncture. Suspicions of scandals involving misuse of Japanese aid funds by the Marcos administration had been present for some time, but were not a cause of public concern in Japan. However, by the early 1980s, these suspicions grew stronger and brought the whole Japan-Philippine relationship into question. Within the Philippines, growing opposition to Marcos also directed its anger against donors who were seen as supporting the regime's excesses and even its survival. Japan was bitterly accused of complicity in the Marcos regime's excesses by many Filipinos and increasingly by concerned Japanese. This opposition increased significantly after the assassination of opposition leader Benigno Aquino in August, 1983.

In the next three years, political opposition to Marcos grew significantly and at the same time, pressure against donors who were seen as helping perpetuate the regime also increased. The Japanese press began critical coverage of events in the Philippines on a more intensive scale.[4] This coverage included investigations of Japanese ODA projects and revelations of scandals involving these projects. During this period, several Japanese businessmen in the Philippines were kidnapped under unclear circumstances. While the kidnappings were blamed on the communist New People's Army, there were strong suspicions that the kidnappings were related to failures by Japanese businesses to pay kickbacks to military and political officials. The effect of these kidnappings was dramatic in Japan where daily news reports speculated on the causes, conditions, and possible outcomes. New Japanese investments in the Philippines slowed down and relationships between the Marcos government and the government of Japan cooled. However, this cooling took place out of public view. In public, Japan's ODA relationship with the Philippines and specifically with the Marcos administration continued and was increasingly the target of criticism.

The Japanese public became increasingly aware that the Marcos administration was suppressing human rights. The Marcos government was not the only regime in Asia that was doing this, but the focus of Japanese press attention was not on the other regimes (with the possible exception of South Korea). As indicated earlier, the Philippines and specifically the Marcoses held a more visible position in the eyes of the Japanese public than did many other countries and their governments. Japan did have the principle that she would not extend ODA to a country where human rights are clearly distorted, although there were no clear criteria or processes for invoking that principle.[5] In the case of the Philippines, opposition groups and civic organizations increasingly asked Japan to stop the ODA flow claiming that it reinforced abuse of the Filipino people by the Marcos regime. Mr. Salvador Laurel, then an opposition leader (later Vice-President under Mrs. Aquino), came to Japan and spoke to the Diet condemning the role of Japanese aid in supporting the Marcos regime. He told Dietmembers that perpetuation of the regime was against the will of the Filipinos.

For Japan, the issue had two dimensions. One issue is judging the legitimacy of the current power in a country. By its very nature as an intergovernmental transaction, ODA tends to support the regime in a recipient country. This support is not simply financial, but it is also political since it represents an external validation of a regime's legitimacy and inevitably can be taken as a sign of support for a recipient country regime by a donor government, not simply validation by a donor government that a recipient country regime was in power. In some cases, however, it is not a simple matter to determine whether a regime has domestic legitimacy. For Japan, and for any other donor, the problem in the Philippines during the 1983-86 period, for example, could not simply be determined by the views of the political opposition in the Philippines or even through an assessment of the strength of revolutionaries.

By early 1986, for example, the political situation in the country was highly ambiguous. In a Central Luzon village where the writer has continued community-level observation for several decades, a majority of the villagers supported the President mainly because of implementation of agrarian reform programs in that area. For any donor, it is one thing to determine there is instability in a country and another thing to determine that a regime lacks legitimacy. For Japan, traditionally hesitant to make judgements about domestic political arrangements in Asian recipient countries and traditionally reluctant to publicly second-guess U.S. judgements especially where the U.S. has significant interests in a country, the legitimacy issue was very difficult indeed. What was clear, however, was that by the 1983-86 period, Japan's ODA relationship with the Philippines had placed Japan in a difficult position. By continuing the aid, Japan was vulnerable to criticisms that it was supporting an illegitimate regime thus possibly endangering future Japan-Philippine relations. To terminate the aid, however, would be viewed by some Filipinos and possibly by other ASEAN governments as interference in domestic Philippine affairs. Such a step would endanger existing relationships with the regime in power and might generate criticisms from other Asian recipient countries concerned by the prospect of a more assertive and interventionist Japan.

The second issue is the problem of the economic security of the people in the recipient country. Here Japan confronted an issue that other donors have also confronted when they face regimes who behave poorly: who is actually hurt by a termination of ODA? There is little doubt that stopping Japanese ODA (e.g. after the events of 1983) would have had harmful effects on the daily lives of the Filipino masses, already strongly affected by deteriorating domestic economic conditions. Moreover, was it right for the Japanese to listen to the Filipino political opposition who after all were themselves economic elites with little direct exposure to risks from termination of ODA?

To understand the issues, it is important to review why Japan was giving aid to the Philippines. The motivations for Japan's ODA to the Philippines have three aspects. One is a sense of guilt for damages caused by the Japanese military during World War II. Particularly at the early stage of Japan's ODA programming, when economic cooperation went together with reparations, this aspect was significant in motivating an enlarging commitment. Grant aid for educational facilities as well as loans for highways were examples although benefits for Japanese business interests were also involved.

A second aspect is enhancement of economic ties to prepare a smoother path for activities of Japan's business interests, especially for securing access to Philippine natural resources and access to Philippine markets for Japan's products and investment. Construction of wharf facilities on the northern coast of Mindanao on grant aid, for example, was apparently connected to concurrent and prospective investments by Japanese steel interests in that same area.

In the 1980's, a third aspect, political considerations in international relations, became more conspicuous. From the perspective of the United States, the Philippines was increasingly regarded as the fragile link in Southeast Asia—exhibiting a poor international image, lagging behind economically, and unable to overcome various domestic insurgencies and venial politics. On the other hand, throughout the period under investigation, the Philippines was viewed by the U.S. as its most reliable ally in Southeast Asia on international security matters. This assessment was both reflected in and rationalized by the presence of significant U.S. military bases in the Philippines, but in addition was supported by the pervasive pro-American orientation of many Filipinos.

For both the U.S. and Japan, therefore, political stability and economic recovery in the Philippines were practically indispensable features of regional political and economic strategies in the 1970s and 1980s. While the U.S. political role in the Philippines was recognized as enormous and while U.S. economic interests in the Philippines were substantial, nevertheless by the mid-1980s, the flows of new U.S. capital—both private and official—to the Philippines were in decline. By the late 1980s, for a variety of reasons, it was also becoming clear that further extension of the U.S. military presence in the Philippines would be expensive[6] for the U.S. and that even if negotiations to renew the bases agreements were successfully concluded, approval of these agreements by the revived Philippine Congress was not assured. In December 1989, a serious coup attempt against President Aquino was defeated at least in part because of symbolic flyovers by U.S. jets from Clark air base. The U.S. gesture, made at Mrs. Aquino's request, ironically broadened opposition to continuation of the base agreement by those who were opposed to the Aquino regime as well as by those who supported the regime but were opposed to excessive U.S. influence in Philippine politics.

The recent expansion of Japan's ODA to the Philippines therefore is understandable only when we take into account the decline of the U.S. economic and military roles and the joint U.S.-Japanese interests in regional stability and security. U.S. interpretations of these joint interests were reflected in pressure on Japan to increase defense expenditures. Japan has resisted this as a general response, but for example in the case of the Philippines, Japan has accepted the concept of "burden-sharing" and has been willing to cooperate with the United States by increasing its share of donor responsibilities for supporting the economic recovery of the Philippines.

Today, Japan's ODA to the Philippines is most clearly an issue of triangular relations among the U.S., the Philippines, and Japan. In this sense, there has been a shift of emphasis in Japanese ODA to the Philippines from a more narrow "business orientation" to a "change of shoulders" (*katagawari*) for carrying the ODA load between the two donors. The U.S. phrase "burden sharing" seems to be too weak to describe the situation since what has happened is less a sharing of an existing burden a more shifting principal responsibility for an expanding burden. This point is further illustrated by looking more closely at Japan's ODA support to the government of Mrs. Corazon Aquino.

Japan's ODA for the Aquino Regime

At the start of the administration of Mrs. Corazon Aquino in February, 1986, Japan immediately expressed support, and offered grants and loans on a larger scale to the new regime in cooperation with the United States. Since the economic situation of the country was critical with negative growth, extensive capital flight, and a dramatic reduction in foreign investment flows, the Philippines urgently needed an inflow of external capital resources. However, as noted above, since the U.S. was in the process of lowering its proportional commitments of ODA to Southeast Asia at the time, Japan took the lead role in assisting the Philippines.

For this purpose, at the end of 1986, the government of Japan organized a committee composed of scholars and staff of ODA implementing agencies, namely JICA, OECF, and the Export Import Bank of Japan, to review the performance of Japanese ODA to the Philippines during the previous two decades, to examine the current state of the economy and development policies of the Philippines, and to prepare recommendations to formulate appropriate assistance policy for an anticipated new era of Japan-Philippine relations. The writer happened to be in the chair of this committee. "The Country Study Group for Development Assistance to the Republic of the Philippines"[7] proposed a "Basic Strategy for Development Assistance" in April of 1987. This was accepted by Japanese government as a guideline in formulating ODA to the Philippines, and was agreed to by the recipient government in principle.

As a basic concept, the report stated that the primary goals of Philippine development policies as indicated in the government's "Medium-Term Development Program (1987-92)" are the generation of productive employment, alleviation of poverty, promotion of equity and social justice, and attainment of sustainable economic growth. The report concluded that while Japan's assistance should be designed and implemented to help attain these goals, it is the Philippine government that is in principle responsible for all aspects of development assistance programming. This means that it is necessary to draw a clear distinction between the respective roles of both parties in implementing the programs.

One implication is that Japan should provide assistance that contributes to the enhancement of the Philippines' capacity to absorb assistance. A second implication is that considering that previous assistance had tended to concentrate on an improvement of basic socio-economic infrastructure, future assistance needed to be focused more clearly on benefitting the poorer stratums of Philippine society. A third implication for Japan is that since Japan's ODA had focused largely on "hardware" inputs (e.g. capital goods and infrastructure), in the future there needed to be a significant increase in "software-oriented" assistance (e.g. human resource and institutional development). This meant, for example, greater assistance for the formulation and administration of appropriate policies. The report also concluded that private sector resources and capacities both in the Philippines and Japan should be positively utilized in implementing programs.

As a short-term goal for Japan's assistance, the report indicated that emphasis needed to be placed on rehabilitation of the Philippine economic base after the damage inflicted during the Marcos period and strengthening the Philippine financial situation. This meant it was desirable to implement programs without delay to attain immediate positive effects on revitalization of production and employment. This was consistent with a U.S. preference at that point for rapid disbursement and rapid impact assistance. Such assistance served a dual purpose of supporting President Aquino's consolidation of power and, at the same time, demonstrating the importance to the Philippines of continuing assistance from the U.S. and other donors. In terms of medium-and long-term objectives, emphasis was placed on job creation and improvement of the rural infrastructure for increasing productivity of various industries and for improving income distribution.

The report also emphasized the following areas as policy priorities.

1. The target group for ODA-supported programs should be the country's poor who form more than 60% of the population.
2. Agrarian reform is indispensable to accomplish economic development and is a prerequisite for social justice and political stability.
3. Productivity of both the agricultural and industrial sectors must be improved.
4. Creation of employment in urban and rural areas is a critical priority. Emergency employment promotion measures, as well as

small- and medium-scale labor intensive industries mainly in rural areas, should be developed. Employment generating investment by the Japanese private sector should be encouraged.

5. Development of human resources committed to community-centered economic development is indispensable for sustainable growth.
6. Cooperation in health care should be provided on a continual basis to realize self-sufficiency in Basic Human Needs.

The report recommended: (1) immediate emergency assistance programs; (2) closer and more systematic interaction between assistance loans, grant aid, and technical cooperation; (3) diversification of assistance through steps such as the introduction of sector loans, peso-denominated loans, structural adjustment loans, international syndicated loans, and flexible management; (4) increasing the ratio of grant aid and technical cooperation components; (5) improved collaboration with other donors; (6) dispatch of advisory and executive experts; (7) exchange of junior corporate executives; (8) formulation and administration of assistance programs through effective use of human resources in the private sector; (9) expansion and improvement of the joint Japanese-Philippine system for evaluating programs; (10) improving the administrative and management capabilities of concerned Japanese ODA organizations in the Philippines; (11) assistance for research that improves identification of needed and feasible projects; (12) increased local-cost financing; (13) more incentives to the private sector; (14) more effective use of Philippine NGOs; and (15) expansion of cultural cooperation.

The study was unique in the history of Japan's ODA. Issues involving a particular recipient country were thoroughly reviewed, basic strategy for a specific country was discussed in detail, all members of the group were experts on Philippine affairs, discussions were based on deep insights about the actual performance of ODA programs in the country, target beneficiary groups of ODA (rather than types of projects) were officially taken into account, and the contents of the report was shared and discussed with the government of a recipient country.

After the start of the new regime, Japan enhanced her assistance to the Philippines enthusiastically. In 1986, ¥49.5 billion in loans were provided to cover essential commodity imports, flood prevention, local water supply, road construction in Manila, irrigation system rehabilitation, and others. ¥10.0 billion was granted for the Trade Training Center, the Metro Manila garbage collection system, strengthened support services for food production, the Labor Safety Center, and other projects. In 1987, ¥120.6 billion in loans was provided primarily to finance improvements in power generation capacities, essential commodity imports, flood control in Manila, and modernization of export industries. ¥11.0 billion was granted for construction of hospitals, improving food storage and marketing systems, and so on. In 1988, the loan amount increased to ¥169.3 billion, including ¥26.4 billion in relief funds to be used to offset international debt obligations and ¥14 billion for highway construction, electrification of poverty districts in Manila and others. ¥12.7 billion was granted for school house buildings and so on. In 1989, the amount of the 16th Yen credit package reached ¥214.9 billion which meant a 30% increase over the previous year.

While Japan was making a significant effort to help the Aquino administration through major expansions in ODA flows, this at a time when other sources of capital—both private and official—were in decline, disharmony nevertheless arose between the two governments on matters of development priorities. One issue was assistance to the Philippine agrarian reform program. During the Presidential campaign, Mrs. Aquino gave strong emphasis to the need for a genuine agrarian reform program, characterizing the land reform programs of President Marcos as tokens. She argued that comprehensive and thorough agrarian reform was needed to achieve social justice and to establish a more egalitarian social foundation. The government of Japan agreed with this assessment and after Mrs. Aquino assumed power, Japan adopted a stance of support for genuine agrarian reform in the Philippines. Japan argued that in the Philippine context, effective agrarian reform was a prerequisite to political stability and economic rehabilitation.

The posture of the political power of the country, however, changed. Throughout 1986, President Aquino deferred from essentially proclaiming a more rigorous agrarian reform program under the executive powers she welded at that time, arguing that even if the objective was justified, undertaking a major social reform through what amounted to dictatorial means (namely an executive order) was inconsistent with efforts to redemocratize the Philippine political system.[8] By 1987, a key element of the President's redemocratization agenda was in place: a new constitution. The constitution addressed the agrarian reform issue in a manner that required that landowners must receive just compensation. This was interpreted as market value. The decisions on land retention limits and program sequencing were left in the hands of the Congress.[9] This was troubling to proponents of agrarian reform because as had been the case before Marcos declared Martial Law, Congress was a stronghold of the landowning interests.

This caused serious controversy in the country with many peasant organizations expressing opposition.

In July of 1987, the government announced a Comprehensive Agrarian Reform Program (CARP). Prior to the start of the program, the Philippine government negotiated with the World Bank, the United States, and Japan in an effort to secure credits to finance the program. The Philippine government request to the donors covered land acquisition, extension, institutional intensification, infrastructure building, database development and monitoring, and regional development. The total cost estimate of the program was estimated at $2.5 billion of which $1,814 billion was expected to be financed by external resources. All three donors turned down the request. In the U.S. case, there was an objection in principle to the economic justification for reform, especially on rice and corn lands, where small farms already dominated. The U.S. indicated a willingness, however, to help support agricultural support services. The World Bank was prepared to support the principle of agrarian reform, but argued that land acquisition costs should be borne by the Philippine government itself since land acquisition was a domestic political matter. Since the Philippine budget was under substantial pressure, however, this meant that the Bank was saying publicly that the Philippine government would have to make serious developmental choices. Privately, however, Bank officials were reminding the government that money was fungible.

In the case of Japan, although the government was eager to assist agrarian reform in general, it was not possible to justify loans to be used to compensate landowners for land acquisition. Japan believed that issues of acquisition and compensation were deeply domestic political matters which the Philippine political system needed to recognize and for which it needed to assume responsibility. Japanese ODA officials indicated it would be entirely inappropriate for Japanese funds and worse, Japanese ODA personnel, to be involved directly in such matters. Beyond that, however, drawing on her own historical experience, Japan emphasized that reform was indeed needed, and that what was required was serious accommodation to this need by Philippine political and economic elites. If the reform were externally financed, Japan doubted that there would really be an alteration in the distribution of political and economic power in the Philippines. Japan was disturbed that there appeared to be little inclination by Philippine political and economic elites to support even a moderate agrarian reform. Japan was also disturbed that plans for agrarian reform support services were only vaguely defined.[10] In effect, the focus was almost exclusively on land acquisition and very little on the support services needed to make land transfer operations viable. Finally, Japan had serious doubts about the capability and integrity of the agency identified to actually lead implementation of the reform. The Japanese position caused some friction between the Philippine and Japanese governments.[11]

Since 1987, the political will of the Philippine government to accomplish the program has been continually toned down by resistance of the congress and landed groups. In addition, there has been frequent turnover in administration of the program, in part because of revelations of corruption in the limited land acquisitions operations that were undertaken. As a result, confidence in the whole scheme tended to weaken among the donors. Still Japan did make commitments to help support service projects as part of its agricultural and rural development assistance.

This is not to suggest that Japan's position has been clearly and consistently in favor of a comprehensive agrarian reform program in the Philippines. In the late 1980s, a controversy developed in the Philippines involving conflicting objectives between the Department of Trade and Industry (DTI) and the Department of Agrarian Reform (DAR). The DAR argued that a wide range of agricultural lands throughout the country were subject to disposition under the terms of the comprehensive agrarian reform law by the Department of Agrarian Reform for agrarian reform purposes. The Department of Trade and Industry argued that it was legally possible to withdraw land from agrarian reform eligibility if the land was scheduled to be used for non-agricultural purposes, primarily as industrial estates. The DTI was attempting to encourage foreign investment into the Philippines through the offer of lands and facilities for industrial estates. A primary target for this offer were Japanese investors and businesses. The problem was that virtually every municipality could designate land as a candidate for an industrial estate, thereby withdrawing that land from the agrarian reform pool.

It was clear that Japanese businesses were significantly interested in the industrial estate possibilities. Official Japanese ODA policy did not get directly embroiled in the controversy (which led to the non-confirmation of a DAR Secretary). More precisely, while Japan was not heard in favor of the estates, neither was Japan heard in favor of the priority of agrarian reform. In the politicized environment in which this debate occurred, Japan's failure to defend agrarian reform, was taken in several quarters of the government and the media as an approval of the DTI strategy.

Philippine Perceptions of Japanese ODA Policy

To understand Japan's ODA relationship with the Philippines, it is important to understand how the Philippines sees the relationship. A starting point for such an assessment, however, is to gauge to what degree Japan is seen distinctly from the United States. A study in 1988 explored this issue.

> Japan's interests in the Philippines are seen primarily as economic. The GOP [Government of the Philippines] senses (and to some degree, as elsewhere in Southeast Asia, is concerned) that there are also distinct Japanese political and security interests in the Philippines, but the GOP appears not to be entirely clear what these are. There are also potentially irritable sociocultural issues (e.g. the status of Filipino service sector workers in Japan, the behavior of Japanese "sex-tours" to Manila and Cebu) between the Philippines and Japan. When these irritants surface, GOP interpretations of Japanese attitudes towards the Philippines can be affected.
>
> There appears to be widespread concern that if the U.S. or Japan can define a basis for long-term economic cooperation with the Philippines, it might not necessarily be in the interests of the Philippines. As one GOP official put it, Japan's interests in the Philippines can be defined as the political in support of the economic, while American interests tend to be the economic in support of the political. In both cases, in the views of many Filipinos, the interests actually tend to be relatively short term and heavily weighted to the Donor's benefit. An example that was often cited is that recent GOP attempts to open discussions on improved market access for Philippine exports in the U.S. and Japan as part of ODA discussions were essentially ignored by the U.S., and Japan. Yet, the GOP is pushed, especially by the U.S., to permit the Philippine economy to be more open to American imports.[12]

Several aspects of the way Japan manages its ODA relationships with the Philippines were viewed critically.

1. Japan's consensus approach in ODA policy-making as well as her allocation criteria were seen as unsynchronized. This is a clear reference to what is seen as competition within Japan's ODA policy system between the Ministry of Finance and the Ministry of Foreign Affairs.
2. Japan's ODA was not seen as especially concessional. The reference is not to interest rates on loans but rather to rigidities in

how program and project loans can be used. For example, Japan tends to look for project activities in the Philippine budget and medium term plan that fit their "style," although these may not be the areas where the Philippines would like external support. Once agreements are signed, amy changes in project details are seen by Japan as problematic.

3. Japan does provide grants, but there are extensive requirements for purchasing goods and services in Japan with these funds. Prices in Japan are very high.

It is important to acknowledge that at the time these perceptions were assessed (1988), the Philippines was urgently attempting to restore economic growth, overcome the beginnings of what was to become a recognized severe domestic debt problem, and to undertake needed developmental public expenditures to restore both foreign investor confidence as well as domestic economic recovery. In these circumstances, the Philippines was looking for responses from donors characterized by rapidity and flexibility.

For Japan the problem was how to respond to what she recognized as a authentic need in a recipient country, but to avoid further misuse of her ODA funds, a concern that remained even with the new government. Finally, while Japan recognized the "relief" nature of some of the needs in the Philippines, Japan was deeply concerned about policy reforms that were needed to support a serious economic rehabilitation. This was especially urgent given the Philippines' external debt problem. The problem for Japan was how to communicate this perceived need for serious reform without engaging in forms of explicit bilateral aid conditionalities. Japan was not comfortable with this practice in part because of sensitivities about interventionism in domestic politics and policies in Asia generally and in part because Japan was concerned that the other side of policy conditionality was long-term obligations by a donor to support a recipient country.

Japan was not necessarily against all forms of policy-based aid conditionalities. Japan's objection was to the employment of this strategy by bilateral rather than multilateral donors. For example, Japan was uncomfortable with what she perceived as too strong a move in the direction of policy-based aid conditionalities by the Americans. In informal aid policy consultations between Japan and the United States in the late 1980s, it was apparent that while the U.S. and Japan might agree in principle that certain economic policy reforms were desirable, Japan was not willing to go as far as the U.S. in making those preferences into aid conditions. On the U.S. side, there were concerns that Japan was undermining the leverage that the U.S. and the multilaterals were attempting to exercise in favor of policy reform on some governments.[13] In the case of the Philippines, however, Japan's ODA policy-makers—especially in the Ministry of Finance—were coming to the conclusion that simply transferring capital resources to the Philippines was not going to be acceptable.

The Multilateral Assistance Initiative

Japan's basic posture for assisting the Philippines is expressed clearly in her positive participation in the Multilateral Assistance Initiative (MAI). The MAI is known in the Philippines as the Philippine Aid Program (PAP). To strengthen the economy of the country as soon as possible and to relieve the Philippines from the developmental burden of a $29 billion external debt, joint efforts in aid provision to the Philippines were proposed by the United States at the summit meeting at Toronto in 1988. The seven member countries agreed.

The MAI was designed to be more than a donor consultative group. Experience in the Philippines and elsewhere has been that the donor consultative groups, most of which were established in the 1980s for debt rescheduling purposes, were not especially effective as mechanisms for linking aid coordination among donors to agreed programs of economic reform by a recipient country. Instead, most donor consultative meetings were basically pledging sessions with perfunctory statements of policy reform intentions by the recipient government but with no clear association between these intentions and frequently discrete donor reactions and commitments. The MAI was supposed to address these shortcomings.

The MAI would involve a commitment by donors to work together as a coordinated group. The Philippines was to reach agreements with the World Bank and the International Monetary Fund (IMF) on economic reform policies. The Bank and the Fund would be responsible for both accepting this package and for monitoring Philippine compliance with it. On the basis of this package and any year to year agreed revisions that were needed, financing requirements would be identified and donors, acting in a coordinated manner, would respond through ODA commitments.

For Japan, the MAI represented a new level of coordination with other donors. Moreover, although the World Bank chaired the MAI, the MAI represented implicitly the significant role that other donors expected Japan to play in this case in providing ODA to the Philippines. In some quarters in Japan, the MAI was seen as an attempt to impose collective donor management and restraint on Japan's ODA.

Some even saw the MIA as an attempt by the U.S. to maintain its influence in the Philippines in effect with money from Japan and the World Bank. For example, one of the critical issues of the MAI/PAP was possible cooptation of MAI ODA programs by U.S. security objectives in the Philippines. In Japan, anxieties were expressed in the media about whether the MAI could be used as tool of *katagawari* between the U.S. and Japan, in effect transforming Japan's ODA into part of the package to pay for the U.S. bases.

However, given the recognized U.S. stake in the Philippines and given the potential financial enormity and political and social sensitivity of Philippine external financing requirements, the MAI was an acceptable collective mechanism for Japan's ODA policy-makers. What was especially attractive to Japan was that the recipient country would reach agreement with the Bank and Fund on a policy reform program and that progress in implementing these reforms would be monitored and assessed by the Bank and the Fund.[14] While Japan agreed with the need for macroeconomic policy reform in the Philippines, Japan was averse to pursue that agenda as a strictly bilateral matter between Japan and the Philippines.

In July 1989, Japan convened an extended donors meeting in Tokyo under terms of the MAI. The Philippine government prepared a medium-term development program for 1989-92 with the help of the IBRD and the IMF as a basis for the MAI. It estimated the amount of necessary `new money' at approximately $7 billion. Delegates of 19 countries (Australia, Belgium, Brunei, Canada, Denmark, Finland, France, West Germany, Italy, Japan, Korea, Netherlands, New Zealand, Singapore, Spain, United Kingdom and the United States plus Sweden and Switzerland as observers) and 8 international organizations (the World Bank, the International Finance Corporation, the Asian Development Bank, the International Fund for Agricultural Development, the IMF, and the United Nations Development Program plus the European Community and Saudi Development Fund as observers) discussed urgent needs, and promised to expand assistance to the Philippines.

On the Philippine side, steps were taken to organize an office for receiving and allocating MAI funds. The Coordinating Committee for the Philippine Aid Program was organized by order of the President to handle planning and implementation of externally assisted programs related to the MAI/PAP.[15] This represented a weakening of connections between economic planning and ODA management since ODA management was transferred away from the National Economic and Development Authority where it had been and placed directly under the Office of the President. The arrangement was politically controversial since it represented a significant weakening of existing administrative arrangements for coordinating external aid. For example, some countries such as the U.S., Japan, and Germany expressed fears regarding the capacity of the Philippines to absorb and utilize large quantities of ODA, especially since there was evidence of a significant backlog of already committed but unutilized ODA (estimated to exceed $2 billion) in the pipeline. The controversy generated claims within the Philippines that the transfer of aid coordination functions was in compliance with Japanese wishes.

Evaluation of Impacts on Local Communities

Together with the execution of development assistance programs, Japan has been attempting to assess the impacts of her ODA projects.[16] Generally, however, as is the case in other countries, project assessment tends to take the form of birds-eye views by dignitaries or audit-type evaluations by the staff of Japanese government agencies. The impacts of the projects on beneficiaries, while a matter of concern in principle, was a matter seldom assessed systematically. In recognition of this point, the Economic Cooperation Bureau and JICA in particular began to take steps to improve impact assessment. One strategy was to team Japanese and local experts together to assess project impacts. In accordance with recommendations in the report of the Philippine country study group described earlier, the Philippines and Thailand were selected as initial cases for joint Japanese-local expert evaluations focused on the impact of Japanese ODA projects on intended project beneficiaries.

A team of scholars and engineering consultants was organized in 1988 to evaluate two grant aid projects and one development loan project in the Philippines.[17] The projects chosen were a local environment and hygienic development project in the central Luzon and southern Tagalog regions, a forestry development project in Nueva Ecija, and a ferry boat system project between the Bicol region and Samar Island. On the Philippine side, staff and consultants from the Development Academy of the Philippines were appointed by the National Economic and Development Authority of the Philippines as counterparts to the Japanese scholars and engineering consultants.

The research was carried out for almost two years. The uniqueness of the evaluation is that it is based on detailed observation of specific projects for a long duration. The lower strata of the impacted communities were given special attention in analyzing impacts. Emphasis was placed on not only those who benefitted from the project but on those also who were negatively affected by the project. Through this evaluation project, many lessons are being learned for planning and implementing projects to meet the local needs, for smoother interrelations among agencies delivering and receiving development assistance, and for building better understanding between donor and recipient nations.

Conclusion

The basic nature of Japan's ODA to the Philippines has given high priority to Japanese business interests. This reflects the genesis of Japan's ODA to the Philippines in a long program of reparations. In recent years, Japan's ODA policy to the Philippines was characterized by political considerations to actively assist the Aquino regime in close collaboration with the United States. However, Japan's business interests remained an important factor.

Japan's current role as the top bilateral donor for the Philippines is likely to continue and even to expand in the future, partly because Japan places high value on political stability and economic welfare in the Philippines and partly because of Japan's relationship with the United States. However, *katagawari* is the right expression to describe the change of roles on the stage of economic cooperation in the Philippines between Japan and the United States.

With rapid growth of ODA in the Philippines as well as other parts of the world, Japan is looking for new horizons by herself. Facing internal and external criticism, and learning from experiences of ODA implementation for three and half decades, the government of Japan is gradually changing its approach in order to improve formulation of basic ODA policies. The late 1980's was the period when substantial renovation started in Japan's ODA. There is little question that Japan's experience in the Philippines has been a significant motivation for this.

One of the new trends is ODA execution based on area understanding. The `country study' approach that was first applied in the Philippines to examine past ODA performance and to prepare directives for future ODA formulation depends on the availability of country-specific expertise. Enhancement of evaluation of ODA projects, again through methods first applied in the Philippines, is another indication of progress in ODA assessment.

Opening of ODA information to the public is also being improved. This too can be traced to the investigative journalism that exposed various anomalies in ODA programming to the Philippines. Because the Japanese public was not well-informed about the purposes and results of Japan's ODA in general, these reports were both disturbing and educational. As a result, strengthening the manpower for ODA planning and execution are now eagerly sought by both public and private sectors groups in Japan. The necessity for a simplified central management system for ODA (to overcome the very diffuse decision-making structure now in place) is openly discussed as a step that is needed to enhance and streamline the administrative framework of Japan's ODA in the field.

Thus, Japan is in the process of reshaping its ODA framework to better meet new challenges.[18] Japan's ODA experience with the Philippines has played an important role in creating constituencies for such reshaping. However, the Philippine case also leaves some important old questions on the table, including the future of Japan's ODA relations with the Philippines—especially in light of the U.S. departure from Clark Air Base in late 1991 and from the Subic naval facilities in 1992.

The writer cannot help noticing the tendency of recipient countries, and especially the Philippines, to be weak in mobilizing local resources for their own development. Any increase of external assistance to the Philippines should not have the effect of enlarging already significant gaps between social strata and should not spoil spontaneous local resource mobilization efforts. In this context, it was very impressive to hear the chairman of a leading *sogo shosha* of Japan at a party held at the gorgeous Manila residence of the chairman of the Coordinating Committee for the PAP. He asked: "Is it necessary for us to extend helping hands to a country where so many tremendously rich families are present?"

Endnotes

1. See for example David Timberman, *A Changeless Land: Continuity and Change in Philippine Politics* (New York: M.E. Sharpe, 1991).

2. Overall American concessional flows were frequently higher than those from Japan, but these included U.S. Economic Support Funds which constituted grant payments to the Philippines in association with U.S. military bases in the Philippines.

3. In October, 1983 the Philippine government indicated it could not make scheduled payments on its outstanding external debt. This announcement came shortly after a similar announcement by Mexico and was thus treated by

the international banking community as part of the unfolding global debt crisis. The Philippine anouncement set in motion an economic decline that included negative overall growth and a contraction in particular of manufacturing. Analysts would say, however, that the collapse began in 1981 with the so-called Dewey Dee scandal as a result of which several banks failed. See Bruce Koppel, "Mercantile Transformations: Understanding the State, Global Debt and Philippine Agriculture," *Development and Change* (October, 1990), Vol. 21, pp. 579-619.

4. Senator Aquino was assassinated as he exited a commercial plane flight at the Manila International Airport. The assassination took place away from public view. However, a Japanese newspaperman and photographer claimed to witness the shooting. His testimony received wide coverage in Japan, all the more because Philippine authorities refused to permit him to return to the Philippines for several years.

5. See the chapters in this book on Burma, China, and South Korea.

6. Philippine demands were calling for annual "rental" payments approximating $1 billion per year (3-4 times more than average payments in the 1980s), trade concessions, and debt restructuring.

7. Japan International Cooperation Agency, *Philippines: Report of the Country Study Group on Aid*, 1987 (Japanese: Summary in English).

8. Bruce Koppel, "Agrarian Problems and Agrarian Reform: Opportunity or Irony?" in Carl Lande, ed. *Rebuilding A Nation: Philippine Challenges and American Policy* (Washington D.C.: Washington Institute Press, 1987), pp. 157-187.

9. Program sequencing was the crucial decision. Four areas for program coverage were identified: (1) rice and corn lands already identified as eligible under the Marcos programs; (2) plantation and other commercial agricultural lands voluntarily offered for sale; (3) plantation and other agricultural lands that would have to be acquired through negotiation; and (4) public lands. Given probable financing capabilities as well as administrative and political constraints, the sense was that those areas for coverage that were deferred were less likely to ever be covered. Sentiment in Congress was to defer plantation areas.

10. Japan and other donors indicated willingness to consider financing support services—such as agricultural credit, technical extension, irrigation and road improvement, etc.

11. Bruce Koppel, Hirohisa Kohama, Akira Takahashi, and Toru Yanagihara, *Japan-U.S. ODA Cooperation: Perspectives from India, Indonesia, and the Philippines*. Background paper for the Conference on ODA Management and Asia's Economic Development, Honolulu: East-West Center, May 10-12, 1988.

12. Koppel, Kohama, Takahashi, and Yanagihara, *Japan-U.S. ODA Cooperation*, p. 7. See also: Filologo Pante, Jr. and Romeo A. Reyes, "Japanese and U.S. Aid to the Philippines: A Recipient Country Perspective," in Shafiqul Islam, ed. *Yen for Development: Japanese Foreign Aid and the Politics of Burden Sharing* (New York: Council on Foreign Relations, 1991), pp. 121-36.

13. Bruce Koppel and Seiji Naya. *ODA Management and Asia's Economic Development: Report of a Japan-United States Aid Policy Dialogue*. (Honolulu: East-West Center, 1988).

14. Interviews with senior officials of the Economic Cooperation Bureau in March, 1990.

15. The Joint Forum for Philippine Progress was established by business groups, ex-government officials, aid-related organizations and scholars of the U.S., Japan and the Philippines, as the private sector group for the MAI/PAP.

16. Akira Takahashi, *The Impact of Japanese Aid on Beneficiaries: Observation in Southeast Asia* (Washington, D.C.: Georgetown University, 1987).

17. Overseas Economic Cooperation Fund, "Philippines: Country Sector Survey," *OECD Research Quarterly*, No. 64 (1989). (Japanese) See also: Akira Takahashi, *Enhancing Economic Cooperation Between the Philippines and Japan* (Manila: Embassy of Japan, 1990.)

18. See: Ministry of International Trade and Industry, *Keizaikyouryoku no genjouto kadai* (White Paper on Economic Cooperation) 1989.

5

PERSPECTIVES ON JAPAN'S ODA RELATIONS WITH THAILAND

Prasert Chittiwatanapong

Introduction

In 1988 and 1989, Thailand's double-digit growth made it the fastest growing economy in the world. Growth in manufactured exports is a key to this performance and this in turn has been driven in significant part by an infusion of Japanese capital and technology. The question for both Thailand and Japan is whether and at what costs this high growth can be sustained. For example, excessive concentration of industry in the Bangkok metropolitan area and inadequate infrastructure throughout the country raise troubling questions about Thailand's abilities to continue to attract and absorb both private and official capital flows in ways that are consistent with broad socioeconomic development.

Japan has a demonstrated commitment to and direct interest in Thailand's economic development, significantly strengthened in recent years, but with several decades of experience behind it. This experience has continued uninterrupted for Japan, despite Thai political change (including the February 23, 1991 military coup) and uninterrupted for Thailand, despite a growing Thai trade deficit with Japan over the last two decades. However, sustaining growth in Thailand in the 1990s presents Japanese economic cooperation policy-makers and Thai economic policy-makers with a complex challenge.

An article in *The Economist* summarized the challenge nicely.

> One solution to these problems could be for Japan to pay for the rebuilding of Thailand in its own image. It already provides 70% of Thailand's aid. And yet politics prevents it from increasing this share. Thais are more relaxed about potential domination by Japan than other South-East Asians, partly because they suffered less at Japanese hands during the second world war. But even they are starting to fret about becoming an economic colony.[1]

TABLE 5.1 Japan's ODA to Thailand, 1984–1988 (US$ millions)

Year	Grant		Loan		Total	
	$	%	$	%	$	%
1984	90.4	8.5	141.6	10.4	232.0	10.3
1985	117.2	9.9	146.9	10.7	264.1	10.3
1986	125.8	7.4	134.7	6.3	260.4	6.8
1987	135.6	6.1	166.9	5.5	302.4	5.8
1988	138.4	4.8	222.2	6.3	360.6	5.6
1989	204.5	6.7	284.4	7.6	488.9	7.2
1990	172.0	5.7	246.0	6.3	419.0	6.0

Source: The Economic Cooperation Bureau, Ministry of Foreign Affairs, *Wagakuni No Seifu Kaihatsu Enjo*, Tokyo, 1989, 1990.

Japan's ODA policy towards Thailand and Thai management of Japan's ODA are important windows on this complex bilateral relationship. Japanese ODA to Thailand during the period of 1984-90 is summarized in Table 5.1. During this period, both grants and loan assistance have increased significantly. Japan's total ODA to Thailand more than doubled between 1984 and 1990. As proportions of Japan's overall ODA, these actually represent declining shares since Japan's overall ODA grew more rapidly. Nevertheless, the totals to Thailand have made Thailand among the top three recipients of Japanese aid since the mid-1980s.

Japanese ODA loans to Thailand have supported infrastructure development projects identified by Thailand's national economic and social development plans. The top three areas for infrastructure support under Japanese loan financing were transportation (35%), power (20%), and telecommunications(15%). Together these three have accounted for 70% of all ODA loans offered by Japan from the beginning of the aid program in 1968 through the fifteenth yen loan in 1990 (Tables 5.2-5.3).

TABLE 5.2 Japanese Loan Assistance to Thailand, 1968–1990 (million yen)

Date of Agreement	Project	Amount	Financial Institution	Rate	Maturity	(grace period)
Jan. 12, 1968	First Yen Credit (I)	5,400	EXIM, CB	5.75	15	(5)
Jan. 12, 1968	First Yen Credit (II)	5,400	EXIM, CB	5.75	18	(5)
Jan. 12, 1968	First Yen Credit (III)	10,800	OECF	4.50	20	(5)
Apr. 12, 1972	Second Yen Credit (I)	1,821	EXIM, CB	5.00	20	(7)
Apr. 12, 1972	Second Yen Credit (II)	4,179	EXIM, CB	5.00	20	(7)
Apr. 12, 1972	Second Yen Credit (III)	6,000	EXIM, CB	4.00	20	(7)
Apr. 12, 1972	Second Yen Credit (IV)	17,000	OECF	3.25	25	(7)
Apr. 12, 1972	Second Yen Credit (V)	17,000	OECF	2.75	25	(7)
Apr. 12, 1972	Second Yen Credit (VII)	8,000	OECF	3.75	20	(7)
Oct. 7, 1975	Third Yen Credit (I)	9,550	OECF	4.00	20	(7)
Oct. 7, 1975	Third Yen Credit (II)	7,290	OECF	2.75	25	(7)
June 10, 1977	Fourth Yen Credit	24,900	OECF	3.25	25	(7)
Mar. 29, 1978	Fifth Yen Credit	32,500	OECF	3.25	25	(7)
Mar. 30, 1979	Special Yen Credit	10,300	OECF	3.25	25	(7)
Apr. 20, 1979	Sixth Yen Credit	39,000	OECF	3.25	30	(10)
July 29, 1980	Seventh Yen Credit	50,000	OECF	3.00	30	(10)
Apr. 21, 1981	Eighth Yen Credit	55,000	OECF	3.00	30	(10)
June 8, 1982	Ninth Yen Credit	55,000	OECF	3.00	30	(10)
June 8, 1982	Special Yen Credit	15,000	OECF	4.25	30	(10)
June 27, 1983	Tenth Yen Credit	67,360	OECF	3.00	30	(10)
June 16, 1984	Eleventh Yen Credit	69,638	OECF	3.50	30	(10)
Sept. 30, 1985	Twelfth Yen Credit	12,077	OECF	3.50	30	(10)
Mar. 4, 1986	Special Yen Credit	1,000	OECF	3.50	30	(10)
Sept. 18, 1987	Thirteenth Yen Credit	80,869	OECF	3.00	30	(10)
Sept. 22, 1988	Fourteenth Yen Credit	75,818	OECF	2.90	30	(10)
Feb. 14, 1990	Fifteenth Yen Credit	81,154	OECF	2.70	30	(10)

Note: Offical exchange note basis.
Source: Ministry of Finance, Bangkok.

Grant assistance increased significantly from $90.4 million in 1984 to a peak of $204.5 million in 1989. Grant assistance to Thailand as a percentage of all grant aid provided by Japan has declined, however, from an 8-9% range to a 5-6% range. Still, the continuing high levels of Japanese grant assistance to Thailand have been viewed by other donors as surprising given Thailand's growing per capita income (over $2500 in the Bangkok area). These levels are leading other donors to consider making Thailand eligible for graduation from such assistance.

The purpose of this chapter is to present a country study of Japanese ODA to Thailand and how Thailand has managed that ODA. The paper will first discuss the origins of Japanese ODA to Thailand with special attention on the economic-political background of the Japanese aid program in Thailand. Discussion will then consider the contents of Japanese aid policy to Thailand, including several factors determining the levels of Japanese aid. Finally, the management of Japanese ODA by Thailand as an aid-recipient country will be considered.

TABLE 5.3 OECF-Financed Projects to Thailand by Sector (1968–90)

Sector	Number of Loans	Loan Amount (million yen)	Share (%)
Power	31	157,140	19.66
Transportation	38	273,230	34.18
Telecommunication	10	115,549	14.46
Irrigation	13	54,840	6.86
Agriculture, forestry and fishery	7	30,051	3.76
Social development	14	53,183	6.65
Industry	11	58,492	7.32
Development loans through banking systems	15	50,839	6.36
Others	2	5,952	0.75
Total	141	799,276	100.00

Source: Fiscal Policy Office OECF, Ministry of Finance, Bangkok, and OECF.

Origins

Japan resumed her postwar trade relations with Thailand in 1948. In 1952, the Japanese-Thai Agreement was concluded to open a new era of economic relations between the two countries. In 1955, an agreement to settle the special yen payment was concluded. During the 1942-1945 period, Japan borrowed from Thailand a total amount of 1.556 billion Bhat (or 1.52 billion yen). After the war, the Thai government demanded the repayment of a total of 135 billion yen, or 90 times more than the original, because of inflation. The negotiations were prolonged and finally in 1954 the Thai government agreed to reduce its demand to 15 billion yen, of which 5.4 billion yen would be repaid in money and the remaining 9.6 billion yen in capital goods and services.

Such was the agreement concluded in July of 1955. However, there was a dispute whether the 9.6 billion yen in capital goods and services was to be transferred as grants, as the Thai government demanded, or as a loan, as the Japanese government argued. In November 1961, during his visit to Bangkok, Japanese Prime Minister Hayato Ikeda met Thai Prime Minister Sarit and agreed to the Thai government's demand that the 9.6 billion yen payment be considered a grant. With this political decision, the new agreement on the special yen problem was concluded in January, 1962.[2] Behind this political decision was the firm belief of Prime Minister Ikeda and the Japanese business community that the repayment would be used to procure Japanese goods and services.

The origins of Japanese ODA to Thailand, as in several other countries in Southeast Asia, were in reparations for war damages, or in this case, for settlements of war-related claims. These origins gave rise to two important legacies. One was the so-called request-basis method of decision-making for determining the volume of ODA each year as well as the specific projects to be supported by the ODA. The second was the deep involvement by Japanese businesses throughout the entire Japanese ODA allocation and programming process including project-identification, consultancy services, construction, and the procurement of equipment and other materials. One Japanese scholar has observed that Japanese "business organizations were quick to see the connection between reparations payment from 1955 to 1976 and the revival of Japanese industries in the 1960s."[3] Indeed, without this close involvement by Japan's business sector, Japan's ODA budget might not have expanded as fast as it did.

Another important origin of the Japanese aid program in Thailand is the Japanese commitment to the Western camp, especially to the United States. The San Francisco Peace Treaty and the U.S.-Japan Security Treaty, both signed in 1951, put Japan into a position of semi-alliance with Southeast Asian countries against the communist revolution in China.[4] For Japan, the loss of the old Chinese market could only be compensated for by the resource-rich and growing Southeast Asian market. At the least, this meant that the reinvigoration of prewar business connections would acquire added importance. In Thailand, Toyomenka and C. Itoh returned in 1953, Marubeni in 1954, and Mitsui, Mitsubishi, and Sumitomo in 1959.[5]

Prime Minister Ikeda was right in his 1961 calculation. In the long run, the question of whether the payment was a loan or grant made little difference as far as the Japanese business community was concerned. The reparation funds were spent to procure numerous goods and services from Japan such as textile plants, railway equipment and rolling stock, feasibility studies for power generation and distribution projects, and the dispatch of Japanese experts. Some money also was transferred to the Industrial Finance Corporation of Thailand (IFCT) to be loaned to private firms for the purchase of goods from Japan.[6]

Such were the origins of Japanese ODA to Thailand. The year 1961 was also the year when the Thai government under Prime Minister Sarit announced the first Five-Year Economic and Social Development Plan. The Plan signalled a shift in Thai economic policy from state capitalism to stronger reliance on private initiatives and foreign investment. However, because of significant weaknesses in Thailand's infrastructure, including power, roads, and port facilities, this shift required large scale improvements and investments in Thailand's infrastructure. Japanese economic assistance eventually helped to finance this five-year plan.

The Expansion of Japanese Aid to Thailand

Six major factors help explain the expansion of Japan's aid to Thailand. The first factor is the end of war reparations and the beginnings of ODA. It is generally believed that the year 1965 was a turning point for Japan's ODA policy in terms of aid volume. It was around this year that several war reparation programs were completed and the Japanese economy continued to grow at an extremely rapid rate. For Thailand, the first OECF yen loan was offered in 1968, in part in anticipation of the expiration of the special yen program in 1969. The first yen loan of 21.6 billion yen ($60 million) was used to finance seven development projects. The second yen loan of $208 million was offered in 1972 to finance Thailand's third Five-Year Economic and Social Development Plan (1971-75).[7]

The ODA doubling plans are a second factor. The overall Japanese ODA budget has expanded rapidly since the late 1970s. Increases in Japanese ODA to Thailand are certainly associated with increases in the size of the overall ODA budget. Trade and investment growth constitute a third factor. During the stagnation period of the Thai economy (1975-1976), Thai imports from Japan increased 1.9 times, exports to Japan increased 1.4 times, and Japanese investment in Thailand increased 3 times, but the ODA volume increased 6.2 times. Comparing the two periods 1970-1976 and 1977-1983, total Japanese private investment volume increased from $1.65 billion to $4.88 billion, but ODA increased even more sharply from 9,376 to 58,414 million yen in grants and loans. In the period 1986-89, Japanese direct foreign investment into Thailand increased from $884 million to $3.27 billion. During that same period, Japanese ODA increased also, although by a smaller magnitude, from $260 million to $489 million.

The association between trade and aid has been a source of some dispute in analyses of Japan's ODA policies. The simplest depiction of the association is that ODA and trade are closely correlated. The Thai case demonstrates an association, but the relationship is more subtle than a one-to-one association. For example, political factors may have played an important role in ODA allocations to Thailand. The economic stagnation period of 1975-1976 was a period of political instability in Thailand. There were border threats after the fall of Saigon in 1975 and domestic political uncertainty after the overthrow of the military dictatorial regime by the "student revolutions" in 1973. As a result, Japanese ODA to Thailand continued to increase to help support Thai economic development and political stability.

However it can be counter-argued that economic considerations were primary. Economic cooperation with an emphasis on infrastructure was calculated to be useful for future Japanese economic activities in Thailand. Also of growing importance was Thailand's trade balance with Japan. In 1975, Thailand had a trade deficit of $425 million with Japan. By 1989, the annual deficit had grown to $4.46 billion. The trade relationship represents a growing point of friction in the Thailand-Japan relationship. Since the mid-1980s, as will be discussed below, Thailand has attempted to undertake discussions with Japan to restructure the bilateral economic relationship. On Japan's side, ODA (as well as private investment) can be viewed as one way to reduce the friction generated by the growing trade deficit.

Political-security considerations constitute a fourth factor explaining the expansion of Japan's ODA to Thailand. The communist takeover of Vietnam in 1975 and the Vietnamese occupation of Cambodia in 1979 influenced Japan to play a more active role in Southeast Asia. Under pressure as well from the United States to assume more responsibility for peace and security in Asia, Japan decided to use its only effective official means, ODA, by increasing economic cooperation to a front line state, Thailand. Beginning in 1976, American aid to Southeast Asia began a decline that lasted until 1985. Japanese ODA to Southeast Asia began to rise in 1977, the year of the first ODA doubling plan and also the year in which the Fukuda Doctrine was announced.

Some experts on Japanese foreign policy offer another explanation for the relationship between political-security considerations and the growth of Japan's ODA program overall. According to one expert, the ODA budget increase rate was the highest among all budget items during the past several years because of one reason: the sharp rise in the defense budget. "It is very simple", said Shiina Motoo, a well-known *Gaiko Zoku* (Diplomacy Tribe) from Iwate Prefecture, "You just add two more percent to the increase rate of the defense budget. Then you have the increase rate of ODA budget each year."[8] Shiina implies that the ODA budget increase was used as a pretext to camouflage the hawkish image of the sharp rise in the defense budget during the Nakasone Administration. Certainly the parallel increase of the two budgets has drawn attention from many observers.[9] However, this does not appear to be a direct factor influencing ODA levels or shares specifically to Thailand.

The Fukuda Doctrine is a fifth factor. Prime Minister Fukuda played an important leadership role in the evolution of Japan's political, economic, and cultural ties with Thailand and other ASEAN states. Following his faction leader Kishi's anti-communist policy, he focussed his Asian diplomacy on ASEAN. It could be argued that the Fukuda Doctrine merely symbolized several trends in Japan at that time: favoring more ODA to ASEAN, more active cultural diplomacy with Asean nations, and strengthening political ties with ASEAN as Indochina came under communist rule. However, Fukuda's personal commitment to ASEAN apparently was sincere. After Fukuda resigned from his premiership, he founded the Japanese Solidarity Committee for Asian Alumni (JASCAA) to strengthen ties with former Japan alumni in ASEAN countries. He also strongly supported the ASEAN Committee for Japan Alumni.[10] Through control of the posts of Minister of Foreign Affairs and Minister of Education after his premiership, Fukuda continued to exert significant influence on Japan's ASEAN diplomacy and ODA activity. For example, Fukuda, his faction in the Liberal Democratic Party, and JASCAA were instrumental in Japanese decisions to support three cultural projects in Thailand. These grant aid projects were: The Japanese Studies Center at Thammasat University in 1983, the Social Education and Cultural Center of the Kingdom of Thailand, later renamed the Thailand Cultural Center, in 1984, and the Ayuthaya History Study Center in 1987.

A sixth factor is the role of Japanese business firms. It is widely believed that the Japanese construction industry plays a big role in the entire ODA process. They play an important role in project identification. They also push for the selection of the projects that they had been involved in developing. The request-basis procedure opened room for them to put pressure both on Tokyo and the aid-recipient countries. In some cases they even drafted the project proposals on behalf of the local government agencies. The traditional Japanese bidding practice of *dango* (taking turns winning the projects) also played a role. Efforts undertaken to initiate a project, pushing the project for selection, establishing connections with influential bureaucrats and politicians, and other investments in social functions were all counted in *dango* negotiations. A race to get the credits and investments was thus a game among various competitors involving many Japanese consultants, trading firms, and contractors. The situation became more complex as Japanese businessmen established close ties with local bureaucrats, politicians, businessmen, and military leaders in Thailand.[11]

Thai Management of Japanese ODA

Institutional Set-Up

There are three agencies administering foreign aid programs in Thailand. The Department of Technical and Economic Cooperation (DTEC) is responsible for the administration of technical and grant assistance. It is the Thai counterpart for JICA. The Loan Policy Division of the Ministry of Finance is responsible for the administration of loan aid. It is the Thai counterpart for OECF. The Overall Planning Division of the National Economic and Social Development Board (NESDB), the economic planning agency of Thailand, is responsible for the screening of all ODA proposals to check whether they follow the Five-Year Plan. DTEC has its own decision-making committee chaired by a Minister of the Prime Minister's Office, called the DTEC Policy Committee, composed of representatives from various agencies. The loan aid proposals must be submitted to the National Debt Policy Committee chaired by the Minister of Finance, to see to it that each year the total Thai government's loan commitments do not exceed the prescribed ceiling. This ceiling was set at $1 billion during the Prem Cabinet (1980-88) but was later increased to $1.2 billion and now to $1.5 billion.

Each year, the Thai Ministry of Finance submits a number of projects to the government of Japan for yen loans. According to the officials of the Loan Policy Division of the Ministry of Finance, the screening process is quite simple. The selection criteria are based on the Five-Year Economic and Social Development Plan.[12]

Unlike many aid-recipient countries, the Thai government has been very cautious in asking for ODA loans. As mentioned earlier, a debt ceiling has been set by the government for total foreign loan commitments each fiscal year. Furthermore, the Thai government sometimes refused to utilize loans even after signing the loan agreement. An example was the Fertilizer Complex Construction project, signed in July, 1986. The amount involved was 20,206 million yen. This was the highest value project among 14 projects that year, or one-fourth of the total of 80,999 million yen in loans. The Thai government determined that this investment was financially unfeasible considering serious economic stagnation and high appreciation of the yen. The latter development was an important consideration because repayment must be in yen. To the surprise of NESDB officials, the Japanese Ambassador in Bangkok gave several press interviews saying that Thailand needed to have that project.

Managing Japan's Aid

In August 1985, the Thai government officially made public a Thai demand to negotiate with Japan in a systematic and comprehensive way on trade, investment, economic cooperation (ODA) and all other bilateral economic issues. This document, officially called *The Restructuring of Economic Relations between Thailand and Japan*, but commonly called the White Paper, was the basis of negotiations in the following years. The first White Paper negotiation was held in Tokyo in December, 1985 and the second one in Bangkok in March, 1988.

There were three points concerning Thai-Japan ODA relations in the White Paper. One was the Thai objective of using Japanese aid to support the expansion of Thai manufactured exports to Japan, this to help reduce the huge trade deficit Thailand had with Japan. A second was the demand for more participation of Thai consultants in engineering consulting services and procurement of equipment and material for Japanese ODA projects in Thailand. The third and last point was a Thai request to extend ODA to the Thai private sector.

At the negotiations, officially called a "consultation," in December 1985, the Thai delegation asked for a review of the terms and conditions of loans for engineering services with an objective of increased participation by Thai contractors. The Thai delegation also asked for Japanese economic cooperation (ODA) for the newly-announced three-year Thai indicative plan. The plan envisaged 50% of Japan's grant and technical assistance going to export-related and other specific areas and assumed an annual increase rate of 30% in total ODA commitments from Japan.[13]

Since the form of the meeting was a "consultation," the answer from the Japanese side was vague. "In extending economic cooperation," the record of the consultation says, "The Japanese side would continue to respect the Thai needs and give as much consideration as possible to the new Thai approach." A less promising reply was given regarding Thailand's Three-Year Indicative Plan.

> Comprehensive allocation to respective areas of cooperation and 30% annual increase of total funds are both institutionally and financially difficult. It is also difficult under the present system for Thai construction firms and consultants to participate in grant aid as prime contractors.[14]

Two years later at the second White Paper meeting in Bangkok, the "consultations" ended in a similar manner. On the question of loans, the Thai delegation again indicated that the bidding procedures for consultancies should allow for more participation of Thai firms and joint-ventures formed between Thai firms and other developed countries' firms. The Thai government proposed that preferential treatment be given to Thai consulting firms. Where possible, Thailand wanted local materials to be used for projects financed by ODA loans. The response from the Japanese delegation stressed that the door was not closed to Thai consultants' participation, and that "market forces" and "competitive natures" would determine the prospects for Thai contractors and for the local procurement of materials and equipment.

As for the question of grant and technical assistance, Thailand again requested Japanese support for the Three-year Indicative Plan (1987-1989) which placed emphasis on ODA for export expansion purposes. The Japanese side stated that grant aid would continue to be addressed to meeting the basic human needs of the poorest sectors of Thai society, while technical cooperation would be "more readily amenable to projects pertaining to Export Promotion and Investment Programmes."[15]

Behind the diplomatic responses of the Japanese government was a strong recommendation from the Japanese private sector, especially the construction industry. They suggested that the Thai demands on ODA relating to consultants and construction should not be accepted. In response to the White Paper, as well as to criticisms from the Thai construction industry, the Japan Chamber of Commerce and Industry in Bangkok quickly formulated its position and made their position known to the Japanese Ambassador to Thailand in a letter dated November 7, 1985. The Chamber's Construction Department took a strong position on the construction aspects of ODA.

> For yen loan, to the White Paper's remark that OECF loan was beneficial to Japanese contraction business, as a donor side, we think that certain string-attached conditions are unavoidable. On the other hand it is natural. They argued that OECF loan's conditions were extremely small, a reason that made the Thai government decide to borrow OECF loan. As for the remark that Japanese firms won a great number of biddings, it was the competitiveness that made difference, so it was very natural. For the remark that it was advantageous to Japanese firms when Japanese consultants won the biddings, again this could not be helped. It would be unnatural if Japanese firms were made disadvantageous by employing third countries' consultants and making the BS standard the industrial standard. As for grant, to the criticisms by the Thai side that the selection of grant aid projects was largely made by the Japanese side, it was due to the absence of aid planning on the part of the Thai government. The White Paper's attempt to make the planning this time was a good indicator, revealing that the Thai government itself was not clear what projects were needed and when would they be needed.[16]

One favorable response eventually did come from the Japanese government. In 1988, OECF rules were changed. Rules governing selection of loan-financed engineering consulting services were changed from LDC untied to general untied.[17] Many claimed this change was pushed by officials in the Loan Aid Division of the Economic Cooperation Bureau in the Ministry of Foreign Affairs, against displeasure from MITI and resistance from the Japanese construction industry. As a result of these differences, while the change was accepted, it has been put into effect only gradually. Thailand was scheduled to be eligible for this new ruling in 1990. However, the fifteenth yen loan signed on February 20, 1990 does not allow general untied criteria for engineering consulting services. Officials at the Loan Policy Division of the Thai Ministry of Finance said that OECF officials mentioned that the untied criterion might be associated with the next yen loan, but they indicated "that it is still not sure."[18]

Japan's ODA Relationships with Thailand: A Case Study

There is a widely shared view among both public and private sectors in Thailand that Japanese ODA is offered with certain conditions to ensure that the money will not leave Japan. In particular, this is a view of the Thai construction industry. Since the mid-1980s, they have utilized mass media to appeal to the Thai general public to pressure both the Thai and Japanese governments. Their fundamental objective has been to gain a greater share of Japanese ODA construction contracts.

Dissatisfaction among Thai contractors about the advance into Thailand of Japanese construction businesses has been clearly expressed in the monthly journal of the Thai Contractors Association. For example, in the July 1987 issue of the monthly *Kahochang* (Thai Contractors News) a headline appeared: "Four Associations Joined Hands to Resist Aliens."[19] According to this emotional article, on June 16, 1987, at the Royal Engineering Institute of Thailand, representatives from the Thai Contractors Association, the Consulting Engineers Association of Thailand, the Association of Siamese Architects, and the Royal Engineering Institute of Thailand, came to discuss ways and means to protest against alien construction firms coming into Thailand, and taking away an increasingly great number of construction contracts. They were opposed in particular to Japanese ODA conditions which strengthened Japanese construction firms' position to the disadvantage of weaker Thai construction firms. Apart from the *Khaochang*, other Thai daily and weekly newspapers also have been used to launch public relations campaigns against Japan.

In 1987, the Thai Contractors Association appealed to the Ministry of Foreign Affairs to raise the issue of loss of contracts to the Japanese government at the White Paper negotiations on Economic Restructuring between Japan and Thailand. They also appealed to the Thai Chamber of Commerce, which is a member of the Government-Private Consultation Conference, to raise the issue to the Thai government. On December 2, 1987, they appealed to the Economic Affairs Committee of the House of Representatives. Finally, during February 4-5, 1988, the Thai Contractors Association, in cooperation with other associations and the National Research Council of Thailand, organized a national conference on "The Development of the Thai Construction Industry." The results of the conference were later submitted to the government.

The Consulting Engineers Association of Thailand was also dissatisfied. In May, 1987, they sponsored a seminar on "The Development of Thai Consultants" and made several proposals to the government. On July 27, 1987, the Economic Ministers Cabinet passed a cabinet resolution in their favor, instructing Thai government agencies receiving foreign loans to "give priority to the Thai consulting firm," or approving the so-called lead firm principle, with exceptions in case of high technology projects. The resolution also instructed the Finance Ministry, the Ministry of Foreign Affairs, and the Department of Technical and Economic Cooperation to negotiate with foreign aid agencies to allow more Thai participation in both loan and grant projects.[20]

Thai architects have been dissatisfied with Japan for offering grant projects with a condition that bidding for architectural design works are open only to Japanese architectural firms. Thai architects were angry to see the Cultural Center of Thailand, completed in early 1987 to commemorate the sixtieth anniversary of His Majesty the King, designed by Japanese architects in such a way that no Thai architectural beauty was expressed either outside or inside the buildings. Moveover, there was an unusual Japanese pavilion, surrounded by a small Japanese garden, standing inside the Center's compound in sharp contrast to the Thai pavilion standing nearby. The main building of the center was called by some Thai architects, "the elephant house," due to its clumsy appearance.

Dissatisfaction from the architects grew further in 1987 when JICA proposed support for the Ayuthaya History Study Center Project under the same conditions as the Cultural Center of Thailand. Thai architects were invited to participate as "commentators" on the finished blueprints. The more appropriate way, in their view, would have been participation from the very initial stage, starting with the problem of site selection for the project in the 417-year-old Ayuthaya capital. The resistance campaign reached a climax on September 26, 1987, the day Prime Minister Nakasone was scheduled to visit the ancient capital to sign the exchange of note documents. Concerned with the emotions surrounding the issue, Nakasone decided to cancel his historic trip.

The Association of Siamese Architects' protest received considerable press coverage. After efforts to mediate the issue by the Ministry of Foreign Affairs of Thailand during early 1988, an "ultimatum" statement was made by the Ministry of Interior. The Ministry of Interior indicated that the JICA project would not be accepted unless the architectural works were done by Thai architects. For the first time, JICA relaxed its grant conditions. A Japanese architectural company lost some work, but Thai public appeared to be very grateful for the recognition of Thai architectural tradition by Japan.[21]

Opinions of Thai Construction Industry Associations

Thai Contractors Association. In order to learn more about Thai private sector views on the impacts of Japan's ODA, 56 managers of Thai construction firms or contractors who are members of the Thai Contractors Association were interviewed during October 1988. Regarding OECF yen loans, Thai contractors felt they were placed in a disadvantageous position for several reasons. Almost all the bidding for engineering consulting works are taken by Japanese consultants as "lead firms." Japanese contractors could bring in tax-free construction machineries and Thai loan-recipient government agencies tended to feel grateful to Japan.

Regarding Japanese grant aid, the majority of Thai contractor respondents felt that Thai contractors were placed in a disadvantageous position. The overwhelming majority of the respondents felt that there existed some kind of Japanese state support to promote overseas bidding activities by Japanese construction firms. They pointed to low interest-rate funding, and the capability of Japanese firms to survive at low bidding prices.[22]

Thai contractors made several suggestions about how to address their grievances. Regarding Japanese ODA loans, the respondents wanted Thai engineering consulting firms to participate as "lead firms" in the construction projects since Thai engineers are technically competent. In OECF-financed construction projects, they wanted Thai contractors, owning 100% of the firms' shares, to participate in the construction projects as joint ventures with not less than 40% of the construction value. Regarding Japanese grant aid, the respondents wished Thai contractors could participate as lead firms. Similarly, for architectural design jobs, they wished that Thai architectural firms could participate as lead firms.

The Consulting Engineers Association of Thailand. Interviews were conducted with members of the Consulting Engineers Association of Thailand (CEAT), which had only eighteen members in 1986-87.[23] According to Thai law, foreign engineers are not allowed to come into Thailand to do their work except in foreign aid projects. Therefore, the opinions of Thai engineering consultants are mostly directed towards the problem of consulting projects under OECF loans. Their views, mostly in the form of questions, are briefly summarized below.

Why does Japan offer loans at lower interest rates than the World Bank and Asian Development Bank? Is it worth receiving Japanese loans if we have to lose something? Loan projects from ADB and World Bank accept Thai requests to allow Thai consultants to be lead firms. OECF maintains keeps tied conditions and has not accepted Thai requests. IN CEAT's opinion, procurement of consulting services under OECF loans should be general untied. They believe it is also beneficial to work with western engineering consultants because western engineering technology is higher than Japan's. Technology transfer is also more likely because there are fewer language barriers. Pacific Consultants International, Nippon Koei, and Sanyu are examples of Japanese engineering consulting firms who have been receiving consultant contracts in Thailand continuously for more than ten years. Fifteen Japanese consultant firms maintain their joint venture offices in Thailand.

OECF's agreement to allow Thai engineering consultants to participate in up to 40% of the total person months of work is not appreciated by CEAT Board members. If it were 40% of the total value, this would be better and closer to an equal footing. If our ability to carry out the works of Thai engineers are not inferior to the Japanese, why should we receive actually only about 15% of the total value? CEAT Board members interviewed also pointed out the problem of Thai engineers who have to work in an inferior position under Japanese consultants, a kind of relationship which will never make Thai engineering consultants grow and develop to a higher stage of technology.

CEAT rejected the idea of trying to negotiate with Japan. In their view, the Thai government should announce a policy of Thai lead firms for all engineering consulting services under foreign aid financing. If another suspension bridge or another international airport are to be constructed, Thai engineers should be the ones who do the engineering consulting work for the entire process. They ask: are we not short-sighed to swallow Japanese foreign aid with strings-attached, despite the fact that the Japanese engineering technology level is lower than that of America and European countries? They conclude: we have been long suffering since our government yielded to Japanese loan conditions.

Association of Siamese Architects. Interviews were conducted with members of the Executive Board of the Association of Siamese Architects (ASA), an association with some 3,100 individual members.[24] As in the case of engineers, foreign architects are not allowed by Thai law to do their work in Thailand except in foreign aid projects. Therefore, the opinions of ASA members are mostly directed towards JICA projects.

ASA has been angry to see JICA's grant projects in Thailand designed by Japanese architects. Their attitudes on this "cultural infiltration" by Japan are very nationalistic. For "cultural" grant projects like the Cultural Center of Thailand and the Ayuthaya History Study Center, Thai architectural beauty must be expressed and only Thai architects are qualified to handle the work. It involves national art and culture and the "faces of Thai people." In their view, the Cultural Center of Thailand is a shame having Thai architectural beauty expressed only in a small pavilion, not in the main building. ASA has been skeptical about the actual construction costs of JICA projects. They raised the question of *dango*. What is the necessity of importing the expensive roof tiles and toilet appliances from Japan?

Conclusion

The future of Japanese ODA to Thailand and the Thai management of that ODA has entered a new stage as Thailand is now following Malaysia, Singapore, and South Korea towards graduation from status as an aid-recipient country—at least according to conventional standards. A few years ago, it appeared that with graduation would come a reduction and ultimately a termination of all grant aid and technical assistance along with significantly reduced access to concessional ODA loans. However, as the continuing rise in Japan's ODA flow to Thailand suggests, this pattern is not inevitable.

The rise in ODA levels across all categories reflects the overall increase in Japan's ODA resources, but it more closely parallels the rapid rise since 1987 of Japanese private investment in Thailand, especially in the Eastern Seaboard area. The Japanese argue that while Thailand is indeed approaching levels of income compatible with graduation, its rapid growth momentum cannot be sustained without significant investment in major infrastructure including ports, roads, power, and communications. These investments are not within reach of Thailand's domestic investment budget nor are they appropriate candidates in most instances for commercial loans.

Does this mean that the association between ODA levels and allocation and Japan's commercial interests in Thailand and the Indochina region are now going to become stronger? Since the rapid increase in Japanese (and Taiwanese) private investment in Thailand is associated with a rapid increase in domestic Thai private investment and an increasing incidence of joint ventures between Thai and Japanese firms, it appears that new constituencies for Japanese ODA to Thailand are developing—both in Japan and in Thailand. What is new is that these are constituencies sensitive more to what ODA finances rather than to the modalities of ODA contracting and disbursements.[25]

The Thailand case certainly illustrates the contributions Japan's ODA can make to economic development. However, the case also illustrates that managing Japan's aid—from both the Japanese side and, in this instance, from the Thai side, is not without problems. While Thailand clearly has benefitted from Japan's aid, there are costs encumbered for that aid. On the Thai side, it appears that the long-range view of officials responsible for aid management have not been completely responsive to the impacts of Japanese aid on certain Thai interests. On Japan's side, there are similar problems of responsiveness to Thai needs and interests.

While the case study reported here can be viewed as a critique of relationships between the Thai construction industry and the Thai government, who after all are the "official" arbiters of the industry's relationships with Japanese ODA, there is a deeper issue involved for the management of Japan's ODA. Japan needs to learn how to pay better attention to forces that can be associated with strengthening civil society in Thailand. In this case, it appears that Japan responded to the short-term interests of Japanese contractors in getting the contracts and the short-term interests of the Thai government in getting the ODA. Japan's ODA policy will need to learn how to consider longer term trends in recipient countries. Japan's weaknesses here in relation to Thailand are not limited to arguments about who should design cultural centers and which sectors of Thai society might feel insulted. In February, 1991 when elements of the Thai military staged a coup and overthrew the democratic government, other donors (e.g. the United States) suspended their assistance programs immediately. Japan's massive program continued without a break. One senior Japanese ODA official described the coup as "a peculiar but traditional Thai political process."[26]

Finally, what the case illustrates is that the ODA relationships are neither stable nor isolated. They are not stable in the sense of what both sides expect or need from the relationship. Failure to recognize that these needs and expectations change—or at least failure to recognize without strong pressure—can have consequences beyond the ODA relationship. Secondly, the ODA relationship is not isolated. It influences and is influenced by wider changes in the roles of government and private sector actors in development financing. In the Thai case, it appears that these wider changes have had much to do with both successes and shortfalls in the ODA relationship.

Endnotes

1. "Japanese Investment in Thailand: Too Good to be True," *The Economist* (June 2, 1990), pp. 74-75. See also: Paul Handley, "Doubts Surface about Japanese Presence: Unequal Partners," *Far Eastern Economic Review* (May 3, 1990), pp. 51-52; Rodney Tasker, "Thais and Japanese Reap the Rewards from Partnership: Wedded to Success," *Far Eastern Economic Review* (May 3, 1990), pp. 49-51.

2. Akira Suehiro, "Nihon Tai Keizai Koryushi: 30 Nen No Ayumi" (Japanese-Thai Economic Relations History: 30 Years of Development), *Tai Keizai Shakai No Ayumi To Tomo Ni)* (Together with the Economic and Social Development of Thailand), (Bangkok: Japan Chamber of Commerce and Industry in Bangkok, 1987), pp. 286-287.

3. Kenjiro Ichikawa, "Japan's Repayment of the Special Yen Account to Thailand During the Second World War," Proceedings of the Joint Symposium on "Thai-Japanese Relations: Development and Future Prospects," Bangkok: Thammasat University, 1988, p. 32.

4. See the argument on the ideological significance of the San Francisco Peace Treaty on Japanese-Southeast Asian relations in Suehiro, p. 257.

5. Suehiro, p. 288.

6. Shigeru Sugitani, "Japan's Economic Assistance to Thailand," 1975, quoted in Patcharee Siroros, "Japanese and U.S. Aid in Thailand: The Thai Perspective," a paper presented at the "Workshop on Japan as No. 1 Donor?" Missoula, Montana: The Maureen and Mike Mansfield Foundation, May 13-17, 1975, pp. 11-12.

7. Ichikawa, p. 33.

8. From an interview with Shiina Motoo, November 3, 1990, in Bangkok, Thailand.

9. The idea that the defense budget is the "other wheel" driving the growth in the ODA budget is widely accepted, including by senior Japanese ODA policy-makers.

10. Fukuda was especially committed to cultural ODA. See Prasert Chittiwatanapong, "Japan's Cultural Foreign Policy," *Thammasat University Journal*, (July 1989), pp. 86-100.

11. See Prasert Chittiwatanapong and others, "Japanese Official Development Assistance to Thailand: Impact on Thai Construction Industry", a research report, Tokyo: Institute of Developing Economies, March 1988.

12. From an interview with officials of the Loan Policy Division, Ministry of Finance, Bangkok, November 2, 1990.

13. Statements by Japanese Delegation (Japan-Thailand Economic Consultations), a document for internal use, pp. 10-11.

14. *Ibid.*, p. 11.

15. The Report of the Meeting on the Restructuring of Economic Relations between Thailand and Japan (in Thai), the second meeting, March 29-31, 1988, at the Ministry of Foreign Affairs, Bangkok, published in June 1988 by the Economic Affairs Department, Ministry of Foreign Affairs, Thailand, p. 8.

16. *Tai Nichi Keizai Kankei Kozo Chosei Ni Kansuru Hakusho* (The White Paper on the Restructuring of Economic Relations between Thailand and Japan), (Bangkok: Japan Chamber of Commerce and Industry in Thailand, Document No. 164, September 1986), p. 83. See also: Alan Rix, *Japan's Economic Aid: Policy Making and Politics*, (London: Croom Helm, 1980), pp. 191-220.

17. LDC untied means that eligibility to bid on engineering and consultancy services or to otherwise provide goods and services for an ODA loan-financed project is open to any firm from a developing country or Japan. General untied means that eligibility is open to firms from all developed and developing countries.

18. From an interview with officials of the Loan Policy Division, Ministry of Finance, Bangkok, November 2, 1990. See also Prasert Chittiwatanapong,

"Towards A Qualitative Improvement of Japan's Official Development Assistance," a paper presented at "The International Symposium on Japan's Economic Role in the Asian Pacific Region: Policy Implementation and Responses," organized by the Centre for Asian Pacific Studies, Lingnan College, Hong Kong, and the International Studies Centre of Thailand, Huahin, Thailand, November 7-9, 1989.

19. *Khao Chang* (Thai Contractors News), Thai Contractors Association, Bangkok, July 1987.

20. *Government House Newsletter*, No. 535/2530, Bangkok, July 27, 1987.

21. Interviews with members of the Ministry of Interior Committee on the Ayuthaya History Study Center Project revealed that the Japanese decision-making process was very time-consuming. This made the final positive response from Tokyo less appreciated.

22. On the question whether there exists some kind of compensation fund for those member firms that bid very low in winning the contracts, the Nikkenren (the Japanese Management Federation) denied the existence of such a fund. They say that if there are such low biddings, it is part of the long-range strategies of individual firms. From an interview with Nikkenren officers at Nikkenren Office, Tokyo, May 31, 1988.

23. Interviews were conducted with CEAT officers in Bangkok on July 30-31, 1988 and November 9, 1988.

24. From interviews with ASA officers in Bangkok, August 7, 11, and 14, 1987.

25. This is also apparently a major reason for the continuation of Japanese ODA despite the military coup in early 1991 and U.S. objections to new aid commitments until civilian rule is restored.

26. Reported by Robert Orr from interviews he held at that time.

6

STICK OR CARROT? JAPANESE AID POLICY AND VIETNAM

Juichi Inada

Introduction

There are two methods of using economic aid as a political and diplomatic measure. One is to use it as a "carrot" and one is to use it as a "stick." In the former case, a donor says "If you do this, we will give aid" or "We will give you aid, so do this." In the latter case, a donor says, "If you do this (or because you did this), we will not give you aid." Such characteristics, albeit crude ones, describe the practice of aid conditionalities utilized by the IMF and the World Bank, especially during the last decade. It has been said as well that such calculations have influenced the distribution of U.S. bilateral aid. Conditionalities can be associated with significant year-to-year variation in the allocation of aid to different countries from donors who practice conditionalities. By contrast, Japan's aid policy builds incrementally—ODA amounts and their distribution are usually closely related to the amounts and allocation of the previous year. Increases and decreases are normally not extreme.

However, there are cases where Japanese aid has been significantly increased or decreased.[1] As described elsewhere in this book, the dramatic rise of Japan's overall ODA budget since 1978 has meant significant proportional and absolute increases in Japanese ODA to many countries and regions. However, there have been exceptions. Two examples of aid suspension are described in the chapters in this book on Burma and China and an example of aid varying year to year as a direct consequence of political judgements by Japan is described in Dr. Kim's chapter on Korea. However, the most dramatic example of a significant reduction in Japanese foreign aid is the freezing of aid to Vietnam.

In October 1975, the Japanese government formally decided to provide economic aid to the Democratic Republic of Vietnam (henceforth referred to as North Vietnam) which was moving toward national reunification after the end of the war with the United States and the liberation of South Vietnam. Japan's aid at that point to North Vietnam was a symbolic political policy which indicated that Japan, in an independent and unique position, was searching for a stable relationship with Indochina now that the long Indochina war was over.

In April and July of 1978, a total of 14 billion yen in economic aid was given to the unified Socialist Republic of Vietnam (henceforth referred to as Vietnam). In December 1978, Japan indicated that it would provide another 14 billion yen in economic aid in 1979. However, Japan changed its aid allocation to Vietnam after the Vietnamese army invaded Cambodia in December, 1978. Spurred by that incident, Japan place a freeze on its aid to Vietnam. This freeze has essentially continued until now.

In recent years, the end of the cold war between the United States and the Soviet Union, the progress of democratization worldwide, the collapse of the East European communist regimes, and finally the disintegration of the Soviet Union have vastly changed Vietnam's international situation. Against this background, with Vietnam's introduction of a domestic economic reform policy (*Doi Moi*) in the early 1980s—one of the earliest socialist economies to undertake such reforms—and withdrawal from Cambodia in September 1989, the Vietnamese expected that Japanese aid would resume and that other important elements of its international situation would normalize.[2] However, aid was not reinstituted because the overall Cambodian problem remained unresolved and because a comprehensive U.S. economic embargo in place since the end of the war remained in force.

In this paper, I analyze changes in Japan's underlying political and diplomatic strategy regarding the freezing of Japanese aid to Vietnam and the problem of reestablishing aid in the future. First, I will describe Japan's aid policy from the time that Japan provided aid to Vietnam after the end of the war in Vietnam until Japan froze the aid.[3] Then, I will analyze what the political constraints have been concerning reestablishment of Japanese aid despite the many changes in

Vietnam's situation. Finally, I will offer some perspectives on how Japanese aid to Vietnam might be reestablished.

Japanese Aid to Vietnam

Japanese aid to Vietnam can be divided into two major periods: the first from 1975, when Japan began to give economic aid to North Vietnam (prior to 1975 it was giving aid to South Vietnam), until December 1978, when all economic aid was suspended owing to the Vietnamese invasion of Cambodia; and the second, the period of the aid freeze that followed.

The Search for a Japanese Role in Indochina (Prior to December 1978)

During the Vietnam War, Japan gave aid to South Vietnam. The Japanese government also expressed support for the American bombing of North Vietnam. This position was criticized by the opposition parties and the anti-war movement in Japan as a "diplomacy of passive obedience to America" and "complicity in the U.S. invasion of Vietnam." In spite of Japan's public positions of support for the U.S., however, the Japanese government took relatively early initiatives in anticipation of the end of the war. In 1971, unofficial contact was made with North Vietnam in Paris. In 1972, just before President Nixon's historic visit to Beijing, Wazusuke Miyake, Director of the First Southeast Asia Division of the Japanese Foreign Ministry, visited Hanoi.[4] In December of that year, Foreign Minister Masayoshi Ohira disclosed to the Seventh Cabinet Ministers' Meeting on Southeast Asian Development that Japan planned to provide economic aid both to North and South Vietnam, reflecting a decision to "carry out international cooperation regardless of differences in political systems."[5]

Japan normalized diplomatic relations with North Vietnam in January, 1973 after the signing of the Paris peace accord between North Vietnam and the United States. In June 1973, Ohira announced before the Japanese Diet three principles on which aid to Vietnam would be based: (1) observation of the Paris Peace Accords by North Vietnam; (2) provision of aid to the entire country (i.e. North and South Vietnam); and (3) no hard selling of Japanese aid. He also revealed that 500 million yen in emergency humanitarian aid had already been given to the entire territory of Vietnam through the International Red Cross.[6]

In April 1975, Saigon fell to the communists, and South Vietnam came under the rule of the Provisional Revolutionary Government. Speaking in the Diet in June 1975, Ohira said:

> No matter what form of ideology is adopted by the government of South Vietnam, as long as it works to upgrade national self-determination, and the living standard of the people, and correction of the imbalance between rich and poor, we would like to maintain friendly relations and provide as much assistance as we can.[7]

On October 11, 1975, Japan provided its first official aid package to North Vietnam: 8.5 billion yen in grants (in the form of bulldozers, trucks, and excavators). On September 14, 1976, another 5 billion yen was given in the form of equipment and materials for a cement plant. In fact, this assistance had been strongly demanded by North Vietnam as World War II reparations.[8] Japan did not formally agree to the request for reparations, but the total of 13.5 billion yen in grant aid closely corresponded to the amount of reparations—14 billion yen—given to the former South Vietnamese government.

In August 1977, Prime Minister Takeo Fukuda proclaimed the "Fukuda doctrine" during a visit to Southeast Asia. The doctrine enunciated the principle that Japan would act "as an equal partner, to cooperate in strengthening the solidarity and resilience of ASEAN, deepen mutual understanding with the nations of Indochina, and thus contribute to the building of peace and prosperity in the entire region of Southeast Asia." This policy reflected Japan's intention to play a political role by acting as a bridge between ASEAN and Indochina.[9]

On April 28, 1978, a further 4 billion yen was given in grants (cotton thread, synthetic fibers, materials and equipment for electrical power networks) to the now united Vietnam. When official notes were signed and exchanged in connection with this aid, a "Memorandum Concerning Payment for Solution of Credit and Debt Problems" was also signed. This agreement was made in order to clear the debts owed by the former government of South Vietnam (a principal of 15.5 billion yen plus interest).[10] After two years of negotiations, the Vietnamese agreed to repay this debt in full. In response, on July 7, 1978, the Japanese government provided 10 billion yen in commodity loans (fertilizer, fibers, electrical equipment, tools, chemicals and pharmaceuticals, cement, rubber, and dyes), and Vietnamese Foreign Minister Nguyen Duy Trinh visited Japan on December 14 of that year.

Thus, after the fall of South Vietnam, Japan was the most forthcoming of the western bloc nations in providing aid to Vietnam, even if aid was connected with the problems of war reparations and debts inherited from South Vietnam. This policy reflected Japan's intention as an advanced Asian nation to play an independent, positive role in stabilizing Indochina after the withdrawal of American troops.

The Freezing of Aid to Vietnam (December 1978 to Mid-1981)

Japan's aid initiatives towards Indochina were brought to a standstill by the Vietnamese invasion of Cambodia in December 1978. Just one week prior to the invasion, the Japanese government had announced its intention to give the same amount of aid to Vietnam in 1979 as in the previous year: a total aid package of 14 billion yen, comprising a loan of 10 billion yen and a grant of 4 billion yen. This commitment had to be suspended because of the invasion.

One reason Japan was keen on providing aid to Vietnam was the desire to prevent Vietnam from leaning too far towards the Soviet Union. The Japanese government suggested that Vietnam pursue a peaceful foreign policy, contributing to the stability of Indochina and Southeast Asia, and that it maintain an independent political position.[11] When Foreign Minister Nguyen Duy Trinh visited Japan in December 1978, Foreign Minister Sunao Sonoda sought reconfirmation of this policy, and Trinh reportedly stated that Vietnam would maintain a peaceful foreign policy and would not allow the Soviet Union to build bases in Vietnam.[12] That same month, however, the Vietnamese army invaded Cambodia, and the Japanese government had no choice but to announce that aid to Vietnam would be "handled cautiously."[13] The government testified before the Diet that "we have told the foreign minister of Vietnam that it will be difficult to provide economic assistance if anxiety is caused to the ASEAN nations."[14]

Relations between China and Vietnam deteriorated decisively between February and March 1979, leading to the Chinese invasion of Vietnam. During this conflict, Soviet vessels continued to dock at Vietnamese ports, making the continuation of aid even more difficult to justify. In spite of this, however, the Japanese government maintained that there "could be no suspension of aid,"[15] and gave no indication of changing its policy of "moving ahead with implementation."[16] The reason for Japan's reluctance to change its policy was that a pledge had already been made to Vietnam and Japan was reluctant to reverse this pledge. Consideration was also given to the possibility that freezing aid would cut off the lines of communication between Japan and Vietnam, thereby weakening Japan's influence on Vietnam. The fact that Vietnam was continuing to request aid was another factor in Japan's reluctance to cut off aid.[17]

In June 1979, when large numbers of refugees began to pour out of Vietnam, the Japanese government announced that "a postponement of aid is possible."[18] In July, the Japanese government announced that "if the outflow of refugees does not stop, suspension of aid will be considered."[19] By this time, with the refugee flow increasing and the government of Vietnam doing little either to acknowledge the problem nor to curb it, many Western nations began to freeze aid to Vietnam as a protest against the Vietnamese government's attitude towards the refugee problem. Norway announced an aid freeze on June 23. Britain announced on July 3 that it would provide no new aid, although it would make available the loans that had already been promised. West Germany announced on July 4 that to continue providing aid would be impossible and that it would therefore reprogram money allocated to Vietnam to assist the refugees. Denmark announced that it would stop all aid on July 9. However, there was still no change in Japan's Vietnamese aid policy. In December 1979, when Saburo Okita was appointed foreign minister in the second Ohira cabinet, he stated that Japan would continue as before to "carry out [aid] while waiting for the situation to settle."[20]

This position of wanting to continue aid began to take on a more negative direction after American diplomats were taken hostage in Iran in November 1979 and the Soviet Union invaded Afghanistan in December 1979. These incidents forced Japan into acting more clearly as "a member of the west."[21] Japan found it difficult to continue providing aid to a country that was supported by the Soviet Union, and in January 1980, the Japanese government announced its intention of "not reopening aid."[22] There was no follow-up statement until the middle of February, when the foreign ministry made it clear that cutting aid completely for 1979 would be unavoidable. The reasons given, in addition to the unstable military situation in Cambodia, were the frequent presence of Soviet naval vessels in Cam Ranh Bay and elsewhere off Vietnam, and the possibility of permanent Soviet bases in Vietnam.[23] Some voices within the Japanese government recommended keeping the promises already made and delivering aid within the year in order to maintain a channel of communication with Vietnam, but the negative reactions of China and ASEAN to the growing Soviet presence proved more influential in the final decision.[24] The aid freeze was thus extended.

Japan's desire to support ASEAN was an element that emerged clearly in Japan's policy on Cambodia. At the ASEAN Post-Ministerial Conference held just after the Vietnamese attack on the Thai border area of Ban Nong Mak Mun in June 1980, Foreign Minister

Okita expressed support for the ASEAN joint statement backing Thailand, saying that the time had come when Japanese diplomacy could no longer exclude political questions.[25] Premier Suzuki, who was installed in July 1980, made his first overseas visit as prime minister to the ASEAN countries in January 1981. This demonstrated the importance his government placed on ASEAN. At a press conference in Manila on January 9,1981 Suzuki stated that Japan "would not unfreeze aid until a peaceful solution is achieved in Cambodia." And in Jakarta, foreign minister Ito stated that "when Japan takes any action in aid towards Vietnam, there will be prior consultations with ASEAN," showing a clearly pro-ASEAN stance.[26] Vietnam expressed dissatisfaction with this Japanese position.[27]

The freezing of Japanese aid to Vietnam, as described above, was not necessarily a deliberate sanction. In Japan's view, a basic policy of continuing aid was being temporarily suspended due to various circumstances. The period of suspension was extended because of the deterioration of the Cambodian situation and the Soviet invasion of Afghanistan, both of which required that Japan take a clear position as "a member of the west." However, as events continued to unfold, Japan eventually began searching for a new Indochina policy.

Offers of Humanitarian Aid to Vietnam (Mid-1981 to Present)

Japan clearly demonstrated a pro-ASEAN position with respect to aid to Vietnam, but its contacts with Vietnam continued, and some officials of the Vietnamese government and communist party visited Japan at the invitation of the Japanese Communist Party in March and April of 1981. On May 1, 1981, Akitane Kiuchi, director-general of the Foreign Ministry's Asian Affairs Bureau, visited Vietnam with the avowed purpose of observing Vietnamese local conditions. This was the first time since 1978, a lapse of three years, that a high-ranking Japanese foreign ministry official had visited Hanoi.

About this time, there was a growing movement within the Liberal Democratic party (LDP) for a reassessment of the aid freeze. In September 1981, members of the LDP's Asia-Africa Study Association visited Vietnam and Cambodia. Having observed the serious economic difficulties there, they advised against continuing a hardline policy towards Vietnam and, instead, advocated the provision of humanitarian aid. In November of the same year, Vietnamese legislators visited Japan at the invitation of the Japan-Vietnam Parliamentarians' League (chaired by LDP Chief Secretary Yoshio Sakurauchi) and met Foreign Minister Sonoda. Japan unofficially communicated to the Vietnamese that it was prepared to provide humanitarian aid (chiefly medicine), separate from the 14 billion yen previously promised.

By the end of 1981, circumstances were changing in a way favorable to a reassessment of relations with Vietnam. As news was received of Vietnam's economic plight, world opinion began to grow in favor of humanitarian aid. France resumed humanitarian aid to Vietnam in December 1981. Worsening economic conditions in Vietnam made it impossible for Hanoi to repay international loans. A hospital built with Japanese assistance in the former Saigon could no longer operate owing to lack of medicine. At the same time, Vietnam announced a new economic policy to deal with its domestic economic difficulties.

In January 1982, during the visit to Hanoi of Hiroaki Fujii, Councillor of the Asian Affairs Bureau, Japan reached an agreement with Vietnam on the provision of humanitarian aid. The agreement called for medicine worth 30 million yen to be delivered by the end of March. Japan sought prior approval from ASEAN for this offer of humanitarian aid. ASEAN's response was not entirely positive, but Japan went ahead with its decision.[28] This was the first specific instance since the aid freeze that Japanese-Vietnamese relations were adjusted despite lack of endorsement by ASEAN. Although the amount was small, this was the first significant development since the aid freeze in December 1978.[29]

Along with the provision of Japanese humanitarian aid, France announced its intention to provide $30 million in aid to Vietnam in March 1983.[30] In April, it concluded an aid agreement for the delivery of $950,000 worth of flour.[31] Likewise, after gaining power in March 1983, the Australian Labor government also announced a resumption of aid to Vietnam.[32]

Japanese humanitarian aid to Vietnam in 1983 was set at the same figure as in 1981: a grant of three million yen in hospital supplies and materials. On December 2, 1983, additional emergency aid of $100,000 was provided for typhoon relief. This too was justified on humanitarian grounds.[33] Behind the scene, the dialogue with Vietnam gradually took on a more positive cast.[34] In March 1983, Vietnam's vice-minister of foreign affairs visited Japan. This was the first visit by a high official of the Vietnamese foreign ministry since December 1978. In April 1984, high level discussions took place between Japanese Foreign Minister Shintaro Abe and Vietnamese Vice-Minister of Foreign Affairs Ha Van Lau, who was attending an ESCAP meeting in Tokyo.[35] In October 1984, on his way back from the UN General Assembly, Foreign Minister Nguyen Co Thach visited Japan for a Japanese-Vietnamese foreign ministers' conference, where an agreement was signed to expand the dialogue between the two countries.[36] This meeting at the foreign ministerial level was the first in six years since the talks between Vietnamese Foreign Minister Trinh and Japanese Foreign Minister Sonoda in December 1978.

While economic aid to Vietnam has remained frozen since December 1978, a nearly constant annual level of humanitarian aid (disaster relief and medicine) and cultural cooperation has been continuously provided since 1983. Since 1983, dialogue between Japan and Vietnam has also continued. Visits were made to Vietnam by Toshio Goto, Director-General of the Asian Affairs Bureau in July 1985; by Hiroshi Fukuda, Councillor of the Asian Affairs Bureau, in July 1986; by Kimio Fujita, Director-General of the Asian Affairs Bureau, in September 1987; by Shoichi Kuriyama, Councillor of the Foreign Ministry, in November 1988; and Sakutaro Tanino, Director-General of the Asian Affairs Bureau, in February 1990. Visits to Japan have also been made on an average of once a year by the Vietnamese foreign minister or a high foreign ministry official, so that there has been continuing dialogue between Japan and Vietnam.

In September 1989, the Vietnamese government announced that it would withdraw Vietnamese troops from Cambodia. An unverified troop withdrawal followed. In the complex international environment surrounding both Cambodia and Vietnam that followed, the reestablishment of Japanese aid became a major diplomatic issue between Japan and Vietnam. In this environment, the Minister of Foreign Affairs, Taro Nakayama, visited Vietnam in May 1991, the first visit to Vietnam by a Japanese Minister of Foreign Affairs since aid was frozen in December 1978. By January, 1992 Japan informed the United States that it was prepared to resume ODA flows directly to Vietnam, despite misgivings expressed by the United States[37] and unsteady progress in the implementation of a Cambodian peace agreement. How Japan got to this point is an interesting illustration of the relationships between Japan's ODA policies and Japan's evolving foreign policies.

Changes in the Circumstances Regarding Aid to Vietnam

After the invasion of Cambodia by Vietnamese troops in December 1978, Japanese aid to Vietnam was frozen except for a small amount of humanitarian aid. In September 1989, Vietnam withdrew its troops from Cambodia and gradually there began to be some developments on the problem of renewing aid to Vietnam. After December 1989, the

Japanese government, which had cut off aid because of the Cambodian invasion, was driven by necessity to a new response regarding the reestablishment of aid. This necessity was further strengthened once it became clear during 1991 that some form of Cambodian peace agreement was likely.

There are several points regarding the problems and progress of the Vietnam aid issue for Japan. The first point is the relationship between the aid issue and the Cambodian problem. This proved to be the biggest roadblock to restoration of economic aid to Vietnam. The second point concerns changes in international relationships surrounding Vietnam. The third point is how economic aid will be related to democratization processes within Vietnam.

The Cambodian Issue and the Vietnam Aid Issue

The primary reason why there were delays in resumption of Japanese economic aid to Vietnam (and in removal of the U.S. trade embargo) was that the Cambodian situation remained (and arguably still remains) unstable. Vietnam declared that it had completely withdrawn its troops from Cambodia by the end of September 1989. However, the withdrawal was carried out without verification by any United Nations observation group. As a result, the withdrawal was not recognized internationally. This was an unfortunate situation and for Vietnam it must have been disappointing, but Japanese economic aid was every bit as stalled despite the withdrawal as Japan awaited "a comprehensive resolution of the Cambodian problem."

The Japanese government cut off aid to Vietnam because of the invasion of Cambodia by Vietnamese troops, and announced that it would be difficult to resume aid as long as Vietnamese troops were in Cambodia. Despite the announcement that Vietnamese troops had completely withdrawn from Cambodia by September 1989, aid was not resumed because the Japanese government, along with the United States and other Western nations, said it was necessary to have "a comprehensive solution to the Cambodian problem," not only the withdrawal of Vietnamese troops but also stable political power among the four Cambodian factions.

This goal of a comprehensive solution remained unmet from the end of 1989 through the first half of 1990. Central to the stand of the administration of Heng Samrin was the removal of Pol Pot's power. This made it nearly impossible to form a coalition government of the four factions, including Pol Pot. On the other hand, the position of

China, as a supporter of Pol Pot, hardened and it appeared that an agreement could not be easily reached.

Japan's true feeling was that aid could possibly be resumed without waiting for a stable Cambodian coalition government. This could be done by carefully tackling the problems and dealing with the various conditions flexibly. However, it was difficult diplomatically for Japan alone to resume large-scale aid before the other Western nations. Japan requested that Vietnam cooperate and conveyed to the Vietnamese that: "We are counting on a situation in which Japan can resume aid to evolve soon."[38] One can interpret the statement "the situation in which Japan can resume aid" to mean three things: stabilization of Cambodia, improvement of Vietnam's relations with the West (especially with the United States), and the acceleration of democratic political evolution in Vietnam.

During 1990, the Japanese government dispatched First Southeast Asia Section Chief Masaharu Kono to Cambodia and he had informal contact with leaders of the Heng Samrin administration. This was the first official contact Japan had with Cambodia since the invasion of Cambodia by Vietnamese troops in December 1978. That same month, the Asian Bureau Chief, Mr. Tanino, visited Vietnam and tried to find a solution to the Cambodian problem. Further, during that visit Japan formally announced financial cooperation of $100,000 through UNESCO for restoration of the historical remains at Hue.

In June of 1990, representatives of the Heng Samrin government and the three coalition parties gathered in Tokyo in order to seek resolution of the Cambodian problem. There were several significant points about this meeting. First, Japan's policy towards Cambodia was shifting its focus to value the pro-Vietnamese government of Heng Samrin rather than supporting the stance of the three anti-Vietnamese parties. The second point about the significance of the meeting was that the meeting revealed that a new alliance had been formed between Tokyo and Bangkok among all the international combinations working towards peace in Cambodia.[39] This meant that Japan was not only going to support reconstruction after the resolution of the Cambodian problem (a point that Japan was making in several forums) but that Japan had also started to contribute to the peace process in Cambodia. This also showed Japan was broadening its choices in developing a Southeast Asian policy by using resumption of aid to Vietnam as a lever.

Meanwhile, in July of 1990, the U.S. government announced it was opening discussions with the Vietnamese government on the Cambodian problem and (like Japan) was modifying its previous policy of supporting the non-communist opposition parties. This approach meant not only that the United States had reconsidered its opposition to Heng

Samrin as "a puppet of Vietnam." It also had the immense significance of showing that the United States would seek direct discussions with the Hanoi government. In September, 1990, the first U.S. and Vietnamese meeting (between Secretary of State Baker and Foreign Minister Nguyen Co Thach) took place.

In September 1990, the results of a study by the U.S. General Accounting Office were revealed by the Southeast Asia and Pacific Affairs Subcommittee of the Senate Foreign Relations Committee. The study concluded there was a high probability that U.S. aid to non-communist opposition factions in Cambodia was benefitting Pol Pot. After hearing this report, the subcommittee chairperson, Alan Cranston, appealed to the Bush administration to remove the embargo against the Heng Samrin administration and to reexamine the issue of aid.[40] In December 1990, U.S. Assistant Secretary of State for Asian and Pacific Affairs, Richard Solomon, said in a Washington speech that the United States was prepared to negotiate the normalization of diplomatic relations with Vietnam once the U.N. mediation plan for peace in Cambodia was signed.[41]

As 1991 came to a close, an agreement was reached among the four factions for the establishment of a transition Supreme National Council (SNC) and UN supervision of a cease-fire, further discussions within the SNC framework, and an election. As these developments unfolded, much uncertainty remained and it is difficult even now to forecast what shape the solution to the Cambodian problem would take. Japan's approach has been to strengthen its contribution to the process of resolving the Cambodian problem while gauging the timing of resumption of economic aid to Vietnam. As one element of this effort, Japan used the prospect of economic aid to Vietnam as a lever to reach its immediate goal of eliciting Vietnam's cooperation on the Cambodian problem. As a second element of this effort, Japan had to be very circumspect given the still-standing U.S. economic embargo on Vietnam and the broader context of growing friction in U.S.-Japan trade relations. Japan understood that numerous American business people were urging the Busch administration to lift the embargo, in part from concerns that Japanese businesses were already laying significant foundations.

International Relations Revolving Around Vietnam

International circumstances surrounding Vietnam have rapidly changed in recent years. Of all these changes, the biggest has been the change in the Soviet Union's policy towards Asia and the impact this has had on relations between Vietnam and the Soviet Union, between Vietnam and the ASEAN nations, and on Vietnam's relations with the United States. International circumstances revolving around Vietnam have the inherent possibility of changing greatly over the long term. This is not just limited to the problem of resumption of aid to Vietnam but may also greatly influence the politics and security of the entire Asia-Pacific region. In that sense, when one considers the issue of aid to Vietnam, one must have a comprehensive view covering not only the situation in Cambodia and Indochina but also the future order in the broad Asia-Pacific region.

One factor which made resumption of Japanese aid to Vietnam difficult, although it has not been openly indicated, has been the Soviet-Vietnamese military relationship. As long as the Soviet Union has a base at Cam Ranh Bay and the United States and ASEAN nations view this as a threat, Japanese aid to Vietnam would be opposed by the United States and the ASEAN countries. However, extremely important and positive changes have been made in the progress of detente between the United States and the Soviet Union, in Soviet moves to improve relations with the other Asian countries, and in the termination of Soviet and East European aid to Vietnam.

In December 1988, the Soviet government proposed the mutual withdrawal of the Soviet base at Cam Ranh Bay and the removal of the U.S. bases in the Philippines. This proposal was interpreted as political propaganda during the early stages of US-Philippine negotiations on possible renewal of the Philippine bases agreement. It was not taken seriously by either the U.S. or the Philippines. However, in a less flamboyant manner, the Soviet Union was in fact reducing its military presence at Cam Ranh Bay. For example, the Soviet Navy began withdrawal of units that had been stationed at Cam Ranh Bay in late 1989.[42] The Soviet Foreign Ministry announced that it had completed withdrawal of its MIG 23 and TLU 16 aircraft from Cam Ranh Bay also during 1989,[43] and also stated its plan to withdraw all Soviet troops stationed in Vietnam by 1992.[44] However, in August, 1992 the Russian Foreign Minister indicated to ASEAN foreign ministers that "we are not necessarily rushing to leave," and that Russia was formally seeking continued access to the aiur and naval facilities formerly used by the Soviet military at Cam Ranh Bay.[45]

Soviet and East European aid and preferential trading arrangements were very important pillars of the Vietnamese economy. The termination of these arrangements created serious problems for Vietnam, but also opened potential opportunities for the re-entry of other donors and the restoration of economic relationships with ASEAN and the West. At first, when the Soviet Union began cutting economic aid to Vietnam, some voices in the Japanese government expressed their opposition to resumption of aid since the appearance would be one of Japan simply replacing the aid that the Soviet Union had supplied. However another argument gradually became increasingly persuasive: it was that the Soviet Union and Eastern Europe were rapidly changing, that these changes had the potential to lead to long-term stability in Asia, and that Japan had an important and constructive role to play in creating and supporting this new long-term stability.[46]

The ASEAN nations have gradually decreased their suspicions of Vietnam. Among them, Thailand is most rapidly strengthening contact between the three nations of Indochina as symbolized by the slogan advocating to changing the three nations of Indochina "from a battlefield to a marketplace." Former Prime Minister Chatichai Choonhavan of Thailand personally requested Japan to resume aid to Vietnam when he visited Japan in April 1990.[47] The attitude of the ASEAN nations regarding Japanese aid to Vietnam has been changing from caution to tolerance and even to anticipation. In November 1990, President Suharto of Indonesia visited Hanoi. In addition to signing an economic and scientific technology agreement, he also made clear at a series of meetings that he would welcome Vietnam's desire to join the ASEAN alliance. In 1991, Singapore strengthened its trade and investment relations with Vietnam.

Among the European nations, the two which have especially been strengthening their contact with Vietnam are France and Italy. The Foreign Minister of France visited Vietnam with representatives of financial circles in February 1990, and formed the first joint French and Vietnamese economic committee. Also while in Vietnam, he formally announced that a government loan of 45 million francs would be granted, and he also agreed on the signing of a peace and friendship pact with Vietnam. Italy also formed a joint economic committee with Vietnam in Rome in April and announced that it would resume economic aid to Vietnam.[48] In addition, Spain and Switzerland moved towards establishing embassies in Vietnam, and Germany is considering the resumption of economic aid.[49]

Investment in Vietnam by the Western nations has been gradually increasing, in part because of a liberalized Vietnamese foreign investment policy first promulgated in January 1988. By the end of 1989, 105 joint enterprises had been approved and a total of $852 million had been invested. The investors included companies from France, West Germany, Australia, and Britain and Asian companies from Korea, Taiwan, Hong Kong, and Thailand. Competition was especially keen regarding development of Vietnam's offshore oil fields. Oil field development has been the area where joint enterprises have made their largest investments.[50]

Before September 1989, Nissho Iwai was the only major Japanese trading company which did business in Hanoi, but by January 1991, Mitsubishi, Tomen, and Kanematsu had established local representative offices in Hanoi. In addition, many other companies, including Sumitomo Shoji and Marubeni, are building the foundation for business in the future.[51] However, not much actual Japanese investment has been made. For example, among the 105 joint enterprises mentioned previously, not one was Japanese.

The U.S. trade embargo continues and the United States continues to oppose financing assistance for Vietnam from the Asian Development Bank, the World Bank, and the International Monetary Fund. The relationship between the United States and Vietnam has not only been a hindrance to resumption of Japanese economic aid to Vietnam but has hindered investment and trade relationships with Vietnam by Japanese companies. However, there are signs that relationships are being improved and that normalization may be possible, particularly if there is continuing satisfactory progress on Cambodia.[52] If and when that happens, it is anticipated that U.S. companies will finally be able to participate in investment and trade with Vietnam. In the interim, Japan is watching the progress of aid resumption by the Western nations as well as the degree to which U.S. and Vietnam relations improve. Japan is continuing to watch for the right time to resume aid and improve Japanese-Vietnamese relations. For example, in January 1992, once the SNC had actually been established and appeared to be functioning in Cambodia, Japan accelerated its discussions with Vietnam on the resumption of aid relations. Several high level visits were made to Vietnam by Japanese Foreign Ministry officials. Publicly, Japan indicated that while resumption was approved in principle, its actual occurrence would depend on the clarification of outstanding Vietnamese debts to Japan. Privately however, both Japan and Vietnam understand that resumption will need to await further progress in restoration of relations between Vietnam and the United States.

Aid to Vietnam and the Democratization Problem

There was no direct link of Japan's aid suspension with the problem of inadequate democratization in Vietnam. However, as progress was made towards resolving the principal factors that supported the suspension, and details about the renewal of Japanese economic aid to

Vietnam come under serious discussion, democratization of Vietnam's political system could prove to be an issue.

For Japan, controversy over how to deal with the problem of democratization in a nation receiving aid has drawn attention as a vital issue since public debate surfaced in Japan about Marcos and the Philippines in 1984 (as described in Professor Takahashi's chapter). Since then, repressive government behavior in Burma and China made the issue of democratization an increasingly major problem for Japan to confront in its aid ideology.[53] The democratization issue has received even greater attention with the rapid development of democratic forces in Eastern Europe and the (former) Soviet Union.

As a result of these developments, Japan moved to make the promotion of democratization both an objective of and condition for its aid. In part, this was seen as a rationalization of any Japanese aid to Eastern Europe and possibly the Soviet Union. The issue and possibly the dilemma for Japanese aid policy is how to apply this criterion in Asia, where Japan has been especially sensitive about interfering in the domestic political choices of recipient countries.

Although Japan had on occasion suspended or stopped the provision of aid for political reasons,[54] and in other cases, the continuation of ODA to nondemocratic regimes has been a focus of criticism, behind Japan's ODA policy was the fundamental if often tacit belief that economic development and modernization would lead to democratization. The assumption was that when Japan helped support the industrialization and modernization of developing countries, Japan was promoting their democratization. In terms of this logic, if Japan pushed especially hard for democracy and made it a condition for providing aid, that could actually have the effect of delaying democratization by delaying industrialization and economic development. Japan recognized there were cases where developing nations formed a political configuration called "a development dictatorship" in order to carry out economic development. Japan recognized the diversity of governmental systems, did not believe it should categorically accept some and reject others based purely on their institutional characteristics, and had not therefore sought political concessions.

After the incident at Tiananmen Square, the Japanese government froze aid to China to express opposition to the Chinese government's reactionary actions against democratization and to act in solidarity with the Western donors. This action was consistent with the freezing of aid to Burma which also occurred because of the Burmese military administration's oppression of a democratization movement. Clearly, the democratization issue has become a vital consideration for Japan in granting aid, and it is not an exaggeration to say that this "democratic conditionality" has become a political condition for aid. However the terms under which the condition is to be applied are not yet entirely clear. For example, the Japanese government announced the resumption of economic aid to China at the Houston Summit in July, 1990. In October of 1990, renewed economic assistance actually began with the third yen loan for specific projects. Vietnam bitterly criticized Japan for the lack of consistent logic in its policies towards China and Vietnam. Japan's response to this criticism was that the Tiananmen incident was an internal affair for China but that the Cambodian problem was of a different order entirely—it involved external aggression and intervention by Vietnam.[55]

Could Vietnam possibly accept political conditions for aid renewal? Vietnam has flirted with democratization, but it appears that in Vietnam (as in Eastern Europe) these developments are the products of internal political forces, not accommodations to prospective aid flows. For example, Vietnam has indicated a willingness to try to expand democracy under socialist principals as recently as the Central Committee General Meeting in March 1990. However, within a few months, Vietnam began to retrench politically after seeing the collapse of socialism in Eastern Europe, calling out for "the building of socialism through party leadership." By late 1990, party leadership was indicating that the establishment of a multi-party system in Vietnam was unthinkable at the present time.[56]

There are voices in the Ministry of Foreign Affairs calling for using economic cooperation as a lever to promote democratization in Vietnam.[57] However, there are also many experts who say that it is not a wise policy to attach political conditions since it would be extremely difficult for Vietnam's internal politics to accept these conditions. In a report by the Japan International Issues Research Institute, the following interpretation is given:

> When the Guen Ban Rin administration instituted "Doi moi" (reform policy), it was appropriate for political stability to be regarded as most important. Our nation should not make it a precondition for aid that the Vietnamese policy quickly promotes democratization. One item of top priority in Japan's aid to Vietnam is eliminating the economic conditions which generate refugees. For that purpose, we supply people, money and technology and have attained the basic position where we can also give advice.[58]

A report by the World Peace Research Institute Tokyo concluded that in "regards to democratization of Asia, Japan can adequately explain the approach taken by the Asian nations to the U.S....It is important that Japan suggest now that democracy should be in Asia."[59] The logic can be summed up as follows. Democracy is a value which is universal. However, the road to democracy differs depending upon the unique circumstances of each country. One must not impatiently force a standardized democratization process. The developing nations of Asia first need economic security and then the political stability that is supported by it. This seems to be the dominant theory in Japan.[60]

The Outlook for Japanese Aid to Vietnam

Vietnam's greatest needs are for economic infrastructure such as roads, harbors, railroads, telegraphs, telephone lines, etc. For example, a large hindrance to the economic development of the Vietnamese economy is the lack of adequate road, rail, and telecommunications linkages between North and South. It is also essential to prepare harbors and other types of infrastructure needed for the expansion of international trading activities. Some of this has already become the object of a preliminary investigation for an aid project by a Japanese consulting company. In the summer of 1989, Nippon Koei Co., Ltd. and several other Japanese companies performed a feasibility study on harbor construction in northern Vietnam.

In Japan's aid scheme, economic infrastructure is usually supported by yen loans. When Japan resumed aid to China in 1979, preparation of railroads and harbors was the most important topic and these projects were supported by yen loans. In the same way, when economic aid is truly resumed to Vietnam, economic infrastructure will be the most important area, the most likely aid modality will be yen loans, and the amounts of money may well be vast.

Some countries in Southeast Asia may be wary because of the large funds likely to be involved. For the Japanese government, it would be difficult diplomatically to quickly provide a large amount of loans for economic infrastructure unless Vietnam rapidly becomes closer to the West. Some Thai researchers have proposed a Japan-ASEAN fund system in which Japan provides the money and ASEAN businesses use the Japanese money to build aid projects in Vietnam.[61] This would certainly benefit ASEAN businesses, but it would also help integrate Vietnam into the ASEAN and the Asia-Pacific economic spheres.

Another area where the needs of the Vietnamese economy are great is in financial aid for fiscal support. At present, Vietnam has a large amount of accumulated debt ($9 billion) to the non-socialist world. When Vietnam has economic transactions with foreign nations, one can anticipate financial restrictions. Normally, Japan responds to this need through commodity loans. A commodity loan provides the funds necessary to import vital materials a developing country needs to sustain its growth.

However, this type of financial aid has proven to be more difficult to provide, both politically and diplomatically, than yen loan aid for economic infrastructure. There have been cases where it was not clear how commodity loans were used. For example, in the past, there has been strong opposition in Japan over commodity loans to China and the Philippines. Consequently, there is a strong possibility that there would be criticism not only from some foreign nations but from inside Japan as well if commodity loans were provided to Vietnam.

The Philippine Multilateral Aid Initiative (MAI) may prove to be a model for the likely strategy. Multilateral agencies, especially the International Monetary Fund, the World Bank, and the Asian Development Bank, will take the lead in reaching agreements with the Vietnamese government on needed levels of fiscal support and associated economic policy reforms. Japan, along with other bilateral donors, would then act in concert to participate in providing these funds-—both directly on a bilateral basis as well as indirectly through special funds donors establish or support in the multilaterals. Until there is some form of multilateral arrangement, it is unlikely that Japan would provide fiscal support to Vietnam by itself.

Japan is already active in providing economic aid to Laos. The Japanese government provides grant aid, dispatches experts as economic consultants to the Laotian government, and accepts foreign students. This is a response to efforts by Laos to move in more market-oriented economic directions, to encourage foreign investment, and to improve relationships with Thailand. In August 1990, Foreign Minister Nakayama visited Laos, the first visit to Laos by a Japanese Foreign Minister in thirty-one years. He announced a policy of total cooperation through economic aid in helping Laos develop a market economy.[62] In 1989, the total amount of aid to Laos including grants and technical cooperation totalled about 2.6 billion yen.

Japanese economic aid to Laos sends a message to Vietnam. It says what concrete effects would result if Vietnam were to promote political democracy and maintain momentum on economic reform. However, the determining factor in deciding the way that Japanese economic aid to Vietnam will be shaped is, to the very end, political and diplomatic. The biggest factors in influencing those decisions are, first of all, maintaining momentum in the Cambodian peace process. After that, the questions will be how Vietnam draws closer first of all to the

ASEAN nations, the United States, and other Western nations; and how Vietnam will move towards democratization.

Japanese aid to Vietnam was like a "stick" when it was frozen in response to the invasion of Cambodia by Vietnamese troops. Now it has changed its role to that of a "carrot," to lead Vietnamese policy in desired directions.

Endnotes

1. Please refer to the following publications regarding the system and process of Japan's policy decisions about ODA (Official Development): Alan Rix, *Japan's Economic Aid: Policy-making and Politics* (London: Croom Helm, 1980); Robert Orr, Jr., *The Emergence of Japan's Foreign Aid Power* (New York: Columbia University Press, 1990); Juichi Inada, "Japan's Aid Diplomacy: Economic, Political, or Strategic?" *Millennium: Journal of International Studies* (1989) Vol. 18, No. 3, pp. 399-414; Juichi Inada, "Japan's Official Development Assistance to ASEAN Countries: Its Objectives and Policy-making Process," *Development and ODA: Japan-ASEAN Forum I* (Tokyo: United Nations University, 1991), pp. 45-75.

2. For example, Vietnam expected a resumption of lending activities by the multilateral development banks and other measurable indicators of progress towards the normalization of relations with the United States.

3. A more detailed analysis of the period up until 1984 can be found in: Juichi Inada, *Aid to Vietnam: Japan's Policy*, Indochina Report No. 20, (Singapore: Information and Resource Center, 1989).

4. Akira Okada, *Mizudori Gaikou Hiwa: Aru Gaikoukan no Shougen*, Chuou-kouron-sha, 1983, pp. 187-195.

5. Minoru Hirano, *Gaikou Kisha Nikki: Ohira Gaikou no Ninen (1)*, Gyousei-tushin-sha, 1978, p. 153.

6. Proceedings of the House of Representatives, Committee on Expenditure, No. 15-3, June 12, 1973.

7. Proceedings of the House of Representatives, Committee on the Budget, No. 23-10, June 9, 1975.

8. Proceedings of the House of Representatives, Committee on Foreign Affairs, No. 1-11, July 9, 1976.

9. The Fukuda speech was seen as a turning point in Japan's diplomacy towards Southeast Asia. Koji Watanabe, "Japan and Southeast Asia: 1980," *Asia Pacific Community* (Fall, 1980), No. 10, pp. 83-97.

10. Proceedings of the House of Representatives, Committee on Foreign Affairs, No. 5-13, October 26, 1976.

11. For example, during talks between the foreign ministers of Japan and Vietnam on December 18, 1979, Foreign Minister Sonoda said, "Japan can provide an appropriate amount of economic aid if Vietnam contributes to the peace and stability of Southeast Asia, but if not, it will be necessary to restrict Japanese cooperation." *Tounanazia Geppo*, December 1978, p. 29.

12. *Yomiuri Shimbun*, April 13, 1979.

13. *Asahi Shimbun*, January 8, 1979 (evening edition).

14. Proceedings of the House of Representatives, Committee on Budget, No. 12-29, February 16, 1979; Proceedings of the House of Representatives, Committee on Foreign Affairs, No. 3-16, February 28, 1979.

15. *Asahi Shimbun*, March 12, 1979.

16. *Nihon Keizai Shimbun*, March 15, 1979.

17. *Asahi Shimbun*, March 12, 1979; *Nihon Keizai Shimbun*, March 15, 1979.

18. *Nihon Keizai Shimbun*, June 24, 1979.

19. *Sankei Shimbun*, July 5, 1979; *Mainichi Shimbun*, July 10, 1979.

20. *Asahi Shimbun*, December 4, 1979.

21. "One member of the west" (Nishigawa no ichiin) is the generally used term. In its 1981 diplomatic blue book (*Gaiko seisho*, p. 14) the Foreign Ministry used the phrase "one member of the advanced democratic community" (*senshin minshushugi shakai no ichiin*). In the 1987 edition (p. 3) the official terminology was "one member of the (community of) free democracies" (*jiyu minshushugi shokuku no ichiin*).

22. *Nihon Keizai Shimbun*, January 9, 1990.

23. *Mainichi Shimbun*, February 13, 1980.

24. *Nihon Keizai Shimbun*, March 12, 1980 (evening edition).

25. *Yomiuri Shimbun*, June 29, 1980.

26. *Yomiuri Shimbun*, January 14, 1981; Seiji Ito, "Tai ASEAN gaikou: kenkyo to hairyo ga fukaketu," *Gekkan Jiyu Minshu* (July, 1985), No. 354, pp. 49-50.

27. *Mainichi Shimbun*, January 12, 1981.

28. *Ibid*.

29. *Mainichi Shimbun*, January 13, 1982.

30. *Mainichi Shimbun*, March 27, 1983.

31. *Nihon Keizai Shimbun*, April 5, 1983.

32. *Mainichi Shimbun*, April 28, 1983.

33. *Mainichi Shimbun*, December 14, 1983.

34. *Mainichi Shimbun*, December 6, 1983.

35. *Asahi Shimbun*, April 25, 1984.

36. *Asahi Shimbun*, April 25, 1984.

37. *Asahi Evening News*, January 6, 1992.

38. Interview (Ministry of Foreign Affairs, Asian Affairs Bureau, Southeast Asia Section 1).

39. *Sankei Shimbun*, June 6, 1990.

40. *Sankei Shimbun*, September 20, 1990.

41. *Nihon Keizai Shimbun*, December 6, 1990 (evening edition).

42. *Sankei Shimbun*, January 11, 1990 (evening edition).

43. *Asahi Shimbun*, January 19, 1990.

44. Report of the U.S. House of Representatives Military Affairs Committee, *Asahi Shimbun*, June 6, 1990.

45. Maria Luz Y. Baguioro, "Russia Intent on Keeping Cam Ranh Bay Naval Base," *The NIkkei Weekly* (August 1, 1992), p. 24.

46. In December of 1989, the Ministry of Foreign Affairs believing that "the changes in relationships between East and West will have various effects on the socialist countries of Asia, especially on China, Vietnam, North Korea and so on," forged a policy to "make vigorous efforts to bring the socialist countries of Southeast Asia into the process of prosperity in Asia and the Pacific." (Page 3 of the December 2, 1989, Ministry of Foreign Affairs document, "World Conditions and Japan's Foreign Relations." Also in *Asahi Shimbun*, December 24, 1989.

47. *Nihon Keizai Shimbun*, April 14, 1990.

48. *Nihon Keizai Shimbun*, March 7, 1990.

49. *Nihon Keizai Shimbun*, May 12, 1990 (evening edition).

50. *Asahi Shimbun*, April 19, 1990.

51. *Asahi Shimbun*, January 17, 1990.

52. For the U.S., the MIA issue remains a difficult problem in terms of domestic American politics.

53. Please refer to the following regarding the relationship between the democratization problem of China and Burma and Japan's aid policy. "Changes in Asian Conditions and Political Guidelines Sought in Japan's ODA," in *Kokusai Mondai*, March 1990 (Number 360).

54. See for examples the chapters in this volume on Burma, China, and Korea.

55. Interview (Ministry of Foreign Affairs, Asian Affairs Bureau, Southeast Asia Section 1).

56. *Asahi Shimbun*, October 12, 1990.

57. *Nihon Keizai Shimbun*, October 21, 1990.

58. Tadashi Mio, "Japan's Policy towards Vietnam," in *Various Problems Regarding Vietnam*, (Tokyo: The Japan International Issues Research Institute, March 1991), p. 157.

59. Nariai Osamu, *Whither the Vietnamese Revolution*, Policy Paper 50, (Tokyo: World Peace Research Institute, March 1991), p. 10.

60. The following essay sums up how to regard the issue of "democratization" in terms of Japan's aid to socialist countries: "Historical Changes in Aid Policy and Future Views—Research on the political guidelines for aid (especially concerning what Japan's aid policy should be towards socialist countries)," FASID (Foundation for Advanced Studies in International Development), *Development and Aid Research*, March 20, 1991.

61. *Yomiuri Shimbun*, January 20, 1990.

62. *Sankei Shimbun*, August 2, 1990.

7

JAPANESE ECONOMIC ASSISTANCE TO BURMA: AID IN THE *TARENAGASHI* MANNER?

David I. Steinberg[1]

Introduction

Japanese economic assistance to Burma (Myanmar)[2] is in some sense an anomaly: the largest provider of foreign aid has been the major supporter of what was and still is potentially the richest nation in Southeast Asia. Japanese aid has not only been the major bilateral or multilateral mainstay of Burma for about two generations, it has arguably been the means by which the military government remained in power during its darkest economic periods, and the critical sustenance of the civilian era. The magnitude of this assistance represents one of the largest worldwide of the Japanese ODA (official development assistance) program annually, and in the aggregate (some $2.2 billion) constitutes one of the largest programs of Japanese assistance on a per capita basis.

Japanese support was provided within the context of internal Japanese political, economic, and developmental policies, and within a foreign policy context that helped shape both its magnitude and its continuity. Japanese aid to Burma has differed from its assistance to other developing states in the region, where in both centrally planned and market economies in Asia, Japanese investment and trade have been more important than ODA. In Burma, however, official assistance has been primary, while trade—other than Japanese imports into Burma under this assistance—has been small, and investment (even when allowed by the Burmese government) has been minuscule. There have been criticisms in the Japanese press concerning the effectiveness of the "self-sustaining" or development impact of this assistance in contrast to its purported *Tarenagashi* character. This subject will be reviewed toward the close of this essay.

In receiving and encouraging Japanese support, Burma has also had a special, if not unique, relationship with this donor. Japanese assistance was given to and embraced by the Burmese for a variety of reasons—economic, political, and personal, but the degree to which any single motivation predominated in either party must be a matter of speculation. In spite of the special conditions surrounding the provision and receipt of such aid, there are important lessons that may be learned from the process and the relationship, lessons that relate to foreign assistance generically, less broadly to the Japanese program as a whole, and to the Burmese development process in particular.

Japanese ODA has been characterized as having five policy objectives. These are:

1. Furthering Japanese economic interests by promoting exports, securing supplies of raw materials, and creating a favorable climate for commercial business activities in the recipient countries;
2. Establishing and strengthening diplomatic relations;
3. Maintaining the stability of the political, economic, and social systems of ODA-receiving countries;
4. Demonstrating Japanese good faith to the other aid-giving western nations; and
5. Establishing Japan's status and influence in both regional and global international affairs.[3]

Another authority[4] noted that Japanese aid has evolved through five stages:

1. Reparations (1954);
2. Lending and investment in economic cooperation (1958);
3. Economic cooperation integrated with Asian foreign policy (1965);
4. Responsibility as an economic power (1980); and
5. Role as a current account surplus country.

Japan's role in Burma mirrored some of the policy objectives and the stages in these broad categorizations, but in several instances the timing and emphases were somewhat different, and Japan's role as an economic power in Burma was only very recently (1988) realized.

Rather than dividing Burma into the periods of Japanese assistance as noted above, it is more effective to consider the critical Japanese decisions or actions that affected the program in Burma. There have been (until July 1990) five such actions taken by the Japanese government in the provision of assistance to Burma. They have been:

1. The decision to provide war reparations in 1954 in conjunction with the peace treaty;
2. The decision to move from reparations to economic cooperation in the 1960s;
3. The decision to increase economic support some tenfold in the 1970s;
4. The decision in March 1988 to enter into a policy dialogue with the Burmese, warning them about the need for economic reforms; and
5. The decision to restart previously approved projects in February 1989.[5]

These past decisions, and the Burmese conditions under which they were made, and their efficacy in both Burmese and Japanese terms are the subject of this essay.

Background

As the independent Union of Burma entered the decade of the 1950s, the state of that union was dire and in marked contrast to its pre-war status. In that earlier period, Burma had been virtually unique among developing countries or colonies as a major exporter of both food and energy. It was the world's leading exporter of rice (3.123 million tons in 1939/40), accounting for about two-fifths of the world's rice exports.[6] Oil production in 1939 was 275 million imperial gallons, and petroleum products accounted for one-quarter of exports.[7]

Before and following independence, Burma suffered from two starkly contrasting periods of war and destruction. In World War II, Burma was the site of the most extensive of the Pacific campaigns, in which it was methodically ravaged twice with scorched earth policies instituted by both victor and vanquished each time. They resulted perhaps in more devastation than in any other Asian state, except perhaps for Japan itself. The physical destruction was estimated at $175 million, but another estimate was K.9400 crores (about $15 billion).[8] Whole population groups were dislocated. More Japanese soldiers died in Burma than in any other Southeast Asian nation, an emotional factor of significance in the Japanese commitment to Burma.

The internal rebellions that began on independence in 1948 were of two varieties: ideological from the left, and ethnic on the part of some minority groups. State power for a short period was virtually reduced to Rangoon. By 1954, however, the government was back in control of most urban centers, even as its power in the peripheral areas was circumscribed. But the civil war had caused havoc in the economy. Burma also lacked sufficient trained manpower to run what virtually all the elite agreed would be a socialist economy. Burmese per capita income was calculated in this period at about $55, but another estimate indicated that although per capita GDP was K. 395.3 (about $84) in 1938/39, it had fallen to K. 218.1 in 1948/49, and had only risen to K. 304 by 1956/57, or about a quarter less than the prewar level.[9]

Aung San, the founder and negotiator of independent Burma who was assassinated in July 1947, had written that Burma should never be dependent on foreign assistance. Yet such assistance was necessary for capital formation and for access to needed technical assistance and technological training. Although the Colombo Plan nations and the United States, as well as the USSR, were prepared to and did provide assistance, Japan seemed the likely major source of support.

Japanese War Reparations

The Union of Burma signed a peace treaty with Japan on November 5, 1954. Under it, Japan agreed to supply reparations and, later, economic cooperation. Japan was to provide Japanese products and technicians with a total value of $200 million over a ten year period, together with an annual grant of $5 million for technical assistance during this decade. Of that latter amount, $2 million annually was set aside for joint ventures between the two countries.[10] Although Japan initially had planned to limit reparations to Burma to $100 million, Burma wanted a far larger settlement. Japan accepted the higher amount as a compromise, with a stipulation in the peace treaty that the magnitude of the payments to Burma could be reconsidered in the light of reparations payments to other nations ($200 million to Indonesia, $400 million to the Philippines).[11]

The purposes of the supply of goods and services under reparations were "economic rehabilitation and development and the advancement of social welfare." Initially, consumer goods were not included in the agreement, but it was agreed they could be added by mutual consent if they did not undercut the normal procurement of such goods by Burma through regular trade channels.

There were a series of problems, essentially connected with the pricing of such goods and services. Most goods were 5-15 percent higher than competitive Japanese prices because the Japanese did not provide tax rebates or favorable interest rates, and technical assistance was charged at two to three times normal Japanese wages.[12] Complaints about the reparations program could be heard in Rangoon during that period on these scores. There was the added internal Burmese issue of how the assistance should be divided: how much would the constituent states receive. This was a major concern to the Shan State, the leaders of which indicated that they were not receiving income commensurate with their contributions to the national economy. Further, there were local pressures for reparations to supply goods (such as automobiles) to senior officials reflecting essentially the perquisites of office.

Japanese motivations for providing this magnitude of assistance (about $10 per capita over that ten year span, or $1 per person annually) in retrospect seems complex. No doubt Burma could not be excluded from any major Asian reparations program, given the funds provided to other Southeast Asian nations. There was also no doubt that the reestablishment of the Japanese position in Asia and the prospects for a lucrative market for Japanese products were partial motivation for all reparations programs, since they were tied to the provision of Japanese goods and services. The under-exploited and even unexplored natural resources of Burma were important attractions. Yet there were emotional and personal ties that were part of the equation, and were later to loom larger.

The Japanese had been an important spur to Burmese independence (as in a number of other colonies in the region) and of early assistance in the anti-colonial struggle. Although in 1945 the Burmese turned against the Japanese when they recognized that the independence the Japanese had granted them was less then complete and that the allies would be victorious, most of the leaders of independent Burma in 1948 had been a part of that Japanese-sponsored wartime government. Perhaps even more important were the personal ties to key leaders created by the Japanese before the war. They had trained the "Thirty Comrades," Burmese with nationalist credentials who provided a core of critically placed individuals who served the Japanese in the early period of the war, and who returned to Burma in the wake of the Japanese invasion. Many became part of the nucleus of the Japanese administration. Aung San was one, but most important over time was

Ne Win. Relations between Japan and Ne Win since that period have been close. All during the critical economic periods since the military coup of 1962, only the Japanese ambassador of all the diplomatic corps had continuous access to Ne Win.

On independence, Ne Win was deputy commander of Burma's army. In 1949 he became commander, and from that period until 1962 he was variously commander, minister of defense, deputy prime minister, and under the first military "constitutional coup" of 1958, prime minister. At that time, he even suggested bringing Japanese farmers into Burma to settle the sparsely populated Yu River valley and to teach the Burmese how to grow irrigated rice more effectively. From 1962, he became the undisputed leader of Burma as Chairman of the Revolutionary Council, then President and concurrently the chairman of the Burma Socialist Programme Party from 1962 until his retirement from the Party on July 23, 1988. Since that date, and although he holds no official title, he still is said to be a salient influence in Burmese policy formation.

The foreign policy context in which Burma operated was also conducive to reliance on Japan. Burma was neutral (the government preferred the term "non-aligned") nation, and it was essentially because of the impeccability of those credentials that U Thant was chosen as Secretary General of the United Nations. Although the Sino-Soviet split had not yet occurred, one in which Burma would have deftly to define its role later, the great power rivalries from which Burma attempted to keep itself aloof made a demilitarized Japan an attractive source of support. In this relatively pluralistic period of civilian rule, Japanese assistance raised fewer internal political issues from the legal left, which was always politically influential, than U.S. or Colombo Plan support.

Japanese aid, beginning with reparations but continuing through about thirty-five years of support, must be placed in the context of overall Japanese policy and its internal political context. Constant themes of Japanese foreign economic and political policies are energy and food security, within the five policy objectives cited above. Completely dependent on foreign sources of oil, Japan has used both its diplomacy and its economic programs to ensure its diverse and continuous supply of oil. Although security in rice production was much discussed in the press in 1990 in relation to the acerbic negotiations with the United States concerning rice imports, in fact some twenty years ago Japan is said to have made the decision to ensure for the future (if need be) alternative foreign sources of rice as it was anticipated that internal production might not keep pace with demands.[13]

Japanese reparations were important in magnitude and in specific projects, although many of the results proved ephemeral. Through September 30, 1960, Japanese assistance to Burma was 49.7 percent of all foreign aid commitments, although it was only 37.8 percent of deliveries.[14] However, the assistance was vital to Burmese stability. In addition to supplying railway rolling stock, electrical goods and appliances, industrial equipment and machinery, Japan also provided construction equipment and vehicles of all types.

By far the most important reparations project, indeed perhaps the most important aid project in Burma since independence, was the Japanese provision of a hydroelectric installation in the Kayah State. The Lawpida, or Beluchaung project, provided about 40 percent of the total electric supply for the country. Built in a remote area of thick jungle, and in an insurgent-influenced territory when built, it is said that the Japanese contractors made payments to the insurgents to ensure that construction was not interrupted. It has proven to be a valuable contribution to modern Burma.

TABLE 7.1 Japanese Reparations Projects in Burma (US$ millions)

1. Beluchaung Hydroelectric		28.8
2. Four industrial projects		29.2
Agricultural machinery plant	[4.4]	
Small vehicle plant	[9.2]	
Electric goods plant	[8.6]	
Bus/truck plant	[7.0]	
3. Railway rehabilitation		20.2
4. Automobiles		17.2
5. Rangoon port rehabilitation		17.2
6. Technical cooperation		7.5
7. Other		76.0
	Total	200.0

Source: Japanese Embassy, Rangoon.

The most "notorious" of the reparations era projects were, however, the four industrial projects (see Table 7.1), which initially cost $29.2 million. They never were self-sustaining, being continuously dependent on Japanese components and material, which have unremittingly been supplied through loans as late as 1987.[15]

Writing in 1962, Walinsky concluded that "Japanese reparations did not register very strongly. Once negotiated, they were taken for granted, and they involved neither repayment nor a sense of obligation."[16] Later evidence indicates that these characteristics were not unique to the reparations program, but covered most assistance. Both loans and grants were taken for granted because grant projects were considered free (most Burmese did not seriously consider in economic terms the local currency or foreign exchange costs assumed by their government for operations, maintenance, and spare parts), and those who ran loan projects were not forced in most cases to cost account the capital investments or amortization.

In 1963, Burma requested a renegotiation of the reparations agreement with the Japanese, as specified in the original treaty. They requested an additional $200 million, of which $150 was to be grant reparations, and $50 million credits. The Japanese were prepared to provide $100 million. Brigadier Aung Gyi, who at that time held several portfolios in the military cabinet and was considered heir apparent to Ne Win, was sent with a twelve-man delegation to Tokyo on January 13, 1963 to negotiate the agreement. The negotiations stalled for a period, but on January 25 agreement was reached for $200 million to begin in 1965 and to last for twelve years. Of this amount, $140 million was reparations (grants), and $60 million was to be concessional loans.[17]

Although Aung Gyi thus seemed successful in achieving the Burmese goals, he had publicly stated in his opening remarks: "We (the Burmese) have come here as a younger brother would to an older brother to consult a certain family problem," and he painted a dour picture of the Burmese economy. This humiliating negotiating stance was said to have angered Ne Win, and on February 7 Aung Gyi "resigned" from all his positions and went into retirement (he was later jailed). The Japanese had noted tensions within the Burmese delegation on negotiating issues, but whether Aung Gyi's resignation was caused by this or ideological factors in economic policy is not known. On February 16, 1963, however, the military government announced a new economic policy allocating all procurement, production, distribution, imports, and exports of all commodities solely to the state. The period of rigid socialism thus began.

Burmese Conditions and Japanese Assistance, 1962-1971

Japanese reparations disbursements continued through 1975, somewhat behind schedule,[18] but the continuity of the Japanese program at approximately the same average level of expenditure was in stark contrast with the changes in the political and economic structure of Burma.

Since the reparations began, Burma had undergone two military coups: the first was a "constitutional" one in 1958 in which the civilian government acquiesced to temporary military rule in the face of yet another potentially disastrous civil war because it involved those at the heart of power. It did not alter the moderately socialist economic stance of the state, even though the military attempted to force bazaar prices down, and expanded a major military conglomerate, the Defense Services Institute, that placed the military at the heart of much of the economy.

The second in 1962 was designed to keep the military in command permanently. It established a thorough socialist state, run by the Burma Socialist Programme Party (BSPP), which in fact meant run by the military. Within two years of the coup, an authoritarian Marxist system was set in place, some 15,000 private firms nationalized, and the foreign business community (Europeans, Chinese, and those from the Indian subcontinent) effectively eliminated from positions of economic dominance, and in the case of the Indians, some 200,000 were forced back to their lands of origin. The "Burmese Way to Socialism," an eclectic mixture of Marxist thought wrapped in a vague mantle of Buddhist theology, was the official basis of policy, but it at least had the charm to specify that, in accordance with Buddhist thought, even that official doctrine was also in flux.[19]

The coup leaders had retired the last vestiges of an apolitical public service, the elite Burma Civil Service. The general bureaucracy, which had been upbraided by U Nu in the 1950s because of divided loyalties (to the state and to the party), and which had become (with notable exceptions) singularly inefficient, became controlled by the military, to which all loyalty was transferred. Political ideology and expediency replaced economic rationality. Burma's economy deteriorated rapidly. Rice exports dropped from 1.7 million tons in 1962 to 0.3 million tons in 1968, while the overall value of exports fell from $218.8 million in 1958 to $111.0 million in 1968.[20] Ne Win said that the country could starve for the first time.

Aside from some United Nations support, which was relatively small, Burma had piecemeal cut itself off from the outside world over this period. Refusing to have any group scrutinizing its economy, it effectively severed relations with the World Bank. Its policies and poor implementation brought an end to the U.S. assistance program. A political dispute with the Chinese in 1967 over the cultural revolution suspended their assistance, which had not been insignificant; and as Burma was fearful of Chinese activities in Burma, the Sino-Soviet dispute resulted in truncating the Russian effort. Japan thus emerged as the major source of assistance to Burma during this period.

Although that support was comparatively small, averaging about $20 million per year, it was not insignificant in the Burmese context. One Japanese analysis noted, in the 1960s "Japan's aid could play an important role in the economy of Burma."[21] Indeed, this is an understatement; it could be argued that without it, the Ne Win government might have completely collapsed. Because Burma is a series of only loosely connected village economies that did not necessarily rely on the center for subsistence, the state could continue even under extreme economic mismanagement, which was evident at that time.

Economic Reconsiderations and the Japanese Response

Even as economic conditions deteriorated, the military felt confident enough to expand the BSPP from a cadre to a mass organization. In June-July 1971, it held its first party congress. In it, the party considered reform of the economic debacle in which it found itself. It presented a stinging critique of the economic situation. Published later, *The Long-Term and Short-Term Economic Policies of the Burma Socialist Programme Party*[22] noted deficiencies in the economy, commented on the lack of employment opportunities due to suppression of the private sector, formulated goals for a Twenty-Year Plan (composed of five, four-year plans) and changed priorities to concentrate on the exploitation of Burma's natural resources—agriculture, forestry, fisheries, mining, and especially oil. This was in contrast to previous planning priorities aiming to establish an urban industrial proletariat. The party attempted some internal administrative reforms of the State Economic Enterprises (the public sector) that were marginally effective. It re-endorsed the state's socialist goals, but explicitly called for "mutually beneficial economic relations" between foreign firms and the Burmese state sector, and approved of official (although not private) foreign assistance.

The Burmese economy did expand in the 1970s. Although statistics in Burma can often be considered whimsical at best, and even though Ne Win himself noted years later that the data had been inflated, there was real growth. It was sparked by two elements. The first was rapid expansion under state encouragement of the agricultural sector, especially rice, through the introduction and spread of the newly developed high-yielding varieties together with increased fertilizer use.

The second reason was the expansion of foreign assistance. Donors responded to Burmese liberalization with enthusiasm, as Burma broadened its approaches to foreign support. Donors seem attracted to

Burma because of its obvious poverty, its manifest economic potential and natural endowments, its relative lack of extravagant income inequalities, its neutrality, and perhaps because it seemed the last exotic major nation in Asia. Burma invited the World Bank back. It joined the Asian Development Bank, and bilateral assistance exploded over the next few years, prodded in 1976 by the formation of the consortium group on Burma chaired by the World Bank.

Over the next few years, total assistance to Burma grew by some twenty times, reaching about $500 million at its peak. Japanese support was about $30 million before the reassessment began to have an effect; it rose to about $178 million by the end of the decade. Burma had been the eighth largest recipient of Japanese ODA before the reforms in 1970, but by 1980 it was the fourth largest. Although by 1987 Burma had once again dropped to eighth, support was $172 million and Burma was third in receipt of grant aid in the 1980s. In 1986, Japanese aid peaked at $244.0 million and represented 6.3 percent of all Japanese assistance (Table 7.2).[23]

There seemed to be more flexibility in Japanese assistance as well. Although Japan introduced Yen credits in 1969, after the reforms Japanese assistance grew and broadened. In 1975, general grants were introduced, and in 1976 grant assistance for cultural projects was initiated. By 1977 support for food aid was introduced and in 1979 debt relief.[24]

The period of the later 1970s and early 1980s was, however, deceptive. Burma, because it was at that time not dependent on foreign oil and because rice production expanded, seemed, *mirabile dictu*, to be economically better off than many other states in the region as it grew and weathered the oil crisis and as agricultural growth led the economy. This period masked structural problems in the state sector, as massive, relatively easy expansion of rice production in the most climatically favorable regions reached a plateau. Less than 13 percent of Burma's agricultural land is irrigated, and most as insurance against drought rather than for double cropping. Consequently, effective production limits, given restricted although expanded fertilizer supply, were soon reached.

TABLE 7.2 Japanese Economic Assistance to Burma: Loans and Grants, Including Reparations (current US$ millions, disbursements)

Year	*Grants*	*Loans*	*Total*
1950–57	45.7	---	45.7
1958	26.0	---	26.0
1959	18.7	---	18.7
1960	21.4	---	21.4
1961	13.6	---	13.6
1962	24.4	---	24.4
1963	27.0	---	27.0
1964	16.6	---	16.6
1965	11.6	---	11.6
1966	10.2	---	10.2
1967	6.4	---	6.4
1968	10.2	---	10.2
1969	---	30.0	30.0
1970	11.9	---	11.9
1971	16.7	7.1	26.7
1972	18.1	11.6	29.6
1973	14.8	41.9	56.3
1974	12.1	34.2	46.4
1975	17.1	7.1	21.6
1976	17.7	21.5	27.3
1977	8.0	12.2	20.6
1978	10.6	96.7	107.3
1979	30.0	153.3	178.1
1980	37.2	122.3	152.5
1981	33.2	100.1	125.4
1982	21.3	76.5	97.8
1983	48.4	65.1	113.4
1984	47.1	47.1	95.4
1985	49.4	104.9	154.1
1986	68.9	175.2	244.1

Table 7.2 (continued)

Table 7.2 (continued)

Year	*Grants*	*Loans*	*Total*
1987	67.3	104.7	172.0
1988	91.3*	168.3	259.6
1989	0.1**	----	0.1
1990	33.0***	----	33.0
Total	886.0	1,380.0	2,266.0

Note: Totals do not add because of rounding and discrepancies. All figures are in current dollars. Some figures are in question, because sources do not sometimes discriminate between commitments and disbursements. Figures do not include repayments. Grants include reparations, semi-reparations, cultural grants, debt relief, and food production programs. Loans include project assistance and commodity loans.

Grant assistance between FY1975–86 included Y. 329 million for culture, and cash grants for debt relief of Y. 3,003 million.

* May not include $450,000 in emergency food aid, and $29 million in debt relief.
** Emergency fire victims relief, $150,000.
*** Untied debt relief of Y. 3.5 billion, announced July 24, 1990 by Kyodo News Agency. FBIS, July 30, 1990.
Reparations grant commitment 1954 $200.0 million
Semi-reparations grant commitment 1963 $131.4 million

Source: Burmese and Japanese data.

Economic Crises in the 1980s

At the same time, internal and external factors created the preconditions for a crisis. There was a major slump in the international commodity markets, which badly hurt Burmese foreign exchange earnings. Prices for virtually all legal Burmese exports, including rice, metals, rubber, and even teak, declined. At the same time, Burmese imports, which had been growing as Burma continued to borrow from abroad to provide capital for industrial expansion, had risen in value. Burmese foreign debt mushroomed, and in part was exacerbated by the revaluation of the Japanese yen and the West German deutsche mark. Burma's external debt, which was a modest $62.3 million in 1955, rose to $319.9 million in 1975, but by 1984 was $3.4 billion. (By 1989, it was $4.3 billion in long-term committed and disbursed debt, $5.6 billion in committed but undisbursed debt.)[25] Further, the state economic enterprises were not producing at capacity, and while Burma was generating increased external debt, it had also incurred massive internal debt. By 1984/85 (the Burmese fiscal year begins on April 1), their internal debt to the government was K. 4.3 billion.

The crisis became more acute because as debt rose. Burma had to drastically cut its imports. This diminished the availability of spare parts and raw materials necessary for the production activities of the public sector, thus exacerbating the internal debt problem. As internal production dropped, demand for consumer goods and necessities increased. More reliance was needed on smuggling, and especially on that from China, which quickly assumed a predominant role (it was regularized, if not completely controlled on October 1, 1988 under a joint Sino-Burmese agreement).

Because of the fall in export values and the rise in external debt, Burma's debt service ratio[26] rose officially to 55 percent, but other, informal calculations reached as high as 91 percent. In December 1987, at the time when Burma became an accredited United Nations "least developed nation."[27] Burma's foreign exchange reserves were down to about $28 million.

In August 1987, Ne Win publicly said that there needed to be changes in the economic, political, and even the constitutional structure of the state, and he called for suggestions from the party faithful for consideration at the scheduled party congress planned for the summer of 1989. However, internal and external events overtook that planned timetable.

Japan's Policy Shift

In March 1988, in events completely unrelated to the political turmoil that was to engulf Burma that year, the Burmese Deputy Prime Minister, who was also Minister of Planning and Finance, visited Tokyo. During that trip, he was informed by the Japanese government that Burma was in dire economic straits, and that the situation could not long continue.[28] More importantly, he was told that if Burma did not make substantive economic reforms, ones that were not specified at that time, then Japan would have to reconsider its economic relations with Burma.

This remonstrance was a major event in Burma's contemporary economic history. From a Japanese perspective, it was a precedent. Perhaps never before had Japan unilaterally laid down the requirement for policy changes on the part of a recipient. Certainly they had never done so in Burma, which had jealously guarded its economic policy autonomy, and at least officially refused to listen to policy advice (although of course at a lower level, and unofficially, advice was sometimes proffered by individual donors, multilateral or bilateral, and even sometimes quietly taken on technical matters). This was undoubtedly the most important economic decision made by the Japanese in Burma since the inauguration of the reparations program in 1954. There seems to have been the gradual and incremental development of a consensus within the Liberal Democratic Party, as well as within such entities as MITI, the Ministries of Foreign Affairs, Finance, and others, that the Burmese government was incapable of implementing effectively foreign assistance and that change was imperative.

Burma had been ripe for reform, as Ne Win had previously noted. On September 1, 1987, Ne Win liberalized the grain trade, a positive step and the most important liberalization move since 1962. But then five days later, in moves that must have strongly disturbed the Japanese, he demonetized some 57 percent of the currency notes without compensation. The economic consequences were disastrous with dangerous longer-term inflation (although short-term deflation), hoarding, smuggling, and the loss of what little economic confidence remained in an economically inept regime. This latter ill-conceived move, motivated, so the rumors in Burma indicated, by Ne Win's astrological whims,[29] so exacerbated the dire economic situation that the price and availability of rice, the critical economic indicators of stability or revolution, reached crisis proportions. Coupled with political frustration and pervasive unemployment problems, especially among youth and the educated, the country exploded beginning in March 1988. Although the spark of crisis was apolitical, excesses, brutality, and general social anomie all contributed to its spread. It ended in tragedy with the military coup of September 18,1988, which shored up the previous, quasi-military administration.[30]

This recognition of the need for change may have had antecedents in private discussions or other fora in which Burmese officials and foreigners talked about needed changes. Significantly, the Japanese did not specify individual changes as long as they were "substantive," for to do so would open them to the Burmese charge of interference in Burmese internal affairs. The opening to the private sector announced at the special party congress held on July 23, 1988 was undoubtedly one such reform.

The traumatic period of the summer of 1988, when the nation was in a state of virtual revolution motivated by a compound of political, economic, and social frustration, effectively stopped foreign aid as embassies evacuated personnel, not because any of the demonstrations were directed against them, but because there was a fear of anarchy in the air. The coup physically stopped foreign assistance.

Aftermath of the Coup

If the coup temporarily truncated foreign assistance, the human rights abuses of the military and the previous civilian government stopped it for a longer period. The United States, West Germany, Great Britain, and other European states as well as the multilateral banks, all terminated support.

The Japanese were in a somewhat different position. Although other nations regarded the military government, the SLORC (State Law and Order Restoration Council, composed of eighteen military leaders), as a continuation of the previous regime by other means, the Japanese were in a different position because of their own internal regulations. They had to make the positive step of actually recognizing the military government, rather than a more passive one.

On September 27, 1988, nine days after the coup, the Japanese Embassy noted publicly that in considering its future assistance, it would be important that:

1. A political settlement of the situation reflecting the general consensus of the Myanmar people be reached and the stability of the domestic situation restored; and
2. Efforts be made for economic reforms and for opening up of the economy.[31]

The Government of Japan was under pressure both internally and externally. The Burmese wanted and needed Japanese assistance, but the foreign donor community (with the notable exception of the Australians) were in favor of a cut off of foreign aid, and Japan did not want to split with the donor community. The Japanese business community also applied pressure. Japanese business was losing considerable money on contracts which they had already signed but on which they could not deliver. On January 25, 1989, twelve major Japanese firms—including such influential ones as Mitsubishi and

Mitsui—formally requested the resumption of recognition, noting that in its absence, others (notably China, Malaysia, Singapore, and Korea) would take economic advantage of the situation.[32] The timing of the ultimate decision was forced by the funeral of Emperor Hirohito in Tokyo on February 25, 1989. In order that the Burmese not lose face and (as influential Japanese put it) have to sit with unrecognized delegations such as the Palestine Liberation Organization, a decision was made on February 17, 1989 to recognize the new government.

There are rumors that this issue created controversy within the Ministry of Foreign Affairs, but that the issue was resolved in favor of recognition from a higher authority. A compromise, in any case, was reached. Although the Burmese wanted a complete resumption of all assistance, including negotiations on new projects, the Japanese agreed only to restarting already approved projects, which were considerable: some five grant projects aggregating about Y.9.2 billion (about $66 million, of which over two-thirds had already been disbursed) and 18 loan projects totalling Y.124,470 billion (about $890 million, of which only about 20 percent had been disbursed).[33] However, many of the larger projects, such as the enlargement of the Rangoon airport,[34] could not be continued because the Burmese government could not produce the local currency or supplies required under previous agreements. The Japanese said that they would await the completion of the elections scheduled for May 27, 1990 before deciding whether to negotiate new projects or programs.

A new complication, however, entered the picture. Although all Burmese governments had been scrupulous in repayment of their foreign debts even in the worst of times, the burden became too great, and the Burmese fell in arrears. By July 1989, Burma was about $100 million in arrears to the Japanese. According to Japanese regulations, this issue had to be resolved before new assistance could be provided. The Burmese Minister of Planning, Finance, and Trade visited Japan in November 1989 to make the case, but the Japanese have still not yet yielded. Newspaper reports[35] indicate that the sale of part of the land of the Burmese Embassy in Tokyo, which will bring in an estimated $239 million, may be used to pay off the arrears so that the program can continue. Of course, some debt may eventually be forgiven because of Burma's least-developed-country status if the arrears are first settled.

The Japanese and other donors watched the elections and judged their "fairness" to determine future actions. The actual voting seems to have been held without great trauma, even though the key leaders of the opposition were not allowed to run, and electioneering was circumscribed. By August 1990, the SLORC still had not allowed the newly elected *Pyithu Hluttaw* (National Assembly) to convene, and were withholding permission for the opposition National League for Democracy, which had won an overwhelming victory at the polls, to form a government. It also continued to hold under house arrest key opposition figures, such as Aung San Suu Kyi, and to continue the detention of others, such as General Tin Oo. The military has indicated that it may not allow a new government to be inaugurated until a new constitution has been approved (under military guidance) by the *Pyithu Hluttaw* and a national referendum held on it.

On the other hand, Japan is under great pressure both internally and from the Burmese to restart its program, but it does not wish to break with the western donor community. Under what objective political conditions in Burma and under what economic stipulations it will be restarted are undecided issues. Some Japanese believe that both the Miyazawa and Watanabe factions of the LDP agree for the need for release of detainees and a transfer of power to civilian authorities. It is said that Mr. Watanabe himself agreed to go to Burma in August 1990, if he could meet with both Saw Maung and Aung San Suu Kyi, but that this request was turned down by the SLORC. Nevertheless, on July 24, 1990, the Japanese announced a $23.3 million debt relief grant, perhaps as a response to an election in which the votes seem to have been fairly counted.[36]

The Effectiveness of Japanese Assistance

The concept of "effectiveness" of foreign aid, is not simple to define and in many ways is culturally determined. This is especially true considering that the motivations for both giving and accepting aid are a composite of political, economic, and other factors. This has been the case for Japanese assistance to Burma. At one level, effectiveness can be defined in terms of the political and economic objectives of the donor. From this perspective, the argument can be made that Japan's ODA to Burma has been effective. Burma fit Japanese planning and policy goals very well, at least in terms of Burmese proven potential in oil and performance in rice exports. The alacrity with which Japanese and other nations bid for on-shore oil exploration rights in 1989 (when for the first time in the independence period such opportunities were provided), the off-shore oil and gas tests that continue, and the perpetual rice export market (although poor Burmese performance in quantity and quality has meant market opportunities have been eroded by the United States and more recently by Vietnam), all indicate that

Japanese strategic planning was well-founded, even if Burmese performance did not equal expectations.

At another level, effectiveness refers to what happens to the ODA once the recipient country has the ODA. Before the various Japanese aid organizations engaged in substantive evaluations, effectiveness was used almost as a technical term to indicate the degree to which, when a country or institution borrowed funds, it used completely the total approved amount. One hundred percent use equalled 100 percent effectiveness. Neither how those funds were used nor the effect of such assistance economically seemed to have been considered. This was, in a sense, a technical matter: so much money was promised or pledged and delivered, and so much was spent.

This situation has changed. Internal Japanese government pressures have called for evaluation of the uses of the assistance, as has the Japanese press. Calls for reform have also come from academic circles. It is now possible to get a clearer view of the Japanese perception of its aid program to Burma, not only one from outside. Recent discussions in the press[37] along with more analytical articles have cogently set forth many of the problems associated with Japanese aid to Burma.[38] Concerns are raised that Japanese aid has failed and has not reached the people or contributed to sustained Burmese growth. Part of the problems, however, stem from the Burmese milieu.

Officials of the Burmese government[39] have admitted that before the economic reforms first discussed in public in 1971 (but after the coup of 1962) there were few, if any, feasibility studies for projects to be funded from any source. Decisions were reached at a higher level, and projects then implemented without due regard for their economic viability or priority need. After that time, such studies were introduced, but they were often regarded as slipshod and manipulated to achieve economic rates of return that were politically defensible and that justified decisions predetermined. Burmese sources claimed that the World Bank had the most rigorous studies, while other donors were less thorough. Many projects were chosen and physically located on the whims of the Burmese leadership.

The success or failure of any of these projects is not the only issue to be considered; what is also important is the "triage" effect, in which the support of one project or sector under restricted funding leads to neglect of another. As much or more may be lost through misplaced support as in an inappropriate project itself. How much Burmese requests were generated by potential Japanese contractors, as has been charged in other countries, is not known in the case of Burma although the issue has been raised.[40] Walinsky[41] has stated that "in almost every case" the joint venture proposals were suggested by the Japanese suppliers of equipment (none were ever approved in that period). They took no risks; originally 40 percent of the capital was planned to be Japanese, but this figure for equity capital was dropped to 10-20 percent, which would come from the profits on plant and equipment. The Japanese firms would also make profits from management contracts for the factories.

The reparations period probably should be considered separately. It seemed important to Japan because it was a part of the peace treaty process and served to reestablish a Japanese presence in Burma, and in other countries in the region, and may have been an attempt to end the unpleasant memories of the wartime period. It was a means to penetrate effectively the Burmese market and to situate the Japanese in a position to develop Burma's raw materials. As noted earlier, in retrospect, the overall Japanese effort seemed politically successful. The economic impact of the program however is more difficult to judge. There seems no question that the Lawpida hydroelectric project responded to a major Burmese need, and that it was a clear developmental priority. It is likely, however, the some of the other reparations assistance was too highly priced (as previously noted) and some of questionable priority. It was of dubious accuracy to state: "It can be pointed out that the aids provided by Japan for industrialization projects so as to stimulate economic recovery have played an important role in the recovery of industrial potential."[42] In fact, these projects have never been effective. The retail costs of many of the consumer items are far higher than comparable imported (smuggled) ones. They have proven to be a drain on foreign exchange, and are continuously resupplied through loans, which although highly concessional, produce little of importance.

What this points to is that the issue of trade relates closely to that of aid. There has been a massive, virtually continuous trade imbalance between Burma and Japan (See Table 7.3). In fact, a major percentage of Japanese exports to Burma since 1972 have been related to the goods and materials supplied both under grants during the period of reparations and semi-reparations, and under commodity loans. Data are not available to allow detailed analysis of the effects of project loans or grants on the trade imbalance, but it seems evident that the Japanese aid program accounted for a major element in Japanese exports to Burma. In many years, commodity loans alone were about half of all imports from Japan.

In 1985, the Burmese minister for trade visited Tokyo and requested a survey mission from Japan to determine how to raise Burmese exports, and which products offered greatest promise. In January 1986, a Japanese survey mission on exportable products visited Burma. As a

TABLE 7.3 Burmese Imports and Exports with Special Reference to Japan (US$ millions)

Year	Total Exports	Exports to Japan	Total Imports	Imports from Japan
1952	227.0	21.2	170.6	29.8
1953	269.4	33.1	182.5	50.2
1954	224.8	45.6	197.3	63.1
1955	232.5	38.3	188.8	45.8
1956	246.7	36.3	181.7	42.4
1957	248.2	75.9	277.6	24.8
1958	193.4	10.0	204.2	45.4
1959	227.7	8.4	221.0	50.5
1960	237.2	11.3	235.5	58.5
1961	226.8	8.8	207.1	45.6
1962	259.4	12.8	222.3	50.0
1963	268.4	15.6	227.0	61.4
1964	227.0	15.8	233.3	46.5
1965	238.6	22.0	208.7	71.5
1966	191.3	12.4	176.2	36.6
1967	127.1	6.6	136.5	17.2
1968	108.6	9.9	176.8	25.2
1969	125.5	10.3	141.7	35.6
1970	117.4	11.5	158.9	42.6
1971	122.6	12.5	141.4	50.3
1972	122.5	14.6	162.5	36.8
1973	152.1	34.5	206.8	30.2
1974	200.7	22.2	233.8	64.6
1975	162.3	17.6	249.3	56.8
1976	172.7	24.9	212.7	73.3
1977	206.3	19.6	307.4	76.3
1978	272.3	46.4	495.4	255.6
1979	362.6	79.7	731.7	113.3
1980	428.6	69.6	788.2	236.5
1981	533.2	57.5	863.1	274.0
1982	422.8	44.3	913.0	253.7
1983	375.2	42.6	728.2	197.3
1984	364.1	29.3	564.5	198.9
1985	310.8	32.0	512.9	204.6
1986	505.4	44.6	669.9	234.8
1987	532.3	31.5	659.6	195.5
1988	587.6	29.3	741.3	202.1
1989	367.1	na	580.3	na

Source: International Monetary Fund, *International Financial Statistics 1988 Yearbook; Direction of Trade Statistics 1989. Economic Survey of Burma.* NOTE: IMF/IBRD Burma trade statistics vary annually by as much as 10 percent. These figures should therefore be regarded as indicative, and not as absolute.

result of this visit and subsequent discussions, the Japanese noted that the Burmese had unduly restricted the entry and stay of Japanese traders (there were only 20 in Burma in the later 1980s), and most were concerned with construction projects, not with Burmese exports.[43] The report suggested that visas for Japanese traders be doubled.

Was the charge that later Japanese aid was essentially *tarenagashi* justified? Viewing the total program as a whole and in light of Japanese strategic concerns as articulated above, that charge is not valid. The Japanese have, essentially, accomplished their purposes of establishing an pre-eminent position in Burma. Their relations are critical to Burma, their support vital to the Burmese economy, and their access exceptional.[44] Should Burma prosper, both Burma and Japan will benefit.

Looking to the Future

The four major Japanese industrial projects started over a generation ago have never been self-sustaining, and probably should never have been initiated. However attractive vehicle assembly, for example, may have been, and however modern such an approach may have seemed, the economies of scale have not warranted such assistance. That project and a variety of others that depended on imported raw materials (65 percent of the vehicle parts came from Japan), imported machinery and a continuous supply of foreign spare parts, and the absence of a market sufficient to justify the capital costs and import substitution effort all indicate a lack of concern for "sustainability." The *Mainichi Shimbun* article, based on an earlier Japanese evaluation of the Burma program, indicated that because of the cut off of Japanese assistance and a lack of materials and parts, the automobile assembly plant was operating at about five percent of capacity, the electrical appliance plant had stopped production, and the agricultural machinery plant was producing at 3-4 percent. In these cases the *tare-nagashi* concept has validity.

The fault, if there is one and it can be assigned, lies first with the Burmese authorities in suggesting or agreeing to non-economic projects. The Japanese were at fault more for not refusing, or not setting Japanese policy guidelines that would have helped better focus assistance.

Saito has made a number of telling points about this in her article. She comments on the lack of an assistance "ideology" or "concept" with which to guide the Japanese program, notes the pressures from the Burmese government on evaluations that were likely to be critical, and the lack of external (third party) evaluations. The onerous debt burden not only has meant that Burma cannot repay it, but has forced Burma into ecologically destructive sales of forest resources along the Thai border. She further deplores the reliance on large projects in major cities, such as Rangoon and Mandalay, and that the assistance is not reaching the people, who have not been involved in the project cycle. She also has been critical of the role of Japanese business in the process of project choice, even though such requests were supposed to come from the Burmese government.

The importance of the future Japanese role in foreign assistance in Burma may be considered by speculating on Burmese needs and foreign responses in general, and then more specifically with regard to Japan, if such Japanese aid is renewed or terminated. First, any economic assistance, including a revived Japanese aid program, will be operating in the context of a new world order, minus the antagonisms of previous cold war and great power rivalries. Movements toward political settlement in Indochina, and a less rigid economic stance will mean a Burma somewhat less dependent on foreign assistance as a whole, and thus on Japan than in the past. The regularization of much of the border trade with China, Bangladesh, and eventually more formally with Thailand decreases Burmese reliance on Japanese goods.

A central issue here is whether the new Burmese government will allow the scrutiny of its economy by the multilateral donor community, thus allowing such assistance to be forthcoming. Further, if Japan chooses not to participate in a Burma aid program (possibly following the lead of other western powers), then other nations, such as Korea, might well be delighted to increase its already growing influence in Burma, especially at Japan's expense.

Japan will probably be influenced by its OECD relationships and the perspectives of the OECD governments on assistance for Burma. For example, the German government has taken a strong position on resolution of political and ethnic tensions in Burma before it will consider the resumption of assistance. Japan may well follow that lead in restarting new programs, although it will in all probability continue implementing its current aid portfolio. A Burmese expatriate organization in Japan in the summer of 1990 has lobbied for withholding assistance until a transfer of power has been achieved and detainees released.

Burma needs Japanese aid, but not to the degree that it had to rely on it in the past. A more open economic system will bring in private investment, so long prevented, but whether that investment, beyond oil exploration and development, will be for longer-term capital needs rather than shorter-term trade relations will depend on the internal political climate and investment guarantees. Thus, Japan's future role in supplying economic assistance to Burma will be important, but not likely as critical as in the past.

Lessons from the Japanese Aid Program to Burma

Japan's earlier role as a modest donor on the world scene, and in its early years in Burma, has implications far different from Japan's position as the world's largest supplier of foreign assistance and as the primary donor in Burma. Japan's role in Burma, thus, is in some sense a microcosm of the world experience for Japan. As long as Japan was one of many donors in Burma in the 1950s, even though its assistance was quite large in percentage, Japan, which was new at the development experience, could realistically and appropriately eschew many policy issues. As Japan took a predominant role, however, its responsibilities changed. As the only bilateral donor with a large enough portfolio to be critical to the recipient, and with the access to the top leadership that only Japan had on a continuing basis, Japan's responsibilities grew exponentially.

Burma has relied on the Japanese, virtually since independence. Burma may today be reluctant to admit this either internally or externally as Brigadier Aung Gyi did in 1963, but the magnitude of the assistance indicates clearly how important Japan has been. Whatever the political future of Burma, its national well-being and the well-being of its people will depend on both the sagacity of the Burmese government's policies and their implementation, and the role of foreign donors. Japan has a special responsibility as the leading donor.

Endnotes

1. "*Tarenagashi*" was a term used in a *Mainichi Shimbun* article on June 11, 1989 to describe Japanese aid to Burma. It means to flow through without control, and implies in this context the act of giving without serious concern about the intended outcome. Earlier versions of this paper appeared as working papers at the East West Center (1989) and at Northern Illinois University (1990).

2. Because Myanmar as a national name was only adopted in 1989, and because some opposition groups within Burma object to the change, the original appellation is maintained here. In addition, "Burman" refers to those who speak Burmese as their native language and who adhere to the cultural norms of that group. "Burmese" refers to any citizen of the country.

3. Hosup Kim, *Policy-Making of Japanese Official Development Assistance to the Republic of Korea, 1965-1983* (Ph.D. Dissertation, University of Michigan, 1987), p. 19.

4. Saburo Okita in *Japan and Third World Agricultural Development* (Washington, D.C.: International Food Policy Research Institute, Policy Briefs #4, 1989).

5. Since the summer of 1990, Japan has faced a sixth critical choice: whether or not to restart new Japanese assistance following the Burmese elections held on May 27, 1990 and the subsequent failure of the military government to participate in an effective transfer of power to a newly elected (and overwhelmingly opposition-oriented) National Assembly, the writing of a new constitution, and the release of opposition figures from detention or house arrest.

6. Luldip Singh Mali, *Financing Economic Development of Burma Since Independence* (Ph.D. Dissertation, Indiana University, 1960), p.33.

7. Mali, p. 37.

8. U Ba Nyein, *Japanese Repatriation* [in Burmese], March 1962, pp. 6-11. This figure seems inflated. U Ba Nyein was later a key advisor to the military Revolutionary Council, Minister of Cooperatives, and a strong advocate of Burmese socialism. I am indebted to Dr. Mya Than (Institute of Southeast Asian Studies, Singapore) for this reference.

9. David I. Steinberg, *Burma's Road Toward Development: Growth and Ideology Under Military Rule* (Boulder: Westview Press,1981), p. 78.

10. Mali, p. 81.

11. Louis J. Walinsky, *Economic Development in Burma 1951-1960* (New York: Twentieth Century Fund, 1962), pp. 512-515.

12. *Ibid.*

13. One may speculate that South Korean moves into Burma in oil exploration and in foreign investment, which accelerated with economic liberalization following the military coup of September 1988, were prompted by considerations similar to those of Japan.

14. Walinsky, pp. 509-511. There were also complications in accounting, as the Japanese fiscal year began April 1, and the Burmese fiscal year October 1. The Burmese later changed their fiscal year to April 1.

15. In 1985 $2.1 million to supplied them under a commodity loan, and In 1987, $3.5 million was supplied. See the OECF annual reports.

16. Walinsky, p. 509.

17. The information on this period is taken from *The Nation* [Rangoon], January 6-February 16, 1963. Aung Gyi discusses his retirement (and much else) in his widely circulated private letter to Ne Win of May 9, 1988.

18. In 1975, grant assistance included Y.72,000 million in reparations and Y.47,336 million in "semi-reparations." "Semi-reparations" refers to grant economic assistance or cooperation essentially provided to ensure Japanese access to markets.

19. For a discussion of "The Burmese Way to Socialism," see Steinberg, 1981.

20. David I. Steinberg, "Neither Silver Nor Gold: The Fortieth Anniversary of the Burmese Economy," In Josef Silverstein, ed., *Independent Burma at Forty Years: Six Assessments* (Ithaca: Cornell University, Southeast Asia Program, 1989).

21. Institute of Developing Economies, "Basic Survey for Promotion of Official Loans to Burma." March 1983. Prepared for the Economic Planning Agency.

22. Rangoon: Planning Department, Ministry of Planning and Finance, December 1973. Publication had to await approval of the party's Central Committee.

23. Ministry of Foreign Affairs, *Japan's Official Development Assistance. 1988 Annual Report* ,Tokyo, 1988.

24. Institute of Developing Economies, *Basic Survey for Promotion of Official Loans to Burma*, Tokyo, March 1983 [prepared for the Economic Planning Agency].

25. See David I. Steinberg, *The Future of Burma: Crisis and Choice in Myanmar* (New York: The Asia Society and the University Press of America, 1990).

26. The ratio of annual external debt payments to the value of export revenues and other inflows of foreign capital.

27. Burma's annual per capita income was said officially to be $200, at the upper edge of qualification. Yet official statistics did not take into account the extensive smuggling trade, which may have reached 40 percent of GNP, the massive illegal internal transfer of goods, as well as an unrealistic exchange rate that was overvalued by about six times. Burma wanted "least developed country" status because it would provide lower interest rates on loans, and some loans might be converted to grants. Burma did not inform its own public about this demeaning status until late March 1989, and then only tangentially in reference to some positive economic indicators.

28. Burma had borrowed expensive Eurodollars so they could continue to meet payments on Japanese loans.

29. Steinberg, 1990, chapter 2.

30. See *Ibid.*, and also David I. Steinberg, *Crisis in Burma: Stasis and Change in a Political Economy in Turmoil* (Bangkok: Chulalongkorn University, Institute of Security and International Studies. Occasional Paper #5, 1989); and Bertil Lintner, *Outrage: Burma's Struggle for Democracy* (Hong Kong: Review Publishing Company, 1989).

31. "Japan's Aid to Myanmar." Rangoon: The Japanese Embassy, August 1989.

32. See *Mainichi Shimbun*, June 11, 1989. Also evident from personal communications with the Japanese Embassy, Rangoon.

33. "Briefing Paper on Japan's Aid to Myanmar." Rangoon, September 1989.

34. In 1984, the Rangoon airport extension consumed about 25 percent of the total Japanese support of Y.891.6 hundred million.

35. See, for example, *The Economist*,February, 1990.

36. Kyodo News Agency, as reported in FBIS, July 31, 1990.

37. *Mainichi Shimbun*, ibid.

38. For an excellent example, see: Teruko Saito, "ODA and Ecological Destruction in Burma: Japan's Responsibility." *Gendai Nogyo* (Contemporary Agriculture), November 1989 (in Japanese).

39. Personal communications. March 1989, Rangoon.

40. Ibid.

41. Walinsky, p. 515.

42. Institute of Developing Economies, p. 35.

43. The Japanese noted that the Japanese members of trading firms resident in Thailand were about 400 (of some 4,400 Japanese in Thailand), and that in 1986 Thai exports to Japan were 28 times Burmese exports, and in 1987 49 times those exports to Japan. The implication is that if the Burmese want more exports, they had to allow more Japanese to be resident in Burma. These and other data are from an undated (but clearly after 1987) and untitled Japanese document.

44. For example, on April 11, 1990, the Burmese and Japanese announced a new joint venture, Myanmar-Japan Concord, which will involve construction of seven major projects, including new international airports in Rangoon and Mandalay. The costs are expected to be about $14 billion over 10-15 years, and will involve 240 Japanese firms. See *Economist Intelligence Unit Burma Country Report*, No.2, 1990, p. 30.

8

JAPAN'S AID DIPLOMACY WITH CHINA

Zhao Quansheng

Introduction

Aid to China illustrates the range of issues confronted by Japan in virtually each of the recipient countries and regions analyzed in this volume. In addition, other than Korea, no country has had as intense a relationship with Japan. Bilateral relationships have erupted into war twice within 100 years, first in the 1890s and later in the 1930s. However, Japan's involvement in Chinese affairs was not limited to military conflict. Japan attempted to use aid as a means of furthering foreign policy objectives as early as World War I. The Nishihara loans, issued beginning in 1916, were used as an inducement for China's declaration of war against Germany. Following World War II, both Chinas renounced reparations. As an ally of the United States, Japan extended assistance to Taiwan from the inception of the aid program until the initiation of diplomatic relations with the People's Republic of China in 1972. Eventually, with the signing of the Peace Treaty in 1978 and the start of Tokyo's ODA program in China, Japan moved into the position of preeminent donor.

This chapter gives an overview of Japan's ODA to China and examines the basic characteristics of Japan's contemporary aid policy towards China. Conventional arguments claim that Japan has no clear aid policy, and that foreign aid receives scant attention from the Japanese people or leaders.[1] This chapter will argue, however, that Japan *does* have clear economic, political, and strategic goals for its foreign aid programs. This can be demonstrated by an examination of Japanese aid to China before and after Tiananmen.

After the Economic Summit of seven major industrialized nations held in July 1990 in Houston, experienced observers of Asian affairs notice that while

> other world leaders kept their distance, it is notable that it was Japan which moved furthest and mostly quickly to restore friendly relations with Beijing in the aftermath of Tiananmen, and that it was Japanese Prime minister Toshiki Kaifu who undertook to act as the spokesman for China's interests at the Group of Seven meeting in Houston.[2]

Japan's actions have inevitably brought forward questions about what Japan wants from the relationship with China, what are the major external constraints (and supports) on how Japan chooses to pursue its objectives, and what are the likely prospects for the future. This chapter will try to answer these questions within the framework of Japan's "aid diplomacy" towards China.

June 4, 1990 marked the first anniversary of the military crackdown on the student-led pro-democracy demonstrations at Tiananmen Square in Beijing. It was also the first anniversary of economic sanctions imposed on China by Western countries and Japan. At the Houston summit of July 1990, Japanese Prime Minister Toshiki Kaifu announced that "Japan will gradually resume" its third package of government loans to China valued at 810 billion yen (US$5.4 billion), thereby ending more than one year of economic sanctions against China.[3] This soft loan package to China is designed to last for five years. Even though Japan's decisions, announced at the Houston summit, received understanding from the United States and other Western economic powers, these countries did not immediately follow Japan's lead in changing their policies towards China.[4]

For more than a year after Tiananmen, Japan refused to restore the loan commitment process, arguing that Tokyo's hands were tied by both domestic public opinion and international obligations.[5] Japan's action, in line with Western economic sanctions (including the suspension of World Bank loans worth $750 million),[6] continued to sour relations between Japan and China. This made it increasingly clear that Japanese ODA to China not only possesses economic significance, but also is a crucial part of Japan's diplomacy towards China, directly affecting overall bilateral relations.

In order to get a better understanding of Japan's aid diplomacy towards China, it is necessary to briefly review the development of

Japan's ODA to China and consider an overall picture of Japan's aid policy and its loan packages to China.

An Overview of Japan's ODA to China

Although the 1972 Sino-Japanese rapprochement and the 1978 Sino-Japanese Peace and Friendship Treaty laid foundations for the rapid development of bilateral relations, it was not until 1979 that China received any Japanese foreign aid. At that time, Beijing signed an agreement with Tokyo to receive an ODA loan. From this beginning, Japanese aid to China grew substantially throughout the 1980s (Table 8.1). From 1982 to 1986, China was the largest recipient of Japanese aid and during the 1987-1990 period, China was the second largest recipient next to Indonesia.

TABLE 8.1 ODA Flows to China from Japan (US$ millions)

Year	*Amount*
1979	2.6
1980	4.3
1981	27.7
1982	368.8
1983	350.2
1984	389.4
1985	387.9
1986	497.0
1987	553.1
1988	673.7
1989	832.2
1990	723.0

Source: Gaimusho, *Wagakuni no Seifu Kaihatsu Enjo*, Tokyo, various volumes.

Japan is now the largest ODA donor to China. For example, Japan's ODA to China accounted for 45 percent of the total amount of aid that China received during the period of 1979 to 1984 from DAC members and international organizations. During the same period, the International Monetary Fund was second (14 percent), with United Nations agencies third (12 percent), and West Germany fourth (9 percent) as aid donors to China.[7] In 1989, Japan's share of aid to China reached nearly 70 percent of the total aid China received before the Tiananmen incident.

An important characteristic of Japan's aid to China is that loan aid has accounted for 85 to 90 percent of the total ODA. The Chinese have been especially interested in acquiring Japanese aid for large-scale infrastructure projects, such as railways, ports, and hydroelectric power plants. From the Japanese perspective, these large-scale projects normally have "high feasibility" status, receive better publicity in the international community, and are favored by an important domestic constituency of Japanese ODA, the engineering and construction firms.

Since 1979, there have been three major packages of Japanese government loans to China. The first ODA loan package was 350 billion yen ($1.5 billion) for China's five-year plan (1979-84) which was pledged by Prime Minister Masayoshi Ohira on his visit to China in December 1979. This was followed by a 470 billion yen (US$2.1 billion) package agreed to by Prime Minister Yasuhiro Nakasone in March 1984 for the five-year period of 1985 to 1990. The third package is the 810 billion yen (US$5.4 billion) covering 1990-95 that was promised by Prime Minister Noboru Takeshita during his visit to Beijing in August 1988. These government loans, known as "soft loans," follow the international standard of providing longer payback periods and lower interest payments. This means the loans are repayable in thirty years at approximately three percent interest with a ten-year grace period. In 1988, the Japanese government announced an interest reduction on yen loans to developing countries to approximately 2.6 percent. China was one of the first countries to receive such a low interest rate.[8]

Economic, Political, and Strategic Considerations

Japan clearly takes into consideration economic factors when formulating its aid policy towards China. Although trade with China has been less than five percent of Japan's total trade, China is economically important to Japan. For years Japan, alternating with Hong Kong, has been China's leading trade partner, accounting for approximately one-fourth of China's total foreign trade. However, Japan's leading position in the China market has constantly been challenged by other industrialized countries, making foreign aid an area of competition between Japan and the Western states.

In 1979, China began its economic reform and open-door policy. For the first time, China showed a willingness to accept foreign aid including loans and grants. The first loan request was for a package of eight infrastructure construction projects which included three hydroelectric power plants, three railroad lines, and two ports. When China began to explore loan possibilities for these projects in the summer of 1979, Tokyo was well aware of the potential for competition from Western countries. For example, there were several private commercial loan offers from France ($7 billion), Britain ($5 billion), Sweden, and Canada. The Japanese also knew of U.S. Vice-President Walter Mondale's promise of $2 billion Eximbank credits to China when he visited Beijing in 1979. The Japanese government understood that ODA project loans would be a convenient and useful way to enhance Japan's long-range economic benefits. The loans would allow Japan, as Chae-Jin Lee, a long-time observer of Sino-Japanese relations, pointed out, "to establish a firm foothold in China's economic infrastructure, and induce a spillover effect to other areas of Sino-Japanese economic cooperation."[9]

From the first loan package (1979) Japan agreed to provide six (out of eight) construction projects for government loans. Railroad line and port projects were selected, while two hydroelectric power plant projects were dropped. This selection clearly reflected Japan's economic interests. The two ports, Shijiusuo and Qinhuangdao, are important ports for exporting coal to Japan. Two of the three railroad lines, the Yanzhou-Shijiusuo Railway and the Beijing-Qinhuangdao Railway, directly connect the two ports. Japan provided 62 percent and 100 percent of requested loan amounts respectively. On the other hand, the third railroad, Hengyang-Guangzhou Railway, was irrelevant for energy exports to Japan. It received only 16 percent of what China asked for. The two hydroelectric power plant projects (Longtan and Shuikou) were rejected by the Japanese, because they were in conflict with Japan's economic interests. The Longtan Hydroelectric Power Plant would have had the capacity to supply electricity to a large aluminum refinery with an annual production capability of 600,000 tons, which was in conflict with Japanese joint venture interests in aluminum production in Indonesia and Brazil.[10] These examples demonstrate that the actual selection from the requested projects reflected, as Greg Story suggested, "the needs of the donor rather than the recipient, that is, it followed Japanese rather than Chinese economic priorities."[11]

Since normalization, Sino-Japanese relations have experienced political frictions. The most notable friction surrounds the charge of Japan's "revived militarism." In 1982 and again in 1985 and 1986, there were large anti-Japanese demonstrations in Beijing and other major Chinese cities. These were inspired by China's sharp criticism of the

Japanese government's revision of Japan's past war behavior in school textbooks (known as the "textbook controversy") and an official visit by Prime Minister Yasuhiro Nakasone to the Yasukuni Shrine to honor Japanese war dead. Other problems included a territorial dispute over Diaoyu Island,[12] and a controversy between China and Taiwan over ownership rights of a student dormitory in Kyoto. A Japanese court decided in favor of Taiwan. During these frictions, Japan's political leaders pledged large scale "soft loans" to China. Although there were no direct connections between the controversies and the loans, the Japanese used government loans as goodwill gestures to cultivate political ties with the Chinese.

Emotional ties towards China also play a part in formulating Japanese aid policy. In public opinion polls taken in Japan over the past several years, China has consistently been second only to the United States as the most "friendly" nation. Because of a shared culture and historical and geographical closeness, the Japanese emotion towards China is sometimes, as Swadesh De Roy suggests, "above reason."[13] There are also wide-spread feelings of regret among the Japanese, especially the older generation, about Japan's past war behavior in China. Chiang Kai-shek in 1951 and Zhou Enlai in 1972 respectively, foreswore Japan's war reparations as goodwill gestures. However, many Japanese believed that Japan could use ODA loans as surrogate reparations.

To further promote the bilateral relationship and increase mutual understanding at the public level, Japan has concentrated most of its grant aid towards humanitarian purposes and cultural exchanges. One of the most important projects was the China-Japan Friendship Hospital in Beijing, which cost 16.4 billion yen and accounted for 57 percent of all grants to China in the 1980-85 period. Other smaller projects included a Sino-Japanese youth exchange center in Beijing (1985),[14] a rehabilitation center in Beijing for the physically handicapped (1986), water purification facilities in Changchun (1986), forest resources restoration (1988), an experimental fishery station in Hebei province (1988), a national library and a foreign language college in Beijing (1988), and preservation of the Dunhuang Mogao Cave on the historic Silk Road (1988). A one billion yen grant for the Mogao Cave was pledged by Prime Minister Noboru Takeshita when he visited China in 1988. The Prime Minister indicated that the grant was to "appeal to the hearts of the Chinese people."[15] Economic assistance to China has also come in the form of technical and training assistance. For example, in 1986, of ten thousand "foreign experts" in China, about 40 percent were Japanese. A management training center funded by the Japanese was opened in Tianjin in 1986.

Japan also has strategic considerations in its aid programs to China. Article nine of Japan's postwar constitution renounces "the right of belligerency." This has been interpreted to mean that Japan cannot use military policy as an explicit instrument of its foreign policy.[16] This leaves economic means, including ODA, as one of the prime ways available to the Japanese government to exercise international influence and to deal with its Asian neighbors, particularly China.[17]

Despite a claim made by Prime Minister Nakasone during a Upper House hearing on ODA that Japan would not bring strategic considerations into the distribution of Japanese foreign aid,[18] nevertheless strategic considerations clearly influence aid policies. Japan's strategic goals have gone through several changes over the past three decades. In the 1960s, ODA was used to promote Japan's exports. After the 1973 oil shocks, Japan's aid policy switched to securing raw-material supplies. China was one of the source countries (together with Indonesia and countries in the Middle East) during this period. Entering the 1980s, Japan tried hard to boost aid to countries which did not necessarily have close links with Japan, such as Egypt, Pakistan, and Turkey, but which were strategically important from the perspectives of the United States and other Western countries.

China has always remained strategically important to Japan. China's natural resources, in particular energy resources, are desirable for Japan. After the oil shocks in the 1970s, Japan became aware of how political instability in the Middle East could jeopardize assured access to that region's energy supplies. This was an important recognition since Japan was highly dependent on energy resources from that area. With rich natural resources such as coal and oil and safer, cheaper, and closer sea routes, China is an ideal source from which Japan can diversify its energy supplies.

Japan's strategic considerations also reflected an awareness of international sensitivities to Japan's aid diplomacy towards China. To smooth other countries' concerns, the Ministry of Foreign Affairs in September 1979 released the "Ohira Three Principles" of aid policy to China. The three principles were aimed at (1) cooperation with the United States and other Western nations (primarily the EC), easing fears expressed that Japan might move to monopolize the China market; (2) balancing aid to China with aid to other Asian countries, especially ASEAN; and (3) avoiding loans to China's defense-related industries. The last principle was to deflect criticism in particular from the Soviet Union, Vietnam, and South Korea.[19]

Post-Tiananmen Dilemma

Japan's initial reaction towards the Tiananmen incident of June 1989 was clear yet cautious. Right after Tiananmen, Tokyo decided to join in the economic sanctions imposed on China by Western industrialized countries, putting a hold on its government loans. Yet, the Japanese government was careful with the aid issue. Instead of calling it a "sanction," Tokyo initially described the holding back of loan disbursements as necessary to protect Japanese aid officials in China due to the violent military actions in Beijing. Both Prime Minister Sousuke Uno and top foreign affair officials either deplored Beijing's armed suppression or called it "morally intolerable." In the immediate post-Tiananmen period, because of a lack of clear direction, Japanese aid officials followed a "case-by-case review" process for approving current loans and grants to China.[20]

Domestic Japanese reactions towards the Tiananmen incident were strong. Economic sanctions were frequently called for and received a wide range of political and public support. This support came not only from the ruling Liberal Democratic Party (LDP) and top government bureaucrats, but also from opposition parties. LDP's Foreign Affairs Department Chairman Koji Kakizawa openly called for economic sanctions saying that Japan should make clear that it is a nation which respects the principles of democracy, freedom, and human rights. The Japan Communist Party (JCP) Secretariat Chief Mitsuhiro Kaneko asked to "immediately halt economic assistance to China," because it is "paid for by the sweat of the Japanese people's brows." Japan's largest labor organization, the Japanese Private Sector Trade Union Confederation known as *Rengo* (with 5.4 million members), and the 4.5 million-strong General Council of Trade Unions, announced that they would suspend exchanges with China to protest Beijing's action.[21]

Japan was the only Asian country that went along with Western industrialized countries to impose economic sanctions against Beijing's military suppression of the pro-democracy movement which left hundreds dead.[22] One of the measures Japan took was to freeze its government loan of 810 billion yen ($5.4 billion) which had been scheduled for April 1990. Other measures included the suspension of high-level government contacts and several scheduled economic and cultural exchange meetings, including the inauguration of an investment-promotion organization for China and a Sino-Japanese meeting on high technology transfer. In addition to emphasizing basic democratic principles, Japan was also deeply concerned with its international obligations. Many observers believe that if Japan had not taken a tough stance on condemning China's military crackdown, Tokyo "might find itself internationally isolated."[23]

This international pressure has slowed Japan's process of lifting economic sanctions against China, and has resulted in some confusion over when Japan should resume government aid to China. For example, a Japanese government source indicated in December 1989 that Japan would extend the 810 billion yen loans ($5.4 billion) once the World Bank lifted its freeze on new loans to China. Finance Minister Ryutaro Hashimoto then promised in early January, 1990 that Japan would unfreeze the loan programs with China if Beijing lifted martial law.[24] Another possible timing for the loan release, according to an official from the Japanese Foreign Ministry, was the resolution of the Fang Lizhi issue. Fang, a well-known dissident and physicist, took refuge in the U.S. Embassy in Beijing for more than a year.[25] Despite these announcements, Japan let several opportunities pass without lifting its freeze on the $5.4 billion loan, such as Beijing's lifting of martial law in January 1990, the resumption of World Bank humanitarian aid to China, Beijing's release of several hundred political prisoners in the first half of 1990, and China's decision to allow Fang Lizhi to go abroad.

Tensions between the two countries eased somewhat in early May 1990 when the Japanese government extradited a Chinese hijacker who seized a Chinese airliner on a flight from Beijing to Fukuoka in western Japan late in 1989. The hijacker claimed to have been involved in the pro-democracy movement. The return of the hijacker to China was seen by some foreign observers as China's only major "diplomatic victory since June 4." China's next objective, according to an Asian diplomat, "is to persuade Japan to restore its official loans and so end sanctions by Western governments."[26]

What concerned the Japanese government had much less to do with domestic public opinions or human right issues. Tokyo's lower priority on human rights issues was demonstrated not only by its policy of sending the hijacker back to China, but also by its reluctance to defend Chinese students in Japan who were allegedly intimidated and harassed by the Chinese Embassy.[27] Rather, Tokyo was waiting for clear signals from its Western partners, notably the United States. As late as July 1990, the atmosphere in Washington was quite negative towards Beijing. Even though President George Bush extended China's most-favored-nation (MFN) status, the U.S. Congress was getting tougher in its posture towards China. The U.S. lawmakers were determined to step up their efforts to limit World Bank loans to China by exercising their influence over the World Bank.[28] The Bush administration also held firm in its policy towards the Japanese loans.

U.S. National Security Adviser Brent Scowcroft told a key LDP leader, former Japanese foreign minister Hiroshi Mitsuzuka, "not to restore the credits too quickly."[29] Under such circumstances, Japan appeared to be cautions in its own policy towards China.

The United States had been ambivalent towards Japanese aid to China even before Tiananmen. On the one hand, the United States itself was explicitly prohibited from extending ODA to China by the Foreign Assistance Act due to the fact that China was "a member of the international communist movement."[30] Conservative lawmakers and the Commerce Department viewed Japan's aid presence in China suspiciously, worrying about Japanese penetration of the Chinese market and the implicit condoning of human rights abuses in China. On the other hand, however, State Department and foreign aid agencies had consistently encouraged Japan to take the lead in the West's relations with China, specifically through foreign aid. They believed that a moderate and open China would serve U.S. interests.[31]

Since June 1989, China's credit rating has fallen and some bankers have speculated that China might have to reschedule some of its $44 billion foreign debt, especially if it is unable to sign new loans. About half of China's debt is owed to Japan, China's largest creditor. The World Bank's outstanding loans to China come to about $8 billion. Even before the crackdown, Japanese big business (industry and commerce in particular) had already shown decreasing enthusiasm about China as a marketplace.[32] For example, Japan ranks a poor third in overseas investment in China (after Hong Kong and the United States) with about eight percent of the total foreign investment into China in 1988.[33] After Tiananmen, commercial bankers became increasingly reluctant to extend new loans to China. Japanese bankers are deeply concerned about China's current economic situation which was affected by the political chaos. "The downhold on loans from Japanese banks has nothing to do with politics," a Japanese banker claimed recently, "it just doesn't look profitable for us at this time."[34]

Despite a reluctance to extend the loans, the Japanese government is cautious to avoid pushing China into further isolation. Immediately after the crackdown, the chief spokesman for the Ministry of Foreign Affairs, Taizo Watanabe, emphasized that, "What the government is taking into account most is the fact that relations between Japan and China are naturally different from those between the U.S. and China," referring to Japan's military's behavior during World War II. He also warned that Japan must be cautious because Beijing might launch a harsh attack against Tokyo's economic sanctions in order to distract domestic attention from the current unrest. The view of the government was supported by many business leaders. For example, Bank of Japan

Governor Satoshi Sumita advocated a "wait and see attitude" right after the Beijing crackdown.[35]

Japan's dual-positions were highlighted by a *Japan Times* editorial on the first anniversary of the Tiananmen incident. The editorial condemned Beijing's repressive policy, but also claimed that "outsiders' one-sided perceptions of China have played an excessive role in isolating China in the international community." It concluded that "it is time to try to pave the way for China's full-fledged return to the international community." As time passed, Japan's business community began to complain that the hold on loans had "seriously affected" exports to China; and the business community wanted the government loans resumed.[36]

This dual-position inevitably produced a diplomatic dilemma and created confusion in Japanese policy towards China. The controversy forced Tokyo to search for a balance among various options, trying to confirm to both the West and China that Japan (1) will continue to be in line with the West, but at the same time (2) will prevent pushing China into further isolation. Therefore, Japan needed to work on two diplomatic fronts—China and the West—in its post-Tiananmen policy towards China.

While refusing to implement new loans, Japan lifted its freeze on ongoing aid to China in August 1989.[37] In October 1989, the World Bank began to resume its lending to China for humanitarian aid including a $30 million loan for earthquake relief (October 1989) and a $60 million credit for agriculture projects (February 1990).[38] Following the World Bank lead, the Japanese government, for the first time after the Tiananmen incident, released new grant aid of $35 million in December 1989 for improving facilities at a Beijing television broadcasting station and a Shanghai hospital.[39]

Japan has since frequently reminded the United States and other Western countries that it was not in their interest to impose continuing heavy sanctions on China. Japan also was reluctant to openly criticize China in July 1989 at the Paris summit of seven major Western industrialized countries.[40] "To isolate China will not be good for world peace and stability," Prime Minister Toshiki Kaifu claimed at a 1990 New Year's news conference.[41] The prospect of a wealthy Japan facing an isolated, chaotic China has long been a nightmare for Japanese decision-makers, and has prompted Japan's willingness to be a mediator between China and the Western world. A Japanese economic official put it this way, "Japan should take one step ahead of other nations in improving its relations with China. Japan can help create a climate for other nations to improve their relations with Beijing."[42]

Two months prior to the Houston summit of July 1990, Japan pledged again to resume the government loan package, when Prime Minister Kaifu met with the Japan Socialist Party (JSP) Secretary General Tsuruo Yamaguchi before his eight-day visit to Beijing. Yamaguchi urged Kaifu to lift the freeze on the loan package. The Prime Minister told the JSP leader that there would be no problem in telling the Chinese leaders that "Japan will certainly honor its promise" in the $5.4 billion loans, but that there were "difficulties in resuming aid immediately."[43]

Political Access in China

The Japanese have attached great importance to building "a multilevel network of cooperative relations in the international community at both the governmental and private levels."[44] Japan's aid diplomacy was fruitful. Even before Tiananmen, American journalists noticed that despite problems surrounding the "textbook controversy," the Japanese still maintained better access to top leaders in China than the U.S. and other Western leaders and diplomats.

There were many networking activities between the Chinese and the Japanese that were helpful in cultivating political ties. For example, in 1984, Chinese Communist Party Secretary General Hu Yaobang invited visiting Japanese Prime Minister Yasuhiro Nakasone to a rare private family dinner.[45] In early 1985, Hu dined with Japanese Ambassador Yosuke Nakae three times in one week, whereas American Ambassador Arthur Hummel during his entire four-year posting met with Hu only once. After signing the agreement transferring Hong Kong over to Chinese sovereignty in 1997, British Prime Minister Margaret Thatcher proudly announced that the Chinese officials agreed to receive a British trade delegation. But when the mission of ten top British industrialists arrived in February 1985, they found themselves outdone by a visit of 100 members of the Japanese Chamber of Commerce. The Japanese delegation met with China's paramount leader Deng Xiaoping; the British did not. A Western journalist concluded, "no other country can compete with Japan for access in China."[46] This greater access to the Chinese leadership can largely be explained (in addition to racial and cultural affinity) as the result of Tokyo's long-time activities of cultivating relations with Beijing.

Tokyo's working style is also noteworthy. The Japanese preferred behind-the-scenes ways to deal with the Chinese. In turn, Beijing felt more comfortable in talking to Tokyo than to Washington, for Americans tend to make bilateral negotiations highly public. In the aftermath of Tiananmen, Japan was careful not to hurt the relations of mutual understanding between the two countries. The following example is one of many actions taken by Tokyo to maintain its political ties with Beijing, and to deliver messages to Chinese leaders with regard to the issue of economic sanctions.

With the decision to suspend high-level official contact between the two countries, current Japanese leaders were banned by the government from visiting China. However, this ban only applied to those who held formal official positions, and not to private citizens. During the immediate post-Tiananmen period, in an urgent need to keep channels open, Tokyo often utilized informal channels (*kuromaku*), notably political actors and organizations in contacting Beijing.

Isami Takeda, a Dokkyo University professor who participated in the first post-Tiananmen informal visit to China and who is author of chapter 11 on the Pacific Islands in this volume, gave this author a detailed account of activities of the first type of *Kuromaku*.[47] In early August 1989, two months after Tiananmen, a Japanese delegation which included Takeda quietly visited Beijing for one week. At that time, few private Japanese would visit Beijing, while government officials were prohibited from visiting by their government and tourists were advised by the foreign ministry not to visit China for safety reasons. The delegation was organized by the Forum for a Liberal Society (FLS), and therefore was considered a private visit.

The FLS is a Tokyo-based, foreign policy-oriented *Kenkyujo* (thinktank), with a membership of more than a dozen LDP *wakate* (young Diet members) from virtually every LDP faction. The Forum's chairman is Takujiro Hamada, a former parliamentary vice minister of foreign affairs, who specializes in foreign policy issues. The Forum conducts research on a wide-range of issues in foreign affairs and maintains close ties to both the Ministry of Foreign Affairs (MFA) and the LDP's Policy Affairs Research Council (PARC). The Forum has a small research staff and runs such programs as the "Asian-Forum Japan," and "Japan-China Policy Dialogue."

The delegation was comprised of six members: two senior FLS policy staff members, two university professors, and two businessmen. Among the two professors, one was a specialist in East Asian affairs, and the other an expert on Japanese foreign aid programs (Takeda). The two businessmen were from All Nippon Airlines (ANA), which had contributed funds to the Forum and had a keen interest in China. One of the businessmen used to be the head of the ANA Beijing office and spoke fluent Chinese. During his years in Beijing, he made many Chinese friends, especially those who were sons or daughters of high-level officials. Before their departure, the two FLS staff members visited MOFA. Although many scheduled trips, official and private alike, were canceled, MOFA gave a clear green-light to this visit. The mission of this delegation was to assess Beijing's situation, to pass "non-official messages," and to conduct "free discussions" with the Chinese.

Upon arrival in Beijing, the first problem encountered by the delegation was the high level of publicity the Chinese press wanted to provide in order to cover the visit. The Japanese refused the publicity in order to keep the visit low profile. Considering the relative low level and non-official nature of the FLS delegation, its activities during the Beijing visit were surprisingly extensive. After a detailed briefing at the Japanese Embassy in Beijing on the current Chinese situation, the delegation was welcomed by Fu Hao, former Chinese Ambassador to Japan, at the Great Hall of the People, a place usually preserved for high-level official activities. Then, the two FLS staff members were received by a vice minister of the Chinese foreign ministry for a lengthy discussion on post-Tiananmen Sino-Japanese relations. In addition, the delegation was initially scheduled to meet with Deng Rong, daughter of China's paramount leader Deng Xiaoping (which was regarded as rather unusual), but the meeting was canceled at the last minute without any explanation given.

The formal host of the delegation was the Chinese Institute of Contemporary International Relations (CICIR), a research institution directly under the supervision of the State Council of China, which was believed to have access to the party-government leadership. Despite the considerable pressure on intellectuals at that time (for example, the office building of the Chinese Academy of Social Science was still under military control), the Chinese participants appeared confident. The Chinese side was headed by the CICIR's director and a deputy director in addition to about a dozen researchers. The Japanese were told that it was rare for the director to attend this kind of discussion with foreign visitors because of his high-level government position and busy schedule. Consequently, his involvement from the beginning to the end showed the importance attached to their visit by the Chinese.

The discussions focused on post-Tiananmen Sino-Japanese relations, particularly the release of the third package of Japanese government loans. The Japanese expressed their "personal opinions" to explain Japan's domestic constraints and international obligations. They mentioned three conditions necessary for moving on the loan issue: (1) lifting martial law in Beijing; (2) release of loans by the World Bank; and (3) signs of improvement in relations between China and the United States. The Japanese explained that changes in American attitudes would be a key issue because of the United States' global influence and that relations with the United States were a foundation of Japanese foreign policy. The Japanese also helped the Chinese understand the difference in perspectives on China policy between the U.S. Congress and the Bush Administration.

The extensive and lengthy discussions lasted for three days, and were frank and cordial. In Beijing, the Japanese were treated as if they were state guests. After returning to Tokyo, the delegation members were invited by the Chinese Embassy for a welcome-back banquet. The two FLS staff members not only gave a detailed report to their own institution, but also paid a visit to the Ministry of Foreign Affairs and reported on the China trip to the vice minister of foreign affairs.

In summing up this trip to Beijing and the *kuromaku* function he and other members played, Professor Isami Takeda stated that "informal contact is always important in Japanese foreign policy," because mutual understanding is more likely developed through "informal channels." He further explained that as informal envoys, the Japanese members could discuss many issues with the Chinese as frank as possible without having official obligation. At the same time, various Japanese government options and opinions were passed on to the Chinese.

These and other informal contacts provide necessary and appropriate social environments for cultivating cordial relationship and facilitating mutual understanding among the parties involved. It is a form of informal consultation, aiming at avoiding open confrontation, and thus making it easier to reach compromise as well as enabling political access. One of the major political considerations of Japan's aid to China was, as former prime minister Takeshita said, to "win the hearts of the Chinese people." This strategy has resulted in greater access for the Japanese to the Chinese political leadership.

China's Position

After the communist victory in 1949, Beijing was suspicious about foreign loans. An exception was $1.5 billion in government loans received from the Soviet Union and East European socialist countries during the period 1953 to 1960. After normalization of relations between China and Japan in 1972, Tokyo on several occasions raised the issue of government loans as a form of economic cooperation, and was rejected unequivocally by Beijing.[48] As late as 1977, the Chinese leadership still insisted that China should not allow any foreign interests or jointly managed companies to develop domestic primary resources, and should not accept any foreign credits.[49]

China's domestic and foreign policy changed drastically after the end of 1978 when Beijing began its open-door and reform policy to promote modernization. While commercial foreign loans were needed to help finance China's economic development, foreign government "soft loans" proved more useful to successive Chinese demands as fiscal crises repeatedly threatened China's key projects. Japan became the first non-communist government to offer government loans to China. Western countries such as Belgium and Denmark and international organizations, including the World Bank, quickly followed suit. China gained valuable knowledge about working with the international financial community through its experience with the Japanese. A senior U.S. official commented that "very clearly, China's most important international relationship is with Japan."[50]

The increasing importance of Japanese government loans prompted Deng Xiaoping in 1988 to say in public that Japanese loans are "extremely significant" when he received Prime Minister Noboru Takeshita, who had just pledged the $5.4 billion loan package to China. Deng claimed, "I want to build a new era like that which we enjoyed during the days of former prime ministers Kakuei Tanaka and Masayoshi Ohira."[51] Deng's remarks clearly reflected the successful momentum of Sino-Japanese relations brought about by Japan's aid diplomacy.

With the benefits that aid has brought, China is facing a potentially serious problem—international debt. This concern was reflected in a remark made in 1987 by Lu Zhongwei, Deputy Director of the China Institute of Contemporary International Relations. He said that "Yen-denominated loans make up 90 percent of Japan's ODA to China. China's future debt problems with Japan will therefore be alarming."[52]

The debt problem has indeed been exacerbated since June 1989. China will have to make an annual debt payment of $6 billion in 1992, much of which will go to Japan. Although Beijing openly stated that the foreign debt of some $40 billion was within China's "repayment limit,"[53] many foreign observers have serious doubts. Tomoo Marukawa, a Japanese economic official, for example, believes that it would be very difficult for a developing nation like China to register a surplus of $6 billion in its current balance of trade.[54]

With its steady although slow economic growth, it is not necessarily likely China will encounter a major economic crisis in the near future. Nevertheless, China has begun to face the problems of capital shortage. The Tiananmen incident and the subsequent political uncertainties have prompted much of the capital which previously flowed through Hong Kong to China to shift its flow either back to

Japan, Taiwan, and Singapore or to be re-routed to Thailand, Indonesia, Malaysia, and the Philippines.[55] According to recent reports, more than $3 billion in foreign loans to China's hotel industry are already in trouble and the Chinese are asking for a rescheduling of payments. Several Japanese commercial banks are involved, such as Sumitomo Bank (a $110 million loan made in 1987) and Bank of Tokyo ($73 million made in 1989).[56]

Alarmed by the worsening economic situation, Chinese leaders pushed hard for Western nations to lift imposed economic sanctions. In this effort, China paid special attention to its top creditor and largest foreign trading partner, Japan. Fully aware of the subtle differences between Japan and the Western nations and the special role Tokyo could play, China watched Japan more closely. Right before the Paris summit of July 1989, Chinese Premier Li Peng praised Japan for its reluctance to further condemn China. After seeing Deng Xiaoping in Beijing in November 1989, Eishiro Saito, Chairman of the Federation of Economic Organizations (*Keidanran*) confirmed that Deng and other Chinese leaders "showed great expectation of Japan."[57] During the same month, in his discussion about Western economic sanctions, Li Peng predicted that the sanctions would be lifted sooner or later. "Some will go first and others later. We'll wait and see which country will make the first move. The country which does so is brave and praiseworthy."[58] The country Li was referring to as making "the first move," clearly was Japan.

But Tokyo did not immediately live up to Beijing's hope of softening its stance over the $5.4 billion loan package, and only made a small grant ($35 million) "for humanitarian reasons" in December. By the end of 1989, Chinese Vice Premier Wu Xueqian showed his disappointment with Japan by criticizing Tokyo as being behind Washington in its China policy, referring to the visit of U.S. National Security Adviser Brent Scowcroft to Beijing.[59]

In a ten-day visit to Japan in January 1990, Zou Jiahua, Chairman of the Chinese State Planning Commission (the highest Chinese official to visit Japan since the Tiananmen incident), conducted extensive diplomacy aimed at improving bilateral relations, and in particular at the government loan package. He held talks with Prime Minister Toshiki Kaifu and Foreign Minister Taro Nakayama, focusing on the $5.4 billion loan issue. However, except for a goodwill gesture that Japan would soon send an aid "study" mission to China, there was no change towards "an immediate extension of pledged loans to China."[60] In a March 1990 statement, Chinese Foreign Minister Qian Qichen emphasized "the historical background, geographical location and cultural heritage" between the two countries and called for "better relations."[61] Yet the annual bilateral subcabinet-level talks held shortly after Qian's statement did not lead to any progress in lifting Japan's economic sanctions.[62]

Nevertheless, Beijing's efforts began to receive positive reaction from Tokyo when both Japan's domestic mood and international sentiment changed gradually in 1990. Prominent political leaders either openly advocated lifting economic sanctions, or visited Beijing themselves to hold discussions with Chinese leaders on problems between the two countries. In mid-April of 1990, LDP Secretary General Ichiro Ozawa asked Foreign Minister Taro Nakayama to prepare for the loan release "even if countries like the United States do not take a similar action."[63] Michio Watanabe, head of one of the LDP's largest factions and former Chairman of the LDP's Policy Affairs Research Council, visited China in early May, 1990 and met with Party Secretary General Jiang Zemin and Premier Li Peng. Watanabe pledged to implement the loans as soon as possible, and told Li, "I can say this clearly, after having conferred with other leaders in Japan." Li thanked Japanese leaders for their efforts to have the loans made available, but also spoke of the harm that could come to Sino-Japanese relations "if the loans are delayed too long." A few days after Watanabe's visit, eighty-eight year old ex-LDP Diet member Yoshimi Furui, who was a well-known China hand in Japan, visited Beijing and met with Li Peng. Li again emphasized that he did not want to see Sino-Japanese relations being damaged [by the loan issue]."[64]

Opposition parties were also active on Japan's aid diplomacy towards China. Whereas the Democratic Socialist Party (DSP) and the JCP remained uncompromised towards Beijing, the JSP and the Clean Government Party (CGP) were ready to push for releasing the loans. Secretary General of the JSP Tsuruo Yamaguchi visited Beijing in mid-May 1990 and met with Jiang Zemin and Politburo Standing Committee member Song Ping. Yamaguchi promised that the "JSP would continue to work hard to resume the third loan package."[65] In May, 1990 Jiang Zemin and Li Peng met in Beijing with the visiting CGP delegation headed by its founder, Honorary President Daisaku Ikeda, with whom he discussed bilateral relations.[66] Equally important was that Japan's business community began to complain that the hold on loans had been "seriously affected" exports to China; and the business community wanted the government loans to be resumed.[67]

Conclusion

With a more than a ten year history, Japan's aid diplomacy towards China has become an indispensable part of Sino-Japanese relations. Aid diplomacy has enabled Japan to utilize its advantageous economic strength. The unexpected political turmoil in China, the Tiananmen incident, and Japan's quick, yet cautious, reaction further demonstrates the importance of Japan's foreign aid for Tokyo's political and strategic goals. Aid diplomacy has served the functions of promoting Japan's international status and smoothing relations with neighboring countries, in this case, China. It also demonstrates that Japan has given priority to maintaining its role as a faithful partner to the West, and to the United States in particular.

Japan's aid diplomacy helped give Japan more leverage in its dealings with China. As a *Beijing Review* article points out, "by using its economic power, Japan seeks to become a political power."[68] One of the reasons behind Beijing's lifting of martial law in January 1990 was concern over negative international reaction and economic sanctions from Western countries. Japan was an important part of this concern. Even though Japan decided in July 1990 to gradually resume its government loan package, the fact that Japan imposed economic sanctions for more than a year demonstrates "Tokyo's increasing efforts to translate economic clout into [political] influence and participation."[69]

On the other hand, Japan's aid diplomacy has its limitations. Even though there have been calls for Japan to follow the example of the Marshall Plan that was carried out in Europe by the United States in the postwar period,[70] the size of Japanese aid to China has never reached a level commensurate with that degree of influence and impact. One reason is that the position of Japan today is quite different than that of United States more than four decades ago. As Bruce Koppel and Michael Plummer point out, "while Japan's influence in Asia through economic cooperation is enormous, levels of interaction in ODA have not advanced to a point where Japan can extract predictable policy outcomes from the commitments."[71]

Despite its relative success, one cannot say that Japan's aid programs are without fault. Many people within and outside of Japan complain that there is a lack of "a grand design for lending."[72] For example, Japan's post-Tiananmen performance demonstrates that Japan's aid decisions are heavily influenced by Western countries, particularly, the United States;[73] and there has been confusion over controversial decisions, such as when and how the economic sanctions towards China should be lifted, and what kind of aid projects can or cannot be advanced.

Economic benefits from aid diplomacy are obvious. Japan has not only ensured itself of long-term raw material supply--energy supplies in particular--but has also broadly and deeply enhanced its position in China's market. From the Chinese perspective, Japan's aid programs provide less expensive capital for China's modernization drive, in particular, its large-scale infrastructure construction projects.

However, loans bring debts which can become a serious problem. As pointed out earlier, China has already encountered difficulties in its foreign debts repayment. These difficulties may be transferred onto Chinese domestic politics. Japan could again be blamed for an "economic invasion" as it was during the Chinese students demonstrations in the mid-1980s. Although economic sanctions have political leverage, they may also produce a backlash. It may stimulate nationalist feelings in China, creating a new-round of anti-Japanese feelings. Indeed, Japan has been in the difficult position of searching for a balanced role in the post-Tiananmen period. On the one hand, Japan has been criticized by the Western countries and China's pro-democracy forces for not being tough enough.[74] On the other hand, Tokyo has been hard-pushed by Beijing to take a lead in improving relations with China.

In sum, the large-scale bilateral economic exchanges and government aid from Japan have helped to strengthen economic interdependence between the two countries. As many observers of international affairs have recognized, Sino-Japanese relations "will assume increasing importance in Asia as both the U.S. presence and Soviet ambitions in the region fade in the post-Cold War era."[75] As long as China pursues its goal of economic modernization and its political future remains uncertain, Japan's aid diplomacy will continue to play a crucial role in Sino-Japanese relations both economically and politically.

Endnotes

1. See Nigel Holloway, "Aid in Search of a Policy," *Far Eastern Economic Review*, November 9, 1989, p. 64.

2. *Far Eastern Economic Review*, August 23, 1990, p. 32.

3. *Japan Times*, July 12, 1990, p. 1.

4. *Far Eastern Economic Review*, July 19, 1990, p. 57-58.

5. For a detailed account see "Sino-Japanese Relations Remain Far from Normal—Ties on Hold," *Far Eastern Economic Review*, May 10, 1990, pp. 16-17.

6. *Japan Times*, May 10, 1990, p. 6.

7. Tasuku Okubo, *China and Japan: Financial Aspects* (Tokyo: Sophia University, 1986), p. 5.

8. *Bangkok Post*, July 21, 1988, p. 28. There are a number of other channels through which China can obtain loans from Japanese sources. The most notable are short-term and higher interest private commercial loans, and Export-Import Bank loans. For example, in May 1979, the Export-Import Bank of Japan agreed to a loan of $2 billion with a fifteen year term at 6.25 percent interest. Three months later, China obtained two commercial loans for a total of $8 billion at a higher rate and with shorter payment periods (six months and four and a half years respectively). Clearly, the ODA loans have much better terms than the commercial and Export-Import Bank loans.

9. Chae-Jin Lee, *China and Japan: New Economic Diplomacy*, (Stanford, California: Hoover Institution Press, 1984), pp. 116-119.

10. *Asahi Shimbun*, December 1, 1979; Chae-Jin Lee, *China and Japan*, p. 121.

11. Greg Story, *Japan's Official Development Assistance to China* (Canberra, Australia: Research School of Pacific Studies, Australian National University, 1987), p. 35.

12. *Senkaku* in Japanese

13. Swadesh De Roy, "Japan Image of China," *Daily Yomiuri*, January 14, 1985.

14. *Japan Times*, October 14, 1985.

15. *Japan Times*, May 7, 1988, p. 7 and August 25, 1988, p. 1.

16. Nigel Holloway, "Aid in Search of a Policy," p. 64.

17. Interview with Masaji Takahashi, Japanese Consul General in Honolulu, Honolulu, July 17, 1990. Takahashi was previously the Deputy Director

General of the Economic Cooperation Bureau and before that a long-time senior official with the Japan International Cooperation Agency.

18. *Asahi Evening News*, January 31, 1985, p. 1.

19. *Asahi Shimbun*, September 3, 4, and 9, 1979; also see Greg Story, *Japan's Official Development Assistance to China*, p. 34, and Chae-Jin Lee, *China and Japan*, pp. 118-119.

20. *New York Times*, June 7, 1989, p. A8.

21. *Japan Times*, June 8, 1989, p. 1; June 25, 1989, p. 1; June 27, 1989, p. 3; and July 1, 1989, p. 3.

22. *Journal of Commerce*, November 30, 1989, p. 5A.

23. *Japan Times*, June 6, 1989, p. 12 and June 7, 1989, p. 10.

24. *Japan Times*, December 23, 1990, p. 9 and January 11, 1990, p. 1.

25. Henry Cutter, "Politicians Prepare to Restore China Aid," *Japan Times* (weekly international edition), May 28-June 3, 1990, p. 1.

26. *Japan Times*, May 3, 1990, p. 7.

27. For the full account, see Mutsuo Fukushima, "Chinese Students Find Tokyo Government Deaf to Their Pleas," *Japan Times*, June 5, 1990, p. 1 and 2.

28. Susumu Awanohara, "No More Favors: U.S. Lawmakers Expected to Maintain Anti-China Stand," *Far Eastern Economic Review*, June 7, 1990, pp. 56-57.

29. Henry Cutter, "Politicians Prepare to Restore China Aid."

30. U.S. Congress, *Legislation on Foreign Relations Through 1985*, vol. 1, p. 171.

31. Robert Orr, *The Emergence of Japan's Foreign Aid Power* (New York: Columbia University Press, 1990), p. 73.

32. Walter Arnold, "Japan and China," in Robert Ozaki and Walter Arnold, ed., *Japan's Foreign Relations: A Global Search for Economic Security* (Boulder, Colorado: Westview, 1985), p. 114.

33. *Journal of Commerce*, August 16, 1988, p. 7A.

34. *Japan Times*, February 2, 1990, p. 10.

35. *Japan Times*, June 6, 1989, p. 12; June 7, 1989, p. 10; 1989; and January 10, 1990, p. 1.

36. *Japan Times*, May 3, 1990, p. 7, and June 4, 1990, p. 20.

37. Steven Weisman, "Foreign Aid Isn't Easy for Japan," *New York Times*, August 20, 1989, p. 3E.

38. *Sing Tao International*, May 11, 1990, p. 15.

39. *China Daily*, December 6, 1989, p. 1. Also see *Japan Times*, November 29, 1989, p. 3.

40. *Japan Times*, July 5, 1989, p. 1 and December 15, 1989, p. 1.

41. *New York Times*, January 15, 1990, p. 5.

42. *Japan Times*, November 9, 1989, p. 12.

43. *Japan Times*, May 11, 1990, p. 1.

44. Masataka Kosaka, *Japan's Choice*. (London and New York: Pinter Publishers, 1989), p 73.

45. Amanda Bennett, "Japan Excels in Relations with China, A Fact that Washington Finds Useful," *Wall Street Journal*, April 13, 1984.

46. Jim Mann, "China and Japan: How They Buried Centuries of Hate," *International Herald Tribune*, May 6, 1985, p. 6.

47. Interview with Isami Takeda, June 6, 1990, Honolulu.

48. Chae-Jin Lee, *China and Japan*, p. 113.

49. A *Renmin Ribao* editorial (January 2, 1977), for example, claimed that "We never permit the use of foreign capital to develop our domestic resources as the Soviet revisionists do, never run undertakings in concert with other

countries and also never accept foreign loans. China has neither domestic nor external debts." The authoritative communist party journal *Hong Qi* (Red Flag) (March 1977) also argued that, "Ours is an independent and sovereign socialist state. We have never allowed, nor will we ever allow, foreign capital to invest in our country. We have never joined capitalist countries in exploring our natural resources; nor will we explore other countries' resources. We never did, nor will we ever, embark on joint ventures with foreign capitalists." Also see Robert Kleinberg, *China's "Opening" to the Outside World* (Boulder, Colorado: Westview, 1990), p. 1.

50. Amanda Bennett, "Japan Excels in Relations with China."

51. *Japan Times*, August 27, 1988, p. 1.

52. *Asahi Evening News*, July 7, 1987, p. 3.

53. "China Expands Economic and Trade Co-operation with Other Countries," *Beijing Review*, Vol. 33, No. 17 (April 23-29, 1990), pp. 30-31.

54. *Japan Times*, November 9, 1989, p. 12. He further predicted that the Chinese economy would continue to have low growth; "China may manage to get by on a short-term basis, but it will be in serious trouble in the long run."

55. Editorial, "Cold Wind from the North," *The Japan Economic Journal*, September 16, 1989, p. 10. Japan is also prepared to turn its ODA programs to Eastern Europe to support democratic changes there. *Japan Times*, December 23, 1989, p. 3.

56. "Ill-starred Ventures: China's Hotel Industry Faces a Foreign Debt Crisis," *Far Eastern Economic Review*, April 26, 1990, p. 54.

57. *Japan Times*, July 4, 1989, p. 1, and November 14, 1989 p. 1.

58. "Li Peng on Domestic and World Issues," *Beijing Review*, Vol. 32, No. 49 (December 4-10, 1989), pp. 12-14.

59. *Japan Times*, December 30, 1989, p. 1.

60. *Japan Times*, January 24, 1990, p. 1.

61. "Foreign Minister Qian Meets the Press," *Beijing Review*, Vol. 33, No. 15 (April 9-15, 1990), p. 17.

62. *Korea Herald*, March 28, 1990, p. 1.

63. *Japan Times*,April 17, 1990, p. 1.

64. *Renmin Ribao*,May 4 (p. 1), 5 (p. 1), and 14 (p. 1), 1990.

65. *Renmin Ribao*,May 19, 1990, p. 1 and May 21, 1990, p. 1.

66. *China Daily*, June 1, 1990, p. 1.

67. *Japan Times*,May 3, 1990, p. 7.

68. Chu Qimen, "Tokyo Seeks More Political Clout," *Beijing Review*,June 18-24, 1990, p. 17.

69. "Japan's New Gospel: Kaifu Signals Tokyo's Desire for Influence in Asia," *Far Eastern Economic Review*, May 17, 1990, p. 13.

70. The original idea of Japan's "Marshall Plan" was floated by former foreign minister Saburo Okita. See Hobart Rowen, "Japan Puts Forward its 'Marshall Plan'," *Japan Times*, October 21, 1986, p. 8. Also see James Robinson, "For a Japanese Equivalent of the Marshall Plan," *New York Times*, May 3, 1986, p. 19.

71. Bruce Koppel and Michael Plummer, "Japan's Ascendancy as a Foreign-Aid Power: Asian Perspective," *Asian Survey*, Vol. 29, No. 11 (November 1989), p. 1055.

72. James Sterngold, "Japan's Foreign Aid Problem," *New York Times*, November 5, 1989.

73. *Japan Times*,December 21, 1989, p. 1.

74. "Friendly Advice on Human Rights," *Japan Times*, July 19, 1989. See also Gerald Segal, "Why the Japanese Are Keeping Quiet," *International Herald Tribune*, July 3, 1989, p. 6.

75. *Far Eastern Economic Review*,August 23, 1990, p. 32.

9

JAPAN'S FOREIGN AID TO BANGLADESH: CHALLENGING THE DEPENDENCY SYNDROME?

Toru Yanagihara

Overview

Bangladesh, with its population of more than 100 million people, is the largest among the least developed countries (LLDCs). This fact, as well as its location in Asia, makes the country of special concern for Japan's ODA. Bangladesh is heavily dependent on external assistance to cover its developmental requirements. Net ODA receipts to Bangladesh amount to roughly one-tenth of GDP, two-thirds of domestic investment, half of total central government expenditures, and no less than nine-tenths of its development outlays.[1]

Japan's economic assistance to Bangladesh started immediately after the latter's independence from Pakistan in 1971. Initially, the focus of aid from Japan as from other donors was on emergency grant aid of food and clothing. Food aid has continued to be an important element of Japan's grant aid to Bangladesh to the present although increased weight has subsequently come to be placed on assistance for food production and agricultural development in general. Loan aid was started in 1973. Initially, the bulk of repayable assistance took the form of commodity loans to respond to acute shortages of basic consumer goods and medical supplies. However, since 1980, commodity loans have increasingly been directed toward the support of productive activities. For example, loans for industrial and infrastructure projects have taken on increased importance.

Since the mid-1980s, Japan's annual ODA to Bangladesh has averaged around 375 million dollars on an annual gross disbursement basis. This has made Japan the leading bilateral donor to Bangladesh. Bangladesh's share of Japan's total ODA each year has placed Bangladesh among the top five recipients, again, since the mid-1980s.[2] A unique and continuing feature of Japan's aid to Bangladesh, compared to the aid coming from other bilateral donors, is the high percentage share (roughly two-thirds) that loans occupy in the total. In fact, Japan is now the only bilateral donor providing loan aid to Bangladesh. However, in practice, the distinction between Japan's grant aid and loan aid to Bangladesh has become meaningless because Japan's practice now is that loans are *ex post* turned into grants through debt relief operations (i.e., provisions of grants to cover debt service payments).[3]

ODA Policy

Japanese ODA to Bangladesh may be viewed in two different contexts, one geographical and the other functional. Initially, Bangladesh's location in South Asia was certainly a decisive factor in Japan's active participation in economic assistance. This geographical emphasis has remained an important consideration. Recently the whole South Asian region has taken on increased importance as a new frontier for Japanese ODA, as the economies of East and Southeast Asia make steady progress on the whole, with some of them ready to graduate from ODA, and as the waves of Asian Pacific dynamism begin to reach the shores of South Asian countries.

No less significant, at least in the recent past, has been Bangladesh's status as one of the least developed countries (LLDC). The fact that it is by far the most populous of all the LLDCs accords Bangladesh a special weight among them. With the primary focus of its ODA squarely placed on economic infrastructure, Japan has been accused of lack of concern with and commitment to poverty alleviation in the developing world. Because Japan has been more familiar and comfortable dealing with Asian nations, compared for example to those in Sub-Saharan Africa, Japan has attached increased significance to Bangladesh as a way of sharing its burden in international efforts toward poverty alleviation.

There hardly exists a significant domestic constituency within Japan in favor of humanitarian aid in general, or to Bangladesh specifically. While officially, humanitarianism is one of the ulterior motivations behind Japanese aid practice, the Japanese aid community has never developed a strong sense of urgency or commitment in dealing with the poverty issue. Beyond these geographical and functional considerations, Bangladesh does not seem to have strategic importance for Japan either from the perspective of military or economic security.

One apparent important purpose of aid from the diplomatic viewpoint is the cultivation of goodwill toward Japan within the international community. In view of this goal, Japan seems to have adopted a policy of being the number one donor for an increasing number of developing countries, including Bangladesh. It is not clear, however, to what extent this motive could be translated into any particular set of diplomatic objectives. On the contrary, the goal seems to be to maintain friendly relationships with and a sense of "indebtedness" on the part of recipients. Bangladesh has been viewed as an important and moderate political leader among the third-world countries and therefore has been considered as a key target for Japanese assistance from this perspective as well.

Based on the preceding discussion, it seems appropriate to characterize Japanese aid to Bangladesh as motivated by its view of Asia as Japan's "zone of responsibility," by its sense of international responsibility for poverty alleviation, and by its pursuit of goodwill among developing countries. All these characteristics are fuzzy, but, as such, they seem to shape the frame of mind of Japanese officials involved in the design of economic assistance to Bangladesh.

Grant Aid

As the largest LLDC, and also because of its location in Asia, Bangladesh has ranked first as the recipient of Japan's grant aid since 1985, accounting for roughly 10 percent of the total of Japan's grant aid. As the growth in the total amount of grant aid is limited, the increase of this category of aid to Bangladesh could only increase at a moderate rate (Table 9.1).

In reviewing Japan's grant aid to Bangladesh the following two characteristics are worth mentioning. First, a number of large infrastructure construction projects, which would typically be provided for by loans, have been financed by grants. These include a bridge, irrigation facilities, and water supply and sewage networks. Secondly, debt relief has come to occupy an increasingly higher percentages of

TABLE 9.1 Trends of Japanese ODA to Bangladesh (gross disbursement in million yen)

FY	*Total Grants*	*Debt Relief*	*Total Loans*[a]	*Commodity Loans*
1971	462	(-)	-	(-)
1972	4,309	(-)	-	(-)
1973	892	(-)	9,000	(9,000)
1974	4,802	(-)	36,013	(36,013)
1975	3,980	(-)	-	(-)
1976	1,230	(-)	-	(-)
1977	3,908	(-)	35,400	(29,000)
1978	6,838	(1,026)	28,040	(15,500)
1979	10,197	(1,292)	16,500	(16,500)
1980	10,172	(1,592)	13,500	(-)
1981	10,877	(847)	34,500	(24,500)
1982	11,568	(1,748)	27,500	(18,000)
1983	11,427	(1,758)	27,500	(16,800)
1984	13,793	(2,372)	6,065	(-)
1985	14,788	(2,810)	54,500	(32,460)
1986	13,065	(3,385)	3,551	(-)
1988	13,642	(5,232)	47,513	(20,800)
1989	15,859	(9,319)	27,500	(9,000)

NOTES:
a. Agregated on the basis of the date of the Exchange of Notes (E/N).
b. Includes debt rescheduling of 24,513 million yen.

Source: Ministry of Foreign Affairs.

grant aid. Debt relief operations were initiated in response to the UNCTAD resolution of 1978 with regard to the debt of LLDCs resulting from bilateral ODA loans. The 1988 Toronto Summit agreement extended the coverage of debt relief to those ODA loan debts incurred since 1978. In the recent past, the amount and the share in total grants of debt relief have increased rather drastically. In fact, grant aid available for other purposes (i.e., socioeconomic assistance) has been on the decline in absolute terms since 1985.

Loans

Japan's ODA loans to Bangladesh are broadly divided into project loans and commodity loans. In principle, project-related procurements are partially untied (goods purchased with ODA funds came from Japan or other developing countries), and commodity loans may be utilized on the basis of general untying. Currently, loans are repayable for 30 years, with a 10-year grace period, and an interest rate of 1 percent per annum. Project loans are heavily concentrated in the energy sector (especially the power subsector) and in the manufacturing sector (especially the fertilizer subsector). In manufacturing, a large percentage of loans are used for the rehabilitation of existing facilities.

With regard to loans, and unlike grants, an overall ceiling is less binding, but there is a constraint of a different kind on Japan's ability to extend ODA loans to Bangladesh. Bangladesh has continuously received debt relief by having loans *de facto* transformed into grant aid *ex post*. This indicates that the country does not have sufficient debt-servicing capacity and that it therefore should not be eligible for loans.

Japan's ODA to Bangladesh in the form of project loans has had tangible impacts in the subsectors where it has been concentrated. Most conspicuous among these is the fertilizer subsector where three projects financed by Japanese loans resulted in a productive capacity of 159 million tons per year (or 69 percent of the total capacity in the country) by 1991. Similarly, power plants financed by Japan will account for 16 percent of the total power-generation capacity by 1992.

Non-Project Loans

Commodity loans have persistently accounted for a large percentage of Japan's ODA loans to Bangladesh. They have dual roles as support for (1) balance of payments and (2) fiscal revenue. As balance of payments support, commodity loans are utilized for importing raw materials and intermediate goods in order to sustain the level of productive activities. As fiscal support, the counterpart funds generated from the sales of foreign exchange are stipulated to contribute to local cost financing of development projects. Through these two channels, commodity loans are expected to assist the recipient country both in the maintenance of current economic activities and in the strengthening of future productive capacities.

In Japan, there are increasing criticisms (especially from the Ministry of Finance) on the perpetuation of commodity loans. There are a number of reasons for this. First, loans are supposed to be repayable. In other words, economic assistance has to be self-liquidating. It is not clear, however, whether this is a realistic prospect for Bangladesh, at least over a foreseeable future. Secondly, as a matter of fact, loans have been converted *ex post* into grants through debt relief. This amounts to a *de facto* recognition that Bangladesh is not creditworthy for loans. Thirdly, there is increased awareness of the need to pay more attention to policy issues both at macroeconomic and microeconomic levels. Concerns are expressed that continued provision of commodity loans without policy conditionality could help perpetuate policies and practices which are detrimental to long-term development.

The Japanese government is extremely cautious about the use of policy conditionality on a bilateral basis, especially in Asia. Japan is aware of the possible sociopolitical risks for recipient countries that can be associated with policy reforms, risks that include unemployment, social unrest, and political instability. There are recognized risks for Japan as well, including fanning nationalist and anti-Japanese feelings to degrees that can harm Japan's international relationships. Japan is also very sensitive to charges of interference in the domestic affairs of recipient countries and is aware that its ODA system does not have the adequate intellectual or administrative infrastructure needed to design, negotiate, and monitor policy conditionality.

On the other hand, Japan is aware that without policy reforms, LLDCs such as Bangladesh can face a future of perpetual aid dependence. By the mid-1980s, in fact, concerns about that prospect generated a palpable "aid fatigue" among several of the principal donors to Bangladesh. While this was not translated into a reduction of aid flows, it did eventually lead to stronger consultation among donors to Bangladesh and increased donor resolve to encourage the government of Bangladesh to undertake several critical policy reforms. Key among these was privatization of fertilizer production and marketing.

Another way Japan has utilized to resolve the dilemmas associated with bilateral donor association with policy reform conditionalities has been co-financing projects with multilateral agencies. The first case of co-financing in Bangladesh involves an energy sector adjustment credit by the World Bank. The decision was announced at the time of Prime Minister Kaifu's visit to Dhaka in May 1990. By going into co-financing arrangements, Japan could, in effect, utilize the technical expertise and claimed political neutrality of multilaterals in the design and execution of policy conditionality.

However, the practice of co-financing with a multilateral, pragmatic and convenient as it may be, certainly invites conclusions by the recipient country that Japan endorses the policy conditionality designed and practiced by the multilateral. In fact, it can be argued that Japan's endorsement is explicit when disbursements of Japan's loans are conditional upon the fulfillment of policy conditionalities—whoever originated those conditionalities.

While perhaps resolving one dilemma (by removing Japan from a direct role in applying policy conditionalities), the practice of co-financing poses a new dilemma to Japanese officials. A problem arises to the extent that Japan does not agree with or is uncertain about policy prescriptions of multilateral institutions. This question has been present as Bangladesh has contracted formal agreements with the IMF and the World Bank with regard to structural adjustment lending. These agreements set constraints on the government's policy options and, indirectly, on the assistance options of other donors. By going into co-financing arrangements, Japan is seen by both the multilateral agencies and the government of Bangladesh to have made an explicit endorsement of the policy conditionalities attached to the multilateral loan in question. When Japan has raised questions expressing concerns about the prescriptions, and especially when Japan is seen as programming its bilateral assistance to Bangladesh in ways that could be interpreted as falling outside the conditionality agreements, the multilateral agencies concerned, as well as other donors privately,[4] complain that Japan is working against the donor community's common effort to encourage needed policy reforms.

It is this dilemma, in fact, one that developed principally in Japan's ODA to Bangladesh, that has led to the chorus of allegations from other donors that Japan's ODA lacks a philosophy, or more precisely, the view that Japan's ODA is principally mercantile. In the late 1980s, this led to serious concerns that Japan did not share the commitment to market-oriented economic reform that was guiding the World Bank, the IMF, and the United States Agency for International Development.

The "Framework" Problem

The Bangladesh case illustrates a broader problem for Japan's ODA policy. Issues of macroeconomic policy management by recipient countries and policy conditionalities by donors are taking on increased importance for Japan's ODA policy system. There are two reasons for the added importance attached to these issues. First, there are increased concerns with the perpetuation of commodity loans in large amounts and also with the continuation of debt relief in large sums. Secondly, the IMF and the World Bank have started lending operations conditioned upon a macroeconomic policy framework agreed upon with the Bangladesh government. These two factors and the weight of Japan's presence as the top donor to Bangladesh have prompted the Japanese government to pay more attention to macroeconomic aspects of economic development and assistance strategy. This question, however, has proved to be a rather difficult one to handle and Japan has failed to clearly determine where it stands (or wants to stand) regarding this issue.

A fundamental reason for such difficulty is the absence of a "framework" approach in Japanese thinking on development and aid. Instead, the dominant school of thought in Japan espouses an "ingredients" approach. The Japanese tend to conceive development in terms of tangible projects and, at most, in terms of a vision of regional development or industrial structure in the future. By comparison, a "framework" approach is best exemplified by the institutionalized economic philosophies of the IMF and the World Bank. Their philosophies are based on doctrines of mainstream Anglo-American economics. The IMF is mostly responsible for overseeing macroeconomic management while the World Bank is primarily concerned with redressing microeconomic frameworks for the management of developing economies.

Economic Assistance as Support to "Self-Help Effort"

The notion of self-help effort has been central in Japan's philosophy of economic assistance. There are a number of contexts within which references to self-help efforts are often made.

1. ***The request principle.*** ODA projects are supposed to be based on the initiative of recipient countries. Projects initiated by recipients are expected to be considered as the recipients' own projects, thus leading to stronger commitment to self-help efforts for project implementation and maintenance.
2. ***Loans rather than grants.*** Debt-servicing obligations incurred as a result of receiving loans are expected to impose more discipline and encourage SHE for better management of projects or for that matter, the development process in general.
3. ***Local cost financing.*** Japan did not, traditionally, provide support for the local cost portions of project construction or for the recurrent costs for operations and maintenance. This decision has been based on the premise that recipients' commitments to self-help are strengthened by having them bear local costs. In practice, however, this principle has not been strictly applied, insofar as local counterpart funds, generated from the sale of goods imported under commodity loans, have been made available to support the local cost components of development projects.
4. ***Policy conditionality.*** As noted above, Japan has traditionally avoided attaching policy conditionalities to its provision of

> ODA. This practice of no conditionality has been maintained although increased emphasis has come to be placed on policy dialogues with recipient countries.

However, Bangladesh does not appear to be a case where Japanese ODA practices have promoted the sorts of self-help efforts Japan's philosophy anticipates from an aid recipient. Several examples support this point. For instance, Japan's commodity loans are made available to countries where commodity imports are urgent and critical for the stability of the economy, provided the recipient's stabilization program, submitted when a commodity loan is requested, is deemed sound and attainable. In reality, it is questionable whether this proviso has always been meaningfully applied in the process of evaluating requests for commodity loans.

In the case of Bangladesh, commodity loans became a regular feature of Japan's economic assistance and seem to have been viewed by the recipient as they were a kind of entitlement available upon request. Japan as a major aid donor to Bangladesh was caught in a dilemma. On the one hand, the perpetuation of conditions in which commodity loans were continually needed implied lack of realism or commitment to stabilization programs by the government of Bangladesh. On the other hand, a decision by Japan to discontinue commodity loans ran the risk of further aggravating already precarious economic and possibly socio-political situations in Bangladesh. Consequently, Japan continued to provide commodity loans to Bangladesh on a request basis while the request principle virtually became void of whatever salutary effect it was supposed to have on the self-help efforts of the recipient.

Second, it is doubtful that the provisions of loans, as against grants, exerted any positive effects on self-help efforts in the case of Bangladesh. As noted earlier, Japan's ODA loans have been converted *ex post* into grants through debt relief. This amounts to a *de facto* recognition that Bangladesh is not creditworthy for loans.

Third, local cost financing has always been a problem for Bangladesh, thus adversely affecting project implementation, disbursements of committed project aid from all donors, and maintenance of completed projects. The situation turned even worse as government increased budgetary allocations for current expenditures at the expense of public investment expenditures during the 1980s. Increases in project and commodity aid over the 1984-89 period were accompanied by drastically reduced commitment by the government to use its own resources for local cost-financing projects.

Fourth, Japan's recognition of limited financial and administrative capacities on the party of the Bangladesh government to effectively maintain projects has often been overwhelmed by the pressure within Japan's ODA system (as within the systems of most other donors) to disburse funds. An evaluation, for example, of the $150 million Narayangang water treatment project, laid out in substantial detail not simply that the Bangladesh government could not afford to maintain and operate the project, but that project design choices were explicitly made which increased the cost of the project and decreased the feasibility of local financial and technical maintenance.[5]

Fifth, in 1990, the Japanese government decided to engage in co-financing with the World Bank in support of the Bank's Energy Sector Adjustment Credit for Bangladesh. This signified a formal endorsement of the policy conditionality attached to that credit, thus breaking the traditional stance of not applying conditionality in the provision of ODA.

What all these examples imply is that the Japanese emphasis, at least in principle, on using ODA to strengthen self-help efforts by recipient countries, a principle reflected in many of the procedures and processes associated with the management of Japan's aid, has often not been effective—on the recipient side in terms of ODA utilization or on the Japanese side in terms of ODA programming.

Aid Coordination

As noted in other chapters in this book (e.g. on Indonesia and the Philippines), Japan's aid policy is often influenced by the presence of consultative arrangements among the donors to a specific country. These arrangements can vary from little more than aid pledging sessions that have no substantial impacts on aid coordination among donors to more synchronized efforts at aid programming. The donor consortium for Bangladesh offers a possibly unique case of institutionalized dialogue and coordination among aid donors. The scope of the consultations may be divided into two broad areas: (1) issues related to policy and institutional reforms and (2) cooperation in the design and execution of large-scale projects.

Opposing Views on Policy and Institutional Reforms

The aid community in Dhaka has developed and maintained active and meaningful dialogues among its members thanks to effective coordination by the local representatives of the World Bank and UNDP. Initially, there were two opposing positions on the questions of agricultural subsidies and privatization of the distribution of agricultural inputs. Both of these questions have philosophical aspects regarding principles of economic management and also involve fundamental issues about the purposes of economic assistance.

The orthodoxy, represented by the IMF, the World Bank, and USAID, espoused greater roles for market mechanisms and the private sector and prescribed elimination of subsidies to inputs, liberalization of product markets, and abolition of the state-run distribution system. The opposing camp, known as the Like-Minded Group (LMG), comprised donors more (or even exclusively) concerned with the protection and promotion of the poor and underprivileged. The LMG was spearheaded by the Scandinavian countries. The LMG opposed the policy prescriptions of the orthodoxy, based on their concerns over the adverse impacts of proposed policy changes on the poor and the weak in the Bangladesh population. Their views also reflected skepticism on the applicability of a market-oriented, private sector-led development model to the realities of a poor, agrarian country like Bangladesh.

Japan found itself somewhere in the middle on this controversy. Japan took a compromising stance of endorsing the orthodoxy in principle but, at the same time, calling attention to actual and possible side-effects of the policy changes. In fact, Japan's stance seems to have moved closer to that of the LMG as the use of agricultural inputs went down after reductions of subsidies and poor and remotely located producers were left to inferior privately operated agricultural extension and distribution systems. In retrospect, it seems fair to say that Japan shared with the LMG the view that agricultural producers should be encouraged to improve their practices through guaranteed access to low-cost inputs and services.

In Japan's case, however, it is difficult to ascertain to what extent there existed, or for that matter exists, explicit official views or positions on those controversial issues. Most of what exist are in the nature of sentiments, which are hardly ever articulated or spelled out but only revealed in response to specific questions at hand. To the extent those sentiments are widely shared among Japanese aid-related officials, however, Japan's responses could be expected to follow a certain systematic pattern. I am inclined to believe that what has been revealed in the context of the controversy on agricultural policy in Bangladesh is not far from the center of collective Japanese sentiments.

Large Projects

There are two extremely large projects to be realized through joint efforts of the donor community. One of them, the first bridge over the Jamuna River, is more concrete in the sense that it is clearly conceptualized and that alternative specifications are articulated. The proposed bridge will provide road, power (and possibly rail) links between the northwest and eastern regions, thus potentially affecting the economic geography and future visions of economic development of Bangladesh. There is now a broad consensus on the feasibility of the project although there are still divergent views on the desirability of a railroad on the bridge. Prime Minister Kaifu expressed Japan's support for the project in principle at the time of his visit to Dhaka in May 1990.

The other mega-project, flood preparedness and control, is not yet well-defined. There are debates on the philosophy and basic premises of the project and alternative approaches are being explored. In fact, it may more appropriately be called a meta-project in that it will be crystallized into a host of specific projects (e.g., physical infrastructure, early warning and quick response systems, etc.). Japan is proposing a practical, step-by-step approach and seems to be critical of the construction of gigantic infrastructure for flood control. Whatever an eventual international consensus might be, Japan will be expected to provide major financial support.

Bilateral Collaboration

Another context in which Bangladesh offers rare examples of inter-country aid coordination is that of bilateral collaboration between the United States Agency for International Development (USAID) and Japan (JICA). One specific instance of project-level collaboration has taken place in technical assistance for advanced agricultural research and training. Kiyushu University and Oregon State University worked together to provide technical support in a joint Japan-U.S. project. On a larger scale, plans for U.S.-Japan collaboration in rural electrification are under study. Furthermore, there have been dialogues on medium-term economic assistance strategies. The timing of the preparation of the Bangladesh Country Development Strategy Statement (CDSS) by USAID and a Bangladesh country study report by JICA coincided and so in 1989, there was a useful and detailed exchange of perspectives on the problems in Bangladesh and the roles of ODA in addressing those problems. The two documents that were being produced and the processes they reflected were not directly comparable.

The CDSS can be seen as a regular programming tool. It identifies major problems, establishes major strategies for addressing these problems, and in effect, requires aid projects to be justified in terms of the problems and strategies outlined in the CDSS. The time frame is usually five years. USAID uses the CDSS to explain to Congress (and to recipient countries) what it is doing in a country and why. A JICA country study is done on an as-needed basis. It can be a review of a country's problems. It can be an estimate of a country's aid requirements. It can also be an indication of the opportunities a country presents for utilizing Japanese technical assistance services. The study is not necessarily binding on JICA or on any of the other prime actors in the Japanese ODA policy system. Consequently, while the dialogues did not result in specific joint projects, it did represent an important sharing of views.

New Developments and Remaining Tasks

Japan's ODA to Bangladesh has exhibited rather clear patterns. On the one hand, commodity loans and debt relief have persistently occupied large shares in the total, reflecting urgent (and lasting) needs for balance of payments and fiscal support. On the other hand, there remains clear emphasis on the building up of productive capacity and infrastructure, especially for food production and power generation.

More recently, attention is being given to improving socioeconomic conditions at the grassroots level. In addition to JICA-backed volunteers, new developments have taken place in the relationship between ODA and non-government organizations (NGOs). During 1989, a new scheme called small-scale grants was initiated in order to provide financial assistance to local NGOs. At the same time, subsidies to Japanese NGOs have been increased. This is an important step for Japanese ODA, since collaboration between Japanese ODA and Japanese NGOs has been very limited. In addition, there are cases of collaboration through division of effort. For example, a rural training center for women was constructed with an ODA grant, but is managed by a Japanese NGO.

During the past few years, the Japanese government, especially the Ministry of Foreign Affairs (MOFA), has been making more systematic efforts to formulate a more systematic economic assistance strategy for Bangladesh. In 1988 a comprehensive country study was commissioned to the International Development Center of Japan (IDCJ). In 1989, a country panel was formed at JICA, for which the IDCJ team served as technical support group, to determine priorities for Japan's economic assistance to Bangladesh. In April 1990, a high-level government mission was sent to Dhaka to participate in an exchange of views between the two governments on general themes of socioeconomic development and the role of economic assistance. This series of studies and policy dialogues paved the way for the visit by Prime Minister Kaifu to Bangladesh in May 1990, the first visit by a Japanese Prime Minister to Bangladesh. Although the Prime Minister's visit itself did not bring immediate tangible benefits, as Japan did not offer any extra assistance as a "special gift" in addition to the regular annual provision, it is nonetheless of symbolic significance as reconfirmation of Japan's commitment to Bangladesh.

Commodity loans in their traditional form are being phased out as a regular feature of Japanese ODA practice. They will be utilized only under exceptional circumstances such as for emergency assistance. Non-project assistance needed to fill balance of payments or fiscal gaps will increasingly be provided through policy-based lending in the form of co-financing with multilateral agencies, the World Bank among others. As noted. in Japan there are widely shared sentiments of discontent with standard policy prescriptions by the World Bank. Nevertheless, for the foreseeable future, Japan, lacking its own viable "framework" approach, will have virtually no choice but to endorse the Bank's prescriptions despite disagreements on some specific points.[6]

This brings us back to a fundamental question regarding economic assistance to Bangladesh: what can ODA do to strengthen long-term developmental prospects more than strengthening the prospects for long-term aid dependence? How long will it take for structural macroeconomic imbalances to be overcome? What combination of "policy framework" and "project ingredients" strategies would be needed for the economy to be transformed into one characterized by self-sustained growth? As the leading donor to Bangladesh, Japan will be expected to play a more important role in defining answers to these questions.

Endnotes

1. Bangladesh's aid dependance has been a source of concern both to donors and to different segments of Bangladesh society. For example, see: Rehman Sobhan, *The Crisis of External Dependance: The Political Economy of Foreign Aid to Bangladesh* (Dhaka: University Press Limited, 1982).

2. Ministry of Foreign Affairs, *Wagakuni no Seifu Kaihatsu Enjo* (Japan's Official Development Assistance), (Tokyo: Kokusai Kyoryoku Suishin Kyokai, 1991).

3. The basic reason for this arrangement is that the agency responsible for commodity aid, OECF, does not have the option of providing grants. OECF funding comes from borrowings from Japan's Postal Savings Bank.

4. For example, at aid policy dialogues between the United States and Japan, the U.S. has raised concerns about whether Japan's aid programming in Bangladesh was undermining the efforts of other donors to support economic policy reform initiatives by the Bangladesh government. See: Bruce Koppel and Seiji Naya, *Honolulu I: ODA Management and Asia's Economic Development* (Honolulu: East-West Center, 1988); Bruce Koppel, *Honolulu II: ODA Management and Asia's Economic Development* (Honolulu: East-West Center, 1989).

5. Bruce Koppel, *An Evaluation of the Narayangang Water Treatment Project* (Tokyo: Ministry of Foreign Affairs. Economic Cooperation Bureau. 1990).

6. See: Toru Yanagihara, "Policy-Based Lending and Japanese Policy," in Ippei Yamazawa and Akira Hirata, ed., *Development Cooperation Policies of Japan, the United States, and Europe* (Tokyo: Institute of Developing Economies, 1992), pp. 77-108.

10

JAPANESE ODA POLICY TO THE REPUBLIC OF KOREA

Hosup Kim

Introduction

There is no nation in Japan's foreign relations which challenges Tokyo's past, present, and future as much as South Korea. Memories on the Korean peninsula of Japan's long colonial occupation which ended in 1945 are bitter and remain close to the surface. They continue to effect the manner, and occasionally the content, of bilateral relations. The potential now growing for Korean reunification and the eventual emergence of an even stronger competitor economically and militarily, poses serious dilemmas for Japan's future regional conduct.

Seoul was the first recipient of Japanese government-to-government loans in 1965. These came about following highly contentious debates in Tokyo over whether and how to establish relations with South Korea. Left wing opposition parties in Japan advocated establishing relations also with the northern communist regime, but this was not seriously discussed. Aid subsequently played a major role in cementing closer ties between Japan and South Korea while stimulating South Korea's ascension into the ranks of the newly industrializing economies.

This chapter will examine why Japan has continued to give official development assistance (ODA) to the Republic of Korea,[1] despite the fact that Korea's economic standing and growth place it well beyond the normal limits of eligibility for development assistance. The answer lies in the "special relationship" Japan has with Korea, a relationship that offers a mix of historical, cultural, economic, political, and security interests. Japan manages the relationship through a complex and unique (for Japan) foreign policy. This context is important for this analysis because the Japanese government recognizes ODA as a foreign policy tool, and uses this tool to attain certain goals and objectives.[2] This chapter will offer an explanation of Japan's ODA goals in Korea through an assessment of the levels and types of ODA provided. Special emphasis is given to analysis of the roles of political factors, such as the broader bilateral relationship between the two countries, and to the reactions and perspectives of the Japanese government to domestic political instability in the Republic of Korea.

Japan's ODA Policy Goals with the Republic of Korea

Japan's ODA flow to Korea is summarized in Table 10.1.[3] As can be seen there, ODA to Korea played a major role in Japan's overall ODA program in the early 1970s. Since the mid-1970s, the levels—in both absolute and proportional terms—have varied considerably. This variation draws attention to Japan's attempts to use ODA as a foreign policy tool and in that context, to Japan's ODA policy goals with the Republic of Korea.

Generally, the Japanese government aims at five policy objectives through its economic cooperation policy.[4] These are: (1) to further Japanese economic interests by promoting exports, securing supplies of raw materials, and creating a favorable climate for commercial business activities in the recipient countries; (2) to establish and strengthen diplomatic relations between Japan and other Asian countries; (3) to contribute to the socioeconomic and political stability of countries receiving ODA, a characteristic that is seen as intrinsically important to Japan's economic and political security; (4) to demonstrate Japanese good faith to the other aid-giving western nations; and (5) to establish Japan's status and influence in both regional and global international affairs. All five of these policy goals have been significant[5] in Japan's ODA relationships with the Republic of Korea.

These objectives are not far different from those of other aid-giving countries except that traditionally Japan has put the highest priority on its own economic interest.[6] Until the early 1980s, commercial motivations such as the promotion of exports to the markets of less developed countries, investment of Japanese capital in the industries of less developed countries, and gaining access to the raw materials of less developed countries were decisive factors in the formulation of

Japanese ODA policies.[7] The Japanese government admits that Japan's economic interests, such as export promotion and raw material supply, have been very important factors historically influencing its ODA policy.[8]

TABLE 10.1 Japanese ODA to South Korea (US$ millions, gross disbursement)

Year	*Japanese ODA to Korea*	*% of Total Bilateral ODA*
1971	124.2	28.8
1972	112.7	23.6
1973	156.6	20.5
1974	167.8	19.1
1975	87.4	10.3
1976	24.2	3.2
1977	84.3	9.4
1978	66.1	4.3
1979	54.2	2.8
1980	76.3	3.9
1981	295.6	13.1
1982	8.3	1.0
1983	180.4	7.4
1984	208.8	6.9
1985	228.1	6.1
1986	264.9	8.1
1987	216.4	6.0
1988	230.2	5.3
1989	234.1	5.3

Source: MITI, *Keizai Kyoryoku no Genjo to Mondaiten;* OECF, *Kaigai Keizai Kyoryoku Benran.*

Normalizing Diplomatic Relations

The first goal of Japan's ODA to Korea was to open diplomatic relationships with South Korea. Discussions on normalization of the relationships between Japan and Korea actually began in 1951, but over the next ten years, little progress was made. In 1961, the negotiations became more serious, in large part because of U.S. pressure.[9] During the latter phase of the normalization negotiations, ODA was employed to support what had become a strong goal for Japan by the early 1960s, a normalized relationship with South Korea. Seoul strongly demanded reparations for Japan's colonial rule over Korea. South Korea considered this a pre-condition for diplomatic normalization. These reparations, called the property and claims fund, amounted to $500 million, and were the first form of Japanese official economic cooperation with South Korea. These reparations were provided over a period of ten years beginning from 1966.

Financing Japanese Exports

The second goal of Japan's ODA to Korea was to finance the export of Japanese goods and services to South Korea. Since the 1960s, the Republic of Korea has implemented successive five-year plans for economic development, including large investments in heavy industry and social overhead capital. From a Japanese perspective, these plans provided good opportunities for exporting Japanese heavy equipment, such as semi-processed industrial parts and heavy plants. Commercial financing for exporting heavy industrial plants was difficult to find because of the huge expense of the plants, the long period of repayment, and the high business risks. Japanese ODA has provided favorable financial sources for exporting heavy equipment to the Republic of Korea. To promote exports of Japanese equipment, the Japanese government, until 1975, restricted use of its ODA to purchasing only Japanese goods and services. Although, since 1976, this restriction has been lifted, Korea has still used most of the Japanese ODA funds for importing Japanese goods and services. However, the importance of Japanese ODA as a financing source to import Japanese heavy equipment gradually became less significant. Commercial economic transactions between the two countries grew sufficiently large to finance most heavy equipment sales.

Diplomatic Pressure: ODA and the Kim Dae Jung Affair

The third policy goal of the Japanese government was to use its ODA to the Republic of Korea as an instrument of diplomatic pressure. The strongest example was the Kim Dae-Jung abduction incident when the Japanese government reduced ODA amounts to Korea to express unhappiness with South Korea's handling of that case and to pressure Seoul for more acceptable behavior. The incident began with Kim's kidnaping from Japan in 1973, and continued to be an issue between the two governments until 1982 when Kim left for the United States to receive medical treatment.[10]

Kim Dae-Jung was a presidential candidate of the opposition party running against incumbent Park Chung-Hee in the 1971 election. He received 46 per cent of the total popular vote and 58 per cent in Seoul. When the Park government suspended the Constitution in October, 1972, and banned all political activity against President Park, Kim was in Japan. Instead of returning home, he remained in Japan and the United States, engaging in very active anti-Park activities. On August 8, 1973, Kim was kidnaped by five men from a hotel in Tokyo, and released five days later in front of his house in Seoul. Agents from the Korea Central Intelligence Agency were suspected. The Japanese government identified Kim Dong-Woon, First Secretary of the Korean embassy in Japan, as a key figure in the kidnaping from his fingerprints left in the abduction spot. The Japanese government demanded that the Korean government (1) cooperate fully with the Japanese government's investigation of the incident, including a full explanation of the first secretary's involvement in the case; and (2) allow the abducted Kim to return to Japan, with the right to stay.[11] The Japanese government saw this incident as a violation of Japan's sovereign jurisdiction by official Korean authorities. Several Japanese intellectuals and representatives of the mass media proclaimed the incident constituted a violation of Kim Dae-Jung's human rights, and was symbolic of the oppression practiced by the Park government.[12]

A diplomatic settlement of the kidnaping case was reached in early November, 1973. The South Korean premier, Kim Jong-Pil, visited Japan to express Seoul's regrets to the Tanaka government. Prime Minister Kim offered apologies for the incident, and promised "utmost efforts" to prevent its recurrence.[13] However, even after the visit of Premier Kim, the South Korean government did not respond positively to the Japanese government's specific demands.

A second round of the Kim case began with his trial by the Korean government in 1976. The government arrested Kim for anti-government activities. His activities in Tokyo were alleged to be communist inspired. This broke one of Prime Minister Kim's promises to the Japanese government. Kim had been reported as earlier guaranteeing that the Korean government would not convict Kim Dae-Jung for his activities in Japan. The Japanese government was also upset by the unsatisfactory investigation of Kim Dong-Won, the Korean embassy official.

Facing the apparent reluctance of the South Korean government to comply with the Japanese government's demands, Japan employed economic pressure, using ODA as a main element. Opposition party politicians first demanded that Japanese ODA to Korea be stopped.[14] Some cabinet members warned that the future of Japanese economic cooperation with South Korea would be influenced by the incident if a Korean government agency was found to have been involved in the kidnaping.[15] Officials of the Ministries of Foreign Affairs, Finance, and International Trade and Industry, and the Economic Planning Agency, urged changes in economic policy to Korea. One official was reported to say that ODA would henceforth be offered mainly for Korea's agricultural development, and that commercial loans would replace governmental economic cooperation for heavy and chemical industry development programs in the Republic of Korea. He disclosed that no working-level negotiations between the two governments for new ODA would be held until the Kim affair was resolved, and that required authorization processes would be suspended on the remaining $155 million of Japanese aid pledged at the ministerial conference of 1972. He added that the government would also reassess its aid plan for South Korea's `New Town Movement (*Saemaul Undong*)' projects.[16]

Japan again expressed its intention to use ODA to influence the Korean government when Kim Dae-Jung was sentenced to death in 1980 by the military government under Chun Doo-Hwan. The Japanese government clearly stated that the future of its ODA loans to Korea were related to the Kim case. The Minister of Foreign Affairs, Masayoshi Itoh, made it clear in the House of Representatives that there would be a change in the Japanese government position on economic cooperation to the Republic of Korea if Kim Dae-Jung were executed.[17]

The Japanese government also used its loans as a means of compensation for Korean compliance with its demands. After Seoul commuted Kim's capital sentence to life imprisonment on January 23, 1981, Japan's Chief Cabinet Secretary, Kiichi Miyazawa, said that the relationship between the two countries would be normalized, including the restoration of yen credits.[18] One official of the Ministry of Foreign Affairs was reported to say that the ministry was now ready to carry out an exchange of notes on the yen credit of 1981, a process which had been suspended because of Kim's trial and capital sentence.[19]

Diplomatic pressure might not have been originally intended as a policy goal for economic aid, but the relationship of giving and receiving between the two countries resulted in a situation in which the Japanese came to employ their ODA to influence Korean policy. Certainly on the Japanese side, a variety of interests including bureaucrats and politicians of both the LDP and opposition parties, seemed to be well aware that ODA could be used to put pressure on the Korean government regarding the Kim Dae-Jung case.

Regime Support

The fourth policy goal of the Japanese government has been to show Japanese governmental commitment to the incumbent regime of the Republic of Korea. Although since the middle of the 1970s, the economic significance of Japanese ODA for Korea's economic development has become less important, the political aspects of ODA are still significant. ODA signifies encouragement to Japanese businessmen who are doing business in Korea or want to do business.

In the early 1960s, the Japanese government's positive response to initiatives by the Park Chung-Hee government for diplomatic normalization gave the impression of a high possibility of future Japanese governmental cooperation. The Japanese government also showed commitment to the stability of the Park government, which was experiencing legitimacy problems right after the military coup. In the wake of the Kim Dae-Jung incident, when the Japanese government announced suspension of its ODA loans to the Republic of Korea, Japanese businessmen interpreted this as a negative sign. Commercial business activities between the two countries decreased. For example, Japanese direct investment in Korea in 1975 sharply decreased to one-fourth the level of 1973. This shrinkage of business activity was partly due to the reduction of the actual amount of the yen credit. However the main reason was that Japanese businessmen carried out their business activities defensively when they recognized their government's intention not to support the Korean government.

Signs of Japan's official commitment were again expressed during the negotiations for the $6 billion package of economic cooperation in 1981. When South Korea's political situation became unstable in 1980 after the sudden death of President Park Chung-Hee, Japanese businessmen were extremely cautious about doing business in South Korea. Some businessmen considered withdrawal of investments. Most of them applied more strict standards to the credit standing of their Korean partners, maintained tighter credit, and postponed business dealings.[20] The amount of trade between the two countries in 1980 decreased for the first time since the 1950s, and Japanese direct investment decreased to one-third the level of a year before. However, the Japanese government's positive response to Korea's request for a $6 billion package of economic cooperation turned this tendency around. The Korean request was thought at first to be an unreasonably large amount with an unprecedented rationale, but the Japanese government responded positively and began to negotiate officially. This action of the Japanese government served as a positive sign of its commitment to the stability of the Chun government.[21]

Regional Security

The fifth policy goal is to show Japan's commitment to the security of the Korean peninsula, an interest closely related to Japan's own security interests. Traditionally, Japan has seen its own security as strongly linked to Korea. This is understandable if one considers the geographical proximity of the two countries, and the geopolitical location of the Korean peninsula in relation to China, the Soviet Union, and Japan. Japan's specific security interests in Korea during the last few decades contributed to stability on the Korean peninsula.[22]

The Japanese government has specified economic cooperation as an important element in its "comprehensive security policy." The comprehensive security policy involves responding to threats to Japanese security not only with military means, but with economic, diplomatic, and cultural means as well.[23] The Japanese government groups efforts to achieve security into two stages: "pre-adjustment" efforts to prevent, in advance, external threats and adverse effects on its security from occurring; and "post-adjustment" efforts to alleviate and absorb external threats and adverse effects which have already happened, and in order to quickly return to normal conditions.[24] The Japanese government believes ODA plays a key role in the "pre-adjustment" stage, because economic cooperation can establish direct interdependent relationships between Japan and numerous countries, and in the "post-adjustment" stage where ODA can prevent harmful effects on Japan's economic security even after a regional dispute has occurred. As a policy measure, economic cooperation includes private as well as governmental level economic activities, but ODA is the most direct policy measure the Japanese government has available. This policy goal is long-term rather and is usually not expected to bring about immediate effects.

Since the initiation of diplomatic relationships between the two countries, it has been Japanese policy to stabilize the Korean peninsula by helping to industrialize the Republic of Korea. One assumption of this policy is that unless Korea is economically prosperous and stable, it will not be able to defend itself against communist subversion and invasion from North Korea. A second assumption is that if South Korea is under communist control, Japan's security will be seriously threatened. Japanese ODA has been employed therefore to demonstrate Japan's commitment to a prosperous and non-communist South Korea.

The policy of stabilizing South Korea has induced the Japanese government to support the incumbent South Korean government, provided it is friendly to Japan. For this purpose, the Japanese government sometimes uses ODA to attempt to achieve immediate effects on domestic Korean politics. For example, when South Korea experienced domestic instability after President Park's sudden death in 1978, the Japanese government began again to export rice on a deferred payment basis (using ODA), a practice it had stopped in 1973. This rice seems to have been exported for the immediate effect of preventing further deterioration in the domestic Korean situation. Rice is a staple food for Koreans, and is one of most important elements for economic stabilization.

Japanese policy on South Korea is aligned with United States policy. From the United States' point of view, there are two policy goals in East Asia: to strengthen the ties of the free world in East Asia;[25] and to encourage a prosperous Japan to take a more active role in sharing some of the U.S. economic burdens in East Asian countries. Since the Nixon administration, it has been U.S. policy to encourage Japan to spend more on defending itself.[26] Shortly after his inauguration in 1981, President Reagan took a policy initiative affecting the Japan-Korea relationship, particularly in terms of ODA loans. In May, 1981, when he met Prime Minister Zenko Suzuki of Japan, they agreed to "promote the maintenance of peace on the Korean peninsula as important for peace and security in East Asia, including Japan," and they "placed high value on the respective role each country is playing in this regard."[27] The two leaders acknowledged the desirability of an appropriate division of roles between Japan and the United States to insure peace and stability in the region, and the defense of Japan.[28] In Japan, this communique was interpreted as a division of roles for the maintenance of security in the Northeast Asian region. However, there was controversy over whether the division of roles had military meaning or not. At first, Suzuki said that the alliance and the division of roles did not include any military meaning. However, later he admitted that "an appropriate division of roles" between the two countries, as mentioned in the joint communique, might include some military aspects, at least from the U.S. standpoint. He thus modified his earlier position that Japan's commitment is to make a non-military contribution to world power and security.[29]

The Korean government interpreted this division of roles between Japan and the United States to mean that it should receive economic assistance from Japan and military support from the United States. In August 1981, when Korea requested loans of $6 billion from Japan, the Korean government used a military and security rationale. Because the security of Japan had benefitted from Korea's defense efforts, Japan had good reason to extend economic assistance to Korea to reduce some of the financial burden Korea carried for its defense efforts.[30] This argument was influenced by the content of the Reagan-Suzuki Joint Communique.[31] When the Korean government encountered strong opposition from the Japanese government about military-related economic assistance, it reiterated Suzuki's position at the summit meeting, and indicated that Japan was violating the spirit of the summit.[32]

Although in the Reagan-Suzuki summit meeting the Japanese government publicly acknowledged the desirability of the "division of roles" to ensure peace and stability in East Asia, and agreed to promote the maintenance of peace on the Korean peninsula as important for the peace and security of Japan, explicitly underwriting Korea's defense efforts by means of ODA was difficult in terms of Japanese domestic politics. Japan had officially announced that it would not provide economic cooperation for military purposes.[33] Japanese public opinion was consistently against government policies involving military implications.[34] The Foreign Affairs Committee of the Diet had passed two resolutions which prohibited economic cooperation from being employed for military use or being used in ways that were conducive to international disputes.[35] The opposition parties erected powerful political barriers against providing ODA with military implications.[36] When the Japanese government officially received the Korean request with the military rationale, its first response was that Japan could not extend ODA loans for military and defense purposes.[37] Neither could Japan accept literally the Korean request to provide large amount of economic assistance because Japan had benefitted for years from Korea's defense efforts.

The issue was solved in the following way. The Japanese government acknowledged the military efforts of the Republic of Korea and the South Korean government dropped the explicit military-related rationale for requesting Japanese public loans. The Japanese government agreed to provide a large ODA loan for Korea's economic development.

Japan does not give ODA to North Korea. From the viewpoint of comprehensive security policy, the goal of which is to establish interdependent relationships with as many countries as possible, and to receive as few harmful effects as possible from regional disputes, it seems to be somewhat out of standard policy that Japan has given up establishing a relationship with North Korea. The reasons why Japan could not establish a relationship with North Korea are: (1) the Japanese government aligns with the United States' Korean policy; (2) the Republic of Korea has maintained strong pressure on the Japanese government not to have diplomatic relationships with North Korea;[38] and (3) North Korea's militaristic approach to international relationships.

Japan's ODA Policy Practices

This section will examine four of the general policy practices the Japanese government applies in giving ODA. The main focus is on how it selectively applied certain policy practices to the Republic of Korea. This selective application results from the subordination of bureaucratically-determined standard operating procedures to security-related political considerations.[39]

There have been four distinct policy practices. These are the principles of graduation, comprehensive commitment, foreign procurement, and commodity loans. First, the graduation principle is that the Japanese government "graduates" a country from the status of eligibility to receive ODA if the country has succeeded in economic development. This principle is not applied to the Republic of Korea.[40]

There are two facets to the graduation principle. First, Japan allocates a larger share of its total ODA to less developed countries, and less ODA to more developed regions. The Japanese government generally keeps to this principle, although it does not guarantee that a particular poorer country will get more Japanese ODA than a particular more developed country. Second, in the case of some countries, as they develop, Japan will gradually give less ODA. The Japanese government applied this principle to Taiwan and Singapore. It stopped giving ODA to Taiwan in 1973 and to Singapore in 1975, except for small amounts of funding for cultural activities and educational exchange.

The Republic of Korea was an exception to the principle in two respects. In 1979, the Japanese government provided 95 per cent of its ODA to countries which had GNP per capita of $1,000 or less. In that year South Korea's GNP per capita was $1,580. When the per capita GNP of the Republic of Korea reached nearly $2,000 in 1983, the Japanese government pledged a new multi-year economic cooperation package of $4 billion.[41] This reflects South Korea's special status among the developing countries which receive Japanese economic cooperation.

In 1975 and 1976, there was an attempt by the Japanese government to decrease its ODA to South Korea. The Japanese rationale for this reduction was the graduation principle.[42] However, the real reason, as discussed earlier, was diplomatic pressure on the South Korean government concerning the Kim Dae Jung case. The flow of Japanese ODA to the Republic of Korea generally reflects the atmosphere of the two countries' bilateral relationship and changes in Korean domestic politic rather than the income level.

The second ODA policy practice is that the Japanese government generally refuses to make a comprehensive long term commitment of governmental loans without specifying projects. Earlier, the Japanese government had extended such commitments in reparations negotiations to Southeast Asian countries and to the Republic of Korea. For example, in 1965 the Japanese government pledged $500 million in reparations to Korea without specifying projects. Since the end of the reparations period, however, Japan has stressed specific commitments, detailing projects or programs to be funded, loan schedules, terms and conditions, etc.

Comprehensive commitments contradict other standard Japanese ODA policies in two respects: the single year principle and the project-based principle. The Japanese government is extremely cautious about long-term financial commitments because they result in budget inflexibilities.[43] Japan is also reluctant to make financial commitments without specifying how the funds will be spent. In ODA relations with South Korea, the Japanese government held to this specific commitment position until 1983. In the late 1960s and early 1970s, when the Republic of Korea pursued its ambitious five-year economic development plans, it pushed the Japanese government to commit comprehensive financial and technical assistance on an amount basis. When it requested such commitments at Ministerial Conferences, the Japanese government never gave in to the Korean request. Keeping to the principle of project by project consideration, the Japanese ministers tried to make as small a specific commitment as possible before full-fledged working level negotiations. However, in 1983, the Japanese government gave in to South Korea's demand for multi-year commitments without specifying projects. Japan pledged to provide ODA amounting to $1.85 billion without specifying projects.

The third practice concerns the commodity loan. Japanese ODA loans are provided in two major modes: project loans and commodity loans. Project loans provide funds needed to procure equipment and services for the completion of specific development projects. Project loans consist of over 80 percent of the whole Japanese ODA. The commodity loan provide Japanese commodities which are then sold in the recipient's domestic market to raise local funds. Various commodities, bilaterally agreed upon, can be exported to the recipient country through commodity loans. Examples have included daily living necessities, industrial capital goods including machinery, industrial raw materials such as steel, raw materials for chemical production, fertilizer, agricultural machinery, agricultural pesticides, and so on.

Japan offers commodity loans only to those underdeveloped countries which have the lowest income levels. To the regular developing countries, it gives project loans. In general, there are three purposes for which receiving countries can ask for commodity loans: (1) to improve their balance of payment position; (2) to overcome serious domestic economic problems such as inflation; and (3) to finance domestic development programs by generating creating counterpart local currency.

Why does Japan restrict commodity loans? First, Japan cannot easily monitor how the recipient government uses the loans. When the recipient government sells the imported commodities to domestic consumers at a domestically decided price, it can create local funds and channel these directly into their general budget. Second, commodity loans are more likely to be related to political corruption in the recipient country. The recipient government can arbitrarily set the domestic price of these commodities because the commodities usually do not have a competitive market. The government is able to distribute them unfairly.

South Korea has had one example exposed of political distribution of an imported commodity under a commodity loan. In 1965, the Korean government imported automobile parts for Toyota passenger cars. The price of the Korean car made with the imported parts was twice as expensive as that in Japan. The president of the car company, Shinjin Jadongcha Kongup, was known to have a close acquaintance with the Chief of Staff of the Presidential Office at the time. This alleged political favor to the company was questioned in Korea's national assembly in February 1966. After the politician was purged in 1980 by the military government, the company went into bankruptcy in 1984.

Since 1973, the Japanese government has not given commodity loans to Korea, contending that Korea is no longer such an underdeveloped country.[44] However, as described before, the Japanese government provided rice to South Korea in 1979 and 1980. In 1981, another case arose in which the commodity loan became an issue between the two countries. During the $4 billion package negotiations from 1981 to 1983, one of the strong demands from Seoul was for commodity loans. At one point during that time, the Japanese Bureau Chief of the Asian Affairs

Bureau of the Ministry of Foreign Affairs expressed an opinion sympathetic to Korea's request.[45] However, the Japanese government finally turned down the request. Instead of regular, untied commodity loans, the Japanese government pledged that Korea could use up to 30 per cent of its ODA for financing local goods and services for projects.[46]

The fourth policy practice is the principle of foreign purchasing (*Gaikashugi*). Here it appears to be MITI's position which prevails. With regard to procurement methods, Japanese ODA has two categories: tied and untied loans. In the case of tied loans, the recipient government only purchases goods and services of Japanese origin, that is, produced or provided by Japanese firms or individuals. In the case of an untied loan, the recipient government may procure goods and services produced or provided by nationals or firms of any eligible source country. However, which countries are eligible as source countries must be agreed on by the government of Japan and the recipient government.

Until 1975, Japanese ODA to South Korea came through tied loans and grants and were therefore limited to the procurement of Japanese goods and services. In 1976, Japanese ODA became officially untied from procurement only of Japanese goods and services.[47] However, Japan's view was and is that the Korean government should not use Japanese ODA for procuring local goods and services. The Japanese government's rationale is that the Korean government should try to procure domestically suppliable goods and services through self-supporting efforts, such as domestic savings. The Japanese government maintains that its economic cooperation is available only to help the self-reliant efforts of the recipient country for the procurement of goods and services that could not be supplied from domestic sources.

Because Japan holds to the principle of foreign procurement, Korean companies are not eligible to participate in tendering for construction of projects, or for supplying facilities necessary for projects which are funded by Japanese ODA even though they may have the capability to supply goods and services for the project.[48] As a result, Korea still uses most of its Japanese ODA loans to procure Japanese goods and services, although it holds internationally open tendering for the projects. If the South Korean government has to put the Korean companies aside and procure foreign goods and services, it is economically advantageous to purchase them from Japanese companies.

The South Korean government has long demanded that Korean companies should not be excluded from participating in tendering for a project which is funded by Japanese ODA. The real problem of the Korean government has become the lack of governmental financial resources to build public projects, not the availability of the goods and services themselves. The Korean government argues that if Japanese economic cooperation is really intended to help the recipient country, Japan should open permit bidding by local suppliers. There are many projects for which local Korean private firms can compete. Also, the Korean government follows the domestic principle that if a local Korean company can supply necessary goods and services for government financed projects, the government should give preference to the local company (buy Korean principle). There have not been many projects recently which can satisfy the principles of both governments at the same time. This is one of the reasons why a smaller amount of Japanese loans in the $4 billion package have been introduced than originally scheduled, although Korea can use up to 30 per cent of the $1.85 billion of ODA for purchasing local good and services.[49]

Japanese Politicians in ODA Policy-Making to South Korea

Analysts who focus on the bureaucrats' roles in Japan's ODA policy argue that politicians have shown little interest in economic cooperation. They say this is the case because ODA is not a major domestic political issue, nor a high budget priority, and because there is little public awareness. It does not attract votes at elections, which results in non-involvement by politicians.[50] However, it is too limited to think that interests of politicians lie only in election results. They are also interested in political funds, and because project contracts financed by ODA are good opportunities for political fund raising, politicians do have roles in ODA policy-making processes.

In the case of ODA to the Republic of Korea, Japanese politicians advocate two different interests. One is the Japanese business firms' interest. Firms which identify some project or try to supply the facilities of the project want Japanese politicians to influence Japanese bureaucrats to approve the foreign government's request for the specific project. A Japanese politician's intervention in economic cooperation policy-making is usually explained as brokerage between business interests and bureaucrats.[51] Japanese conservative politicians function frequently as brokers, and ability at brokerage has been an important precondition for success in modern Japanese politics. Brokerage ability in Japan derives preeminently from stable, institutionalized ties with the bureaucracy which allow a politician to consistently deliver resources formally controlled by government ministries into the hands of private-sector groups.[52]

Japanese politicians also connect Japanese firms to the South Korean government. During tendering and contracting for a project, Japanese politicians contact Korean politicians and bureaucrats to relay the interests of Japanese firms. One example was the Seoul First Subway project of 1971, for which construction was financed by Japanese ODA. Nobusuke Kishi connected the interests of the Japanese firms wanting to supply subway facilities to the Korean politicians. Kishi's Korean counterpart was Kim Sung-Kon, who served as a Chairman of the Financial Committee of the ruling party in Korea at the time. They widely intervened in the bidding, tendering, and purchasing of the necessary materials for the Seoul subway. For example, when the Korean government procured 186 subway cars, it paid about 64 million yen per car in 1971, while the same cars were delivered to the subway public corporations of Tokyo for about 48 million yen each at the same time. The difference of 16 million yen per unit, or 2.2 billion yen in total, was believed to have been distributed among Korean and Japanese politicians, and Japanese supplying companies.[53] Kim was known to have received $2.5 million, or about 780 million yen. He was responsible for raising campaign funds for the presidential election in 1971, and for the national assembly election in 1972.[54] The Chairman of the Pohang Iron and Steel Corporation (POSCO), Park Tae-Joon, also disclosed that he had been pressured by the same Chairman of the Finance Committee of the ruling party to procure facilities from specific Japanese firms. The first stage of the POSCO project was financed by Japanese ODA. Park Tae-Joon said that he managed to evade this politician's intervention by going directly to President Park Chung-Hee to report the pressure.[55]

Japanese politicians also represented South Korean interests to their top leadership and Japanese bureaucrats. For example, in the case of a controversial Korean request which needed political consideration for a decision, the Korean government approached the Japanese decision-making administration for ODA, using not only official channels, but also the personal relationships between the two countries' politicians.[56]

South Korea's Policy Goals for Receiving Japanese ODA

By receiving Japanese ODA, the Korean government has achieved three types of policy goals: economic, security, and domestic political goals. First, South Korea received Japanese ODA to acquire foreign capital necessary for its development planning. After the military coup in May 1961, the Republic of Korea began a long-range economic development plan. It declared that one of its major objectives was to relieve the people of poverty and desperation, and to concentrate its efforts on the attainment of a self-sustaining national economy for a better standard of living in the near future.[57] The success or failure of the economic development plan depended primarily upon whether or not the required capital could be obtained. There was a paucity of domestic savings to finance large and growing investment programs.[58] Thus, one of the major goals of the government's policy was to attract foreign capital. The reason why the military government pressed so hard for diplomatic normalization with Japan was that it wanted to receive financial and technical resources from Japan to support its economic development plans.

In the middle of the 1960s, Korea needed Japanese resources more urgently because American grant-aid had rapidly decreased. American aid had been the main support of the Korean economy since 1945, and especially after the Korean war, which destroyed most of South Korea's industrial facilities. The war also brought millions of war refugees from North Korea into South Korea. Aid from the United States had financed most of the post-Korean war reconstruction. However, since the early 1960s, when the United States began to be seriously involved in the Vietnam War, it gradually reduced its aid to Korea. For example, American aid in 1965 amounted to approximately $131 million, which was about one half of the 1960 amount. The Korean government needed another financial source to replace the United States, and Japan was a good substitute. Until the mid-1970s, Japanese ODA made up a large part of this capital, and directly supplied part of the foreign financing for several large development projects, such as a steel mill, multi-purpose dams, and fertilizer plants.

The economic significance of Japanese ODA for South Korea's economic development has diminished over twenty years. As Korea's economy has rapidly grown, Japanese ODA loans have become less important to Korea's economy. In twenty years, the size of the Korean economy has increased radically. The proportion of Japan's ODA to the total economic transactions between the two countries has drastically diminished during the same period. While the amount of Japanese ODA loans to Korea in 1980 doubled that of 1966, the amount of trade between the two countries in 1980 increased forty times since 1965, and commercial direct investment increased about one hundred times during the same period.

The second policy goal of the South Korean government as a recipient of Japanese ODA has been its security interest. South Korea gains no direct security advantage from Japanese ODA. Its government has not used Japanese ODA for the military budget, nor for investment in the defense industry. However, Japanese ODA contributes, although indirectly, to Korea's security in two respects. Japanese ODA has helped build an economically stable South Korea which can better sustain the financial burdens of its defense. Also, the Korean government could save domestic resources for military defense spending in an amount equivalent to levels of Japanese ODA. Finally, Japan's ODA is an expression of the Japan-U.S.-South Korea triangular cooperation for Korean security.

The third South Korean policy goal as a recipient of Japanese ODA is its domestic political interest. Generally, leaders in less developed countries welcome ODA because the increased availability of financial resources can be used to consolidate domestic political control. In South Korea, development projects financed by Japanese ODA have been interpreted as the incumbent government's achievement. Japanese ODA has also become a sign of the Japanese government's commitment to the stability of the incumbent government in Seoul. When the government experienced domestic problems concerning its legitimacy, foreign support was sometimes sought to help re-establish the regime's legitimacy claims.

One example is Park Chung-Hee's military government in 1961. The military government emphasized economic development and industrialization as its top priority for two reasons: the military leaders believed that industrialization was urgently needed to strengthen national security, and economic development was needed to legitimize the new military government. Carrying out the economic development plan became the foundation of the regime's claim to legitimacy. The Japanese government cooperated through its reparations.[59] A second example comes from the Chun Doo Hwan government in 1981. The Japanese government's responsive attitude to a $6 billion request was taken not only by the Korean people but also by foreign businessmen as a sign of Japanese support for the incumbent South Korean government. ODA did not always have a positive effect, however. As discussed earlier, fluctuating levels of Japanese ODA during the 1970s were seen inside and outside South Korea as signs of the Japanese government's changing support for President Park.

In general, during the last 20 years, the economic importance of Japanese ODA for South Korea's economic development has been getting less significant. The significance of Japan's ODA has become mostly political. For the Japanese government, ODA loans to Korea have become an aspect of the comprehensive security policy aimed at stabilizing the Korean peninsula. For the Republic of Korea, Japanese ODA has become a demonstration of Japanese support to the incumbent government, and has been used domestically to increase the political prestige of the Seoul government.

This diminished economic importance of Japan's ODA has gradually strengthened the bargaining position of Seoul with the Japanese government on ODA loans. The South Korean government sometimes uses the security relationship between the two countries in order to pressure the Japanese government for favorable consideration of ODA requests which do not conform to Japan's standard ODA policy. For example, it demanded ODA because of Korea's contribution to Japan's military security. This is the logic which Seoul applied in requesting a $6 billion ODA package from Japan. In the case of the Pohang Iron Mill in 1969, a project which had been evaluated as economically infeasible by western steel companies, the Korean government employed the security argument to persuade the Japanese government to fund the steel mill.[60] What can be seen, then, is that Korea has tried to change its status from the one-way beneficiary of Japanese ODA to the two-way contributor to Japan's security. As a contributor, Korea then can claim some right to charge for that contribution.

Conclusion

It has been argued that in general, Japan's economic interest is the most decisive factor in formulating ODA policy. However, Japan's security interests are more important than economic interests as principal influences on its ODA policy toward the Republic of Korea. This makes the Korean case unique in terms of ODA policy. It has also been argued that in general, bureaucratic agencies and stable routines dominate the great bulk of Japanese ODA decisions.[61] The South Korean case is exceptional in this instance also because political considerations are more important than bureaucratic inertia.

The importance of particular ODA policy goals has changed during the last 20 years as the economic significance of Japanese ODA for South Korea has diminished and the relationships between the two countries have fluctuated. For the Japanese government, ODA to South Korea has become more a symbol of Japan's comprehensive security policy than a source of economic benefit. The review of the application of general Japanese aid principles to Korea indicates that the distinctive characteristics of the Japan-Korea relationship have led to compromise and adjustments in response to Korean pressure. Concerning the formal rationale for accepting Japanese ODA, South Korea has tried to change its status from the one-way beneficiary of Japanese

ODA to the two-way contributor to Japan's security, so that it has some right to charge for that contribution.

After 1991, the Japanese government will no longer pledge any new ODA to the Republic of Korea. As a result South Korea will "graduate" from the status of a recipient of Japanese ODA. However, this does not mean that the Korean government will lose all interest in the Japanese ODA system. In providing bilateral ODA to developing countries since 1987, the Korean government has modelled its own efforts after the Japanese ODA system (at the early stage of its development) in terms of objectives, organization, and policy-making structure.[62]

Endnotes

1. In this chapter, the Republic of Korea will also be referred to as South Korea or Korea.

2. Dennis T. Yasutomo, "Why Aid?: Japan as an `Aid Great Power'," *Pacific Affairs* (Winter 1989/90), pp. 500-03.

3. The figures in Table 1 should be interpreted carefully. Japan's economic cooperation packages with Korea have been a mix of grants, ODA loans, and other forms of concessional finance. Gross disbursement figures are used in the table to convey the levels of new funds being provided. Actually, during the 1980s, Korea's repayment of past ODA loans often roughly equalled or surpassed the inflows of new ODA funds.

4.John White, *Japanese Aid*, (London: Overseas Development Institute, 1964), p. 9; Sukehiro Hasegawa, *Japanese Foreign Aid: Policy and Practice*, (New York: Praeger, 1975), p. 11; Kazuo Nishi, *Keizai Kyoryoku* (*Economic Cooperation*), (Tokyo: Chuo Koronsha, 1970), pp. 45-73; Kajima Heiwa Kenkyujo, *Taigai Keizai Kyoryoku Taikei Daigoken: Nihon no Keizai Kyoryoku* (*A Series of Overseas Economic Cooperation vol. 5: Japan's Economic Cooperation*) (Tokyo: Kajima Kenkyujo Shupankai, 1973), pp. 26-54; Ken Matsui, *Keizai Kyoryoku: Towareru Nihon no Keizai Gaiko* (*Economic Cooperation: Questioned Japan's Economic Diplomacy*), (Tokyo: Yuhikaku, 1983), pp. 43-73; Ken Matsui and Takeshi Mori, "A Dialog: Aid to Developing Nations," *The Wheel Extended* (July/September, 1983), pp. 2-9; Asahi Shimbun Enjo Shuzaiban, *Enjo Tojokoku Nippon* (*Aid Giving Nation, Japan*), (Tokyo: Asahi Shimbunsha, 1985), pp. 69-108.

5. Hosup Kim, "Policy-making of Japanese Official Development Assistance to the Republic of Korea, 1965-1983," (Ph.D dissertation, University of Michigan, 1987).

6. David H. Blake and Robert S. Walters, *The Politics of Global Economic Relations* (Englewood Cliffs: Prentice Hall, 1976), pp. 132-33; Wolfgang F. Friedmann, George Kalmanoff, and Robert F. Meagher, *International Financial Aid* (New York: Columbia University Press, 1966), p. 389; Jon Halliday and Gavan McCormack, *Japanese Imperialism Today* (New York: Monthly Review Press, 1973), pp. 25-31; Edgar C. Harrell, "Japan's Postwar Aid Policies," (Ph. D. dissertation, Columbia University, 1973), p. 271; I.M.D. Little and J.M. Clifford, *International Aid* (London: George Allen and Unwin Ltd., 1965), p. 20; Edward S. Mason, *Foreign Aid and Foreign Policy* (New York: Harper and Row, 1964), p. 4; Alan G. Rix, "Future of Japanese Aid," *Australian Outlook* 31 (Dec. 1977), p. 418; White, *Japanese Aid*, pp. 9-10.

7. Yasutomo, "Why Aid?," p. 493. For economic interest as a policy goal of Japanese ODA loans to China, see Chae-Jin Lee, *China and Japan: New Economic Diplomacy*, (Stanford: Hoover Institution Press, 1984), pp. 119, 124; Philip Gregory Story, "Japanese Official Assistance in Chinese Development: The Politics of Japanese Aid Decision-Making," (Ph. D. dissertation, Griffith University, Australia, 1988). See also Zhao's chapter on China in this volume.

8. Ministry of Foreign Affairs, Japan, *Nihon Gaiko Sanjunenshi* (*Thirty Years History of Japan's Diplomacy*), Tokyo: 1982, pp. 158-59.

9. Overseas Economic Cooperation Fund, *Kaigai Keizai kyoryoku kikin 20 nen shi* (Twenty Years History of the Overseas Economic Cooperation) (Tokyo: Overseas Economic Cooperation Fund, 1982); Ken'ichi Imai, Yumiko Okamoto, Kazuhiko Yokota, and Akira Hirata, "Evolution of Japan's ODA," pp. 20-54 in Ippei Yamazawa and Akira Hirata, ed., *Development Cooperation Policies of Japan, United States, and Europe*. (Tokyo, Japan: Institute of Developing Economies, 1992).

10. His political programs are briefly expressed in Dae Jung Kim, *Mass-Participatory Economy: A Democratic Alternative for Korea* (Cambridge: Harvard University, 1985).

11. *Japan Times*, 15 August 1973.

12. Haruki Wada, "Nikkan Kankei Jijitsu no Omomi (*Graveness of Facts in the Japanese-Korean Relationship*)," *Nihon Dokusho Shimbun*, 26 November 1973; Shin Aochi, "Genronjin nimo Sekininga (*News-media Person is also Responsible*)," in Haruki Wada and Shin Aochi, ed., *Nikkan Rentai no Shiso to Kodo* (*The Thought and Action of the Japanese-Korean Alliance*), (Tokyo: Gendaihyoronsha, 1977), pp. 64-67; "Seimei (*Statement*)" (August 23, 1973) in the same book, p. 62.

13. *Japan Times*, November 2-3, 1973.

14.Interpellation of Kiyomasa Kato of the Japan Socialist Party in the House of Representative. *Japan Times*, 25 August 1973; Interpellation of Tetsuzo Fuwa, General Secretariat of the Japan Communist Party. *Japan Times*, 2 September 1973.

15. For example, Reply of Yasuhiro Nakasone, Minister of International Trade and Industry, in the House of Representative. *Japan Times*, 25 August 1973; Talks of Susumu Nikkaido, Chief Cabinet Secretary. *Japan Times*, 24 August 1973.

16. *Japan Times*,2 September 1973.

17. *Nihon Keizai Shimbun*, 20 August 1980; 28 November 1980.

18. *Nihon Keizai*, 25, 27, and 28 January, 1981.

19. *Nihon Keizai*, 23 January 1981.

20. *Nihon Keizai*, 22 May 1980.

21. See Yoshihiko Kohno, "Nikkan Keizai Kyoryoku Nijunen no Ayumi to Kongo no Kadai (*Twenty Years History of Japan--Korea Economic Cooperation and Its Future Tasks*)," *Gendai Korea* (November 1985): 34.

22. Ralph N. Clough, *East Asia and U. S. Security* (Washington, D. C.: Brookings Institution, 1978), pp. 170--72; Nathan White "Japan's Security Interests in Korea," *Asian Survey* (April 1976), p. 300; Franklin B. Weinstein and Fuji Kamiya, eds., *Security of Korea* (Boulder: Westview Press, 1980); Franklin B. Weinstein, ed., *U.S.-Japan Relations and the Security of East Asia* (Boulder: Westview Press, 1978).

23. Japan Institute of International Affairs (JIIA), *White Papers of Japan* (1980--81), p. 94.

24.*Ibid.*, pp. 93-94.

25. Japanese progressive intellectuals often emphasized this point, and interpreted the treaty signed in 1965 as the framework for setting up as international system among South Korea, Japan, and the United States against the Soviet Union. However, a conservative scholar such as Masao Okonogi is also of the same view that the treaty is the start of the security system of the three countries. See "Japan-Korea Relations," p. 73.

26. Chong-Sik Lee, *Japan and Korea: The Political Dimension* (Stanford: Hoover Institution Press, 1985), p. 113.

27.Joint Communique, *New York Times*, 9 May 1981.

28.*Ibid.*

29. *Japan Times*,10 May 1981.

30. *Japan Times*,20 August 1981; *Dong A Ilbo*,20 August 1981.

31.In an interview, one South Korean foreign official disclosed that the United States government asked the Korean government, before the Reagan-Suzuki meeting, on which level the Korean government wanted the U.S. to mention the economic assistance issue. The Korean government replied "on the level of President and Prime Minister."

32. *Dong A Ilbo*, 29 August 1981.

33. OECF, *Keizai Kyoryoku Yogoshu* (*Dictionary of economic cooperation*), (1982), p. 128.

34. For example, in the public opinion polls conducted by the Yomiuri Shimbunsha, in October 1980, about 39 per cent of the respondents said that the defense budget should be cut from the present amount. Source; Office of Prime Minister, *Seronchosa Nenkan* (*Yearbook of Public Polls*), (Tokyo: Naikaku Soridaijin Kanbokohoshitsuhen, 1981, p. 559). In polls conducted one year later, about 57 per cent of the respondents said that the defense budget should be kept under the present level. *Seronchosa Nenkan* (1982), p. 571.

35."Resolution on Foreign Economic Cooperation," the Committee of Foreign Affairs, the House of Representative, April 5, 1978, and the same resolution of the same committee, March 30, 1981.

36. For example, the Chairman of the Socialist Party, Ichio Asukata, criticized the Suzuki administration in the Diet. "Because the Suzuki administration admitted that Korean security is closely related to the security of Japan and that the division of roles with the United States in ensuring the security of East Asia was desirable, the Korean government put such a request to share its defense burden with Japan." 95th Diet, Japan, Representative Question of the JSP, the House of Representative, September 30 1981. Source: *Gekkan Shakaito* (Monthly of the Japan Socialist Party) (November 1981): 80-87.

37. *Japan Times*,20 August 1981.

38. Nevertheless, there have been arguments within Japan that it should have a relationship with North Korea as well. The Japan Socialist Party, the Japan Communist Party, and the liberal faction in the Liberal Democratic Party have held this opinion. This is a major reason why the South Korean government did not have a good relationship with the liberal faction of the LDP, led by Masayoshi Ohira and Zenko Suzuki. For example, when Toshio Kimura, Minister of Foreign Affairs, expressed in the Diet on August 30, 1974, that the security of the whole Korean peninsula was important to that of Japan, and that he believed that North Korea did not have aggressive intentions toward South Korea, his statements enraged the South Korean government, and developed into a diplomatic dispute. He was a member of Ohira's faction. *Japan Times*,31 August 1974.

39. This relationship is called a special relationship by Alan Rix. See: Alan Rix, *Japan's Economic Aid*, (New York: St. Martin's Press, 1980), p. 235.

40.Kohno, "Nikkan Keizai Kyoryoku," p. 33.

41. This included ODA plus various mixed credits from the Export-Import Bank and other banks.

42.See the Joint communique of the seventh Ministerial Conference, which did not include any clause on governmental economic cooperation but indicated the intention to broaden private economic cooperation. *Japan Times*, 27 December 1973.

43. This reluctance reflects the position of the Ministry of Finance. See, John C. Campbell, *Contemporary Japanese Budget Politics*, (Berkeley: University of California Press, 1977).

44. This is also a graduation principle.

45. *Nihon Keizai*, 27 February 1982.

46. *Dong A Ilbo*, 12 January 1983.

47.An interview with a minister of Japanese Embassy to the Republic of Korea in September, 1984; Kohno, "Nikkan Keizai Kyoryoku," p. 33.

48. See the chapter on Thailand for a case study of Japan's ODA and the Thai domestic construction industry.

49.An interview in October 1985 with an official of Japanese OECF.

50. Rix, "Future of Japanese Aid," p. 423.

51. Kent E. Calder, "Kanryo vs. Shomin: Contrasting Dynamics of Conservative Leadership in Postwar Japan," in Terry E. MacDougall, ed., *Political Leadership in Contemporary Japan* (Ann Arbor: Center for Japanese Studies, University of Michigan, 1982), p. 8.

52. Chalmers Johnson, "Tanaka Kakuei, Structural Corruption, and the Advent of Machine Politics in Japan," *The Journal of Japanese Studies* (Winter 1986): 1-28.

53. *Mainichi*, 17 and 18 February 1978; Sangmoon Lee, "Jihachul: Kummaek oe Naemak (*Subway: Inside Story of Capital Flow*)," *Jungkyungmoonhwa* (July 1984): 302-15.

54. *Ibid*.

55. *Dong A Ilbo*, 19 February 1981; *Chosun Ilbo*, 19 February 1981; *Kyunghyang Shinmun*, 10 February 1981.

56. Alan Rix calls this relationship the "special relationship" in which economic feasibility was easily subordinated to political necessity. See: Rix, *Japan's Aid*, p. 235.

57. *Korea Annual* (1964), pp. 197-98.

58. Government of the Republic of South Korea, *The Second Five--Year Economic Development Plan: 1967-71* (1966), pp. 28-29.

59. Chairman Park pointed out a main reason why he led the military coup. "...For the first time after the foundation of the government in the ROK, we established a five--year economic development plan, thus, making a large forward stride...This plan, which was destined to remain buried in desks for ten or more years under the former regimes, was a great achievement." He continued, "It is essential to have strong political stability, a new social order, and the determined concentration of our power in the field of economic improvement in order to win ultimate victory against Communism." In Chung-Hee Park, *The Country, The Revolution, and I* (Seoul: Hollym Publisher, 1962), pp. 64-65, 164.

60. The argument was, "The steel mill is essential for ROK's economic development, which is prerequisite for its security."

61. Rix, *Japan's Aid*.

62. On June 1, 1987, Korea launched the Economic Development Cooperation Fund (EDCF), the purpose of which is to enhance Korea's international economic cooperation by providing concessional loans for industrial development and economic stabilization in developing countries. The EDCF will also be used to facilitate the activities of Korean firms with regard to industrial development projects in developing countries. For Korea, the concept of `economic cooperation' has been used to describe attempts to further economic relations with developing nations in order to promote the export of Korean goods and services.

11

JAPAN'S AID TO THE PACIFIC ISLAND STATES

Isami Takeda

Introduction

Contrary to the low-key perceptions that many Japanese have of the Pacific island nations, Japan's importance and role in the Pacific is immense. For the Pacific islanders, Japanese aid policy directions in particular are crucial for their nation-building. This is true despite the fact that Japan's trade with the Pacific islands is small. Similarly, the strategic economic significance of the region for Japan is small. The Pacific island's share of Japanese bilateral ODA is currently less than two percent, although it has significantly increased from 0.6 percent in 1980.

This chapter describes the recent evolution of Japan's ODA policy to the Pacific Island states. The first sections deal with Japan's past and present aid performance in the region, its perception of the region in an historical context, and constraints affecting Japanese aid policy to the Pacific in the 1970s. The following sections analyze new international and domestic factors in Japanese aid policy-making in the 1980s. Finally this chapter closes with comments on Japan's role in the 1990s and the specter of a new problem: aid dependence and Japan's dominant position in the Pacific.

The Pacific Islands in Japan's Aid Program

Since 1980, Japan's aid to the Pacific region as a proportion of Japan's total aid has more than doubled (Table 11.1). However, in absolute terms, the increase has been almost ten times the 1980 level. While Japan is often criticized for the heavy concentration of its aid to Asian nations, and in particular to ASEAN nations, Japan's performance in the Pacific is characterized by widespread distribution of its aid across the region (Table 11.2).

TABLE 11.1 Net Volume of Japan's Bilateral Aid to the South Pacific

Year	*US$ millions*	*% Japan's Total Aid*
1975	5	0.6
1980	12	0.6
1984	25	1.0
1985	24	0.9
1986	55	1.4
1987	68	1.3
1988	93	1.4
1990	114	1.6

Source: Gaimusho, *Wagakuni no Seifu Kaihatsu Enjo*, Tokyo, various volumes.

Aid relationships between donors and recipients in the Pacific traditionally have been determined by historical colonial relations. Australia has allocated more than 50 percent of its total bilateral ODA to the Pacific Island nations throughout the 1980s. The principal recipients of Australian aid are Papua New Guinea (PNG), Fiji, and the Solomon Islands. PNG was a former Australian colony and became independent in 1975. Fiji and the Solomon Islands were under British colonial rule and gained their independent status in 1970 within the Commonwealth.

The principal recipients of New Zealand's aid are the Cook Islands, Tokelau, Niue, Western Samoa, and Tuvalu. Between 1983 and 1987, New Zealand distributed 79 percent of its total ODA budget to these islands. The first three are in free association with New Zealand. Western Samoa, which was a former New Zealand territory, became independent in 1962. Tuvalu was a former British colony which became independent in 1978. The major Pacific recipients of American aid are the former territories of the United States. For example, in 1987, the United States accounted for 94 percent of the total bilateral aid in the Micronesian region except for Kiribati which, as a former British colony, received no aid from the United States.

TABLE 11.2 Recipients of Japan's Bilateral ODA (100 million yen, cumulative net disbursement to 1988)

	Total	*Loan*	*Grant*	*Technical Assistance*
1. Papua New Guinea	451.29	340.21	62.30	48.78
2. Fiji	101.21		51.06	50.15
3. Western Samoa	88.82		67.30	21.52
4. Solomon Islands	57.09		45.84	11.25
5. Tonga	55.45		37.22	18.23
6. Kiribati	48.87		39.65	9.22
7. Micronesia	42.96		36.04	6.92
8. Marshall Islands	37.64		36.16	1.48
9. Palau	22.56		20.97	1.59
10. Vanuatu	20.06		18.64	3.42
11. Tuvalu	12.56		6.65	5.91
12. Cook Islands	0.63		0.10	0.53

Source: Compiled from Gaimusho, *Wagakuni o Seifu Kaihatsu Enjo* [Japan's ODA], Vol. 2, 1989, p. 751.

The leading recipients of Japanese aid in the Pacific are Melanesian nations such as Papua New Guinea, Fiji, the Solomon Islands, and Vanuatu. The second major group of recipients are the Polynesian nations such as Western Samoa, Tonga, and Tuvalu. The third major group of recipients are the Micronesian nations such as Kiribati, the Federated States of Micronesia, the Marshall Islands, and Palau.

While Japan maintains a high level of loan aid to Asian nations, bilateral aid to the Pacific region, except for PNG, is all grant aid and technical assistance. PNG, the biggest island nation in the Pacific and rich in mineral resources, is "the only nation which is able to request"[1] ODA loans and in fact receives Japanese ODA yen loans.[2] In the future, Fiji may be eligible to request ODA yen loans from Japan.[3] However, since most of the Pacific Island nations are small island states with small populations and fragile economies, they are not in a position to request Japanese yen loans.[4]

The two major uses of aid in the Pacific are for development projects relating to agriculture, forestry and fisheries; and infrastructure-type projects relating to land, marine, and aviation transportation. Grant aid for fisheries, such as the construction of fishery training facilities, training boats, and marine research facilities, is one of the most important types of Japanese aid in the South Pacific. This particular type of aid started in 1974 to cope with the evolution of the then new international 200-mile exclusive economic zone marine regime. The Japanese government estimated at that time that if every country would declare its 200-mile exclusive economic zone, "36 percent of total Japanese fishing catches would be affected."[5] In order to minimize the anticipated negative effects from the declaration of 200-mile economic zones on Japan's fishing industry in the Pacific, the Japanese government decided to initiate a new category of grant aid focused on fisheries.

Since marine resources are the most important income source for many of the Pacific islands, Japan regarded grant aid for Pacific Island fishery development as one way of contributing to socioeconomic development in the Pacific islands. In Japan's view, offering grant aid was also a way to obtain assurance of continued access to fishing rights by Japanese fishing fleets in the Pacific. Japan's assumption was that for the islanders, receiving Japanese grant aid would strengthen their own economic development. This perspective has been maintained by Japan. For example, currently Japan hopes to use its aid as a diplomatic tool to ease tension between Japan and the Pacific islands over issues such as drift-net fishing and the ocean dumping of toxic and nuclear wastes.

However, Japan's ODA role in the Pacific is presenting a problem of growing concern to Japan's ODA decision-makers. By 1987, Japan had already acquired a position as top donor in Kiribati and Western Samoa, and was the number two donor in Tonga, Nauru, PNG, Fiji, French Polynesia, and the U.S. territories. If aid commitments by Australia and New Zealand should weaken in the future, a possibly Japan sees as realistic given the economic problems those two donors have, Japan was not in the past and is not prepared at this point to replace them as sources of bilateral ODA. In Japan, there is no clear sign of willingness to accept a position as principal aid donor in the Pacific. In several quarters, there are concerns that if Japan should slip into that position, the commitment will be interminable because of the fundamental weakness of most of the Island economies and the peripheral interest other donors might have, especially as their feelings of post-colonial obligation wane.

Japanese Perceptions of the Pacific Island Region

There are five different stages of Japanese perceptions about the Pacific Island region: (1) World War I, (2) World War II, (3) the post-war period until the late 1970s, (4) the evolution of the Pacific community concept and Asia-Pacific regionalism, and (5) the region's political decade in the 1980s. Japan's ODA commitments to the Pacific region got underway during the fourth stage and significantly grew during the fifth stage.

Before the first stage (World War I), there was an intellectual movement in Japan calling for Japanese nationalism to expand the Japanese frontier into the Pacific as well as Southeast Asia. Shigetaka Shiga, who published "Nanyo Jijo" (Current Affairs in the South Seas) in 1887, is an example of a Meiji intellectual who wanted to foster greater Japanese understanding of the Pacific islands. This intellectual movement, however, did not have any substantial impact on Japan's foreign policy orientation to the Pacific, since Japan was so preoccupied with continental Asian affairs.[6] The two different wars with China in 1894 and Russia in 1904 illustrate this. It was not until World War I that the Japanese government recognized, for the first time, the political significance of the Pacific islands and the possibility of colonial expansion into this region.

During the first and second stages (the period covering the two World Wars), Japan occupied and ruled the Pacific islands known as the inner South Seas ("Uchi-Nanyo"), geographically and ethnically defined as Micronesia. In 1914, just after World War I broke out, Japan occupied the former German possessions north of the equator in the Pacific. These islands were mandated to Japan by the League of Nations in 1921 as an integral part of the Japanese empire. Japan continued to administer these islands until defeated in World War II. Between the two wars, Japan regarded these territories as colonial development sites and as potential battlefields.

During the third stage postwar period, Japan disengaged itself from Pacific Island affairs. After World War II, Japan lost all overseas colonial territories, including the islands in the Pacific. Since the Pacific islands had been a fierce battleground between Japanese and Allied forces during World War II, there was a dark image of the Pacific Islands among the general public in Japan. This was to remain for decades. Since all of the Pacific islands had come under the rule of Western powers, Japan did not see any way to relate to the islands, either politically or commercially, even as late as the 1960s. During this same period, Japan strengthened its political, diplomatic, and commercial relations with the Southeast Asian nations through war reparation arrangements. There were few chances for Japan and the Pacific islands to develop comparable relationships. Japan did not enter any war reparation arrangements with the Pacific islands states except for Micronesia, for which Japan and the United States signed a special agreement in 1969.[7]

The Pacific Islands came to be a Japanese concern within the vague framework of the Pacific community concept. When inaugurated by the Ohira government, the Pacific community concept did does not seem to include the Pacific Island nations. However, the concept generated broader interests and concerns among intellectuals and bureaucrats about the wide range of Pacific affairs. These concerns were sharpened and the Japanese became aware of the political dimensions of Pacific Island regional affairs as results of the collective action of Pacific Island nations against French nuclear testing in French Polynesia and against Japanese proposals for dumping nuclear waste in the Pacific. The formulation of the South Pacific Forum (SPF) and its economic cooperation agency, the South Pacific Bureau for Economic Cooperation (SPEC), in the 1970s were important signs of Pacific regionalism and came gradually to Japanese attention.[8] The Forum was created, in large part, as an alternative to the South Pacific Commission. The membership of the South Pacific Commission, which still exists, includes the Island States and former and current colonial powers. SPF was designed to be a purer expression of Pacific regionalism.

The fifth stage is the present situation which started in the early 1980s. It was not until this stage that Japan became seriously aware of the political significance of the Pacific Islands.[9] There were several factors. Soviet diplomatic initiatives in the Pacific received major news coverage in Japan, especially when Kiribati entered into a fishing agreement with Moscow. Signs of political instability were also apparent. These included coups in Fiji, factional and tribal conflicts in PNG, and the independence movement in New Caledonia. The 1980s were also a decade of growing nationalism in the Islands. In addition, Japan was becoming increasingly aware that global power politics were operating in the Pacific and that the outcomes of these politics could be important for Japan. Japan had to acknowledge that the situation was new in the sense that more than before, the Islanders themselves had become political actors as well and were prepared to pursue their own interests, regardless of Western interests.[10] In this complex context of change due to factors both external and internal to the Pacific Island region, Japan ventured to increase and improve relationships, with ODA policy as the primary instrument.

Constraints on Japan's Aid in the 1970s

Japan first initiated aid to the Pacific following Western Samoa's independence in 1962. However, the share of bilateral aid to the Pacific as a percentage of Japan's total aid remained less than 0.5 percent throughout the 1960s and 1970s. There were four major constraints on Japan's aid commitments to the Pacific Islands.

1. No Reparation Scheme

Japan developed its postwar diplomatic and commercial relations with Asian nations first through war reparation arrangements, second through Japanese ODA yen loans, and third through trade. Japan served as a supplier of capital goods and finance to Asia, while Asian nations became suppliers of natural resources and served as export markets for Japan. War reparation arrangements were frequently the first step in the process of rebuilding relationships.

With the exception of Micronesia, which entered a kind of war reparation arrangement with Japan in 1969 and received 5.84 million U.S. dollars from Japan, there were no war reparation arrangements between Japan and the Pacific Island states. Since during the 1950s and in most cases the 1960s, the Islands were not independent nations but were under Western colonial powers, they were not entitled to claim war reparations from the Japanese government.

2. Nontariff Barriers

Both Australia and New Zealand have strong presences in the Melanesian and Polynesian regions, respectively. Both nations have established long and close relationships with the islanders, and have penetrated deeply into every sector of economic life.[11] Japan was reluctant to be involved in development projects in the region, especially in PNG and Fiji, since Australia regarded this region as its sphere of influence and interests. Australia's presence in the government sector, especially in PNG,[12] served as a nontariff barrier for Japanese consultants who might try to find, formulate, and implement development projects.

3. *Few Independent Nations*

There were only two independent nations in the 1960s: Western Samoa in 1962 and Nauru in 1968.[13] From 1970 to 1980, eight island states achieved political independence: Fiji and Tonga in 1970, Niue (free association with New Zealand) in 1974, PNG in 1975, the Solomon Islands and Tuvalu in 1978, Kiribati in 1979, and Vanuatu in 1980. All of these islands were under the colonial rule of Britain, Australia, New Zealand or France. All this was important because Japan could not consider initiating aid relations with Pacific island nations until they achieved political independence.

4. *Smallness*

Japan has had difficulty finding development projects in the Pacific that it could finance. Japan's style of economic assistance does not readily fit the economic needs of these small countries, with economies that are too small to justify the bigger projects of interest to Japanese contractors. Japan also found it difficult more generally to assist economic development in the island nations, since to Japanese eyes, there seemed to be no blueprint for nation-building.[14]

New International Setting in the 1980s

A combination of political and economic factors led Japan to increase its aid to the Pacific Island region in the 1980s.

Political Factors

The decade of the 1970s was a period of independence and nation-building in the Pacific while the 1980s was a period of political change. Among the issues that surfaced in the 1980s were: the Soviet diplomatic approaches, Vanuatu's diplomatic connection with Libya and Cuba, formation of the Melanesian Spearhead Group, the signing of the South Pacific Nuclear Free Zone Treaty (the Rarotonga Treaty) in 1986, the Rainbow Warrior Affair in 1985, New Zealand's anti-nuclear policy and its diplomatic friction with the United States under the ANZUS agreement in 1985, military coups in Fiji in 1987, expulsion of Vanuatu's president in 1988, domestic political turmoil in PNG, the Bougainville crisis in 1989, an alleged coup plan in Tonga in 1989, and an independence movement and assassination of a political leader in New Caledonia in 1989. Although New Zealand's ANZUS case does not have to be treated as a Pacific Island affair, nevertheless it strengthened the image outside the region and in Japan that the Pacific region was politically unstable. For Japan, therefore, the most important policy issue was to restore and maintain political stability from a Western point of view. Foreign aid was regarded as one of the best means to achieve this purpose.

Among the international political factors, the Soviet factor was the most important. The Soviet diplomatic initiatives in the Pacific contributed to the rise of Japanese public interest in the Pacific and had effects on the evolution of Japan's diplomatic commitments in the region. As Hamish McDonald, a columnist writing in the *Far Eastern Economic Review*, commented in 1986: "Japan is moving, with strong encouragement from the U.S., to expand its economic assistance to the small nations of the South Pacific as a counter to Soviet attempts to build a presence through fishing and trade deals."[15]

The Soviet Union had made diplomatic approaches to a number of island nations beginning in the late 1970s. It attempted to sign fishery and commercial agreements with PNG, Fiji, Tuvalu, and the Solomon Islands. All of these island nations had Anglo-Saxon colonial heritages and had close contacts with either Britain, Australia, or New Zealand. Australia and New Zealand successfully prevented the Soviet Union from concluding any official agreements with those island nations. The Kiribati government, however, ignored the western diplomatic protests and proceeded to sign a fishing agreement with Moscow in its own economic interests. The Soviet Union concluded two different fishery agreements with Kiribati in August 1985 and with Vanuatu in January 1987. The terms of this agreement were: (1) up to 16 fishing vessels can operate within the 200-mile exclusive economic zone, (2) operating permits would be valid for one year, (3) the Soviet vessels are not allowed to enter 12-mile territorial waters, (4) and the license fee is 2.4 million Australian dollars.[16]

Kiribati's decision was economic with no political or strategic consideration behind it. The major reason Kiribati signed the fishing agreement with the Soviet Union was an American refusal to accept a similar agreement when the U.S.-Kiribati tuna fishing agreement expired in December 1984. The Soviet-Kiribati negotiations started when U.S.-Kiribati relations were in the critical stage. Underestimation by the United States of Kiribati's economic interests and determination were decisive factors in the Soviet diplomatic success.[17] An additional factor was the gradual withdrawal of aid commitments by Britain, the top aid donor. Kiribati realized that it was losing a major source of revenue from the United States and a major development fund from Britain.

The fishing agreement was an important source of Kiribati's government revenue, but was not regarded as a vital economic agreement for the Soviet Union, since it could not expect substantial economic benefits from catching fish in Kiribati waters. Western observers held a common view that Soviet motives for concluding the agreement were not wholly economic, but were also politico-strategic. Soviet trawlers were often used for intelligence collection. The United States had an MX missile testing ground in the Marshall Islands, which are close to Kiribati, and a space tracking station on nearby Canton Island.[18]

The Soviet-Kiribati agreement was a shock to the Western powers. In reaction, what emerged was a political consensus that Western interests in Pacific should be maintained. One result was an increase of foreign aid to Kiribati by the United States, Australia, New Zealand, and even China. However, it was Japan that provided the largest volume of bilateral aid to Kiribati after the signing of the fishing agreement. Britain, which had been the top donor to Kiribati since independence, was replaced as top donor by Japan in 1986. By 1987, Japan ODA to Kiribati represented 45 percent of Kiribati's total bilateral aid receipts.[19]

It is possible to conclude that Japanese aid was filling the gap between Kiribati's economic demands and what the Western donors could provide. However, that view would be too simple. Japanese aid policy has always paid keen attention to other Western donors, and particularly to the U.S. This has been rationalized by the concept of "burden sharing" or "responsibility sharing." Since the Soviet invasion of Afghanistan and Vietnam's invasion of Kampuchea in the late 1970s, Japan has made relationships between its ODA policies and its foreign policy much clearer and has been increasingly more willing to relate its aid programs to broadly defined security objectives. On various occasions, the United States has suggested that Japan should take more responsibility for maintaining Western security interests, such as by providing aid to politically and strategically unstable areas.

> Under the rubric of comprehensive security, Tokyo aimed to integrate diplomacy, aid, and defence efforts into a foreign policy framework designed to meet its own as well as western security interests. Lacking a military security option, Japan's policy makers decided to use economic assistance as a major foreign policy tool. They reasoned that by wise application of sufficient economic aid to crucial countries or regions, enough political, social, and economic resiliency could be promoted so

> that conditions leading to internal disorder, disputes, or external intervention might never develop.[20]

It is important to note that the Kuranari doctrine, an important clarification of Japanese Pacific Island policy which will be explained further below, was proposed at a time when U.S.-Japan trade relations were becoming problematic, when the United States faced the Soviet diplomatic challenges in the Asia-Pacific, and when Japan was expected to do something for the maintenance of Western security in the Pacific.

> Concerned about Soviet efforts at expanding its presence and influence in the Pacific, the U.S. has urged Japan to play a greater role in the region....Diplomatic sources confirmed that in recent U.S.-Japan consultations--notably U.S. Secretary of State George Shultz meeting with then Japanese foreign minister Shintaro Abe in Manila in June—American officials have emphasized the need of Japan offering increased economic aid to the islands in the South Pacific. In view of the budgetary difficulties faced by the U.S. and problems it has had with the Pacific states over fishing rights and nuclear policy, the U.S. has asked other Western powers and Japan to take greater responsibility in countering the Soviet drive.[21]

Economic Factors

There are three economic factors which led Japan to increase aid to the Pacific Island region in the 1980s. These are: development needs of the island economies, the decline of traditional donors' economic power, and the rise of aid requests to Japan.

Every Pacific island nation is, without exception, dependent upon foreign assistance for its nation-building and current economic management. Foreign aid forms an important component of government budget making. The island nations receive aid mainly from their traditional colonial powers: PNG from Australia, the Solomon Islands and Kiribati from Britain and Australia; Fiji from Australia and New Zealand; Tuvalu from Britain, Australia and New Zealand. However, in the 1980s, these island nations faced a new common problem—decreasing foreign aid from their traditional donors.

Papua New Guinea is an example. PNG has had to think seriously of diversifying its sources of aid from Australia to other nations. Australia used to provide direct financial assistance amounting to more than 60 percent of the total PNG budget, but by the late 1980s, had reduced the size of its financial assistance by 30 percent.[22] Until 1985, successive PNG governments had refused grant aid offers from Japan, believing that such aid would mainly contribute to Japan's commercial interests, and not to the development of the PNG economy.[23] However, with a reduction of Australia's financial assistance to PNG,[24] the PNG government under Paias Wingti relaxed its attitudes to Japan's grant aid and proceeded to put some development project proposals to Japan.

In the mid-1980s, it was not only PNG but also other island nations which welcomed Japan's new role in the development of the South Pacific region. In view of the economic difficulties in Australia, New Zealand, and Britain, there were increasing expectations in the Pacific that Japan should and would make more efforts to assist the economies of the small island nations. The 17th South Pacific Forum meeting held in August 1986 in Fiji endorsed Japan's growing aid role in the Pacific.

> The Forum strongly endorsed the efforts of the director in developing the dialogue with Japan and others which was called for at the Rarotonga Forum. It noted the increasing significance of Japan in helping to meet the development requirements of the Forum island countries and encouraged continuation of efforts to secure greater Japanese assistance particularly in the areas of telecommunication, regional shipping and assistance to the smaller island countries' development.[25]

New Domestic Political Factors in the 1980s

There are four major domestic political factors which help explain why Japan made the decision to increase its aid to the Pacific region during the 1980s. These are (1) the expanding ODA budget, (2) the concept of an Asia-Pacific community, (3) Nakasone's leadership and LDP factional diplomacy, and (4) bureaucratic initiatives.

The Expanding ODA Budget

As discussed in the opening chapter by Bruce Koppel and Robert Orr, successive Japanese governments made commitments to significantly increase the ODA budget. The first ODA doubling plan (a 3-year term) was initiated by Prime Minister Fukuda at the Bonn Summit meeting in 1978 when Japanese ODA was 2.2 billion dollars. After attaining the Fukuda plan goals in 1980, Japan adopted a second ODA doubling plan (a 5-year Medium-Term Target) in January 1981. Despite an increase in the national budget deficit, the ODA and defence budgets received special treatment. In September, 1985, Japan announced a third doubling plan. The third medium-term ODA target (a 7-year term) from 1986 to 1992 aimed at increasing the total amount of ODA during the seven years to more than 40 billion dollars, and to reach an ODA level in 1992 double the 1985 level. This expansion of ODA required expanding the number of projects that were candidates for ODA support. This made project identification and support in the Pacific Islands a more attractive proposition to the ODA bureaucracy, although the relatively small funding requirements of typical projects were often a source of disappointment from this perspective.

The Concept of Asia-Pacific Community

Much has been said and written about the Asia-Pacific community concept. This chapter does not deal with the historical development of this concept, which had its origins in the 1960s. It is enough to point out here that there are some common understandings about the importance of Asia-Pacific cooperation.[26] In this sense, Japan's expanded aid commitments to the Pacific reflects Japan's support for the Asia-Pacific community concept. It was Prime Minister Nakasone who made the Asia-Pacific community concept a centerpiece of his diplomacy and attempted to use it to demonstrate Japan's diplomatic role in the international community.

Nakasone's Leadership and LDP Factional Diplomacy

Yasuhiro Nakasone was the first Japanese Prime Minister to show serious concerns about the Pacific region and to visit Fiji and PNG in 1985 during his term in office. During the Nakasone government, two foreign ministers, Shintaro Abe and Tadashi Kuranari, paid official visits to the Pacific nations. It was the Nakasone government which strengthened Japan's official relations with the island nations and made major ODA commitments to the Pacific.[27]

It is possible to argue that the Nakasone government saw the Pacific as its factional sphere of influence and interests. In some Asian countries, there exist political relations between Japanese development projects and the factional activities of Japan's Liberal Democratic Party (LDP). The former Tanaka faction established its presence in China and was strong in arranging development projects there. It was also active in Indonesia. The former prime minister Shinsuke Kishi, father-in-law of Shintaro Abe, who once declared Japan's new policy towards Asia under the Abe doctrine, built his strong relations with the Southeast Asian countries through reparation programs. More recently, frequent visits by Michio Watanabe to Latin America and Indochina indicate that the Watanabe faction is establishing its factional strength through sponsoring development projects in these regions. Kanamaru's visit to North Korea in 1990 is another example. By comparison to these other areas, the Pacific was a new area of development with no traditional LDP factions having yet built their footholds there. The then Nakasone factions, now incorporated by the Watanabe faction, found the Pacific to be a new frontier for LDP factional influence through foreign aid.

Bureaucratic Initiatives

Bureaucratic initiatives in strategic alliance with domestic political support can and have acted to expand Japan's official relations with both the Pacific island nations and regional organizations in the Pacific such as the South Pacific Forum. Policy decision-makers in the Ministry of Foreign Affairs played important roles in this process. Two important sections of the ministry took the lead: the Economic Cooperation Bureau, which is responsible for ODA policy, and the Office of Oceania Affairs, which is an international relations office. Outcomes of these political and bureaucratic initiatives included the Kuranari doctrine in 1987, increased ODA flows, the creation of a new diplomatic framework between Japan and the Pacific, and support for the Tuvalu Trust Fund.

New Doctrine, New Framework, New Aid Scheme

The Kuranari Doctrine

In January 1987, Foreign Minister Kuranari[28] of the Nakasone government made official visits to Australia, New Zealand, Fiji, Vanuatu, and Papua New Guinea. At Suva, the capital city of Fiji, he delivered a speech in English outlining Japan's intentions towards the Pacific Island region. What has since been called the Kuranari Doctrine represented a statement by Japan of what it could do to assist in preserving the political stability of the Pacific islands.[29] There are five major points to the Kuranari Doctrine.

1. Japan will take every precaution not to encroach on the independence or hamper the autonomous initiatives of the Pacific Island states;
2. Japan will support and assist existing arrangements for regional cooperation among the island states;
3. Japan will do its utmost to assist in preserving the political stability of the region;
4. Japan will provide as much aid assistance as possible to make the region economically more prosperous; and
5. Japan highly values face-to-face contacts among nations and intends to promote exchange of people at all levels.

The Foreign Minister talked of Japan's political role in the region, prompted without doubt by the general concern over Soviet penetration into the Pacific region and the weakening influence of the Western powers.[30] It is important to note that Kuranari presented his diplomatic doctrine in the framework of East-West tension. It was the first speech which officially declared Japanese commitment to development issues in the Pacific island region, but linked those issues to the maintenance of political stability. This falls into the category of what Dennis Yasutomo has called "the strategic aid"[31] characteristic of Japanese ODA. It is clear that the significance of the Kuranari doctrine is definitely found in its political nature. The existence of the Kuranari doctrine explicitly indicates that Soviet encroachment in the region played a major role in making the Pacific a larger recipient of Japanese foreign aid.[32] This explicitness of this linkage was unprecedented in the history of Japanese aid policy. Successive Japanese governments had restricted themselves to economic issues in international relations generally and ODA policy specifically.

The issue of Soviet activities in the Pacific was seen in a cold war framework. After his speech in Fiji, Kuranari visited Port Villa, the capital of Vanuatu, towards which the Soviet Union was requesting landing rights for Aeroflot and offering to pay fishing license fees.[33] The Soviet approach to Vanuatu attracted international attention and alarmed Western policy-makers. This was a rather sensitive issue for Japan since Vanuatu had a plan to request Japanese aid in order to expand its airport capacity. For Japan, it would have been unacceptable that Japanese ODA would be used to expand an airstrip when the Soviet Union would be a principal beneficiary.[34]

The Kuranari doctrine was a turning-point in Japanese aid policy. It represented an indication of Japan's intentions to participate as a political actor, and through its ODA policy, in Pacific regional politics. Foreign Minister Kuranari, with strong support from within the Japanese bureaucracy, declared that Japan was prepared to contribute to political stability in regional affairs. To do this, Japan was prepared to provide foreign aid in sufficient amounts to remove destabilizing factors in the region. Kuranari also made it clear that he believed every bilateral and multilateral aid arrangement should be based on the will and request of the aid recipients. With this development philosophy, Japan was encouraged by SPF nations to play an increasing role as a principal donor in the region. More generally, political leaders in the Pacific Island region accepted the political as well as economic nature of the Kuranari doctrine and on that basis, expected Japan's continuing commitment to the region's development. Australia and the United States were also pleased.[35]

The Japan-Australia Aid Dialogue

A new ingredient in the framework for Japan's ODA to the Pacific is a series of bilateral arrangements with Australia, a donor with long developmental experience in the Pacific.[36] Since 1985, Japan and Australia have held an annual bilateral dialogue on aid programs in the Pacific region and have attempted to reach a framework of understanding on Pacific Island development issues.[37] Since Australian consulting firms have been playing major roles in the region, Japan was prepared to take advantage of these services in its aid program.[38]

Japan and Australia have developed a model for collaboration in which each donor has its own task in one big project. For example, in Western Samoa's international airport project, Japan constructed the airport building while Australia completed the construction of the airstrip.[39]

The Tuvalu Trust Fund

Tuvalu is the smallest island nation in the Pacific, with a population of 8,500. The people depend largely upon subsistence activities, mainly fishing and agriculture.[40] The public sector is the largest employer. Since Tuvalu achieved its independence from Britain in 1978, it relied upon annual recurrent budgetary support from Britain. However, the British government felt that financial support would be only a temporary measure, and that Tuvalu should overcome its heavy dependence on foreign aid and achieve a measure of economic viability.

Soon after independence, the Tuvalu government started to study the possibility of setting up a Tuvalu fund. When Tuvalu initially made a proposal to Britain in 1982, it was not accepted by Britain, mainly because the proposal only aimed to reduce the overdraft position of the Tuvalu government. By 1984, the Tuvalu government refined the proposal and broached the concept of a reserve fund. Political leaders of Tuvalu proposed the establishment of a multilateral trust fund which would be substantially self-perpetuating financially.

By 1986, Australia and New Zealand had agreed in principle to the concept of a multilateral trust fund.[41] Britain also considered supporting the scheme. With the positive assistance of the United Nations Development Programme (UNDP), a draft agreement establishing the International Trust Fund for Tuvalu was drawn up and signed on June 16, 1987 by 4 parties: Tuvalu, Australia, New Zealand, and Britain.[42]

> According to the agreement, the purposes of the fund are to support:the long-term financial viability of Tuvalu by providing an additional source of revenue for recurrent expenses of the government in order to: (a) assist the government to achieve greater financial autonomy in the management of its recurrent budget; (b) enable the government to maintain and if possible improve existing levels of social infrastructure and services; (c) enhance the capacity of the government to receive and effectively utilize external capital development and technical assistance; (d) enable the government to meet long-term maintenance and operating costs of social and economic infrastructure and services; and (e) assist the government to develop the economy of Tuvalu.[43]

Japan was not a formal signatory member and was prohibited from providing direct financial support. However, Japan contributed about $700,000 to the Tuvalu fund in 1987 through a multilateral channel of the UNDP special fund. Although Japan's financial contribution to the Tuvalu fund is relatively small compared to the other donor countries (who contributed about $24.5 million), this is still a unique aid initiative in Japanese aid policy and may be a model of budgetary-support-type aid for future Japanese aid programs towards mini-states in the Pacific, Indian Ocean, and the Caribbean region.

Conclusion

When Japan initially attempted to become involved in development projects in the Pacific island region during the 1960s and 1970s, there were several constraints which restricted Japan's regional commitment. However, new international developments in the Pacific and changes in Japan's ODA policy objectives combined to remove some constraints, and paved the way for establishing Japan's new role in the Pacific. In this process, the Kuranari doctrine represented a turning point for Japan's regional policy in the South Pacific.

However, the road ahead is not clear. Pacific island states' concerns about Japan's fishing fleets and fishing technologies, Japan's interests in ocean dumping, and the transhipment of nuclear wastes remain as sources of potential friction along with complex concerns about the impacts of expanding Japanese investment and, in some cases, tourism. While the end of the Cold War reduces the importance of the Pacific in strategic terms defined by East-West confrontation, continuing prospects for political instability in the region create concerns among Japanese policy makers for the security of important shipping lanes.

The difficulties that Japan has in finding fundable projects is complicated now by the increasing roles of the Asian Development Bank and the World Bank in the region. In effect, there are too many donors chasing too few projects. On the other hand, an increasing number of Pacific Island governments are sending missions to Tokyo in search of more Japanese aid. The Pacific islands will continue to have special importance for Japan, but Japan will find defining a role that is comfortable for all parties to be a continuing challenge.

Endnotes

1. Interview with an official of the OECF (Overseas Economic Cooperation Fund).

2. Regarding ODA yen loans to Papua New Guinea, see *OECF Nenji Hokikusho 1990* [Overseas Economic Cooperation Fund, Annual Report 1990], p. 77; Ajia Keizai Kenkyujo [The Institute of Developing Economies], *Hatten Tojoukoku hokusetu Shakkan Suishin Kisochosa: Papual Nyuginia Houkokusho* [Basic Study on the Promotion of Direct Yen Loan to Developing Countries: Papua New Guinea], 1986, commissioned by Economic Planning Agency, Tokyo. Further analysis of Papua New Guinea's economic situation can be found in Australian International Development Assistance Bureau (AIDAB), *Papua New Guinea: Economic Situation and Outlook (International Development Issue)*, No. 4, 1988; No. 5, 1989; No. 16, 1991.

3. To evaluate Fiji's economic situation, see Rodney Cole and Helen Hughes, *The Fiji Economy, May 1987: Problems and Prospects* (Canberra: National Center for Development Studies, Australian National University, 1988).

4. Kokusai Kaihatsu Senta, *Minamitaiheiyo no Toushokokka nitaisuru Wagakunino Keizaikyoryoku* [Japan's Economic Cooperation towards Island Nations in the South Pacific], 1984, commissioned by the Japanese Ministry of Foreign Affairs.

5. Kiyoaki Kikuchi, ed., *Nanboku Monai to Kaihatu Enjo* [The North-South Problem and Development Assistance], Vol. 2, 1989, p. 803.

6. Toru Yano, *Nanshin no Keifu* [Study on Japan's Movement to the South Sea], Tokyo: Chuokoron; Kenichiro Shoda, ed., *Kindai Nihon no Tonan Ajia kan* [Modern Japan's Views on Southeast Asia], Tokyo: Ajia Keizai Kenkyujo, 1978.

7. Gaimusho Baishobu [Reparation Section of Foreign Ministry], Baisho Mondai Kenkyukai [Study Group of Reparation Problems], ed., *Nishon no Baisho* [Japan's Reparation], Tokyo: Sekai Janarusha, 1963; Kashima Heiwa Kekyujo, ed., *Nihon Gaikoshi* [Japan's Diplomatic History], Vol. 30, Tokyo: Kashima Kenkyujo Shuppankai, 1972.

8. For a general account of Japan's role in the South Pacific, see: Gaimusho, *Kokusaikankei niokeru Minamitaiheiyo no Chii* [The Position of the South Pacific in International Relations], 1979; Alan Rix, "Japan's Role in the South Pacific Region," *Australian Foreign Affairs Record*, June 1981.

9. See, Akio Watanabe, "Minamitaiheiyo no Kokusaiseijijouno Chii" [The South Pacific in the International Politics], *Kokusai Mondai*, No. 284, November 1983; Terutaro Nishino, "Taiheiyo Toshokoku to Nihon" [The Pacific Islands Nations and Japan], *Ibid.*; Isami Takeda, "Kawaru Niho no Taigaienjo to Minamitaiheiyo Chiiki" [Japan's Changing Foreign Aid Policy to the South Pacific Region], *Toa Asia Monthly* (published by Kazan kai), February 1987; Gaimusho, *Hachiju nendai no Wagakuni Taiyoushu Gaiko* [Japan's Diplomacy to Oceania in 1980s], 1981. To compare Japanese aid approach with Australia's one, see Nancy Viviani, "Australia and Japan: Approaches to Development Assistance Policy," *Research paper* (Australia Japan Research Centre, Australian National University), No. 37, 1976.

10. Robert C. Kiste, "The Island States as Actors in the Region," H. Albinski, R. Herr, R. Kiste, R. Babbage, and D. McLean, *The South Pacific: Political, Economic, and Military Trends* (Washington, D.C.: Brassey's, 1989), Izumi Kobayashi, "Kaiyo no mattadanakano Kuniguni" [Nations in the Midst of

Pacific Ocean], A. Masuda, ed., *Taiheiyo Kyoudoutai* [The Pacific Community], Tokyo: Hara Shobu, 1989.

11. Regarding Australian involvement in the Pacific, see Isami Takeda, "Osutoraria no Minamitaiheiyo kanyoto Chiiki Seisaku no Tenkai" [Australia's Commitment to the South Pacific Region and Its Regional Policy], in K. Miwa and T. Nishino, eds., *Oceania: Toshokoku to Taikoku* [Oceania: Islands and Powers], Tokyo: Sairyu sha, 1990; Joint Committee on Foreign Affairs, Defence and Trade, *Australia's Relations with the South Pacific* (Canberra: Australian Government Publications Service, 1989).

12. Australian consultants were located in numerous senior positions in the PNG government, as were other expatriates. In addition, many District officers were Australian.

13. If the Cook Islands, entering into free association with the New Zealand government in 1965, are included, the number of independent nations was only three in the 1960s.

14. Interview with Japanese consultants and JICA officials.

15. Hamish McDonald, "Checking the Soviets: Nakasone Prepares for a Southern Initiative," *Far Eastern Economic Review*, Vol. 134, (October 2, 1986). pp. 26-27.

16. Research Institute of Peace and Security, *Asian Security 1986* (London: Brassey's, 1987), pp. 142-44.

17. Thomas-Durell Young, "U.S. Policy and the South and Southwest Pacific," *Asian Survey*, (1988) Vol. XXVIII, No. 7, pp. 775-88. The United States maintained an attitude of "benign neglect" towards the region. See: Thomas A. Layman, "Southwest Pacific-U.S. Economic Relations: Issues and Options," *Asian Survey*, (1987) Vol. XXVII, No. 10, pp. 1127-44.

18. *Nihon Keizai Shimbun*, August 27, 1986 (morning ed.).

19. Gaimusho, *Wagakuni no Seifu Kaihatsu Enjo* [Japan's ODA], 1989, Vol. 2, p. 746.

20. W.L. Brooks and R.M. Orr, Jr., "Japan's Foreign Economic Assistance," *Asian Survey*, (1985) Vol. XXV, No. 3, pp. 322-40.

21. Nayan Chanda, "No More Free Rides: The U.S. Wants Japan to Play a Major Political Role," *Far Eastern Economic Review*, Vol. 134, (October 2, 1986), pp. 27-28.

22. *Report from the Committee to Review the Australian Overseas Aid Program (The Jackson Report)*, (Canberra: Australian Government Publications Service, 1984).

23. Hiroshi Aoki, "Minamitaiheiyo: Papua Nyuginia" [The South Pacific: Papua New Guinea], *Asahi Shimbun*, September 2, 1987 (morning ed.).

24. *Nihon Keizai Shimbun*, August 16, 1989 (morning ed.).

25. The 17th South Pacific Forum Communique (News Release, Department of Foreign Affairs, Australia), Suva, Fiji, August 11, 1986.

26. Isami Takeda, "Jokyo toshiteno Ajia Taiheiyo Kyoryoku" [Asia-Pacific Cooperation Situation: The First Stage of Political Development Process], paper read at the National Conference, the Japan Association of Political Science, October 7, 1989.

27. Nakasone's attitudes to the South Pacific are assessed in: "Japan's Nakasone States Isle Policies," *Pacific Magazine (Hawaii)*, October 1986, pp. 62-64.

28. Kuranari is one of the few Japanese politicians to be seriously concerned about Pacific Island affairs. Kuranari started his career in 1951 as a bureaucrat in the Nagasaki local government where he was in charge of remote islands' development affairs. He was an prime advocate of the remote islands development bill which was passed as an act (Ritou-Shinkou-Hou) in July, 1953.

29. For a brief explanation of this doctrine by a Japanese government official, see: Kenji Kanasugi, "Japanese Aid Policy in the South Pacific Region," *Pacific Economic Bulletin* (Australian National University, National Center for Development Studies), Vol. 3, No. 1, 1988, pp. 44-45.

30. *Nihon Keizai Shimbun*, January 6, 1987 (morning ed.). As early as 1985, K. Arai, the then Bureau Chief of Information and Research, in the Japanese Ministry of Foreign Affairs, admitted openly at the research committee on diplomacy and security (House of Councilors) that "the Soviet intentions in the South Pacific is considerably political" and expressed the view that the West should be prepared to guard against the Soviet activities. *Yomiuri Shimbun*, October 9, 1985 (early morning ed.).

31. Dennis T. Yasutomo, *The Manner of Giving: Strategic Aid and Japanese Foreign Policy* (Lexington: Lexington Books, 1986).

32. The Tass News Agency of the Soviet Union criticized the Kuranari visit to the South Pacific as having anti-Soviet motives. *Nihon Keizai Shimbun*, January 6, 1987 (evening ed.).

33. *The Australian*, September 5, 1986.

34. Kuranari later recalled that when he was flying to Vanuatu as the first Japanese foreign minister to visit there, he felt somewhat nervous about his visit given various international political factors. See: Tadashi Kuranari, *Ayausano nakano Nihon Gaiko* [Japanese Diplomacy in Crisis], Tokyo: Shogaku kan, 1988, p. 70.

35. George Shultz, then Secretary of State, also signaled U.S. support for the Kuranari initiative in the Pacific. "U.S. Pleased," *The Japan Times*, January 16, 1987. See also: Robert M. Orr, Jr., *The Emergence of Japan's Foreign Aid Power*, p. 90.

36. Australian Foreign Minister Bill Hayden welcomed Japan's aid commitments to the Pacific. *Nihon Keizai Shimbun*, January 10, 1987 (morning ed.).

37. D. Humphries, "Australia, Japan to Link on Pacific Aid Program," *The Age*, September 9, 1989. The first meeting was held at Canberra in August 1985. *Asahi Shimbun*, August 24, 1985 (morning ed.). The early policy proposal appeared in a report on Australia-Japan relations, commissioned by the Japanese Ministry of Foreign Affairs. See, Yujiro Eguchi, "Minamitaiheiyo womeguru Nichigo Kankei" [Japan-Australia Relations on the South Pacific] in Gaimusho, ed., *Hachiju nendaino Nichigo Kankei* (Japan-Australia Relations in 1980s), 1980, pp. 192-204. The Japan Australia aid dialogue on the Pacific supplements aid dialogues with New Zealand and the United States which also have relevance for the Pacific.

38. Isami Takeda, "Japan Seeks Aid Joint Venture," *The Canberra Times*, August 25, 1988.

39. Isami Takeda, "South Pacific as Testing Ground," *The Japan Times*, January 18, 1987.

40. For the country profile, see Australian International Development Assistance Bureau (AIDAB), *Tuvalu Country Paper*, March 1990.

41. For a detailed account of the scheme, see: Department of Foreign Affairs, Australia, *Tuvalu Trust Fund Appraisal Study*, July 1986.

42. Regarding a general evaluation of Trust Fund, see D. McManus, "The Mouse that Roared," *Pacific Islands Monthly*, April 1990, p. 19.

43. Tuvalu government report, *Tuvalu Trust Fund*, April 1990, p. 4.

12

WHY AID AND WHY NOT? JAPAN AND SUB-SAHARAN AFRICA

Ichiro Inukai

Introduction

There are 45 developing nations in the region of Sub-Saharan Africa (SSA).[1] All countries, except for Ethiopia and Liberia, have attained their independence one after another since the late 1950s, and the decolonization of Sub-Saharan Africa as a whole was finally completed with the independence of Namibia in March 1990. Although Japan has established its diplomatic relationships with each of these new nations, the economic relationships between Japan and these countries are relatively insignificant as compared to its massive economic inroads into the countries in East and Southeast Asia.

Until the end of the 1960s, Sub-Saharan Africa received low priority in Japan's bilateral official development assistance (ODA). However, as Japan grew to become a major industrial power, it sharply increased its bilateral ODA to Sub-Saharan Africa. The net disbursements to SSA expanded from eight million dollars in 1970, to $223 million in 1980, and further to $1.04 billion in 1989. Its share in Japan's total ODA rose from 2.2% in 1970 to 15.3% in 1988. By the beginning of the 1990s, Japan had become among the top five donors in Sub-Saharan Africa.[2]

The emergence of Japan as a major donor in Sub-Saharan Africa raises two contrasting questions: "Why is Japan in Africa?" and "Why is Japan not in Africa?" The first question is primarily concerned with the motivation of Japan's ODA to Sub-Saharan Africa. Japan is a newcomer to the SSA region but is having a strong influence on political and economic affairs in the region where previously only the Western powers had been playing important roles in development assistance. The second question, why is Japan not in Africa, is mainly concerned with the magnitude of Japan's ODA to Sub-Saharan Africa. It assumes that Japan, as an economic superpower in the world, should provide more ODA to alleviate the poverty and hunger prevailing in SSA. As will be seen, these two questions are closely related to each other.

According to the official explanation concerning Japan's increased aid to the developing countries as a whole, five points are given. They are Japan's (1) status as an economic superpower; (2) position as the world's leading creditor nation; (3) high external dependence on natural resources; (4) position as a peaceful nation; and (5) status as a non-Western developed nation.[3] According to this explanation, Japan's ODA is based upon recognition of interdependence in the context of North-South relations and humanitarian concerns about the poor living standards of people in the South. It stresses that aid to Africa is based primarily on humanitarian considerations, particularly concerns about poverty and hunger. This approach does not exclude the possibility that countries with which Japan has closer bilateral relationships will be given special consideration.

Bilateral ODA is undoubtedly one of the principal diplomatic instruments through which political relationships between a donor and a recipient country can be cemented. However, Japan provides its ODA unevenly to the countries in the SSA region. What are the criteria for the distribution of its ODA? Examining this question may offer answers to the two questions. "Why is Japan in Africa?" And "Why is Japan not in Africa?"

Why Is Japan in Africa?

Bilateral ODA is a matter of inter-governmental relationships. When the former African colonies of the European powers began to attain independence one after another in the late 1950s, Japan quickly opened diplomatic relations with the governments of the new born nations. Broadly speaking, however, Japan's economic inroads into the new nations of Sub-Saharan Africa had different features in each of the subsequent three decades. It is possible to argue that the characteristics of Japan's expanded presence in Sub-Saharan Africa are the result of the interactions of the following three factors: (1) Japan's own economic growth, (2) the economic and social problems of the countries in Sub-Saharan Africa, and (3) the general political and economic international environment surrounding both Japan and the countries in Sub-Saharan Africa.

The 1960s

In the beginning of the 1960s, Japan was still considered to be one of the developing countries, but, by the end of the decade, it emerged as one of the major industrial nations. During the 1960s, Japan allocated its ODA almost exclusively to Asia, in particular Southeast Asia. At that time, it was the former suzerain countries—France, the United Kingdom, and Belgium in particular—and the European countries, in general, that offered financial and technical assistance to the new nations in Sub-Saharan Africa.

Japan had few economic relations with Africa during the period of European colonial rule. After the colonies attained independence, one after another, the region appeared to be a promising export market for diversified manufactured goods from Japan. Thus, Japan rapidly increased both the volume and variety of the goods exported to the region. At that time, however, the economic relationships between Japan and the new nations in Sub-Saharan Africa were constrained by the colonial heritage of trade restrictions. The former suzerain states imposed an import restrictive policy applying GATT Article 35 against Japan. Article 35 permits poorer developing countries to utilize discriminatory import restrictions to protect their balance of payments positions. Although Ghana and the Federation of Rhodesia and Nyasaland (now Zimbabwe and Zambia) withdrew the restriction in March 1963 and in August 1963, respectively, the rest of the new countries in Sub-Saharan Africa, in particular the French-speaking countries, continued to apply restrictive trade practices against Japan. Therefore, it was an urgent matter for Japan's trade expansion to encourage them to revise their trade policies.[4]

It should be noted that despite these restrictions, the Japan-SSA economic relationships were characterized by one-way trade in favor of Japan. Protests against this trade imbalance gained momentum to such an extent that a number of African countries began to adopt a policy of import-banning against Japan. The case of Ghana illustrates this problem. Ghana, which achieved independence on 6 March 1957, continued to apply GATT Article 35 against Japan. It was in this situation that for the first time, the government of Japan began to think that it must provide economic cooperation to Sub-Saharan Africa in order to make inroads into the African markets.[5]

Facing strong protests against its trade surpluses from Ghana, Nigeria, Kenya, Tanzania, and Uganda, Japan decided to offer yen loans and technical cooperation to these countries. Thus, in 1966, Japan provided loans of two billion yen each to Kenya and Tanzania, a one billion yen loan to Uganda, and a 10.8 billion yen loan to Nigeria. On the other hand, in 1968, Japan decided to reschedule Ghana's commercial credits amounting to $5.2 million.[6] In terms of technical cooperation, Japan offered grant-aid assistance for the establishment of the Ghana Textile Industry Training Center, the Kenya Industrial Training Institute, and the Uganda Vocational Training Center in the mid-1960s.[7] All this assistance ended up further promoting Japan's exports to these countries since the assistance was tied to procurement from Japan.

Sub-Saharan Africa embraces a number of resource-rich countries. Japan's private capital sought opportunities to expand its development-cum-import schemes in order to make the region an important additional source of raw materials for Japan in the future. Toward the end of the 1960s, Japanese trade missions seemed to be in almost perpetual circulation around the African capitals.[8] It was thought that the promotion of ODA to Sub-Saharan Africa would help Japan expand its markets and secure necessary resource supplies. However, the Japanese government at that time did not have a clear policy concerning the use of ODA for economic development in the Sub-Saharan Africa countries. Instead Japan held a view that private direct investments should be the most effective means for economic cooperation and that ODA would be used for preparing a politically conducive environment for private investment in recipient SSA countries.[9]

It can be concluded that in the 1960s the initial Japanese economic thrust to Africa was made by private businesses through trade and investment. ODA was used for making the political and economic environments more conducive to private sector entry to and activities in the region. In this sense, the trinity of aid, investment, and trade functioned in Sub-Saharan Africa as it did in Asia.

The 1970s

In 1970, growing interest in Africa within Japan took concrete forms.

> The Federation of Economic Organizations, the country's most powerful business organization, has set up a special Africa Committee while among members of the Diet (Parliament) an

"association for economic co-operation and development in Africa" has been established to concentrate interest with the political world.[10]

In February 1970, a high-powered group including eight top executives from Japanese industry did the rounds in nine Sub-Saharan African countries (Ethiopia, Kenya, Tanzania, Zambia, Congo, Nigeria, Ghana, the Ivory Coast, and Senegal). Before the trip, Humihiko Kono, chairman of Mitsubishi Heavy Industries and the leader of the mission, clearly stated its objective as follows: "We have tried every possible means in Southeast Asia. If there were any new world left for Japan, it is none but Africa."[11] After the trip to Africa, he reached the following conclusion:

> If Japan really wants to approach Africa with the consideration of the importance of underground resources of Africa, Japan must extend fairly substantial economic aid to these countries. At present the African nations are friendly towards Japan. However, this can well change if Japan fails to show its sincere attitude concerning its economic aid to them because other advanced countries of the world have been giving assistance on a large scale."[12]

The Japanese government's actions towards Sub-Saharan Africa in the 1970s began with a strong concern to remove the trade barriers prevailing in a number of the new African countries. In order to request them to withdraw the application of GATT Article 35 and other restrictive policies against Japan, two government missions were dispatched to Sub-Saharan Africa. The first went to French-speaking countries in April 1971, and the second went to English-speaking countries in April 1972.

The 1973 Oil Crisis demonstrated the power of resource nationalism. North-south relationships entered a new phase of confrontation in a number of international arenas. The Fourth Summit of the Non-Aligned Countries held in Algiers adopted the *Economic Declaration and Action Programme for Economic Co-operation* on 9 September 1973; the *Declaration on the Establishment of a New International Economic Order (NIEO)* was adopted at the 6th Special General Assembly of the United Nations on 1 May 1974; and the *Charter of Economic Rights and Duties of the States* was also adopted by the 29th General Assembly of the United Nations on 12 December 1974. In these international arenas, Sub-Saharan Africa, as a developing region embracing more than 40 countries, displayed significant solidarity.

The initial mood of confrontation between the North and the South turned to one of cooperation and accommodation at the Seventh Special United Nations General Assembly in 1975, which adopted by consensus the *Declaration on Development and International Economic Cooperation* on 16 September 1975. The Conference on International Economic Cooperation in 1977 reaffirmed the political necessity of improving cooperation between developed and developing countries.[13]

After the confrontation, cooperation, and accommodations of the early 1970s, the international community experienced widely diverse development processes in the latter half of the decade. The North became a tripolar world represented by the United States, Japan, and the European Economic Community, while the South diversified into a number of groups ranging from a cluster of least developed countries (LLDCs) to a group of Newly Industrializing Economies (NIEs). Economic stagnation of the newly independent countries in Sub-Saharan Africa changed the outlook of the region from a region of promising young nations in the 1960s to a cluster of LLDCs by the end of the 1970s. According to the Organization for Economic Cooperation and Development, out of 45 of the "most seriously affected countries by the oil crisis, 27 countries were in Sub-Saharan Africa, while 17 of the 29 LLDCs were also concentrated in Sub-Saharan Africa."[14]

The donor community therefore began to pay special attention to increasing economic assistance to Sub-Saharan Africa, and expected Japan, as a major economic power, to allocate more ODA to Sub-Saharan Africa. Responding to these international concerns, Japan changed its policy for the regional distribution of ODA during the latter part of the 1970s. In 1970, 93.3% of Japan's ODA went to Asia with 3.3% to the Middle East and 2.3% to Africa. However, by 1980, 70.6% went to Asia with 2.5% to the Middle East and 18.9% to Africa according to MITI's regional classification.[15]

There are a number of factors responsible for this change in the distribution of Japan's ODA. First, by 1980, Japan had become the second biggest economic power next to the United States, and also the second largest donor among DAC member countries. Japan could no longer maintain a low posture in development cooperation to the most impoverished region in the Third World. Japan had to strengthen its contributions to the economic and social development of developing countries in order to fulfill its responsibility as a major developed country as well as in order to secure its own long-term prosperity and peace.[16]

Secondly, Japan recognized the diplomatic importance of Sub-Saharan Africa in international arenas. By the mid-1970s, the number of countries in Sub-Saharan Africa increased to 42. The solidarity among the nations in Sub-Saharan Africa was having a growing influence on the handling of important problems, both political and economic, at many international meetings, such as the United Nations General Assembly (UNGA) and the United Nations Conference on Trade and Development (UNCTAD).

Thirdly, resource nationalism among developing countries was reaffirming Japan's vulnerability as a resource-poor country. As the Japanese economy grows, the more dependent is Japan on external resources. The 1973 Diplomatic Blue Book stressed that economic cooperation for the development of natural resources should be mutually beneficial for Japan and the resource-rich African countries as well.[17] This policy was more clearly stated as follows: "The economic cooperation should help Japan secure the steady supply of resources and energy which are necessary to keep its economy moving."[18] According to Richard Synge:

> Africa's interest for Japan is in its extensive raw materials for industry. The current thrust of Japanese policy is to get a share in as many mining consortiums as possible, thereby overcome their disadvantage vis-a-vis established French, Belgian, British and American corporations.[19]

Fourthly, it should not be overlooked that the tragic food crisis in Africa in the early 1970s attracted global humanitarian concern. Japan offered its first food aid to Ethiopia in March 1974, and to the Sahelian countries (Senegal, Mali, Mauritania, Burkina Faso, Chad, and Niger) in 1975. In fact, Japan was alarmed at the seriousness of the poverty and hunger prevailing in Sub-Saharan Africa, and began to provide economic assistance on the basis of humanitarian concern to Africa. "One cannot remain aloof and indifferent to such suffering, and in such compelling urges can we find the spiritual fuel the fires engine of economic cooperation."[20] Denis Yasutomo comments that Japan's ODA to Sub-Saharan Africa is largely based on humanitarian concerns.[21] This tendency began with the Sahel food crisis, and continued into the 1980s.

Fifth, Japan's handling of the political and economic problems related to the international sanctions against Apartheid in South Africa and the racist minority rule in Rhodesia (later Zimbabwe) was under bitter criticism by many African countries. Although the Government of Japan declared a policy of economic and political sanctions against South Africa, Japanese private businesses continued to violate the international economic sanctions.[22] An increase in ODA was politically necessary to at least partly accommodate the strong protests of African countries.

During the 1970s, there was a transition in African reactions to Japan's foreign policy towards Sub-Saharan Africa from passive reactions to protests on trade imbalances and Japan's South African policy. This encouraged Japan to a more active voluntary involvement in African affairs. During the 1970s, there were two official visits by Japan's Foreign Minister to Sub-Saharan Africa. The Kimura Mission of 1974 to Ghana, Nigeria, Zaire, Tanzania, and Egypt was the first official travel of a Japanese Foreign Minister to Sub-Saharan Africa. The second was the Sonoda Mission to Nigeria, the Ivory Coast, Senegal, Tanzania, and Kenya in 1979. Although both of these high-powered government missions took place in the years following the 1973 and 1978 oil crises, their objectives were much wider than the narrowly defined economic interest of Japan.[23]

The 1980s

The World economy in the 1980s began on a low ebb. Recessions among the DAC countries generated a sense of "aid fatigue" in the early 1980s.[24] However, the sustained growth of the Japanese economy allowed Japan to increase its ODA. As a result, Japan exceeded by a wide margin the target set in 1978 of doubling ODA in U.S. dollars between 1977 and 1980. Public opinion in Japan was in favor of economic cooperation to the developing countries. A 1983 poll on future economic cooperation showed that around 40% were in favor of increasing ODA as compared to 7% for reducing it.[25]

In order to deal with uncertainty in the global economic outlook in the 1980s and also to manage an increased degree of interdependent relationships with both the developed and developing countries, economic cooperation was seen as an effective measure for Japan's economic security. The then Prime Minister Zenko Suzuki established the Ministerial Council of Comprehensive Security in December 1980. The Diplomatic Blue Book of 1981 outlined the concept of comprehensive national security as follows:

> Although the objective of Japan's economic cooperation is stabilizing and improving the people's welfare in the developing countries, the government will implement the economic cooperation on the basis of Japan's own initiatives which will be determined by taking into account diplomatic, political and economic considerations in order that Japan can ensure and maintain its own comprehensive national security.[26]

This principle made it possible for Japan to accommodate the external pressures which urged Japan to diversify the regional distribution of its ODA. Because the maintenance of close relationships with the United States has been one of the elements of utmost importance in Japan's foreign policy, analysts have argued that Japan's ODA allocation favors those countries where the American government places strategic importance.[27] From this perspective, it can be argued that Japan engages in strategic ODA, that is, aid to supplement the American strategic aid programs in "the front line states" of regional conflicts.[28] However, this interpretation does not fit well with Japan's ODA to Sub-Saharan Africa.

Two decisive events were taking place in the Sub-Saharan region in the early 1980s. First, the last decolonization struggles in Southern Africa, specifically in Zimbabwe, Mozambique, Angola, and Namibia, resulted in closer relations with the USSR and the People's Republic of China. Since Southern Africa has been one of the major suppliers of rare minerals to Japanese industries, Japan could not remain aloof from political developments in the region.

More importantly, however, the extremely severe drought and famine which affected vast areas of Sub-Saharan Africa from the Sahel to Eastern and Southern Africa in 1983-85 awakened again Japanese humanitarian concerns. Scenes of famine and starvation came into the living rooms of Japanese families through the media of television. Many Japanese responded quickly to the urgent need for emergency food relief. Waves of relief fund-raising campaigns sprang up all over the country. Human compassion went to such an extent that many primary school children sacrificed their own lunches in order to donate food to famine-stricken African people.[29] Although the enthusiasm was short-lived as the news coverage on the African famine disappeared from the mainstream of news coverage, it greatly supported the government's attempts to take initiatives in economic cooperation to Sub-Saharan Africa.

The 39th UNGA adopted the *Declaration on the Critical Economic Situation* in Africa on 3 December 1984. Japan welcomed the opportunity to serve, at the request of African countries, as coordinator of consultations and to work for the adoption by consensus of that historic declaration. At that UNGA, Shintaro Abe, the then Minister of Foreign Affairs, made a strong appeal in his speech, "Urgent Appeal for Assistance to Africa." He stressed the critical importance of assisting Africa for medium- and long-term economic development. When the Special Session of the UNGA on the Critical Situation in Africa was held in New York in May 1986, Saburo Okita, Head of the

Japanese delegation to the Assembly, announced Japan's continued and expanded economic assistance to Africa.

Why Japan Is in Africa

Japan has no political ambitions in Sub-Saharan Africa and its economic relationships with Sub-Saharan Africa are of minor importance to its own economic prosperity. The cumulative total of Japan's direct investments in Sub-Saharan Africa during 1951-88 was $2.5 billion which accounted for only 2.4% of the total overseas investments of Japan during this period. In 1988, SSA's share in Japan's total exports was only 0.9%, and SSA's share in Japan's imports was only 0.8%.[30]

Japan's increased presence in Sub-Saharan Africa, therefore, cannot be explained by the traditional trinity of aid, investment, and trade in North-South relations. No single-factor explanations can provide a valid answer to the question: "Why is Japan in Africa?" Although the manifold economic and social handicaps of Sub-Saharan Africa have been accepted as a major challenge to the international development assistance community since 1960, Japan was still a minor donor in the 1960s. In the 1970s, Japan acquired a capacity to extend its ODA to Sub-Saharan Africa. In the 1980s, the poverty-hunger crisis in Sub-Saharan Africa compelled Japan to join its economic power with collective international assistance to alleviate the suffering of the people in that region. Thus, the evolution of Japan's ODA to Sub-Saharan Africa reflects not only economic concerns primarily associated with natural resources and export markets, but also the humanitarian concerns of the Japanese people and of a government policy backed by popular support.

Why Is Japan Not in Africa?

Sub-Saharan Africa was marginal in Japan's ODA until the mid-1970s. In 1969, net disbursements of Japan's ODA to SSA were $4 million. This accounted for only 1.1% of the total net disbursement in that year. As Table 12.1 shows, in 1974, Japan started to take Sub-Saharan Africa more seriously in its regional allocation of ODA. The volume of net disbursements of bilateral ODA to Sub-Saharan Africa more than quadrupled from $8 million in 1970 to $36 million in 1974, when Japan's Foreign Minister visited Sub-Saharan Africa for the first time. It sharply increased further to $187 million in 1979 when the

Foreign Minister's second mission to Sub-Saharan Africa took place. From 1980 to 1989 it increased from $223 million to $1,040 million, reaching 15.3% of Japan's total bilateral ODA by 1989. Because of this rapid increase in the net disbursements of ODA, Japan became one of the major bilateral donors to the region. In terms of its share in total DAC ODA to Sub-Saharan Africa, Japan increased its rank from 8th in 1980 to 7th in 1985, to 5th in 1986, and 1987, and to 4th in 1988 accounting for 9% of the total DAC ODA to Sub-Saharan Africa.

TABLE 12.1 Japan's Bilateral ODA to SSA, 1969–1989 (net disbursements, US$ millions and percentage)

Year	ODA to SSA	SSA's Share
1969	4	1.1
1970	8	2.2
1971	13	2.9
1972	5	1.0
1973	18	2.4
1974	36	4.1
1975	59	6.9
1976	46	6.1
1977	56	6.3
1978	105	6.9
1979	187	9.7
1980	223	11.4
1981	211	9.3
1982	268	11.3
1983	261	10.8
1984	212	8.7
1985	252	9.9
1986	418	10.9
1987	518	9.9
1988	884	13.4
1989	1,040	15.3
1990	792	11.4

Source: Gaimusho, *Wagakuni*, 1989, 1990, 1991.

The modalities of Japan's ODA to Sub-Saharan Africa also changed. Japan placed greater emphasis on grant-aid to Sub-Saharan Africa in the 1980s. The cumulative total of ODA to Sub-Saharan Africa as of 1979 amounted to 183.4 billion yen, of which yen loans accounted for 154.6 billion yen or 84% of the total. This meant grant-aid consisted of only 28.8 billion yen or 16% of the total ODA to Sub-Saharan Africa. In the period 1980-88, however, the cumulative total of ODA increased to 638.8 billion yen and the share of grant-aid exceeded that of yen loans: 59% for grant-aid and 41% for loan-aid.

TABLE 12.2 Priority Countries in Japan's ODA to SSA: Cumulative Total Bilateral ODA as of FY1988 (in billion yen)

Country	*Loans*	*Grants*	*Technical Aid*	*Grant Subtotal*	*Total*
Total	484.4	442.6	114.2	556.8	1,041.1
Kenya	83.4	31.8	26.0	57.7	141.2
Tanzania[a]	38.2	39.9	16.1	56.0	94.2
Zambia	49.5	28.9	16.1	56.0	94.2
Nigeria	68.7	7.2	5.5	12.7	81.4
Ghana	47.0	20.8	8.1	28.9	75.9
Sudan[a]	10.7	55.9	3.5	59.4	70.2
Zaire	39.1	17.3	5.5	22.8	61.9
Madagascar	27.1	16.6	2.1	18.7	45.8
Senegal	6.6	25.3	5.2	30.6	37.1
Malawi[a]	16.6	7.0	6.4	13.4	30.3
Somalia[a]	6.6	15.6	8.0	23.6	30.2
Niger[a]	3.2	21.5	2.3	23.8	27.0
Guinea[a]	12.1	8.1	2.0	10.1	22.2
Mozambique[a]	4.0	16.1	0.2	16.3	20.3
Zimbabwe	6.6	10.9	1.4	12.3	18.9
Share in each modality (%)					
First 5	59.2	29.1	56.3	34.6	46.1
Second 5	20.7	27.6	19.9	26.0	23.6
Third 5	6.7	16.3	11.2	15.5	11.4
Remaining 30	13.4	27.0	12.6	23.9	18.9
Total	100.0	100.0	100.0	100.0	100.0
Structure of modalities (%)					
First 5	59.8	26.9	13.4	40.2	100.0
Second 5	40.9	49.8	9.3	59.1	100.0
Third 5	27.4	60.9	11.7	72.6	100.0
Remaining 30	32.4	60.6	6.7	68.3	100.0

Note: This table includes Sudan.
[a]Indicates LLDC.
Source: Gaimusho, *Wagakuni*,1989.

Another interesting point about the modality of Japan's ODA to Sub-Saharan Africa is that the share of yen loans in total ODA is lower for countries in Sub-Saharan Africa that receive less ODA. On average, yen loans represent 60% of all Japanese ODA for the top five recipient countries, 41% for the second five, and 23% for the third five (Table 12.2). The bottom ten countries received no yen loans but a small amount of grant-aid only.[31]

One of the measures of the quality of ODA is the grant share (grant-aid/total ODA ratio). According to DAC's estimate, the grant share of Japan's total bilateral ODA in 1987-88 was 29.8% compared to the DAC average of 71.1%.[32] However, as far as Japan's ODA to Sub-Saharan Africa is concerned, the grant share increased from 52.9% in 1987 to 72% in 1988, which is comparable to that of the DAC average.[33] In fact, 14 Sub-Saharan African countries received 100% in grant-aid in their cumulative total receipts of Japan's ODA as of 1988. In Japan's ODA disbursements to 44 Sub-Saharan African countries in 1988, 30 countries received grant aid alone.[34] Most of these are small countries with less than 10 million people each. The sectoral distribution of general grant-aid in FY 1988 was 46% for agriculture, 36% for Public Welfare and Improvement of the Environment, and 33% for Communication and Transportation.[35] In providing grant-aid to Sub-Saharan Africa, Japan has emphasized such areas as public welfare, improved provision of water supply for household use, communication and transportation (including rural electrification and the construction of rural roads), and agriculture, with an emphasis on irrigation.

In May 1987, Japan decided to introduce untied non-project grant-aid in the package of "Emergency Economic Measures." This is an innovation in Japan's ODA and has three special features. First, procurement of goods and services with aid funds is not restricted to Japanese sources. Second, it is disbursed fast. Third, it is explicitly intended to help poor countries buy urgently-needed imports of spare parts or raw materials. The objective of this non-project grant program was to support structural adjustment programs in African countries and LLDCs by providing around 61.7 billion yen over the three-year period from FY 1987 to FY 1989.[36] Under this program, a total of 26 African countries received non-project grant-aid amounting to 61.7 billion yen. This became the largest single component of grant-aid offered to Sub-Saharan Africa in the period 1987-89. Japan has decided to extend an additional 600 million yen of non-project assistance for the period 1990-92.[37]

Sub-Saharan Africa's share in total DAC bilateral ODA increased from 23.3% in 1975/76 to 32.6% in 1987/88. However, there has been a substantial variation in percentage distribution of ODA to Sub-

Saharan Africa among the individual DAC countries. The countries which allocated more than 50% of bilateral ODA to Sub-Saharan Africa in 1987/88 were Ireland (95%), Belgium (75%), Norway (67%), Italy (66%), Finland (65%), Denmark (64%), Sweden (62%), and France (52%). The United Kingdom and Switzerland distributed about 48-49% of their ODA to Sub-Saharan Africa. Generally speaking, it is the European countries which have given highest priority to Sub-Saharan Africa in the distribution of their ODA. This is understandable because of their historical, geographical, and economic linkages with the countries in Sub-Saharan Africa.[38] Japan, like Australia and New Zealand, is geographically far distant from the African continent, and between Japan and Africa are the vast developing regions of East, Southeast, and West Asia with which Japan has had to maintain close political and economic relationships. It is natural for Japan to be occupied with these developing regions as Australia and New Zealand have been occupied maintaining close political and economic relationships with the new nations in the South Pacific.

"Why is Japan not in Africa?" This question is derived from an expectation that Japan should be able to further increase its share of ODA to Sub-Saharan Africa. Japan, at the end of the 1980s, became the second largest economic power and the top donor among the DAC countries and there have been rising expectations about Japan's role in combating Third World development crises. For example, J. Robbinson III says, "We need a new Marshal Plan - a Global Security Initiative... No nation is better positioned to spearhead the Global Security Initiative than Japan."[39] E.V.K. Jaycox, Vice President of the World Bank, argued that:

> We commend Japan on having increased its assistance to Sub-Saharan Africa in recent years...But given the special challenges facing Africa, and considering the potential that now exists to make a development breakthrough there, I believe that Japan could be an even bigger friend to Africa.[40]

General Olusegun Obasanjo, the former Head of State of Nigeria, claims that at least 25 percent of the Japanese ODA should be allocated to Africa.[41]

On the other hand, Japan can no longer say that it is unable to expand its ODA to Sub-Saharan Africa because it has neither sufficient interactions with nor knowledge of Africa. With economic cooperation with SSA countries lasting almost three decades by 1992, Japan had dispatched 5,814 experts for development studies and surveys; 3,268 members of Japanese Overseas Cooperation Volunteers; 2,058 experts in various technical cooperation programs to the region; and received 5,408 trainees from the Sub-Saharan African countries.[42]

In fact, by the late 1980s, Japan had become one of the major donors to a number of the countries in Sub-Saharan Africa. In 1987, for example, Japan ranked as the top donor in Nigeria, Zambia, Malawi, and Kenya. The top five countries in Japan's ODA to Sub-Saharan Africa are Kenya, Tanzania, Zambia, Nigeria, and Ghana, and these five countries, as a whole, received nearly 46% of the cumulative total ODA to Sub-Saharan Africa as of FY 1988 (Table 12.2). The next top five recipients are Sudan, Zaire, Madagascar, Senegal, and Malawi. The aggregate total of these top 10 countries account for 70% of the total ODA to Sub-Saharan Africa. The rest of Japan's ODA was thinly dispersed over the remaining 35 countries.[43]

Table 12.3 reveals how Japan expanded its ODA to a number of selected countries in Sub-Saharan Africa. For example, Japan was the fourth leading donor to Nigeria in 1986 but rose to become the top donor in 1987 and 1988. Its share in total DAC bilateral ODA to Nigeria has steadily increased from 10.9% in 1986 to 35.3% in 1987 and further to 55.3% in 1988. In the same year the share of Japan in total DAC bilateral ODA exceeded 20% in Nigeria, Ghana, Kenya, Zambia, and Malawi. In the second group of five countries, Japan was the second largest donor among the DAC countries.

Examining Table 12.2, which shows Japan's accumulated total bilateral ODA as of the end of 1988, and Table 12.3, which shows recent developments in Japan's ODA to Sub-Saharan Africa, it can be seen that there are many resource-rich countries among the major recipients of Japan's ODA: oil in Nigeria, cobalt and copper in Zambia and Zaire, chrome and fisheries in Madagascar, manganese in Ghana, iron ore in Liberia, uranium in Niger, bauxite in Guinea, diamond and nickel in Botswana, and phosphate and fisheries in Senegal. It can also be argued that Tanzania and Kenya in East Africa; Nigeria, Ghana, and Senegal in West Africa; and Zaire and Zambia in Central and Southern Africa are all leading countries in the Organization of African Unity (OAU).

In fact, Japan tends to concentrate its ODA to resource-rich, politically influential, relatively better developed countries in Sub-Saharan Africa by providing more yen loans than grant-aid. On the other hand, under the name of humanitarian concern, it extends ODA to other African countries by offering relatively small amounts of grant-aid. Therefore, the question, "Why is Japan not in Africa?" in one sense is inappropriate. Japan *is* in Africa and has been there for some time. In another sense, however, the question is appropriate and as such must be related to two aspects of the *manner of giving* in Japan's ODA. First, the international community expects Japan to increase its share of ODA to Sub-Saharan Africa. Currently, Japan distributes 10 to 15% of its ODA to Sub-Saharan Africa. Secondly, African countries, particularly the large recipients of Japanese ODA, are expecting Japan to increase grant assistance rather than loans.

TABLE 12.3 Recent Development of Japan's ODA to SSA (percentage)

	Rank in DAC Bilateral ODA			*Share in DAC Bilateral ODA*		
Country	*1986*	*1987*	*1988*	*1986*	*1987*	*1988*
Nigeria	4	1	1	10.9	35.3	55.3
Ghana	1	2	1	25.1	16.0	26.8
Kenya	4	1	1	9.5	14.6	23.7
Zambia	1	1	1	19.4	12.1	22.2
Malawi[a]	5	1	2	9.2	30.3	21.0
Madagascar	4	5	2	9.0	4.6	19.1
Liberia	3	2	2	2.4	19.8	18.3
Niger[a]	6	4	2	4.5	11.0	17.3
Guinea[a]	5	3	2	9.5	18.8	16.6
Botswana[a]	14	14	2	0.0	0.1	16.4

[a]Indicates LLDC.

Source: Gaimusho, *Wagakuni no Seihu Kaihatsu Enjyo, Kunibetsu Jiseeki* [Japan's ODA by Country], 1988, 1989, 1990.

Perspectives

The marginalization of Sub-Saharan Africa in the global aid business has been quietly taking place. As Wilson puts it: "Third World aid will probably be the main victim of the breathtaking political changes going on in Europe. Africa will be the biggest loser, while Latin America and southern Asia will also find their expectation disappointed."[44] In fact, the post Cold War era may be robbing Africa of whatever strategic significance superpower rivalry provided it. Then, the Gulf crisis took place. "It is unimaginable," says Salim Lone, "that any inter-African crisis would lead to a similarly strong international reaction."[45]

Japan has already decided to extend its economic cooperation to East European countries. It will be making significant contributions to Gulf reconstruction with probable concentration on Kuwait, Egypt, Turkey, and Jordan. This "globalization" of Japan's economic cooperation has generated serious concerns among the Asian countries, the traditional partners in Japan's aid, as well as among Japan's new partners, mostly in Sub-Saharan Africa. In August 1990, therefore, a LLDC cabinet mission, which was composed of foreign ministers of Bangladesh, Sudan, Somalia, and Togo, paid a visit to Japan to seek further cooperation for LLDCs. Bangladesh Foreign Affairs Minister A.I. Mahmud, Head of the mission, expressed serious concerns that Japan would be providing more financial assistance in the future to East Europe than to LLDCs.[46]

As far as the geographical distribution of ODA to Sub-Saharan Africa in the 1990s is concerned, it may be realistic to assume a two-phase approach for expansion of Sub-Saharan Africa's share in Japan's ODA: Phase 1 (1991-95) and Phase 2 (1996-2000).

What would be the characteristics of Phase 1? To answer this question, several points need to be made. First, it is important to emphasize that a substantial share of Japan's ODA is already directed to Sub-Saharan Africa, much of it as part of Japan's support (through multilateral aid) of structural adjustment programs (SAPs). Secondly, there is an increasing degree of inertia in management of aid from all sources by Sub-Saharan Africa's recipient countries. What is immediately needed by the African countries therefore may not necessarily be increased external assistance, but rather more effective utilization of current levels of foreign aid.

Thirdly, Japan's own capacity to handle large magnitudes of ODA may have already reached its limit. For example, the overall budget for JICA technical cooperation increased 4.6 times from 1974 to 1989, and its total budget, including concessional grant-aid operations, increased more than 10 times. Nevertheless, the number of JICA regular personnel increased by only two persons, from 994 in 1974 to 996 in 1989![47] As of the end of 1987, JICA has only seven local offices in Sub-Saharan Africa and each local office has to manage ODA business in neighboring countries. The number of JICA regular staff in the local offices is appallingly small: six in Kenya, four in Tanzania, two in Zambia and one each in Ethiopia, Ghana, Nigeria, and Malawi.[48] The Overseas Economic Cooperation Fund (OECF), which is responsible for handling Japan's yen loans, has only one office in the Sub-Saharan Africa region (in Kenya) where 45 countries are looking for aid from Japan; and the Kenya Office has a staff of only two. The Ministry of Foreign Affairs states:

> The number of aid-related personnel in Japanese embassies and aid-implementing agency offices in developing countries is grossly insufficient compared with other major donor nations, and improvement of the situation is to be given most urgent priority.[49]

In fact, there are two limitations. One limitation is the lack of administrative staff. The second limitation is the lack of private sector people familiar enough with SSA conditions. To date, Japan has circumvented this problem by subcontracting administrative responsibilities for implementing Japanese ODA to SSA to other agencies, notably the British firm, Crown Agents. However, it is not practical for Japan to increase ODA to SSA through this arrangement in part since unlike the relationship with ADB, Japan is not prepared to have the implementing agencies engaging in project identification.[50] It is not an exaggeration to say, therefore, that Japan will be hard pressed to increase its ODA to the Sub-Saharan Africa countries with this limited number of operational staff.

Therefore, Phase 1 (1991-95) can be regarded as a period in which the countries in Sub-Saharan Africa will enhance their capacities to productively absorb and manage aid, while Japan will improve its capacity to handle an increased amount of ODA to Sub-Saharan Africa.

The development of Japan's ODA to Sub-Saharan Africa in Phase 2 (1996-2000) will be largely determined by three factors: (1) intensified needs for external resources in the African countries, (2) the political will of Japan to improve its ODA capacity, both in terms of the aid administrative structure and the resources for aid, and (3) the international environment and Sub-Saharan Africa.

First, the need for economic cooperation in Sub-Saharan Africa will increase further since the economic policy reforms currently being undertaken by African countries require both medium and long-term external assistance. Although the World Bank advocates "sustainable growth with equity" in its assistance for the structural adjustment programs in Sub-Saharan Africa, there are still concerns about the social costs of adjustment policies.

Secondly, Japan's ODA/GNP ratio (0.32%) in 1989 ranks 12th and its ODA per capita ($72.8) 10th among the DAC countries.[51] An improvement of the ODA/GNP ration by 0.1% annually in Phase 2 in order to achieve the 0.7 percent target would generate an enormous volume of aid resources. In other words, Japan still has ample room for expanding its overall ODA volume, provided that changes in administrative capabilities are made commensurate with an expanded volume.

In coming years, the European Community will be busy consolidating its own integration and supporting liberalization and democratization processes in the East European countries. The U.S. will still be struggling to manage its enormous Federal budget deficits. In these international circumstances, the "marginalization" of the Sub-Saharan region in terms of ODA among the major Western donors seems to be unavoidable. On the other hand, Japan's traditional partners in ODA, the Asian NIEs and the ASEAN countries, have entered a self-sustaining dynamic growth path.

The "globalization" of Japan's ODA is a measure designed to meet the needs of the time. It is the Sub-Saharan African countries which are looking for a larger share of ODA from Japan. Japan's ODA in Phase 2 should be directed to intensify its economic cooperation to the increasingly "marginalized" Sub-Saharan region.

Endnotes

1. The Ministry of Foreign Affairs (MOFA) excludes Sudan from the region of Sub-Saharan Africa, and places it in the region of North Africa and the Middle East while the Ministry of International Trade and Industry (MITI) includes Sudan in Sub-Saharan Africa. In this paper, MOFA's grouping of the countries in Sub-Saharan Africa is adopted unless specifically mentioned.

2. Gaimusho, *Wagakuni no Seifu Kaihatsu Enjo 1990 Gekan* (Official Development Assistance of Japan 1990) Vol. II, Tokyo, 1990, p. 354.

3. Ministry of Foreign Affairs, *Japan's Official Development Assistance 1989 Annual Report*, (Tokyo: Ministry of Foreign Affairs, 1990), pp. 15-17.

4. Gaimusho, *Wagakuni Gaiko no Kinkyo 1959* (Diplomatic Blue Book 1959) Tokyo, 1960, p. 102.

5. Kaigai Gijyutsu Kyoryoku Jigyodan (Overseas Technical Cooperation Agency, OTCA), *Gijyutsu kyoryoku Nenpo 1965* (Annual Report of Technical Cooperation 1965), Tokyo, 1966, p. 223.

6. Gaimusho, *Wagakuni Gaiko no Kinkyo 1963* (Diplomatic Blue Book 1963), Tokyo, 1964, pp. 149-150.

7. Kaigai Gijyutsu Kyoryoku Jigyodan, *Gijyutsu Kyoryoku Nenpo 1971* (Annual Report of Technical Cooperation 1971), Tokyo, 1972, pp. 125-127.

8. Kazuo Nishi, *Keizai Kyoryoku—Seiji Taikoku Nihon eno Michi* (Economic Cooperation—A Way Toward Japan as a Political Giant) (Tokyo: Chuo Koronsya, 1970), pp. 142-150.

9. Gaimusho, *Wagakuni Gaiko no Kinkyo 1964* (Diplomatic Blue Book 1964) Tokyo, 1965, pp. 139-140.

10. Godfrey Morrison, "Japan's Year in Africa," in Colin Legum, ed., *Africa Contemporary Record: Annual Survey and Documents* (London: Africana Publishing Company, 1972), p. 81.

11. Nishi, p. 143.

12. Morrison, p. 84.

13. Ichiro Inukai, "Nanboku 'tomodaore' kara 'tomoiki' e (From 'common ruin' to 'common survival' in the North-South relations), in Saburo Okita, ed., *Nanboku Mondai - Taiketsu to Kyocyo* (The North-South Problems - Confrontation and Accommodation), (Tokyo: Cyuo Koronsha, 1974), pp. 3-40.

14. Organization for Economic Cooperation and Development (OECD), *Development Cooperation 1976 Review* (Paris: OECD,1976), pp. 197-198.

15. Tsusho-sangyosho, *Keizai Kyoryoku no Genjy to Mondaiten 1986 Kakuron*, (Present Situation and Problems of Economic Cooperation 1986 Vol. II), Tokyo 1986, p. 90.

16. Gaimusho, *Wagakuni Gaiko no Kinkyo 1973* (Diplomatic Blue Book 1973), Tokyo, 1974.

17. Gaimusho, 1974.

18. Japan External Trade Organization (JETRO), *Economic Cooperation of Japan 1978*, Tokyo, 1979, p.22.

19. Richard Synge, "Raw materials pull in the Japanese investment," *African Development* (June 1975), pp. 5-7.

20. JETRO, 1979, p. 22.

21. Dennis Yasutomo, *Senryaku Enjyo to Nihon Gaikou* (The Manner of Giving—Strategic Aid and Japanese Foreign Policy), (Tokyo: Dobunkan, 1987), p. 166.

22. Japan Economic Institute (JEI), "Japan and Sub-Saharan Africa: Economic and Political Relations," JEI Report No. 344, 19 September 1986, p. 3. Japan's trade with South Africa has been largest in Japan's trade with African countries. The 1988 UNGA Resolution censured Japan for its increasing trade with South Africa.

23. Khalil Darwish, "Keizai Enjyo to Nihon no tai Ahurika Seisaku," (Economic Assistance and Japan's African Policy) *Kokusai Mondai* (International Affairs), No. 326, May 1987, p. 73.

24. "Senshin-koku ha enjyo tsukare" (Aid fatigue in developed countries), *Asahi Shimbun* (December 24, 1982).

25. Organization for Economic Cooperation and Development (OECD), *Development Cooperation 1984 Review* (Paris: OECD,1984), p. 129.

26. Gaimusho, *Wagakuni Gaiko no Kinkyo 1981* (Diplomatic Blue Book 1981) Tokyo, 1982 and Ministry of International Trade and Industry, *Economic Cooperation of Japan 1981*, Tokyo, 1982, pp. 16-17.

27. Alan Rix, *Japan's Aid Program, A New Global Agenda* (Canberra: Australian Government Publishing Service, 1990), pp. 28-29; Robert M. Orr, Jr., *The Emergence of Japan's Foreign Aid Power*, (New York: Columbia University Press, 1990).

28. For example, Japan's ODA to "the countries bordering areas of conflicts" (*funso shuhen koku*) such as Pakistan, Turkey, Egypt, and Thailand in the late 1970s and the early 1980s may have been decided in accord with American strategy. In any case, we cannot deny the fact that diplomatic relations with the United States are predominant in the aid decision-making process in Japan.

29. "Ahurika nanmin ni kakehasi o," (Help African refugees) *Asahi Shimbun* (May 23,1983); and "Sukunasugiru ahurika enjyo, obei karano zogaku yokyu hisshi," (Too small aid to Africa, inevitable demand for its increase by Western countries) *Asahi Shimbun*(March 24,1984).

30. Gaimusho (Ministry of Foreign Affairs, MOFA), *Wagakuni no Seifu Kaihatsu Enjyo 1989 Gekan*, (Official Development Assistance of Japan 1989) Vol. II, Tokyo, 1989, p. 208.

31. Gaimusho, 1989, p. 338.

32. OECD, *Development Cooperation 1989 Review*, p. 208.

33. Gaimusho, 1989, p. 354.

34. *Ibid.*

35. Ministry of Foreign Affairs, *Japan's Official Development Assistance 1989 Annual Report*,Tokyo, 1990, p. 17.

36. "Aiding Africa", *The Economist*, (November 27,1989), p. 59. Also see: Kyoshi Komachi, "Ahurika syokoku e shien kappatsu ni" (Increase support for African countries), *Nihon Keizai Shimbun*,(January 19,1988).

37. MOFA 1989, pp. 78-79.

38. OECD, *Development Cooperation 1989 Review*, (Paris: OECD, 1989), p. 212.

39. Jim Robinson III, "Time for Japan to launch a Marshall Plan," *Financial Times*,(October 1, 1986).

40. Edward V.K. Jaycox, "Japan's role in African development: Challenges and Opportunities," Keynote Address to the African Symposium in Tokyo held on 27-28 October 1988.

41. Olusegun Obasanjo, "Japan and Africa," Keynote address to the Japan International Cooperation Agency and United Nations Development Program Joint Seminar on African Development held in Tokyo on 21 May 1990.

42. Gaimusho, *Wagakuni Gaiko no Kinkyo 1963* (Diplomatic Blue Book 1963) Tokyo, 1964, p. 346.

43. *Ibid.*, pp. 354-355.

44. Dick Wilson, "Will Aid-Squeeze Chill Africa's Hope?" *The Japan Times*,(March 5,1990).

45. Salim Lone, "Africa Needs a Good Dose of Aid Without Fetters," *The Japan Times*,27 August 1990

46. *Japan ODA Outlook*,N. 33, September 1990, p. 4.

47. Kokusai Kyoryoku Jigyodan (Japan International Cooperation Agency, JICA), *Kokusai Kyoryoku Jigyodan Nenpo 1989* (JICA Annual Report 1989), Tokyo, 1990, p. 157.

48. Somucho (Office of Administration and Management), *ODA* (Seifu Kaihatsu Enjyo) *no Genjyo to Kadai - Soumucyou no daiichiji gyosei kansatsu kekka (musyou shikin kyoryoku, Gijyutsu kyoryoku).* (Present situation and tasks of ODA, the results of the first administrative inspection on grant financial assistance and technical assistance), Tokyo, 1988, p. 349.

49. Ministry of Foreign Affairs 1989, p. 33. Also, Somucho, 1988 (pp. 316-73) strongly recommends improvement in ODA administration and structure.

50. It is also the case that Japan does not have the confidence in the African Development Bank that it has in the Asian Development Bank. See chapter 15 on ADB by Dennis Yasutomo in this book.

51. Gaimusho, *Wagakuni no Seifu Kaihatsu Enjyo 1990 Gekan* (Official Development Assistance of Japan 1990) Vol. II, Tokyo, 1990, p. 7.

13

LATIN AMERICA: JAPAN'S COMPLEMENTARY STRATEGY IN ODA?

Stephen J. Anderson

Introduction

Latin America includes countries that are part of a global shift to open elections and political participation. Debt is a leading concern for Latin Americans who support development of the region's democracies. Japan can offer aid and debt relief to help Latin America's developing countries in their search for sustainable economic growth and political change. In fact, finance forms the backdrop for recent Japanese relations and economic cooperation with the region. For example, in November 1989, Latin American bankers met with officials in Japan to discuss financial relief. Japan's credits can meet critical needs of the debt-ridden states, especially as Japanese bankers' relations with debtor countries create strong interests in support of Official Development Assistance (ODA).

This chapter will address Japanese ODA flows, bilateral relations, and the variations among Japanese policies towards Latin American countries. The central argument is that the international context provided by U.S. leadership provides a key influence on Japan, its foreign policy, and particularly ODA flows. The institutional factors in Japanese ODA, such as country-specific policy goals, are secondary factors that can further explain ODA variations. To account for

Japanese responses to U.S. activities, this chapter asks whether Japan has a "complementary strategy" in giving aid to Latin America.

In Latin America, Japan has significant presence and capabilities. Nevertheless, Japanese initiatives including ODA remain sensitive to U.S. goals, interests, and leadership. Japanese efforts in Latin America avoid offending Washington's sensibilities. Japan complements the United States in the Latin American region with Japanese flows of aid most prominent in the Southern Cone, precisely where U.S. interests are the least assertive. The working hypothesis of this chapter therefore is that the bilateral relationship with the United States remains the most crucial variable for determining Japan's ODA priorities in Latin America.

Are ODA Institutions Dependent Variables?

Japanese foreign policy strategies emerge through and are reflected by Japan's ODA institutions. As a dependent variable, ODA is the result of various factors. Taking ODA as an amount or flow that differs among regions, areas, and countries, how is this variation of response best explained? As context for examining this question with specific reference to Latin America, it is important to recall the expansion in Japan's overall ODA budget. For the five-year period 1988-92, Japan pledged to spend $50 billion on aid which doubles the amounts in the previous five years. Compared to other government expenditures that rose by only 6% during 1980-87, foreign aid rose by 87%.[1]

Latin America's share in Japan's ODA has not been constant nor has it changed in a constant direction. For example, as a region in 1988, Latin America alone had the dubious distinction of a decrease in Japanese ODA flows—from $416.63 million in 1987 to $399.29 million in 1988.[2] Latin America's share of Japan's overall ODA dropped from 9.9% in 1983 to 6.2% in 1988. The Ministry of Foreign Affairs (MOFA) gave the following reasons for the decreases:

> Latin America's share is low because income levels are generally high in those countries compared with other developing regions, with the result that few countries qualify for financial assistance, and because many of the countries that are eligible for repayable financial assistance cannot be provided with ODA loans due to their massive accumulated debt and involvement in debt rescheduling.[3]

The scale and distribution of Japanese ODA to Latin America is comparatively limited. Brazil, as the leading recipient, received a

1987 total of $82.1 million which fell in the next year by 19.2%. Due to the concentration of Japanese-Brazilians around Sao Paulo and the closer economic relations of Brazil and Japan, Brazil has long led the region's Japanese ODA recipients. In 1988, eleven countries received over $10 million each, and the top five received over half of all ODA disbursements in Latin America.

By 1990, Latin America's share of Japan's total ODA rose to 8.1%, representing a real increase to $561 million. The leading recipients were Bolivia, Honduras, Brazil, and Jamaica. In 1990, eleven countries still received over $10 million each but now the top *four* received over half of all Japanese ODA disbursements in Latin America.

Japanese Economic Strategy in Latin America

The varying flow of ODA to Latin America can be explained by several factors associated principally with Japanese international economic relations with the region.[4] Characterizations of Japanese economic strategy in the region range broadly from alarmist views about Japanese dominance to benign views of harmonious cooperation and development. Where past research findings are consistent is in pointing to increased economic involvement in the region over the past two decades.

Since the 1970s, changes in natural resource supplies and finance increased Japan's interdependence with Latin America. Interdependence is often a cliche, but specific relationships illustrate how links developed between Japan and Latin America. First, the Japanese foreign policy of comprehensive economic security diversified both partners and forms of security priorities. Japan especially improved relations with natural resource suppliers throughout the region, and emerging national interests urged closer economic relations. Second, bilateral relations increased the range of Japanese private interests in contact with Latin American countries through increased investments, loans, and trade.

In the 1970s, Japanese comprehensive security policy meant broad economic cooperation with Latin America. "Economic cooperation" here as elsewhere resulted in the blurring of public and private Japanese efforts, and the widespread perceptions of concessional and non-concessional aid as parts of an undivided whole.[5] Natural resource suppliers among Latin American countries received the most investment, trade, and assistance. Latin Americans saw many problems with Japan's economic cooperation, and critics interpreted the more than trivial problems as new forms of dependence and neo-colonialism.

For neo-Marxist critics in Latin America, Japanese-style economic cooperation is no different from the economic imperialism that *dependencia* theorists see in all relationships with the developed Northern Hemisphere. Mainstream economic researchers implicitly acknowledge the criticisms. For example, the publication of "Towards New Forms of Economic Co-operation between Latin America and Japan" considers new means for Latin American development in minerals, agriculture, and maritime transport.[6] The efforts of groups such as the United Nations Economic Commission for Latin America and the Caribbean (CEPAL) explore ways to broaden the relations with Japan to include technology transfer, capital investment, and trade in Latin American manufactures.

Many organizational differences remain between Japanese and other countries' economic institutions and banking systems. In Japanese banking, the central bureaucrats practice comparatively extensive, strong regulation of bank activities and institutional arrangements that encourage household saving. In international banking, the Ministry of Finance (MOF) seeks to coordinate international activities by Japanese banks. For example, during the 1970s, the bureaucrats ordered Japanese banks to pull back after each oil shock to control Japan's balance of payments. After July 1977, MOF reformed regulation of Japanese bank overseas activities. Overseas lending by Japanese banks no longer required prior permission from the MOF for every overseas loan. Japan's mammoth banks, now including the world's ten largest in deposit assets, became free to pursue international lending.

The Japanese banks became aggressive competitors with American banks, particularly in Brazil where the bankers used low spreads to increase their market shares.[7] In addition to large multi-purpose syndicated loans and the purchasing of loan shares, some loans went for national projects such as Brazil's Cerrado agricultural complex and the Carajas multi-resource project on the Amazon River.[8] National projects linked the government with Japanese banks like Mitsubishi that in turn deal with a Japanese trading company. These loans help to accomplish three goals: (1) Japanese government development assistance projects are promoted, (2) profits for the trading company are linked to the bank as a result of the loans, and finally (3) the bank earns interest on the outstanding loan. By 1980, the Bank of Tokyo had the most exposure of any Japanese bank in Latin America. In comparison, other banks had a much lower exposure by choosing to buy shares of syndicates, and many did not act as lead managers in Latin America despite their extensive resources.

In the 1980s, Latin America faced its massive debt problem. Beginning with Mexico's August 1982 default, a combination of factors led to the crisis. Critical factors included the drop in commodity prices, the overextension of loans by private banks from the U.S., Japan, and Europe, and the leadership problems among Latin American policy-makers.

Japanese exposure in the debt crisis rivals that of the United States.[9] Breaking down Latin American loans as a percentage of total Third World loans by Japan, the percentage to Latin America is 70.3%. As a percentage of GNP, Japan's exposure in Latin America is slightly higher than that of the United States. Japanese banks held about 16% of Latin America's 1982 debt. The Japanese involvement in Latin America lending is based in 28 institutions that participate in international lending. Among these, the Bank of Tokyo alone has a long history of international experience. Through foreign offices all over the globe, The Bank of Tokyo relays a wide variety of international information to the government, and many observers see the Bank as an arm of the Ministry of Finance (MOF).[10] Competitors also argue that the Bank of Tokyo has more influence with the MOF than other city banks. The Bank of Tokyo relies on international transactions for over two-thirds of the bank's income.

After August 1982, Japanese bank activity in Latin America came to an abrupt halt with the announcement by Mexico that it could not continue to repay its debt under the originally agreed upon terms. With the onset of the debt crisis, the banks were in a state of panic. The U.S. ambassador to Brazil, Langhorne Motley, wrote, "Japanese banks are out of the market, European banks are scared, regional U.S. banks don't want to hear about Latin America, and major U.S. banks are proceeding with extreme caution."[11] The initial response to the debt crisis was self-protection.

Japan's continued involvement in Latin America is critical because of the financial resources Japan has available for debt rescheduling. After 1982, foreign lenders were slow to organize a response. The Japanese government had little experience with this kind of situation, and along with the rest of the world, Japan looked to the U.S. for a remedy to the problem. In the Baker Plan, the U.S. and the IMF came up with a rescheduling strategy that required the banks to lend more money to Latin America. Because U.S.-Japan issues such as trade imbalances were more pressing, compliance with U.S. debt strategy was used to ease tensions with the United States. Japanese banks resisted the idea of lending more money to Latin America, but cooperated with Japanese MOF policy in the broader scheme of completing U.S. policies. Japanese capital holds continued promise for the region, and the Miyazawa Plan offered by Japan's Minister of Finance fulfilled expectations of Japanese initiatives. Features from the Miyazawa Plan later appeared in the adopted Brady Plan, such as debt-equity swaps under multilateral institutions where one part of the debt is exchanged for bonds and the other part is rescheduled.[12]

Japan's on-going bilateral relations with Brazil illustrate connections with a single country in the region. Leon Hollerman argues that Japan operates as a "headquarters country" that pursues "economic strategy" which coordinates among Japanese government agencies, general trading companies, industrial groups, and other economic interests related to Brazil.[13] Hollerman sees Japanese planning as far more coherent than U.S. positions, and contends that Japan has an independent global position. In economic adjustments, according to this scenario, Japan achieved postwar recovery under the domestic control of "Japan, Inc.," then overcame two decades of chaotic adjustments dealing with oil shocks, reduced tariffs, and structural adjustment within a "Japan Disincorporated," and now appears to be emerging as the world's economic leader and headquarters in a "Japan, Reincorporated."

A problem for research findings on Japan's incorporating of Latin America is to document the specifics of strategy. Most writers seeking patterns within Japanese planning processes, corporate activities, and government decision-making cannot cite specific documents, expenditure figures, and decision-makers that account for Japanese strategy. The results leave the field open for two extremes of revisionism. One extreme sees no one in Japan in charge, and the result is a rudderless ship-of-state without guidance in the world system.[14] The other extreme is an overemphasis on the conspiratorial success of *keiretsu*-style industrial cartels, the consequences of collusive relations among industrial leaders and trade and industry policy-makers, and the requirements for firm reactions by U.S. and other world powers.[15] To their credit, the revisionists are quick to point to non-Japanese problems in global affairs such as American indebtedness and declining competitiveness.

Various revisionist views of Japanese strategies in economic cooperation also raise intriguing questions about Japan in Latin America. These region-specific questions also represent a "critical case" in assessing changes of Japanese global strategies in economic and ODA relations. Does an economic strategy exist that is reflected in recent ODA disbursement flows to Latin America?

Complementary Strategy Illustrated

Latin America offers a particular case to test the extent of Japan's emergence as an "aid power" and, at the same time, shows the boundaries of Japanese prerogatives. The hypothesis here is that American bilateral relationships (and interests) limit Japanese ODA prerogatives in Latin America. In bilateral relations with the U.S., the region experiences continued involvement and occasionally open intervention by American interests. In these circumstances, Japan's ODA role is likely to be eclipsed by the U.S. role. Where American interests are less pronounced, or at least are less emphatically pursued, Japan has more leeway to pursue its own interests. These efforts will often include ODA as a part of efforts to build and maintain broader relations with the region.

Patterns Vary by Geographical Proximity to the United States

Japan is reluctant to challenge leadership by the U.S. in countries close to the U.S., especially by giving more ODA to those countries than the U.S. does. Japanese caution arises from the U.S. tradition of the Monroe Doctrine, U.S. postwar dominance in the region, and periodic regional interventions, most recently in Grenada, Nicaragua, and Panama. In fact, Japan's ODA flows show an indirect relationship between geographical proximity to the U.S. and the Japanese ODA role: within Latin America, distance from North America increases Japanese aid.

Three specific findings support the notion of complementary strategy in Japanese ODA. First, U.S. ODA leads in the geographic areas close to the North American mainland. Second, what appears to be a cooperative relationship between Japanese and U.S. ODA is most prominent in an intermediate zone of Central and South America. Third, Japanese ODA is most prominent furthest from the U.S. in the Southern Cone.

United States Leads Close to Its Borders

Patterns of ODA giving show the U.S. leading in flows to countries that are nearest to North America. On the mainland, U.S. ODA giving is from 50% to 90% of the DAC total in many Central American states (Table 13.1). Recent changes in Japan's relations to Mexico and Panama marked a greater prominence for Japan in these countries, but the

United States remains the largest giver. The Mexican case especially reflects increased involvement through Japanese direct investment in the "maquiladoras" or foreign-owned plants in special economic zones near the U.S. border.[16] Panama also receives large amounts of Japanese

TABLE 13.1 U.S. and Japanese Aid to Central American Countries (as percentage of DAC aid)

Country	*U.S. ODA*	*Japanese ODA*
Belize	60.40	0.1
Costa Rica	76.90	3.0
El Salvador	87.90	0.8
Guatemala	72.50	1.2
Honduras	68.80	15.7
Mexico	41.00	23.1
Panama	52.40	20.8

Sources: Japan's ODA: 1989 Annual Report (Tokyo: Ministry of Foreign Affairs, March 1990, Bureau of Economic Analysis); U.S. Commerce Department.

TABLE 13.2 U.S. and Japanese Aid to Caribbean Countries (as percentage of DAC aid)

Country	*U.S. ODA*	*Japanese ODA*
Antigua/Barbados	41.50	1.9
Dominican Republic	57.90	17.3
Grenada	29.90	0.5
Guyana	53.60	5.2
Haiti	62.30	6.8
Jamaica	60.80	2.2
St. Vincent	38.00	3.2
Cuba	0.0	7.1

Sources: Japan's ODA: 1989 Annual Report (Tokyo: Ministry of Foreign Affairs, March 1990, Bureau of Economic Analysis); U.S. Commerce Department.

aid with 1987 ODA totalling 20.8% of the DAC total. Aid and involvement fell during the Noriega administration in Panama and U.S. intervention, but Japanese shipping interests that register in Panama and banks that seek tax and regulatory havens there are likely to continue as bases for bilateral ODA relations. Honduras offers compelling economic needs for aid, and Japanese policy emphasizes the humanitarian aspects of aid to Honduran projects.

With the notable exception of Cuba, the Caribbean islands also support the pattern of U.S. aid leadership (Table 13.2). Because of the legacy of colonial activities, European post-colonial relations with various Caribbean islands also explain variations in U.S. as well as Japanese involvement. These observations mark limits to Japan's Caribbean activities, with some notable exceptions.

Japanese activities in the Cayman Islands illustrate the increased prominence of private interests in the Caribbean. Seeking a tax haven, Japanese banks used the debt crisis to their advantage to gain greater autonomy from the government when the MOF tried to encourage them to cooperate in debt rescheduling and the bankers in turn asked relief on tax issues.[17] Japanese banks independently formed a Cayman Islands company called JBA Investment Incorporated, and gained approval from the MOF on the condition that the banks continue to lend new money to Latin America.[18] Jointly owned by 28 Japanese banks that each contributed $84,000 initial capital, this company allowed the banks to sell their debt at a discount and to write off the loss of their taxes. The scheme improved the banks' taxes and balance sheets by freeing up large amounts of capital that once supported uncertain Latin American loans.

Despite the presence of Japanese private interests in the Caribbean, Japan's ODA is not dominant. Again, reasons given in interviews are that Japan defers to U.S. influence in the area.

Cooperation in Northern South America

Patterns associated with a cooperative ODA relationship between the U.S. and Japan appear most clearly in the countries of northern and Andean South America (Table 13.3). Cooperative patterns may be best explained by country-specific factors than by any other factors. With cautions about spurious connections, the geographic proximity of Colombia, Ecuador, Peru, and Venezuela offer shared characteristics for showing the limits on Japanese ODA efforts. Here, Japan has some interest in Japanese immigrant communities, and embassies have long acted to handle individual and humanitarian concerns that arise for these communities. The linkage of ODA to such groups are tenuous, and economic cooperation or resource security issues were the main reasons to increase early Japanese ODA-giving. Recent changes for Japanese ODA as a whole have impacts on South America, and surpass the compelling country-specific reasons that at first appear dominant.

TABLE 13.3 U.S. and Japanese Aid to Northern South America (as percentage of DAC aid)

Country	*U.S. ODA*	*Japanese ODA*
Colombia	5.20	6.6
Ecuador	28.00	29.9
Peru	24.20	14.4
Venezuela	0.01	10.4

Source: Japan's ODA: 1989 Annual Report (Tokyo: Ministry of Foreign Affairs, March 1990. Bureau of Economic Analysis), U.S. Commerce Department.

The exceptional pattern of Peru is a telling case to test country-specific factors that encourage Japan to increase ODA. Long-standing relations exist due to Japanese immigrants, and incentives of a major pipeline project enhanced Japanese economic involvement. When Alberto Fujimori, the son of Japanese immigrants, won the Peruvian Presidency in 1990, many could again offer reasons to increase Japanese involvement and ODA, as well as again bring Peruvian exceptionalism among these South American states.[19] Yet the immediate Japanese reactions to the 1990 election victory promised no new assistance, and both business and government circles remained gloomy on Peruvian economic prospects.[20] By 1992 a sequence of events had led to a suspension of technical assistance aid. These included the abduction and murder of three JICA aid workers in Peru by the Shining Path (*Sendero Luminoso*) guerillas, and then a suspension of representative institutions and assumption of dictatorial powers by Fujimori (purportedly because of resistance to economic reform measures).

Japanese Initiatives in the Southern Cone

Of all areas in Latin America, Japanese leadership in ODA disbursements is most prominent in the far South (Table 13.4). In Japanese foreign economic policy, Brazil, Argentina, and Chile played prominent roles in meeting Japan's goals to diversify food grains and fishing, oil, mineral, and other resource security aims that emerged in the 1970s. The Southern Cone states, with increasing contacts with Japan in resource development, debt relief, and trade relations, benefit most from Japanese priorities to grant increased levels of ODA.

TABLE 13.4 U.S. and Japanese Aid to Southern South America (as percentage of DAC aid)

Country	*U.S. ODA*	*Japanese ODA*
Argentina	0.01	32.4
Bolivia	36.20	25.3
Brazil	7.00	32.1
Chile	10.00	19.4
Paraguay	0.01	72.2
Uruguay	0.02	17.2

Source: Japan's ODA: 1989 Annual Report (Tokyo: Ministry of Foreign Affairs, March 1990. Bureau of Economic Analysis), U.S. Commerce Department.

Japanese ODA giving accounts for 17.2% to 32.4% of DAC giving in the Southern Cone, except in Paraguay where Japan accounted for 72.2% of all DAC aid in 1989. The reasons for the high level in Paraguay are institutional and policy-based, as the country is poorer and meets Japanese requirements for humanitarian aid. In the Southern cone, only Bolivia receives more from the U.S. than Japan, and here, country-specific factors may be crucial because of U.S. efforts at drug interdiction in Bolivia.

Complementary Strategy and Divergent Interests: Are ODA Institutions Independent Variables?

Through a complementary strategy, Japanese ODA flows complete the priorities of the United States. By completing the patterns of U.S.

and DAC giving, Japan can pursue missions of development and assistance. However, in policy processes rather than flows, Japanese aid priorities are less easily analyzed. The stated policy goals of Japanese foreign aid are ideals rather than realities of policy outcomes. Paraguay, Nicaragua, and Honduras are examples of locations where Japanese aid policy goals of humanitarian initiatives and rapid diplomatic response preceded disbursed ODA funds. However, Japanese ODA politics includes the battling of Japanese bureaucracies over the control of Japanese foreign aid policies. These bureaucratic politics complicate the picture of Japan's regional priorities. These politics, along with other issues ranging from ODA staffing that cannot keep pace with budgets to the emerging independent roles of business and engineering interests invite speculation about economic manipulation and the exercise of international corporate power in explaining the motives of Japan's ODA policies in Latin America (and elsewhere). However, a finding here is that while institutional politics may have limited independent influence in specific countries and projects, their influence is small compared to a broader regional policy guideline that sets ODA allocation relative to U.S. interests.

Clarity in the aid policy process is needed for coherence in Japanese foreign relations. If foreign aid is Japan's foremost effort to enhance its international responsibility, then the coherence of policy goals should precede patterns that emerge in ODA disbursements. Japanese ODA policy-makers are not likely to emphasize that Japan, a sovereign nation, is complementing U.S. goals in Latin America although the evidence shows a large degree of complement. Japanese officials emphasize humanitarian goals, and some evidence occurs throughout the region. Yet the future of Japanese bilateral aid demands hard choices. Should humanitarian aid go to Cuba, Nicaragua, El Salvador, and Peru regardless of political situations in the countries, or should Japan favor Peru where a Japanese immigrant's son is President? Should economic relations with Brazil and Mexico as the region's two largest countries get precedence?

For bilateral and multilateral ODA activities, the significance of both complementing and diverging by Japan goes beyond the management of cooperation or coordination. By "complementary strategy," this chapter suggests that future changes in ODA flows and policies are double-edged. On the one hand, the vacuum of declining U.S. hegemony in foreign aid is being filled by a close ally and trading partner. On the other hand, decline means the further gradual replacement by other nations in influence, leverage, and direct economic benefits. The independence of Japan from the United States is likely to increase, and the emergence of increasingly divergent interests between the two leading aid givers is imminent. Within Japanese policy processes, critical decisions about policy-making are being made. Among the Ministry of Finance, Ministry of Foreign Affairs, and other government agencies as well as with economic interests, conflicts will continue over the future of independent Japanese goals for ODA. This chapter leaves the possible breakdown of complementary efforts in Japanese ODA strategy as the subject for further study. The continuing, striking feature in Japanese ODA to Latin America is the persistence of a complementary strategy with independent Japanese interests only beginning to diverge.

Endnotes

1. Robert M. Orr, Jr., "Being a Team Player: Japanese Foreign Aid Decision-making, Foreign Pressure, and International Responsiveness," Paper presented at Association of Asian Studies Meeting, San Francisco, 1988, and Ministry of Foreign Affairs (MOFA), *ODA Annual Report, 1987*, p. 66. All figures for Japanese foreign aid are in terms of fiscal year disbursements unless otherwise indicated.

2. MOFA, pp. 61-62.

3. Ministry of Foreign Affairs, p. 62.

4. This is not to suggest an absence of a wider context. However, while Japanese ODA overall expanded throughout the 1980s, Latin America's share remained relatively low. The real reallocation within the overall program, although this too was relatively marginal, was from Asia to Africa.

5. On the blurring of public and private in economic cooperation, see Robert M. Orr, "The Rising Sum: What Makes Japan Give?" *The International Economy*, September/October 1989, pp. 80-83.

6. Economic Commission for Latin America and the Caribbean, Santiago, Chile, United Nations, 1987.

7. Leon Hollerman, *Japan's Economic Strategy in Brazil: Challenge for the United States* (Lexington: Lexington Books, 1988), p. 156.

8. Japanese national projects in Latin America are surveyed in the United Nations Economic Commission for Latin America and the Caribbean, *Towards*

New Forms of Economic Co-operation Between Latin America and Japan (Santiago, Chile: ECLAC, 1987).

9. Barbara Stallings, *Banker to the Third World*, (Berkeley: University of California, 1987), and an unpublished manuscript entitled "The Reluctant Giant: Japan and the Latin American Debt Crisis." On the political implications of the region's debt, see Barbara Stallings and Robert Kaufmann, editors, *Debt and Democracy in Latin America* (Boulder: Westview Press, 1988).

10. Stephen Bronte, "The Astonishing Influence of the Bank of Tokyo," *Euromoney*, January 1979, p. 10.

11. Leon Hollerman, *Japan's Economic Strategy in Brazil*, p. 170.

12. Stephen J. Anderson, "Japan's Views of Latin American in the Pacific Basin," *World Policy Report*, Santiago, Chile: CEPAL, 1990, (in Spanish only). The Miyazawa and Brady proposals are also compared in Gretchen Green, "Japan and Latin America," *JEI Report*, No. 15A, April 13, 1990.

13. Leon Hollerman, *Japan's Economic Strategy in Brazil* and *Japan, Disincorporated: The Economic Liberalization Process* (Stanford: Hoover, 1988).

14. Karel van Woferen, *The Enigma of Japanese Power* (New York: Knopf, 1988).

15. James Fallows, "Containing Japan" *The Atlantic Monthly*, May 1989, pp. 40-54.

16. Frank J. Macchiarola, "Mexico as a Trading Partner," pp. 90-109 in his edited volume, *International Trade: The Changing Role of the United States* (New York: Academy of Political Science, 1990).

17. *Economist*, March 14, 1987, p. 78.

18. Karin Lissakers, "A Lesson From Japanese Banks," *New York Times*, March 24, 1987, p. A31.

19. *Yomiuri Shimbun*, July 28, 1990, p. 5.

20. *Nikkei Keizai Shimbun*, June 13, 1990, pp. 1 and 3.

14

JAPANESE FOREIGN AID: OVER A BARREL IN THE MIDDLE EAST

Robert M. Orr, Jr.

Background

In some ways Japan has several advantages over European and American donors in its dealings with the Middle East. Unlike the European powers, Japan does not carry the legacy of colonialism in the region, and unlike the United States, Japan does not carry a legacy of direct association with the Arab-Israeli conflict. However, Japan also wields fewer policy tools such as arms exports or as the Persian Gulf war showed, the threat of dispatching military forces. Therefore Japan has had to depend almost exclusively upon aid and trade in order to attempt to influence policies by Middle Eastern governments in directions favorable to her national interests.[1]

Japan has urgent energy needs and the Middle East remains the largest source, although it should be noted that the share of oil in Japan's energy supply mix has declined since the early 1970s. In 1988, 57.3% of Japan's energy was supplied by crude oil, of which 99.6% had to be imported, 68% from the Middle East alone. Thus, the Middle East is responsible for supplying 40% of Japan's overall energy requirements. As Douglas Ostrom has argued "Japan's economy remains extraordinarily susceptible to serious disruptions in supply or increases in the price of raw materials."[2]

The rising Japanese demand for crude oil has meant that Japan has had to export more in order to pay for the energy, a fact with impacts on U.S.-Japan relations. Despite the appreciation of the yen since 1985, the trade deficit has not declined enough to satisfy Washington. As a result Tokyo often attempts to placate American trade demands by being more responsive to U.S. strategic interests. The conflict between assuaging Japan's oil suppliers and the United States has forced Tokyo to walk a delicate tightrope between both interests.

These factors are critical in understanding what has shaped the content and direction of Japanese foreign aid to the Middle East, and as a consequence this chapter proposes two fundamental arguments. First, natural resource security played a critical role in defining Japanese interests in the region and thus motivating Tokyo to extend economic assistance. If Japanese aid to the Middle East region was only dictated by energy needs, the aid levels might actually be higher. While aid levels did steadily increase in the 1970s, Japan's ODA policy-making and implementation system, as has been argued in chapter one, has not changed appreciably since 1974. As a consequence, the aid system is frequently rife with bureaucratic in-fighting which can have significant impacts on the directions and consistency of ODA policies in the region.

Difficulties in particular in obtaining consensus has meant that Japanese aid policy to the Middle East often appears, to use Kent Calder's application, reactive.[3] Different government institutions can interpret pressure, for example from the United States or other governments to suit their own bureaucratic interests. It is important to keep the reactive policy hypothesis in mind considering that Japan's initial foray into aid diplomacy in the Middle East occurred *after* the nation was threatened by an oil cutoff. The reactive policy hypothesis also explains the effectiveness of U.S. pressure on Japan in the 1980s to extend and sustain aid levels to countries deemed strategically important to western interests. Certainly the Gulf Crisis and War in 1990-91 showed once again just how reactive Japanese aid policy is in the region. For example, the Foreign Ministry has frequently shared foreign views of the need to increase Japan's role in the Middle East through economic cooperation, but has had to rely on external pressure to move a more intransigent Finance Ministry along.[4]

It is significant that humanitarian concerns are rarely articulated as a priority for providing aid to the region, with the notable exception of assistance to Palestinian refugees. Thus, the themes outlined above are finely interwoven into the tapestry of the Japanese aid story in the Middle East as this chapter intends to demonstrate.

The Roots of Japanese Aid to the Region

The outbreak of the Yom Kippur War and the subsequent usage of oil as a diplomatic weapon against the West by the Organization of Petroleum Exporting Countries (OPEC) brought Japan headlong into it's first bona fide international crisis since the end of the second World War. Japan's dependence on OPEC oil had crept upwards in line with Japan's rise as an economic power. Japan, like the United States, took inexpensive oil for granted until 1973.[5] By that time, 77.6% of Japan's energy requirements were supplied by crude oil. 77.4% of Japan's total oil imports came from the Middle East with 46.4% coming from Arab OPEC members and 31% from Iran. When OPEC launched its oil embargo, Japan was not only directly effected but also could not depend on support from other Western nations which suffered the same fate. As Mark Seralnick has noted, with 55 days of crude oil stockpiled, OPEC had Japan "over a barrel."[6]

The OPEC Arab nations wanted Japan to be more sympathetic to their cause vis-a-vis Israel. Japanese policy-makers, particularly the Foreign Ministry and Foreign Minister Masayoshi Ohira, walked a tightrope between moving too far to the Arab side and angering the Americans, who regarded Israel as a key regional ally, and making sure that Japan would not be shut down by a lack of petroleum. Kuwaiti Ambassador Al Ghossein expressed his frustration with "Japan's unclear attitude" toward the Arab cause during the height of the crisis.[7]

This may have been complicated by a bribery scandal in MITI, which seriously distracted policy-making in the Petroleum Department.[8] With MITI at least partially disabled by the scandal, the Foreign Ministry was increasingly able to assert itself. A verbal note to the Arab Embassies on October 25, 1973 amounted to a concrete promise, (as opposed for example to a study plan), for a dramatic expansion of foreign aid to the region. The Economic Cooperation Bureau made the decision to appropriate the initial funds for this purpose.[9] This suggests that the major ingredients in the package were being formulated in the bureaucracy even before the politicians began to consider aid as a means of mollifying the OPEC Arab states.

The imperative of winning over the Finance Ministry was achieved by the obvious gravity of the situation. In December 1973, Prime Minister Kakuei Tanaka dispatched an entourage to the Middle East, led by high ranking LDP member Takeo Miki, with a major foreign aid package. The plan was clearly designed as a palliative toward Japan's Arab critics. It was seen as a means to show Tokyo's "concern." The package included $3 billion in aid overall, including $1 billion each to Iran and Iraq.[10]

The magnitude of the Miki mission's aid gift and the way in which it was handled show that a "request basis" for Japan's ODA is not always necessary. As a government official related to me, "no request was involved, there was no procedure...it was a violation of the usual Japanese approach."[11] I would suggest this demonstrates the extent to which Japan is willing to forego "procedures" in order to "react" to a situation regarded as critical to national survival. With no military tool and little else but money, the stage was set for foreign aid to take on wider applications.

TABLE 14.1 Percentage of Overall Aid Disbursed to the Middle East, 1972–1990

Year	*Percentage*
1972	0.8
1973	1.4
1975	10.6
1977	24.5
1979	10.6
1981	8.4
1983	8.3
1985	7.9
1987	10.0
1988	9.1
1989	5.4
1990	10.2

Source: Wagakuni, various volumes.

The Nature and Volume of Japanese Aid

As Table 14.1 shows, Japanese aid to the Middle East zoomed upward and then stabilized, marginally increasing and subsiding with the ebbs and flows of oil politics reaching as high as 24.5% of overall ODA flows in 1977 but fluctuating around 10% per annum since then with the exception of 1989 due to disbursement bottlenecks. According to Japanese government officials, one of the largest problems now confronting aid policy-makers is that the Middle East region is home to nations with high incomes.[12] This makes it difficult to justify concessional aid to many of these countries. Accepting and applying this criterion, however, can result in bureaucratic conflict between the ministries.[13] As will be brought out more clearly later, while the foreign Ministry sees ODA in terms of the political and strategic implications of Japan's foreign policy in the region, the Ministry of Finance is more concerned about a nation's ability to repay loans. Poorer countries justify concessional loans because of their limited ability to pay. If a country has what the Ministry of Finance regards as a higher income, it prefers either private sector or non-concessional government loans from the Export-Import Bank of Japan.

Grant assistance from Japan to Middle Eastern countries amounted to almost 29.7% of all Japanese aid extended to the region in 1990. Yen loans accounted for the remaining 70.3%.[14] In 1989, among all donors in the Middle East, Japan ranked fourth behind the United States, West Germany, and France. The United States extended $2,368 million to the region, while Japan provided $368.49 million.[15] Almost half of America's Middle East aid went to Israel in that year ($1,152 million). Egypt was another principal recipient of American aid at $905 million.[16] Combined, these amount to $2,057 million which equals 86.8% of all U.S. foreign aid to the Middle East. In contrast, Japan provided $78.65 or 21.3% of it's aid volume in the Middle East to Egypt in 1989 and does not extend any assistance to Israel. These figures suggest that while Tokyo's aid program in the region is significantly smaller, it is more evenly distributed.[17]

Rationalizing Aid to the Region

Subject to bureaucratic bickering, three basic justifications are used for aid to the Middle East. These are (1) resource diplomacy, (2) strategic aid and foreign pressure, and (3) humanitarian "rationalizations." As a result, the dividing line between what constitutes "resource diplomacy aid" and "strategic aid" is often an exceedingly thin one.

Resource Diplomacy

Over 70% of Japan's oil imports from the Middle East emanate from the Persian Gulf region. When the Iran-Iraq War erupted in September of 1980, Japan once again faced the prospects of having it's vital natural resource cut off and was forced into yet another balancing act, except this time both were major oil suppliers. Iraq had become an important recipient of Japanese aid following the 1973 Oil shock when Japan started extending mixed credits to Baghdad.[18] Right from the start, the Foreign Ministry emphasized the importance of oil in it's internal arguments in favor of providing aid to Iraq. MITI and MOF favored mixed credits. In early 1990, the Japanese government reached an informal agreement with Baghdad that roughly 45% of Iraq's debt to Japan would be paid in oil if Iraq could not otherwise service the debt.[19] Despite promises to help rebuild both Iran and Iraq following the war[20], the Finance Ministry hesitated approving further loans until this agreement was struck.

Differing Ministerial perceptions regarding aid to regional resource-rich states have caused ripples in Japan's approach to Oman and Iran as well. In the case of Oman, the Japanese government extended $200 million in credits at concessional rates but the internal bickering over which agency would administer at least part of the funds was substantial. With Japan under considerable trade pressure, officials in the Export-Import Bank of Japan, which was created to stimulate Tokyo's overseas markets, have sometimes worried that they were losing their *raison d'etre*. As Japan's aid volumes mushroomed, bureaucrats in MOF, which solely controls the Bank, as well as in the Bank itself, began to push the idea that Ex-Im would be an ideal institution to help implement concessional credits, something which only the OECF had done before. The other ministries strongly opposed this fearing that it would lead to a dramatic expansion in MOF's influence over foreign aid policy. As a result, the package for Oman, a key nation under the resource diplomacy rationalization, was held up for months as the bureaucrats attempted to settle the issue. Eventually, MOF partially won its way and Oman became the first country to receive concessional loans from the Ex-Im Bank under Japan's foreign aid system.

The Ministry of Foreign Affairs as well as MITI has wanted to expand assistance to Iran for sometime. For many years Tokyo and Tehran were locked in an imbroglio over how to dispose of the Mitsui built, partially OECF yen loan funded Bandar-Khomeini Petrochemical project which the Iraqis had used for "target practice" for much of the war.[21] However a settlement between Mitsui and the Iranian government was finally reached in November 1989 allowing Mitsui to pull out of the project.

With this issue behind, on the surface Iran would seem to be an ideal candidate for more aid under the rubric of resource diplomacy. MOFA has certainly tried to make the case. As Matsuura has noted, the Iranian domestic economy was and is in trouble, with inflation running at approximately 50%.[22] MOFA, in particular has been interested in providing more technical aid and supporting Iranian agriculture.

But here again, bureaucratic disagreement has a role. With an estimated per capita GNP of $2,800, Iran exceeds the minimum figure required for yen loan eligibility under Japanese government guidelines. Some in MOFA believe that the number is artificially high. Nonetheless the Finance Ministry accepts these statistics as a basis for arguing that Iran ought not to receive concessional loans.[23]

It is quite clear in these cases that even when Japanese interests in extending aid are clearly defined for purposes of resource diplomacy by one ministry, that does not necessarily mean that the rationale is accepted by all. Also bureaucratic discord over the type of aid extended and which entity will be responsible for its implementation, can cause considerable delays in disbursement.

Strategic Aid and Foreign Pressure

For a nation like Japan that, until now, has been unwilling or unable to exercise significant political influence in the world, the concept of strategic aid has proven to be very difficult to articulate. More frequently than not, opposition parties in the Diet view strategic aid as simply following America's "global designs."

In the early 1980's, the Nakasone government tried to break this opposition by creating an explicit rationalization to wed the strategic concept with the resource diplomacy concept. This was in part brought about by what some policy-makers in MOFA, as well as Nakasone himself, saw as the need to contribute more assistance to nations in the Middle East or at least on the region's periphery.

Thus, the short lived "Comprehensive Security" approach was launched. This defined aid as one of a triad of foreign policy tools that also included defense and diplomacy. As it relates to aid, this policy was broken down further to rationalize assistance to countries important to western strategic interests. The terms employed were *funso shuhen koku*, literally "nations which border conflict areas" and it did almost nothing to alleviate fears by the policy's opponents that Japan was simply following America's agenda. Again, the government was doing a balancing act since much of the strategic aid was in response to American pressure and employed at least partially as a means of deflecting criticism of Japanese defense and trade policies.[24] Consequently "Comprehensive Security" is a description that has practically been dropped from the government's vocabulary. Instead, MOFA in particular prefers to publicly use *sogo izon* or "interdependence" to justify requests for aid funds to the Middle East.[25]

As Dennis Yasutomo has pointed out, countries in the Middle East which have few if any oil reserves but receive aid—such as Turkey, Egypt, Sudan, and Lebanon—must be placed in the strategic category.[26] Some of this aid can take some rather bizarre forms, such as the construction of an opera house in Cairo through grant assistance. The project was roundly criticized in the Japanese press. Also, bureaucratic differences have been present in Japan's aid policy to Egypt. MOFA sees Egypt as a key player in the Middle East peace process. Peace in the Middle East reduces the likelihood of the oil "pipeline" being threatened. Thus MOFA quite clearly acknowledges the "strategic" importance of Egypt. There is also the feeling that major oil suppliers such as Saudi Arabia "appreciate" Japanese assistance to Cairo.[27] However, the MOF regards Egypt as a "bad boy"—slow to absorb funds, slow to repay loans, and not properly anointed by the International Monetary Fund (IMF). In this sense, the MOF is also susceptible to foreign pressure from International Financial Institutions and the U.S. Department of Treasury. The positions of both are sometimes used internally to counteract the MOFA's use of State Department pressure.

While the Japanese Constitution explicitly forbids maintaining any kind of "land, sea or air force," Japan nonetheless has consistently expanded defense spending in the 1970s and 1980s, largely at American behest. Japan spends more on defense than any nation in Asia, including China. Indeed, Japan's defense budget is 1.3 times the size of the entire South Korean government budget.[28] During the Iran-Iraq war, despite calls on Japan to play a greater role in protecting the oil lifeline, Tokyo depended on the United States, Britain, and France. One contribution, through aid, intended for the protection of open sea lanes was the government's grant assistance to purchase a Precise Navigation System from a British concern to help guide tankers through the mine fields that had been planted by the protagonists.[29]

A difference between "resource diplomacy aid" and "strategic aid" is that the latter is to a much greater extent driven by pressure from the United States. The former is driven by pressure from "resource states." But the policies generated by both influences appear "reactive" rather than "proactive." The complex nature of the aid decision-making process merely ensures that cohesive policy is hamstrung.

Humanitarian Aid

All foreign aid to some extent includes a "humanitarian" component and Japan's aid is no different. In fact, MOFA has a tendency to emphasize this angle in parliamentary discussions. The telltale difference is whether the rationalization is *tatemae* or "officialese" or *honne* meaning "reality." One barometer is the level of foreign aid extended to regional nations with low GNP per capita, indicating a real need for a Basic Human Needs type of assistance. Judging from this perspective, Japan does not come out too well. In 1989 of the eight nations in the Middle East with GNP's per capita under $2,000, Japan was the largest donor in only Yemen while ranking third or below in most of the other countries. Even in this case, Japan expected Yemen to repay almost 84% of this assistance at concessional rates since it was extended in the form of yen loans. The United States is the largest donor in three (Egypt, Jordan, and Sudan), and is ranked third or higher in three others. Moreover, since the United States has moved to a full grant aid program in most of the countries in the region, most of the development assistance was not expected to be repaid.[30]

At least one clear cut case of humanitarian aid, albeit directly related to concerns over Japan's relations with other Arab states, is financial support for Palestinian refugees through multilateral channels. Japan first offered assistance to Palestinian refugees following the oil shock in 1973. Since Japan does not recognize the Palestinian Liberation Organization (PLO) as a state, it cannot offer direct bilateral aid but rather supports refugees through United Nations organizations. Principal among these are the United Nations Development Program (UNDP) and the United Nations Relief and Works Agency for Palestine Refugees in the Near East (UNRWA). MOFA is adamant that these arrangements remain, even though several European donors do provide direct assistance.[31] In 1990, Japanese assistance through UNRWA amounted to $20 million, 8.2% of the total in contrast with the 23.4% of the total provided by the United States.[32] While Israel does not officially object to humanitarian assistance to the Palestinians, some MOFA officials claim that Israeli authorities have not always been cooperative and in fact have been disruptive of efforts to aid the refugees.[33]

In April 1990, Japan and the PLO conducted their first ever consultations in Tokyo. Japan confirmed that it would go forward and support the establishment of a 200 bed hospital in the Gaza Strip to be built by UNRWA. The PLO also called upon Japan to assist in the creation of a new development bank and vocational program for Palestinians. With Japan's reluctance to extend direct bilateral aid, Tokyo again walks the balance beam. If the government sways too far and is perceived as catering to the PLO, it risks the wrath of Washington. If Japan ignores the Palestinians, anger might be triggered in the Arab world.

The Second War in the Persian Gulf

Japan's policy response to Sadaam Hussein's takeover of Kuwait once again demonstrated Tokyo's follower foreign policy.[34] Japan responded to the crisis and subsequent war with a series of aid packages, each time waiting to see how they would be received and when it appeared that the West was less than satisfied, struggled to formulate yet another package.

In this case, the difficulty in going along with the West's campaign to oust Sadaam Hussein from Kuwait should not be underestimated. As late as 1989 Japan was importing 217,000 barrels of crude oil a day from Iraq and another 167,000 from Kuwait, making up 6 and 4.6 percent of Japan's total oil imports respectively.[35] Against this background, the first U.S. request for Japan to formulate an aid package came in a phone call from President George Bush to then Prime Minister Toshiki Kaifu on August 14, almost two weeks after the Iraqi invasion.[36] Three weeks later Tokyo announced it's first aid package which included emergency assistance to Jordan, Egypt, and Turkey amounting to $1 billion. U.S. officials were not shy in pointing out their disappointment. The State Department indicated that it wanted to talk to Japan about "further steps and contributions" and one official was quoted as saying "this is not what we had in mind."[37] Polls in America suggested that the public felt Japan was making the weakest contribution of all the allies.[38] Much of Washington's frustration was that a contribution seemingly had to be dragged out of Japan. There appeared to be no sense of shared commitment coming from Tokyo to "defend democracy" and the international order, an order from which Japan had benefitted greatly.

Confusion reigned in Tokyo. The Finance Ministry indicated that the $1 billion package would be Japan's last contribution for Fiscal Year 1990. The Prime Minister, in announcing the package, said it contained the "maximum" effort Tokyo could make under the Constitution.[39] However, almost simultaneously, the Foreign Ministry was saying that the package was merely a first step.[40] The Foreign Ministry warned that problems in U.S.-Japan relations loomed on the horizon if Japan did not do more. On September 14, a little over two weeks after the first aid package, Kaifu announced a second commitment, this one valued at $3 billion and thus boosting Japan's overall assistance to $4 billion, the largest among all donors. Aid was disbursed through the newly created Gulf Peace Fund.

The Japanese public was largely apathetic about the crisis and subsequent war.[41] Most of the public supported Kaifu's "checkbook diplomacy," particularly if it meant that Japan could avoid a physical presence in the region. For many in the West, however, the lack of a Japanese "flag" in the crisis represented a serious irritant.

Japan's third large commitment of assistance was announced on January 24, following the initiation of hostilities in the Gulf. Once again this package, which totaled $9 billion, came about "only after the United States repeatedly pressured Japan to assume these kinds of responsibilities."[42] Despite considerable difficulty in getting this approved in the Diet, Tokyo's aid rose to $13 billion, the highest of all donors in the conflict. The United States welcomed this pledge as "generous and timely."[43] However, friction remained. Tokyo was initially unwilling to disburse the total dollar amount of their pledge, claiming that due to a fluctuation in the exchange rate, Japan actually really would pay out roughly $8.5 billion. This only supported the American impression that Japan was in reality not a committed ally.

In the post-war period, Japan appeared to be much more willing and able to participate and even have a physical presence. The war wreaked havoc on the environment and Japan offered a fourth mini-aid package to address this problem by pledging $2.6 million for environmental clean-up as well as dispatching two teams of experts. Of the amount pledged $1.1 million was earmarked for a United Nations Environment Program trust fund.

Japan's aid performance in the Gulf war was consistent with the overall problems faced by the program. Bureaucratic and political conflict as well as an inability to formulate concrete policy goals marked Japan's efforts to deal with a crisis of global magnitude. As a consequence, Tokyo was largely reactive to American pressure.

The Future of Japanese Foreign Aid to the Middle East

The future of Japanese ODA in the Middle East will be influenced by several factors. Japan's economic relationships with the MIddle East are becoming increasingly complicated. Traditionally, that relationship has beeen defined in terms of Japan's dependence on Middle East Oil. That perspective will remain relevant. Japan's attempts to diversify energy sources do not appear to be working as well as hoped. Demand for oil increased by almost five percent annually in 1990 and 1991 and the growth rate for energy has exceeded the growth rate for the gross domestic product. Japanese government officials believe dependence on Middle East oil will gradually increase.[44] This could mean that Japan will continue to step up assistance to the region, although Matsuura believes that the ratio of roughly 10% of Japan's overall aid program currently earmarked for the Middle East will remain basically unchanged.[44] However, there are important new elements in the economic relationship. Construction and modernization of several Japanese refineries will be financed in large part by multi-billion dollar investment *from* the Middle East, especially Saudi Arabia.[45] This may generate expectations not simply for more ODA, but for broader access to Japanese technology, goods, and markets and greater leverage on Japan's international political roles.

It is possible, however, that the revolutions of 1989 in Eastern Europe and the collapse of communism in the Soviet Union may have direct consequences on the extent to which Japan increases or decreases foreign aid to the Middle East. If a rapprochement between the Russian Republic and Japan were to be achieved as result of compromise over the Northern Territories issue, then Siberia's vast natural resources could open up for Japan, eventually reducing Japan's dependence on the Middle East and therefore the need for a larger aid role in the Middle East.[46]

Another factor is the extent to which Japan attempts to become more of a global power broker. Tokyo's initial experiences as a mediator in the Middle East during the Iran-Iraq War appeared clumsy. Unless stronger political leadership asserts itself domestically, Japan will remain a very wary and reluctant global political power. Nevertheless, the Gulf War did at least open up the most soul-searching domestic debate about Japan's world role as a political power that has been seen in Japan since the end of World War II. If a way can be found out of some of the structural problems which inhibit the policy-making apparatus, it is possible to imagine some kind of greater Japanese political activism in the future.

This chapter has argued that Japan's aid policy in the region has unfolded mainly as a reaction to events and as a result of foreign pressure. Japan's position has been further complicated by having to walk a delicate balance between securing the nation's energy needs and risking the wrath of the United States if Tokyo runs counter to U.S. policy goals in the region. The system itself makes it difficult to develop a proactive approach to foreign aid. How Japan handles it's complicated policy in the Middle East may well become a bellwether for the manner in which Tokyo comes to terms with it's global position.

Endnotes

1. Ronald A. Morse, "Japan and OPEC in the Global Energy Market," in Edward J. Lincoln, ed. *Japan and the Middle East* (Washington, D.C.: The Middle East Institute, 1990), p. 13.

2. Douglas R. Ostrom, "Trends in Japanese Trade with the Middle East," in Edward J. Lincoln, ed., *Japan and the Middle East* (Washington, D.C.: The Middle East Institute, 1990,) p.18.

3. Kent E. Calder, "Japanese Foreign Economic Policy Formation: Explaining the Reactive State," *World Politics*, vol.XL, Number 4, July 1988, p.519.

4. See Robert M. Orr, Jr., *The Emergence of Japan's Foreign Aid Power* (New York: Columbia University Press, 1990), chapter five.

5.Yasumasa Kuroda, "Japan and the Israeli-Palestinian Conflict," in Edward J. Lincoln, ed., *Japan and the Middle East* (Washington, D.C.: The Middle East Institute, 1990), p.41.

6. Mark Seralnick, "Over a Barrel: Japanese Crisis Decision-making and the Oil Shock of 1973," (Ph.D. dissertation, University of Tokyo, 1987).

7. *Mainichi Shimbun*, (evening) October 19, 1973, quoted in Seralnick, p.87.

8. Seralnick, p.84.

9. *Ibid*, p.92.

10. Dennis Yasutomo, *The Manner of Giving: Strategic Aid and Japanese Foreign Policy* (Lexington, Mass.: Lexington Books, 1986), p.88.

11. Interview, April 17, 1990, Tokyo with former high ranking official in the Middle East/Africa Bureau of MOFA.

12. Interviews, Ministry of Foreign Affairs, April 18, 26, 1990, Ministry of International Trade and Industry, April 20 and Ministry of Finance, March 20, 1990.

13. Koichiro Matsuura, *Enjo Gaiko no Zaizensen de Kangaeta koto* (On the Front Lines of Aid Diplomacy), (Tokyo: Association for the Promotion of International Cooperation, 1990), p.209.

14. Ministry of Foreign Affairs, Economic Cooperation Bureau, *Wagakuni no Seifu Kaihatsu Enjo* (Our Country's Official Development Assistance) v. 2, (Tokyo: Association for the Promotion of International Cooperation, 1991) p. 234. Hereafter cited as *Wagakuni*.

15. *Wagakuni*, v.2, 1991, p.239

16. *Wagakuni*, v.1, 1991, p.314.

17. *Wagakuni*, v.2, 1991, p.278.

18. Matsuura, p.207. Mixed credits have been defined as "using aid to subsidize exports." See Desmond McNeill, *The Contradictions of Foreign Aid* (London: Croom Helm, 1981), p.31.

19. Interviews, with Ministry of Foreign Affairs official and American Embassy officer, Tokyo, April 26, 1990.

20. "Japan Pledges to help with Mideast peace efforts," *The Japan Times*, August 10, 1988, p.1.

21. Officially known as the Iran-Japan Petrochemical Company project located at the Persian Gulf port of Bandar-Khomeini, it was 85% completed when the war began.

22. Matsuura, p.204.

23. Interview with former Director-General of the Middle East-Africa Bureau, April 16, 1990. He commented that the real GNP per capita is probably closer to $1,000 and should be redefined. Also, see Matsuura, p. 206.

24. For an explicit case see Orr, *The Emergence of Japan's Foreign Aid Power*, pp. 117-119.

25. Interview, Ministry of Foreign Affairs, April 18, 1990.

26. Yasutomo, *The Manner of Giving*, p.122.

27. Interviews, Ministry of Foreign Affairs, April 18 and 26, 1990.

28. Jeffrey T. Bergner, *The New Superpowers* (New York: St. Martin's Press, 1991), pp. 174-175.

29. Beacon lights were purchased with Japanese aid funds and installed by a British firm so that ships could navigate easier. "Kuwait, Saudi Arabia to host Navigation Project funded by Japan to help ships safely ply Gulf," *The Japan Times*, July 16, 1988, p.3.

30. Calculated from *Wagakuni*, v.2, 1991, pp.229-344.

31. "PLO seeks direct aid from Japan," *The Japan Times*, April 28, 1990, p.3.

32. *Wagakuni*, v.1, 1991, p.389.

33. Interviews, Ministry of Foreign Affairs, April 26, 1990.

34. Or as Prime Minister Kiichi Miyazawa once put it "We watch the world situation and follow the trends," see Kenneth B. Pyle "The Burden of Japanese History and the Politics of Burden Sharing," in John H. Makin and Donald C. Hellman, eds. *Sharing World Leadership? A New Era for America and Japan* (Washington, D.C.: The American Enterprise Institute, 1989), p.51. Former Japanese Ambassador to the United States Nobuo Matsunaga has observed that, "Japan only makes decisions after foreign countries exert pressure," see Robert Delfs, "Carry the Can," *Far Eastern Economic Review*, July 18, 1991, p. 19.

35. "Tokyo freezes Kuwaiti assets may ban Iraqi oil imports," *The Japan Times*, August 4, 1991, p.1.

36. "Bush calls on Kaifu to step up economic aid for Gulf nations," *The Japan Times*, August 15, 1991, p.1.

37. "U.S. sees Japan's Gulf aid package as inadequate," *The Japan Times*, August 31, 1991, p. 4.

38. "Japan's Mideast Stance 'Insufficient'," *The Japan Times*, August 28, 1991, p.3.

39. Courtney Purrington and A.K., "Tokyo's Responses During the Gulf Crisis," *Asian Survey*, vol XXXI, No.4, April 1991, p. 309. Also see "Prime Minister announces 'maximum' Gulf package," *The Japan Times*, August 30, 1991, p.1.

40. See "U.S. sees Japan's Gulf aid package as inadequate," *The Japan Times*, August 30, 1991, p. 1.

41. See Purrington and A.K., p. 322 for a concurring view.

42. Japan Eçonomic Institute report, No. 4B, February 1, 1991, p.1.

43. *Ibid*, p.3.

44. Tomio Uchida (former Deputy Director General, Middle East Bureau), "Japanese Perspectives with Emphasis on Economic Aspects," unpublished paper, March 1990, p.3.

44. Matsuura, p.211.

45. Interview with Fereidun Fesheraki, Director of the East-West Center Energy Program.

46. Four main islands north of Hokkaido captured and occupied by the Soviet Union since the last days of World War II have remained the principal stumbling block to improved Soviet-Japan relations. Tokyo has demanded their return throughout most of the post-war period.

15

JAPAN AND THE ASIAN DEVELOPMENT BANK: MULTILATERAL AID POLICY IN TRANSITION

Dennis T. Yasutomo

Introduction

The Asian Development Bank has become a fixture on the international development scene since its founding in November of 1966. The Bank's history has been characterized by steady expansion and evolution over the past two and a half decades. Initially capitalized at $1 billion, the ADB's authorized capital stood at $22.1 billion by the end of 1989. Approximately $29 billion had been committed to 942 projects since its founding. The Asian Development Fund, the Bank's soft loan window, had mobilized $13 billion, and the Technical Assistance Special Fund raised $173.2 million.[1]

The ADB also started direct equity investment in the private sector in 1983, and began lending to private sector institutions without government guarantees in 1985. As of the end of 1988, $85 million had been committed to nine private institutions, $52.4 million to 25 equity investment operations, and $25 million to three equity underwritings.[2] And in 1989, the Bank established the Asian Finance and Investment Corporation, with the ADB contributing 25% of the funds to complement Bank efforts promoting private sector growth in the region.[3]

Total membership in the ADB stands at 50 countries, with the entrance of Vanuatu, Bhutan, Spain and the People's Republic of China in the 1980s, and Turkey, Micronesia and the Marshall Islands in 1990. Bank membership will expand to 51 with the entrance of Mongolia in the early 1990s. In 1990, regional members totalled 34, with nonregionals at 16. Nineteen members are developed countries, and developing member countries (DMCs) stand at 31.

A significant development by the 1990s has been the graduation from borrower status of Taiwan, Hong Kong, Singapore, and South Korea. Thailand and Malaysia are expected to join this exclusive group within a few years. This reflects the emergence of the Newly Industrializing Economies (NIEs) and quasi-NIEs in the region since the 1970s, making the Asia Pacific region the fastest growing region economically in the world. While four countries graduated, two new borrowers appeared on the scene in the last half of the 1980s: India, a founding Bank member, converted to borrowing status, and China entered as a borrowing member in 1986.

The Bank also expanded management and staff positions. The ADB began in 1966 with a Japanese president and an Indian vice president. By the early 1980s, two additional vice presidential slots had been created. The Japanese president had been joined by American and German vice presidents, while a Korean replaced the Indian vice president.[4] The Bank's professional staff stood at 605 at the end of 1988 coming from all member nations, and support staff numbered 1,037.

Amid expansion and growth, the ADB suffered strong criticism in the 1980s on several fronts, including a controversial president and policies. For example, critics assailed the president's insistence on loan commitment quotas against the backdrop of a fall in loan demand.[5] The Bank's policies large investments in agricultural projects were criticized for failing to narrow income gaps, increase employment, or provide adequate essential agricultural support services to the poorest peoples.[6] Some of the harshest criticism came from inside the Bank, when information leaks resulted in serious charges of mismanagement. The indictment included complaints that the Bank relied too heavily on outside consultants for new ideas (i.e., too many project engineers and analysts on the staff); distortion of facts and invention of data; withholding crucial information; political machinations in loan preparations; deviations from existing policies and procedures; management cover-up attempts; and retaliatory firing of those who called attention to or opposed alleged infractions or abuses of Bank policy practices.[7]

Through it all, Japan has remained a steadfast bulwark of the ADB. Tokyo's relationship with the Bank is the most intimate of all its ties with international organizations. Critics have often identified the ADB as Japan's international development bank, or the "JDB," and blame Japan for its ills. On the other hand, the Bank has also been regarded as the most successful and efficient of the regional multilateral development banks, and Japan has garnered credit for its success. In either case, Japanese prestige has been closely linked with the Bank's fortunes and reputation from the beginning. As the ADB celebrated its 25th anniversary in 1991, the Japanese seem poised to intensify further their commitment to the Bank's functioning and reputation.

The Japanese approach toward the ADB has tended to reflect its overall postwar foreign policy, often derided as a diplomacy of "silence, smile, and sleep." Throughout the postwar period, Japanese diplomacy typically exhibited passivity and reactiveness to external events and forces, concern only for its own economic welfare, deference to U.S. foreign policy interests, the separation of political from economic matters, attention to Asia, and a near-obsession with national prestige. Japan lacked a grand strategy or international vision, as critics have long urged Tokyo to "do something" or "do more" in international relations.

In some ways, ADB policy was an exception to the rule of passivity: Japan did "do something." Japanese were actively involved in the conceptualization, foundation, shaping, and management of the Bank. Tokyo supplied all Bank presidents, dispatched a large number of professional staff members, oversaw the drafting of the by-laws, took keen interest in staffing and budgeting questions, and took the lead in funding Bank coffers. Tokyo greatly influenced the early Bank's personality and procedures. In this sense, Japan was deeply involved in rule-making and agenda-setting activities from the critical inaugural period.[8]

However, the Japanese government had initially been a reluctant activist in the founding process, with involvement triggered and shaped considerably by the idiosyncratic initiatives of interested individuals. It did take an active role in the actual shaping of the Bank's organization and practices in the early years, but it was not the only influence. Throughout the 1970s and into the early 1980s, Japan's approach remained basically low key and narrowly focused. It lacked a concrete policy agenda or vision, with government representatives remaining silent at Board of Directors meetings.[9] Japan concentrated primarily on: (1) insuring the financial health of the Bank; (2) supplying and supporting the Japanese president; (3) overseeing the smooth operation of the Bank, especially budget and personnel policies, including supplying a large number of seconded professional staff members; (4) working in concert especially with the United States; and (5) maintaining the Bank's image and reputation. In many ways, Japan's objectives were defensive in nature--making sure the ADB survived, prospered, and functioned well enough to maintain not only the Bank's image but Japan's reputation as well.[10]

These traditional concerns remain constant into the 1990s, but they have been shaken by new foreign policy themes engendered by Japan's emergence as an aspiring "international state." A foreign policy debate ensued on Japan's appropriate international role and on the means to fulfill its international responsibilities. The substance of this debate remains murky, but there seems to be a growing consensus on the need for a new course different from the old diplomacy.[11] The Japanese hope to fashion a diplomacy that is more activist than passive, nonmilitary rather than military, focused on political as well as economic issues, global rather than merely regional, and a diplomacy that takes the form of collective management of world problems rather than a hegemonic "Pax Nipponica."[12]

In the 1980s, the Japanese came to realize that one foreign policy tool seems especially appropriate and effective in the pursuit of these aspirations: economic assistance. Since the late 1970s, Japan has embarked on four aid doubling plans. These pushed Japan to the status of the second largest aid-giving nation by the mid-1980s, and the number one position in the early 1990s.[13] In the last half of the 1980s, as Japan attained the status of the world's largest creditor nation, the Japanese focused especially on multilateral development banks as part of its new activism in the search for mitigation of the international debt crisis.

Japan's ADB policy has reflected these new activist currents in multilateral aid policy since 1985. Tokyo's involvement is no longer as low-profile and passive. Japan has begun to define more clearly the ADB's purpose and uses as a foreign policy tool, especially in the area of recycling Japanese surpluses to debtor countries. It has reaffirmed and intensified its commitment to fund the Bank and has demanded recognition for this through an increase in its vote share. It has sent to Manila a new breed of representatives who have been more articulate and assertive, and it has shown greater willingness to participate actively in shaping Bank policy. In other words, Japan gives the appearance of having amended its past policy approach of passivity and anonymity in an effort to gain a preeminent position in the Bank, even differing openly at times with its principal partner, the United States.

Aid policy activism, however, brings new difficulties. The basic problem is that aid policy still reflects the low-posture and passive tendencies of the "old" diplomacy. Its aspirations are forward-looking, but it cannot easily shake off traditional attitudes and preferences. Japanese foreign policy has entered a transitional era, and aid policy is both a reflection of and a catalyst for this transition from the old passive to the new activist diplomacy. But activism still seems to go against the grain of traditional aid and foreign policy, and these strains are causing serious adjustment problems for the Japanese.

As a result, ADB policy in the late 1980s and early 1990s appears almost schizophrenic, a mixture of two different personalities, one passive and reticent and the other active and assertive. The ADB thus serves as an instructive case study of the clash between Japan's traditional low-posture aid policy and the newly emerging high-posture aspirations that must reject these old behavioral patterns and preferences.

Japan's Aid Policy and the ADB

Japan's traditional approach to the ADB reflected its traditional aid policy. Japanese ODA policy evolved within the framework of a specific set of characteristics, including:

1. an emphasis on aid amounts primarily for prestige reasons, reflecting also the absence of an aid philosophy to otherwise justify the extension of aid for commercial objectives;
2. a reactive "request-based" process, reflecting a Japanese preference for "self-help," which places the onus on the aid recipient for finding and presenting aid projects to Japan for consideration;
3. a preference for value-free, nonpolitical aid, resulting in hesitation on conditionality and reflecting the basic pragmatism and reticence that characterizes Japanese diplomacy in general;
4. a preference for Asia, reflecting a sense of responsibility for and identification with the region and a feeling that its global interests and reach are limited; and
5. deference to U.S. aid policy objectives, reflecting the long-standing bilateral alliance in which Japan considered itself the subordinate partner.

These characteristics can provide an adequate framework for understanding Japan's ADB policy into the 1980s, but they also explain the flux in Japanese ADB policy today. Japan is now responding to internal and external calls to revise this type of low-posture policy approach. A struggle has ensued between Japan's preference for this comfortable traditional approach and the imperatives of a riskier, pro-active course necessitated by the nation's newly acquired status as an economic and financial great power.

Preference for Aid Quantity

Japan's contributions to the ADB reflect its overall focus on aid quantity. Tokyo has, from the beginning, exhibited a willingness to be the main financial support of the Bank, while leaving the use of those funds primarily to the Bank's discretion. Washington and Tokyo each contributed $200 million initially, the first time that any nation had matched an American contribution to an international organization. From the beginning, Japan sought to maintain funding parity with the United States. Contributions to Ordinary Capital Resources (OCR) still reflect this concern, but Japan gradually evolved as the preeminent funding source for the Bank through its support for the concessional windows. Since the early 1970s, Japan has pledged to provide at least one-third of Asian Development Fund (ADF) resources, usually surpassing that figure (e.g. 47% in 1989), and since 1978, especially, the Japanese have made up short-falls in the ADF caused by American reluctance to contribute its full share.

In the 1980s, the Japanese not only came consistently to the defense of the ADF but also pushed for an increased OCR share and found new ways to funnel capital into the Bank. As of December 31, 1988, Japan had contributed $3.24 billion to the Ordinary Capital Resources, or 15% of total contributions $6.99 billion to the Asian Development Fund, or 37% of total contributions (the figure reached 47% in 1989); and $47.7 million to the Technical Assistance Special Fund (TASF), or 56.9% of total contributions.[14]

In addition, in 1988, Japan established a Japan Special Fund within the Bank, pledging about $100 million to help recycle Japanese surpluses to debtor developing member nations through technical assistance for project preparation feasibility studies and advisory services in certain key sectors. In 1988, Tokyo established a 94.5 million yen ($700,000) Asian Development Bank-Japan Scholarship Program for one to three years of graduate training for eligible candidates at 11 institutions in nine member countries.[15] At the May 1990 annual meeting, Japan proposed a new environmental preservation fund, offering to set aside $4 million (about 600 million yen) out of a planned $59 million (about 8 billion yen) allocation to the Japan Special Fund.[16] Japanese financial institutions also supported the creation of the ADB's Asian Finance and Investment Corporation (AFIC), offering initially to contribute 40% of the pool and settling for 30% because of fears on the part of some participants of Japanese dominance.

Japan's focus on levels of funding has resulted in criticism that Japan is merely throwing money at problems. "When you don't have a policy, it can't be helped," according to a Finance Ministry official. "The problem is that Japan has no [bilateral aid] strategy. It gives technical assistance and money, but without a strategy or system," he continues. "Japan is considered a great power, but it has no real [aid] policy. It contributes, gives out money," explains another MOF official.[17]

In the past, Japan's lack of a clear policy strategy explains, in part, Japan's willingness to focus on amounts and to follow the lead of the ADB management on policy directions.[18] This was one of the attractive features of multilateral banks in general. They compensated for Japan's lack of a development philosophy and expertise in the development problems of the Third World, including Asia. The Ministry of Finance is the headquarters of Japan's multilateral development bank (MDB) policy, but it lacks expertise in development issues and in the cultures of the developing nations. MDBs can provide that specialized knowledge about developing nations' cultures and development policies. In fact, the smooth and efficient extension of resources to needy areas is one of the official justifications for reliance on MDBs.[19] However, multilateral aid is attractive precisely because Japanese aid policy lacks a clear philosophy. MDBs offer the opportunity to match Japanese money with someone else's philosophy.

Japanese aid officials are painfully aware of the need to move away from the focus on quantity, and to develop a more substantive and coherent aid philosophy or strategy. They have been wrestling with this problem throughout the 1980s, with the Foreign Ministry's formulation in 1980 of Japan's first "aid philosophy," which stressed humanitarian, interdependence, and comprehensive security rationales.[20] Aid rationales remain ambiguous, however, partly because the Japanese have not been able to smoothly mesh aid policy within the nation's overall foreign policy.[21]

In the last half of the 1980s, the Japanese have apparently responded to the need for greater clarity and coherence in its economic cooperation policy. Japan still does not possess an aid philosophy, but the Ministry of Finance is apparently fashioning a development strategy. The following assumptions seem to constitute its main tenets:

1. ODA and Other Official Flows (OOF) are important but not enough. The problems faced by the developing world, especially the debt problem, cannot be solved through reliance on meager

ODA flows alone. Besides, the Japanese budget deficit makes it increasingly difficult to increase aid substantially indefinitely.

2. The private sector is important. Japanese savings are generated in the private sector, and after all, Japan's huge surplus is in the private sector's hands. Financial institutions are hesitant, however, to invest heavily in developing nations, worried about the debt trap, and are attracted by more profitable investment in the United States. Private flows must be coaxed into the Third World.
3. Multilateral organizations are important. These institutions can enhance the impact of Japanese surplus funds. They have other uses as well, including the guarantee of private flows through such institutions as the World Bank's MIGA (Multilateral Investment Guarantee Agency) and ADB's AFIC.

Japan's strategy is to combine these elements into a "comprehensive development strategy" or "comprehensive economic cooperation" policy. The main feature of this strategy or policy is to have the Japanese government take the lead through the use of ODA to induce a flow of private sector funds flowing to the developing world. This will result in "a new, hybrid form of economic cooperation, a combination of official aid alongside private sector transfers of productive capacities, for the most part in the form of foreign direct investment,"[22] but also co-financing arrangements with MDBs. The government's role is important in insuring that the surplus is redirected to developing nations rather than remaining in company coffers or flowing to North America: "The hybrid approach is therefore designed to redirect some of the profit-motivated private flows into a policy-guided, publicly desirable direction by using official flows as inducements."[23]

The Japanese have learned a lesson from the oil 1973-74 crisis:

> In contrast to the oil money, that was held by the governments of the oil-exporting countries, today's surplus capital is largely held by the private sector, and the private sector has learned from the experiences of the 1970s to be extremely wary of investing in or lending to the high risk, heavily indebted developing countries. It is thus especially important that the governments of the trade-surplus countries take the initiative in promoting recycling.[24]

The most significant manifestation of this hybrid ODA-OOF-private flow-MDB form of economic cooperation is Japan's capital recycling efforts in the last half of the 1980s. In 1986, Japan announced a three-year $10 billion multilateral aid package which included establishing a $2 billion Special Fund in the World Bank; $3.6 billion for a special facility in the IMF; and $3.9 billion for other MDBs, including $1.3 billion for the ADF. In 1987, Japan pledged a further $20 billion: $8 billion in additional funds for MDBs, including the ADB; $9 billion for loans co-financed with MDBs, the Export Import Bank of Japan, the Overseas Economic Cooperation Fund (OECF) and private banks; and $3 billion in untied Export Import Bank loans to developing countries.[25] In 1989, Japan pledged a further $35 billion in addition to the previous $30 billion. This program consists of: $14.5 billion in contributions to MDBs and private sector funds; $13.5 billion for Export Import Bank loans for parallel lending with the IMF and co-financing with the World Bank; and $7 billion for ODA loans through the OECF. Of the $35 billion, $10 billion will be set aside for contributions to the American Brady Plan for relief of the global debt crisis.[26]

Only one-sixth of the $20 billion program and one-third of the $30 billion package consists of ODA, and of the $65 billion total package, only 20% will be ODA. The program reflects the Japan's government's effort to use ODA as a catalyst to divert private investment from North America to the developing world: "The Japanese government intends to change that if it can, and is prepared to put some money of its own just as a catalyst."[27] Japan's effort is directed at merging all financial flows, especially private flows, into a "comprehensive" package, with multilateral organizations constituting a pillar of the approach. Finance Minister Miyazawa Kiichi articulated this approach to the debt problem (stressing market-oriented measures and an expanded role for international organizations) at the 1988 World Bank-IMF meeting. The United States strongly criticized the proposal, but proceeded to adopt some of its main tenets in its Brady Plan of 1989.

Japan has concentrated most of its attention on the World Bank and IMF in its allocation of recycling funds because the debt crisis has hit other regions harder than Asia. But the ADB also became a part of this comprehensive development strategy approach from 1987, including a new Japan Special Fund, and much of the recycling funds initially went to Asian nations.

The Japanese stress that comprehensive aid is not for the sole purpose of enriching Japanese companies. They stress in particular the untied nature of recycled funds, and the utilization of a third party (MDBs) as the conduit of funds to the Third World, either through special funds and/or co-financing.[28] In the ADB, for example, the Japan Special Fund, with $100 million pledged over three-years, is intended to enable the ADB to double technical assistance outlays each year. The Japanese assume that technical assistance will result in the formulation of development projects which will increase borrowing from the ADB, which had suffered a decrease in loan requests from the mid-1980s.[29] The Japanese also point to the decrease in their share of ADB procurement awards, consistently a sore spot in Japan's relations with the Bank.[30] AFIC represents the latest effort to combine official and private funds through a multilateral channel. And Japan has strongly supported the Bank's effort to expand co-financing activities in the 1980s.

ADB co-financing in the 1970s consisted of ADB joint ventures with national governments and other international institutions, but President Masao Fujioka (1981-89) brought a commitment to more co-financing with the private sector. While some attribute his interest in the private sector's role to the impact of the Reagan administration's emphasis on the "magic of the marketplace," Fujioka developed his ideas as a Japanese Finance Ministry and Export Import Bank official in the 1970s.

Fujioka's presence was also fortuitous for the Japanese since he seemed to share Japan's focus on amounts as well. Fujioka reportedly instituted a quota for loan commitments of 15% and then 21% a year.[31] The issue became especially acute in the mid-1980s, when the ADB was awash with liquidity because of a drop in loan requests from DMCs. The quotas triggered opposition from some donor countries, notably the United States, and from ADB staff members who charged that careers depended on the quantitative increase of loan commitments. This policy allegedly resulted in a weakening of project quality and departures from standard Bank practices. A senior official asserted that one-third of Bank projects are "cooked in one way or another." The problem stemmed from this "lend or perish" policy. "Fujioka has a reparations mentality. He just wants to shovel the money out."[32]

One ADB staff member disputes the existence of quotas and its effects on promotions and firings, attributing this view to outside (i.e., journalistic) sources, but does concede that Fujioka did institute lending targets.[33] Another staffer points out that Fujioka, despite some opposition, enjoyed the broad support of the Board of Directors: "This was the majority view of the Board, when ADB's performance had been stagnant in 1984-85."[34] India and China eventually shored up loan demand in late 1980s, and in 1989, loan approvals increased by 15% (without China, after loans were halted in the wake of the Tiananmen incident).

Both the Japanese and the ADB are sensitive to these types of charges associated with aid quality. The Japanese government has repeatedly stressed the theme of aid quality in the 1980s, pledging to improve aid conditions and terms and expanding project evaluation efforts. This refrain of quality as well as quantity is often heard in discussions of Japan's overall ODA policy. For Fujioka, "one of his key agenda items was the quality of bank lending. He would get angry and lash out [at critics of his lending targets], accusing the U.S. of being idealogues on this issue."[35]

The marriage in Japan's ADB policy between the emphasis on aid amounts and a new aid strategy remains difficult. Old tendencies remain inviting in an era when involvement requires more than just giving money.[36]

Preference for Reactive and Nonpolitical Aid

Japanese aid policy has basically exhibited passivity in its approach and procedures. Potential aid recipients must approach the Japanese government with aid requests. This "request-based" (*yosei-shugi*) process accords well with Japan's overall foreign policy approach through the 1970s, and it reflects one of Japan's basic aid policy tenets--the belief in the efficacy of self-help rather than aid conditionality.

The Japanese have traditionally hesitated to engage in explicit policy dialogue and to attach conditions in aid negotiations. The request-based approach allows the recipient to take the initiative:

> The so-called "request basis" principle is a vivid reflection of Japan's self-help approach efforts to developing countries. In line with this principle, Japan's approach is to avoid prescriptive aid, and to assist only projects given high priority by any recipient nation.

The Japanese consciously strive to avoid any appearance of interference in the domestic affairs of the recipient nation through the use of aid not only in political matters but even in the economic sphere: "Aid is a cooperative joint work by two countries....Starting from this philosophy, we as a donor should be careful not to force certain economic policies on the recipients."[37]

Part of Japan's concern stems from the fact that Japanese aid policy concentrated on Asia from the beginning. Japanese remain wary of being perceived as intrusive in Asian domestic matters, a legacy of World War II: "Japan has tried to avoid exercising political influence in developing countries especially because of the unfortunate history of Japan's colonial management."[38] Also, they are alert not only to recipient nation sensitivities but also to the concerns of developed nations that see Japan as an economic competitor: "Furthermore, other developed nations could be alerted, seeing it [aid] as another attempt of Japan to strengthen economic dominance over the LDCs by using economic assistance as leverage."[39]

Multilateral development banks follow both request-based procedures and nonpoliticization strictures in principle. The ADB's concern with noninterference and nonpoliticization accords well with Japanese preferences. "We are an economic and financial organization," states President Fujioka. "I don't want to be involved in politics."[40] The Bank Charter officially prohibits the use of political criteria in project formulation, and a panel of outside experts noted in its report that:

> The Bank has been careful to ensure that such covenants are realistic in terms of content and of time frame for implementation. The Bank has also taken into account the competing objectives of the DMCs and has avoided adopting rigid or dogmatic policy stances."[41]

However, MDBs are, in truth, political institutions with explicit or implicit political agendas and impact. At the least, MDBs are vulnerable to developments in international politics. Fujioka's recent book is sprinkled with examples of the ADB bending to external political winds.[42] Under such circumstances, he states, the Bank can play an intermediary role: "Occasionally, the unbiased and apolitical stand of the Bank can exert a stabilizing influence on the principal partners in the venture, with the Bank acting as a bridge or a buffer."[43]

The Bank often does more. It takes political stands, responding to the interests of its member nations, both donors and DMCs. It has suspended aid to certain countries in the wake of invasions: Afghanistan, Kampuchea, Vietnam. It halted loans to China after the Tiananmen incident. It ceased loans to the Philippines during Ferdinand Marcos' last year and decided to extend $100 million to the new Cory Aquino government in a record two month period.[44] The Bank is currently poised to extend aid to Kampuchea and Vietnam with the unfolding peace settlement in Kampuchea, and to China as the furor occasioned by the Tiananmen massacre dies down.[45]

The Japanese consider the ability of multilateral organizations to maintain the political neutrality of aid a major attraction. However, in the 1980s, they recognized the utility of MDBs for diplomatic purposes, with their ability to provide a convenient means of pursuing sensitive political objectives under the guise of political neutrality. Japan has found political uses for bilateral aid in the 1980s, under the slogans of "aid to countries bordering conflict," comprehensive security and aid to "areas which are important to the maintenance of peace and stability of the world."[46] In May of 1988, Prime Minister Noboru Takeshita announced an "international cooperation initiative," in which he designated ODA as "the most valued aspect of Japan's international cooperation."[47] Japan has used aid for diplomatic purposes in recent years especially in the Middle East, the Persian Gulf, Southwest Asia, and Southeast Asia.

Japan has begun to respond to the imperative of formulating a wider foreign policy rationale for ODA, which includes the use of multilateral aid for diplomatic purposes. The Japanese regard aid as a major pillar in a foreign policy that aspires to activism, a nonmilitary diplomacy utilizing nonmilitary diplomatic tools and collective management of international issues.[48] In this quest, aid can no longer be totally politically neutral, except perhaps in form.

The Bank has played the role of buffer in Japan's Asia diplomacy in recent years. For example, while Tokyo suspended bilateral aid to Vietnam in 1979 after Hanoi's invasion of Kampuchea, it lobbied for the Socialist Republic of Vietnam's accession to the seat held by the former South Vietnamese government and for the resumption of ADB loans to Vietnam. The Bank proposed a reconstruction fund for Vietnam prior to the invasion, and it is likely to propose funding for Kampuchea and Vietnam in the early 1990s.

Japan had also favored the inclusion of China as an ADB member against Taiwan's protests. Japan has supported reformist elements in China since Deng Xiaoping's solidification of power, initiating bilateral aid in 1979. China became the top recipient of Japanese bilateral aid in the 1980s. Tokyo thus supported Fujioka's shuttle diplomacy in support of Beijing's entry. Fujioka details his efforts on the China issue in his memoirs, and noteworthy is the frequency of his stops in Tokyo en route to and from Beijing and Taipei, often noting his meetings with the Japanese ministers of finance and foreign affairs.[49] Japan's Ministry of Foreign Affairs also responded to Fujioka's request to second an MFA official to the ADB -- Fujioka specifically requested a China expert.[50] A Finance Ministry official put Fujioka's successful efforts on the China affair at the top of his list of the president's accomplishments.[51]

Japan followed international efforts to economically sanction the Chinese for the Tiananmen massacre by freezing a $5.5 billion bilateral aid package and by supporting the ADB's cessation of loans. However, at the Houston Summit of July 1990, Japan took the lead in efforts to resume aid to Beijing. The Japanese viewed the World Bank's decision in the spring of 1990 to provide China with concessional funds with interest. Japan will more than likely support the resumption of OCR loans to Beijing and support limited access to concessional funds, when and if the Board allows China access to the ADF.

The ADB can therefore serve as a foreign policy tool in the pursuit of Japanese diplomatic interests. It may be easier for Japan to utilize the ADB than other MDBs because of its close ties with the Bank and especially its Japanese presidents, who tend to be ex-Finance Ministry officials. The relationship between the Japanese government and the president has been intimate from the beginning of the Bank's existence.

However, as noted in my previous study of ADB-Japan relations, it has often been the president who shaped Japanese policy. Fujioka was not an exception to the rule. He is quoted as saying of the MOF, "In the end I can go (directly) to the Ministry of Finance. They are my boys; I trained them." An MOF official referred to Fujioka as "*sempai*" (i.e., his senior).[52] As an MOF official notes, his ministry would not have been as cooperative with the controversial Fujioka had he not been an MOF "old boy."[53]

Fujioka may have influenced Japan's policy toward the Bank more overtly than most of his predecessors because of his strong personality, and because he possessed a definite agenda for Asian development. At times, Fujioka exerted naked power over the Finance Ministry. For example, Fujioka presided over the MOF's loss of control over ADB's Budget, Personnel, and Management Systems Department, which had been in the MOF's hands since Fujioka served in that position at the Bank's founding. Presumably Fujioka was piqued with the MOF for seconding a candidate he felt too junior for the position,[54] and because of his preference for a long-time, non-Japanese colleague.

In the end, however, the relationship is not antagonistic. Japan found Fujioka's positions compatible and supportive of its views, and normally the president's view and Japan's policy positions become one. The president expects Japanese support for his position, and the Japanese seek, on the whole, to provide that support. Any major differences of opinion are settled privately, as policies become meshed. The relationship is one of interdependence and mutual support.

However, ultimate political power and influence remain in the hands of the Japanese government. The MOF has the power to nominate the president, and its support provides a crucial foundation for any president's tenure. Fujioka relied heavily on Japan's backing, though often taking it for-granted, and observers note that Fujioka backtracked when confronted with Japanese (and American) opposition. Board members knew where power lay. Representatives of countries that had difficulties with Fujioka reportedly approached the MOF directly in an effort to get the MOF to moderate the president's policy or behavior. Perhaps the ultimate confirmation of the MOF's power was Fujioka's resignation. Fujioka was elected for a second five year term in 1986, but suddenly announced his retirement with two years left to serve, citing age as the principal reason. There is ample evidence that an angry Fujioka did not resign voluntarily, and that the Japanese government was instrumental in easing out the controversial president in order to mitigate the increasingly contentious atmosphere within the Bank.

The Japanese continue to profess support for the political neutrality of the ADB, but the Bank does have a political role to play in the region, whether promoting Kampuchean and Vietnamese reconstruction and reforms, influencing events in an unstable Burma, encouraging liberal policies in China or bolstering Cory Aquino's government. Japan's debt policy, as discussed previously, reveals a definite and sharper view of the diplomatic uses of MDBs, including the ADB, and the political neutrality of the Bank serves as a convenient multilateral cover to draw fire away from Japan and enhance the nation's impact and prestige.

Preference for Asia-Centric Aid

Japanese aid concentrated on Asia from the 1960s, but since the 1970s and especially the 1980s, there is an imperative to disperse ODA to other Third World regions. MDBs and multilateral aid play a major role in globalizing Japan's aid and influence, while the ADB allows Japan to remain focused on Asia.

In the 1960s, almost 100% of Japanese aid flowed to the Asian region. In the 1970s, Asia's share was in the high 60s as aid to Latin America, Africa, and especially the Middle East expanded following the first oil shock of 1973. In the 1980s, Asia's share of Japan's bilateral ODA remained in the 60-70% range. The Japanese find it difficult to break away from Asia. In the early 1980s, they instituted a policy of maintaining a 70-10-10-10 ratio of aid to Asia and the other Third World regions. In the first two years of the $30 billion recycling plan, 90% and 70% of funds flowed to the Asia Pacific region. However, Japan's acceptance of international responsibilities as a global power requires greater attention to the developing world beyond Asia. Multilateral institutions offer Japan a means of reaching the other developing regions despite less interest and even less expertise.

The imperative to globalize aid policy has accounted for many of the problems in the administration of Japanese aid policy. The administrative procedures and structures have strained to keep up with the explosion of aid quantity, but remain hampered by three problems. Tokyo must cope with the insufficiency of personnel, the lack of expertise about specific developing countries and regions and the lack of knowledge about specific development policies of various countries, especially those outside of Asia. While the Foreign Ministry possesses, or has access to, some knowledge about these regions because of its mandate to represent Japan throughout the globe, the Finance Ministry suffers from all three problems. This is a major problem for the MOF since it is the command center for MDB and debt policies.

MDBs can compensate for some of the weaknesses in Japan's aid administration. MDBs can help expand Japan's global interest and impact. They can help Japan reach nations with which contact is weak bilaterally. They provide country and regional experts, familiar with Third World languages, politics, and development policies--thus supplementing the inadequate number of Japanese aid officials and their lack of familiarity with developing regions. This explains in part the utility of and Japanese activism in the World Bank and IMF, which reach countries beyond Asia, especially those hardest hit by accumulated debt. In this sense, the ADB plays a secondary role in Japan's recycling effort.

However, these advantages apply to the ADB and Asia as well, for as one MOF official notes, the MOF is more familiar with the workings of the ADB than with Asian nations. The MOF has, throughout the history of the Bank, found it difficult to promote specific development policies in Asia because it lacked its own development philosophy. This partially accounts for the MOF's emphasis on Japan's development experience as a model for Asian development, which today emphasizes self-help and, in the early years, the solidification of an agricultural base for industrialization. The MOF has thus tended to support the lead of the ADB Board of Directors and management without making strong demands or many substantive suggestions. As one MOF official puts it, "When you don't know Asia very well, why make trouble on the Board?"[55]

Some observers claim that the principal beneficiary of the ADB's professional development role is the private sector. They focus on the seconding of personnel to the ADB by private sector firms. Japanese professional staff members are among the two most numerous nationalities, accounting for 10% of the 600 staff members (Table 15.1) and representing a wide variety of Japanese private sector institutions (Table 15.2). According to one Bank source, current Japanese staffers tend to be younger than those in previous years, but still tend to be seconded by Japanese institutions.[56] Critics have consistently charged

Japanese firms with using the ADB as a training institute and source of inside information about Asian development projects, slighting the contributions these individuals make to the Bank. Many Japanese firms do second personnel to the Bank, but recent years have seen the increase (to about one-third) of Japanese recruited independently and staffers who do not return to their home institutions.

TABLE 15.1 ADB Professional Staff from Countries with Ten or More Members (as of December 31, 1989)

	Country	*Number*[a]
1.	United States	63
2.	Japan	62
3.	India	48
4.	Australia	42
5.	Philippines	41
6.	Canada	39
7.	Republic of Korea	31
8.	United Kingdom	24
9.	Malaysia	21
10.	Germany	20
11.	Indonesia	19
12.	Pakistan	18
13.	New Zealand	15
	Singapore	15
14.	Sri Lanka	13
	France	13
15.	Netherlands	12
16.	People's Republic of China	11

[a]President and Vice Presidents excluded.

[Compiled from unofficial sources]

TABLE 15.2 Previous Employment of Japanese Staff Members (as of February 15, 1990)

Previous Employment	*Number*
Ministry of Finance	5
World Bank	1
Ministry of Foreign Affairs	1
Sumitomo Bank	1
Export Import Bank	3
Japan International Cooperation Agency	1
Engineering Consulting Firms Association	3
Bank of Japan	1
International Development Center of Japan	1
Dai-Ichi Kangyo Bank	1
C. Itoh and Company	1
Fuji Bank	1
Food and Agricultural Organization	1
National Diet Library	1
UN Development Program	1
Ministry of Agriculture, Forestry & Fisheries	2
Aquaculture Development Project, Thailand	1
Sanwa Bank	1
International Labor Organization	1
Pacific Consultants, KK	1
LTCB Research & Management Institute	1
Environment Agency of Japan	1
Ministry of Construction	2
Japan Highway Public Corporation	1
International University of Japan	1
Nippon Koei Company	1
Ministry of Transportation	1
UNDP Bangkok	1
Nippon Telegraph & Telephone Corporation	2
United Nations	1
Small Business Finance Corporation	1
Mitsubishi Research Institute	1
Toyo Engineering Corporation	1
Electric Power Development Company	1

Table 15.2 (continued)

Table 15.2 (continued)

Previous Employment	*Number*
Ministry of International Trade & Industry	1
Bank of America, Tokyo Branch	1
Industrial Bank of Japan	1
Manufacturers Hanover Trust Company, Tokyo Branch	1
Fugro Japan Company	1
Overseas Economic Cooperation Fund	1
UNICEF	1
Canadian Embassy, Tokyo	1
JETRO	1
Inter-American Development Bank	1
Bank of Tokyo	1
Morgan Guaranty Trust Company, Tokyo Branch	1
University of Ryukyu	1
Mainichi Newspaper	1
Board of Audit	1
University of Houston Law School	1
TOTAL	61

[Compiled from unofficial sources]

Critics also assume that Japanese control of the Bank through the presidency and top positions also tilts the playing field toward Japanese firms. Their occupation of top positions obviates the need for suggestions or "making trouble." In other words, they control the agenda. Japanese presence in the management, however, has weakened by 1990. In December of 1988, out of a total of 83 management positions (including the president and vice presidents), nine Japanese held top management positions: The president, three directors/chief, three deputy directors and two managers.[57] Two Japanese recently retired from the Bank (a director and a deputy director), thus depleting the Japanese contingent in the management.

Despite the attention given to advantages for private firms, the long-term utility of the ADB for public sector institutions should not be overlooked. The secondment of government officials expanded in the late 1980s, constituting about one-third of Japanese at the Bank. Japanese aid-related institutions (e.g., OECF, JICA, Export Import Bank) and various ministries (e.g., Transportation, Construction, Foreign Affairs, International Trade and Industry) send personnel.

For the Finance Ministry, in particular, the ADB can serve as training ground for its officials in international finance and Asian development. One could note that many MOF officials seconded to the ADB return to serve in the International Finance Bureau (IFB), the hub of Japan's MDB policy. Fujioka served as the founding personnel director at the ADB and later served as director general of the IFB. The former vice minister for international affairs, Gyohten Toyoo, served as assistant to the founding ADB president. The two most recent ADB executive directors for Japan are serving in the IFB, one of whom is deputy director general. The current executive director previously served as deputy director of the ADB's Budget, Personnel and Management Systems Department before returning to Manila from the IFB, and a former director of the ADB's Budget Department is now serving in the MOF Minister's Secretariat.

This pattern reflects a personnel policy change within the MOF. The ADB executive director position had previously been reserved for a career official on the verge of retirement. Since 1985, the post has been filled by section chief (*kacho*) level personnel, that is, younger officials who will return to the ministry to continue rising up the ranks. In some ways, this represents a downgrading of the position, and makes it more difficult for a younger MOF official to contradict a senior ex-MOF ADB president. However, their stint in the ADB familiarizes them with the Bank, its operations, and senior officials of member nations. In the long-run, the ministry and the nation can thus benefit from this acquisition of knowledge and experience in formulating future MDB and international policies.

MDBs can supplement the Japanese aid administration's deficiencies in personnel and expertise. They can permit Japan to respond to the imperative to reach out globally in aid policy through the World Bank, IMF and other regional development banks. At the same time, the ADB can expand aid policy-makers' knowledge of Asian conditions and supplement the already 70% Asian share of Japan's bilateral ODA. Japan can maintain its traditional focus on Asia while expanding its global involvement. In this area, the two goals are complementary rather than conflictual.

Deference to U.S. Policy

U.S.-Japan cooperation has constituted a major pillar of Japan's traditional policy toward the ADB since the inaugural period. In the 1980s, this relationship in particular illustrates the difficulty in Japanese efforts to move away from past tendencies and preferences and to accept new responsibilities as a regional and global power. The ADB serves as a microcosm of the broader issue of Japan's long-standing deference to the U.S. and the need to act more independently in the world. The problems involve a complex and volatile mixture of personality clashes, differing policy approaches, ideology, and a transformation of Japanese and American international status.

Japan's support for the ADB president presented a problem throughout Fujioka's tenure. Fujioka, according to one observer, is " a Japanese national of undoubted talent but with a reputation for assertiveness, even acerbic, leadership." "That guy doesn't listen to anyone," according to his main antagonist in the mid-1980s, American Executive Director Joe Rogers.[58] Japan was caught between its policy of supporting the president, especially a Finance Ministry "old boy," and working closely with the United States in the Bank.

Fujioka was criticized for both his policies and for his personality and temperament, earning the nick-name "Shogun." Many disagreed with his lending quotas/targets, as previously mentioned. Others focused on his managerial skills. According to one critic, "He had an unfailing ability to promote incompetents and an unfailing ability to fire competent people." Another observer noted that he showed favoritism, promoting "yes men" and individuals whom he had hired when he was the Bank's first director of administration.[59]

On the other side, Joe Rogers was criticized as a young (in his 30s), acerbic, inexperienced representative. According to some observers, he possessed neither knowledge of Asia nor training in Asian development issues. He thus combined a strong personality with a reliance on tough, inflexible ideological positions. According to an MOF reaction to Roger's approach, nonregional countries should not look at Asian development issues "in a textbook fashion, with textbook knowledge."

Another observer insists that the problem was not ideology, but Rogers' personality.

> Policy dialogue was the approach of the Reagan administration, but he took it to extremes. It reflected his personal biases. If you look at all the other [American] directors at [other] MDBs, you will see that the [U.S.] policy position was the same, but Rogers represented his portfolio differently. Personality does make a difference.[60]

A former Japanese director did find it difficult to differentiate between U.S. policy and Roger's personal views.[61] According to many observers, both Fujioka and Rogers would have been much more effective in pursuing their agendas had their personalities been more accommodative and flexible.

The MOF officially sided with Fujioka, admitting in private its difficulties with his strong leadership style. Ironically, Fujioka was chosen as Japan's nominee by the MOF partly to bring strong leadership into the president's position following criticisms of the low-key management style of two of Fujioka's predecessors. Fujioka was just the type of executive Japan desired in 1981, and the MOF was committed to supporting its former Finance director general through all trials and tribulations, although not expecting the storm that would arise, especially with the Americans. Personality differences did exacerbate national difficulties within the Bank.[62]

On policy issues and approaches, American and Japanese aid policies exhibit several general differences.[63] The U.S. and Japan in Manila provide a study in contrasts:

> While Japan emphasizes commercial interests, the U.S. has placed notable emphasis in its policy to the ADB on long-term and short-term political objectives. U.S. initiatives in the Bank have concentrated on ensuring a high level of lending to countries of political and strategic importance to the U.S., and on promoting policies and projects developing market economics and promoting the role of the private sector.[64]

The U.S. has thus promoted policies that supported its efforts in Vietnam under Lyndon Johnson and Richard Nixon, and human rights under Jimmy Carter. Washington has also blocked funding for palm oil, sugar and citrus crops in deference to domestic lobby interests. During the early years of the Reagan administration, the U.S. emphasized bilateral, politically-oriented aid rather than multilateral, development assistance. In later years, the administration focused more on MDBs and strongly stressed policy conditionality (especially privatization as a criterion for MDB funding).[65] The Bush administration is following the previous administrations's emphasis on the private sector, coupled with greater confidence in MDBs and less reliance on ideology.

The current issue for many observers is America's right to flex its muscles in the Bank in view of Washington's failure to fulfill its funding commitment. Because of Congressional inaction, the U.S. remains in arrears on its contributions, again in contrast with Japan, which has paid up and wishes to contribute even more. Americans insist that they have a right to be heard in the Bank anyway. The U.S. is a Pacific nation and has a policy agenda, a development philosophy, and it has a responsibility to American taxpayers in an era of economic difficulties and belt tightening. The U.S. has also assumed responsibilities in Asia beyond participation in the ADB, including the maintenance of open markets for products from developing nations (suffering a trade deficit with Asia in the process), the promotion of direct investment, the provision of bilateral ODA, and the assumption of heavy responsibilities for the security of the Asian region. The U.S. is not in it for the money, profiting from Bank procurement less than the Japanese and Europeans.[66]

Some observers feel that the U.S. exerts more influence in the Bank than Japan: "I do not believe Japan exercises her power strongly in formulating Bank policies....On the contrary, the U.S. does and says a lot on Bank policies."[67] According to Bank observers, the U.S. has increasingly abstained or voted against certain projects. Senior staff members are quoted as stating that U.S. assertiveness accounts for many of Fujioka's agenda items: improving loan quality, promoting the private sector, engaging in more policy dialogue. One U.S. Treasury Department official is said to have requested from Fujioka a written commitment to such policies.[68] In this view, Fujioka was more responsive to American criticism than Japanese policy.

As noted before, Japan's natural inclination is to avoid engaging in policy dialogue and conditionality. In the ADB, the Japanese found the American emphasis on conditionality based on ideology simplistic and inflexible. They agreed with Fujioka's view, that development policies must be tailor-made: "This means making slim clothes for a slim type and appropriate clothing for an obese type."[69] As the Japanese delegate to an annual meeting echoed: "The great diversity of the Asia-Pacific region demands responses individually tailored to fit the geographical circumstances and developmental stage of each of the DMCs."[70]

The underlying Japanese position is that policy dialogue should be based on recognition of Asia's distinctiveness and diversity. The American insistence on support for the private sector and the application of free market principles accords with Japan's preferences. However, the across-the-board application of these demands in policy dialogues strikes the Japanese as overly inflexible--especially in a region that is doing remarkably well economically. As an MOF official pointedly noted:

> It is not good to do what the U.S. does by pressuring DMCs based on ideology. This is not Latin America. There, the U.S. acts as a consultant or doctor and intervenes in a country's management--and look what happened....Asia is doing well. Latin America followed U.S. philosophy, and it has become the world's baggage [*sekai no nimotsu*].[71]

a forceful Japanese representative to the Board during the Bank's inaugural years, followed in the early 1970s by successive directors who tended to be low-key and completely supportive of the president and management, speaking during Board meetings only at the end of the meetings and always in support of the management, with English language difficulties.

The MOF broke this pattern in 1985. As the increasingly bitter and vocal battle between President Fujioka and American Director Rogers threatened to engulf the Bank, the Japanese began sending a "new breed" of "young turk" directors to Manila. With the appointment of Takatoshi Kato in August of 1985 and Shoji Mori in July of 1987, Japan has "come out of the shadows." According to a close observer, "They are young, articulate, skilled in English."[76] The current director, Ken Yagi, is even younger than Kato and Mori, and is knowledgeable about Bank operations, having been seconded to the budget and personnel department in the late 1980s.

These representatives actively countered the American director at Board meetings, and began speaking out on specific policy issues, ranging from support for environmental policies and poverty alleviation to program-based lending and concerns on women and development. And they apparently differed openly on occasion with the Japanese president, though more often in private than in public.[77] In other words, Japan continues to placate critics of Japanese Bank presidents by appointing acceptable candidates to that position, but it has also taken steps through the executive director to insure that its voice on the Board is heard, its policies considered and its presence more visible.

Finally, the Japanese have responded to American assertiveness on Bank policy by forging a closer relationship with borrowing countries. From the beginning of the ADB's history, Japan had envisioned its role as coordinator or balancer because of its status as both an Asian and a donor nation. Japan's preferences were pivotal, for its vote could tilt the balance toward either the DMCs or the nonregional donor members. In the 1970s and early 1980s, the Japanese basically leaned toward the U.S., attempting in particular to induce contributions that would maintain U.S.-Japan voting parity in the Bank, insure the survival of the ADF, and tone down political issues raised by the U.S. In the late 1980s, American and Japanese positions are more in accord than antagonistic, often differing in nuance, but the Japanese are bothered by the style Americans use in presenting their positions. But these stylistic and nuance differences are important, for they also induce strong resentment from many of the Bank's developing member countries and some Europeans.[78]

Asian and Japanese preferences do coincide in several areas. Both Japanese and Asians find strong insistence on conditionality and policy dialogue unappealing. Both find the "Asian management style" preferable, with its emphasis on consensus, conciliation, and compromise rather than contention, politicization, and ideological rigidity. Both agree on the need to keep ADF coffers full and functioning. Asians appreciate Japan's willingness to take responsibility for the financial health of the Bank. They see the U.S. making insistent policy demands without providing contributions, while Japan contributes generously without making strong demands.

The Japanese continue to support active partnership with the U.S. in the Bank, but they find themselves focusing more on DMCs because of concern about the impact of U.S. policies on the ADB. In addition, Asia's importance is enhanced by creeping protectionism in the U.S. and the potential threat of the European Community in 1992. Japanese activities in the region have increased throughout the 1980s economically and politically, and the ADB can reinforce Tokyo's bilateral ODA emphasis on Asia. And Japan's aspiration for a leadership position in Asia always remains close to the surface of its foreign policy.

On the other hand, Japan's tilt toward Asia goes only so far. The Japanese would not side with Asians if the donor nations were united on a policy issue, especially if the U.S. took a strong stand. And after the difficulties with the U.S. under Fujioka, the Japanese have sided more with the U.S. than with DMCs. For example, the Japanese supported America's nominee for ADB vice president against opposition from European and some DMC members, and against hesitation on the part of Tarumizu. Japan also hesitates in expressing a position on the issue of replenishing the Asian Development Fund. The U.S. rejects the Bank's estimated need for $10 billion in new funds for the early 1990s. Japan had also supported American hesitation on resuming lending to China, and has not expressed an official opinion on allowing China (and India) to borrow from the soft loan window. Many ADB staffers assume Japanese positions result from a desire to placate the U.S. after the problems in the 1980s, and from a desire to avoid exacerbating bilateral trade friction.

And yet this tactic conceals Japan's true policy wishes. Beneath the facade of solidarity, Japanese and American positions do differ. Japan feels uncomfortable supporting America's Vice Presidential candidate; Japan wanted to resume lending to China while the U.S. insisted on a suspension; Japan supports Chinese and Indian borrowing from the ADF, provided traditional borrowers are not sacrificed; and since this requires a large increase in ADF funds, Japan supports the Bank's wish to increase ADF coffers substantially. Japan's interests dictate an independent course, but it cannot seem to shake its traditional deference toward the U.S.

In the ADB, Japan and the U.S. started out as equals in status. In the 1980s, Japan sought preeminence, and as the 1990s begin, Tokyo seems willing to settle once again for nominal parity. It is an exaggeration to designate Japan and the U.S. as antagonists in the Bank, but greater competitiveness is visible. It is a struggle between American reluctance to surrender its influence, and Japan's hesitation to wield its power. U.S.-Japan relations in the Bank thus exhibits again the clash between old habits and new aspirations, between passivity and preeminence, between something old and something new.

Conclusion

Japan's ADB policy is a reflection of its economic aid policy, and economic aid policy is a reflection of its overall foreign policy in the late 1980s and early 1990s. It is a policy in transition, a hybrid policy characterized by an uneasy mixture of the familiar and traditional behavioral pattern of a small, insular island country and the new imperatives and aspirations of an economic and aid great power. ADB policy reflects a clash between preferences for reactive, econocentric, nonpolitical, Asia-focused and U.S.-centric policies, and the realization that their diplomacy and aid policy must respond to external demands and internal calls for pro-activism, a trans-economic political role, global involvement, and more independence from the U.S.

ADB policy reflects much that is old. The Japanese maintain their traditional commitment to the financial health of the Bank, support for the president and management, the dispatch of qualified professional staff members, a preference for a nonpolitical approach and cooperation with the United States. One still detects considerable hesitation, caution and defensiveness in Japan's ADB policy. It is still basically reactive, whether in appointing a certain type of president or responding to the issues brought up by Bank critics.

There is also much that is new within the old framework, reflecting Japan's new status in the international system. Tokyo has greatly expanded its financial support of the Bank, by bolstering the old windows and creating new funds, utilizing not only multilateral ODA but private sources as well. The Japanese have developed a clearer conception of the Bank's role and utility in pursuit of specific policy goals, especially in the area of debt relief and the importance of Asia in an era of creeping protectionism among Western trade partners. The Bank thus allows Japan to claim a more active concern for global issues, and it also becomes a diplomatic mechanism and buffer in the pursuit of sensitive political objectives in the region, as seen in policy toward China and Vietnam. Ironically, Japan's political activism is often designed to dampen the politicization of the Bank, especially by the U.S., by attempting to maintain a separation of politics from economics in Bank decisions.

Japan wants recognition for its extra efforts in the form of greater weight in ADB voting power. Tokyo began to push for greater preeminence within the Bank during the 1980s. Unlike the past, Japan is willing to take a more visible leadership role within the Bank, moving gradually away from its past concern that Japan not be identified too closely with Bank affairs. It appears to want not only identification with the Bank but also the power to do something with the Bank.

In either case, Japan seems slightly less dedicated to its policy of maintaining the facade of an equal partnership in the Bank with the U.S., which Tokyo defended and maintained from the beginning. One can detect a subtle divergence of Japan's agenda from American objectives, for many of the problems Japan encounters in the Bank seem to originate in U.S. policy; or else, at a minimum, one can point to similar interests but a dramatic clash of diplomatic styles. The pursuit of Japan's national interests seems to require increasingly a more vocal assertion of Japanese policy, which in turn requires the crystallization of their own distinctive policy to assert.

In the absence of a concrete aid philosophy or development strategy, and wrapped in a reactive diplomatic cloak, Japan's past approach to the ADB focused heavily on national prestige considerations. Japan's reputation and the ADB's status were intimately linked, and Tokyo thus endeavored to insure the Bank's survival and smooth functioning. This concern remains a pillar of ADB policy. But this, too, has evolved, for the Japanese no longer worry as much about the Bank's status. The ADB has established a respectable reputation in the region and in international financial markets, and Tokyo will continue to guarantee the Bank's financial future. In this sense, the Japanese are breathing more easily about their reputation.

On the other hand, Japan's new status as a global economic and financial power has changed the requirements for attaining or maintaining national prestige. For great powers, prestige is determined by deeds, not only by position. Japan today is being judged not by its wealth alone but also by the utilization of that wealth. The ADB thus represents more than Japan's multilateral aid policy toward one multilateral development bank. It reflects the coming of age of an economic and financial great power, an aid great power. Japan's ADB policy will more than likely continue to reflect this greater activism in its aid and foreign policy, but it is also likely to exhibit all the awkwardness of adolescence. ADB policy reflects the clash between old tendencies and new imperatives in overall aid policy, which reflect, in turn, the unresolved foreign policy debate in Japan.

Finally, one thing has remained constant in the two and a half decade relationship between Japan and the ADB: criticism. Japan has been attacked for dominating, mismanaging, exploiting and neglecting the Bank; it has been attacked for not doing enough and for doing too much. Criticism is likely to continue into the 1990s, and may increase with greater Japanese involvement and prominence in Bank affairs. But this is the price a great power must pay for preeminence, and besides, Japan is already quite familiar with criticism of its foreign aid policies. This is something old, nothing new.

Endnotes

1. From Asian Development Bank, *Annual Report* (Manila, 1989).

2. *Ibid*,, 1988.

3. See "Inaugural Meeting of the Asian Finance and Investment Corporation; Statement by Masao Fujioka, President, Asian Development Bank," September 4, 1989.

4. During the 1966 negotiations establishing the Bank, the general belief held that an Indian would be appointed vice president on the condition that India enter the Bank as a non-borrowing member. I presume that the replacement of the Indian vice president by a Korean in part reflected India's interest in becoming a borrowing member as well as Korea's rise as a significant economic power in the region.

5. See James Clad, "Last-Resort Lender," *Far Eastern Economic Review* (May 15, 1986), p. 64, and Robert Wihtol, *The Asian Development Bank and Rural Development* (New York: St. Martin's Press, 1988), pp. 82-83.

6. Wihtol concludes that the Bank has had "little tangible impact on rural poverty." *Ibid*., p. 6.

7. These charges surfaced in particular in 1986, when the Far Eastern Economic Review exposed information it had received from Bank sources. The controversy centered especially on three projects: an aquaculture project

by the Nepal Agricultural Development Bank, an edible oil project in Burma and the Tamil Nadu Electricity power station project in India. See "Unpalatable Loan to Burmese Cooperatives" (pp. 64-65) and "Midstream Reversal" (pp. 66-67) in the Far Eastern Economic Review of November 17, 1986. See also Roy Barun, "The Juggernaut Needs a Big, Hard Push," *Asian Finance*, April 15, 1987, pp. 34-36, for charges of distortion of facts, data invention, and political criteria for loan decisions.

8. For background, see Dennis T. Yasutomo, *Japan and the Asian Development Bank* (New York: Praeger Special Studies, 1983).

9. For a different view, see Wihtol, *Asian Development Bank*. Wihtol argues that Japan pursues specific commercial interests through the use of the ADB and that Japan possessed, in particular, a policy agenda in the field of agricultural development and food production.

10. Japan's interest in the Bank's survival may have been heightened in the 1970s when two other major regional organizations became defunct. The ADB was inaugurated in 1966 along with the Asian and Pacific Council, a South Korean initiative in which Japan played a major role, and the Ministerial Conference for the Economic Development of Southeast Asia, which was the first international conference called by Japan in the postwar period. Both spawned functional regional organizations but the parent bodies disbanded.

11. For a taste of this debate, see Kenneth B. Pyle, "Japan, the World, and the Twenty-first Century," in Takashi Inoguchi and Daniel I. Okimoto (eds.), *The Political Economy of Japan*. Volume 2, *The Changing International Context* (Stanford: Stanford University Press, 1988), pp. 446-86. He identifies various schools of thought that have emerged with the fulfillment of the national goals established by Prime Minister Shigeru Yoshida during the occupation years, namely, economic recovery, minimal defense efforts, and reliance on the United States.

12. These themes can be found, for example, in Yasusuke Murakami and Yutaka Kosai (eds.), *Japan in the Global Community: its Role and Contribution on the eve of the 21st Century* (Tokyo: University of Tokyo Press, 1986).

13. For a discussion of the "fit" between Japan's foreign policy aspirations for the next century and economic aid policy, see Dennis T. Yasutomo, "Why Aid? Japan as an 'Aid Great Power,'" *Pacific Affairs*, vol. 62 (Winter 1989-90), pp. 490-503.

14. Okurasho Kokusai Kinyu Kyoku, "Dai-22 Kai Ajia Kaihatsu Ginko (ADB) Nenji Sokai Supesharu Gesuto Shotai Chosokkai Haifu Shiryo," May 1989; and Asian Development Bank, *Annual Report* (Manila, 1988).

15. See "ADB Invites Students to Apply for Scholarships," *ADB News Release*, (April 3, 1989).

16. *JEI Report*, May 4, 1990, pp. 6-8.

17. Interviews with Finance Ministry officials in August of 1989.

18. For the influence of ADB presidents in shaping Japan's policy, especially in the 1970s, see my *Japan and the Asian Development Bank*.

19. See Ministry of Foreign Affairs, *Japan's ODA 1988* (Tokyo: Association for Promotion of International Cooperation, 1989), p. 7.

20. See Gaimusho, Keizai Kyoryoku Kyoku, Keizai Kyoryoku Kenkyukai, *Keizai Kyoryoku no Rinen: Seifu Kaihatsu Enjo wa Naze Okonau no ka* (Tokyo: Kokusai Kyoryoku Suishin Kyokai, 1981).

21. See Dennis T. Yasutomo, *The Manner of Giving: Strategic Aid and Japanese Foreign Policy* (Lexington: Lexington Books, 1986).

22. Terutomo Ozawa, *Recycling Japan's Surpluses for Developing Countries* (Paris: OECD, 1989), p. 11. Ozawa notes that "The big drawback of market-mediated transactions is that they transfer development resources only in a direction that ensures private benefits" (p. 99).

23. *Ibid*.

24. "Toward a New Perspective for International Cooperation: A Proposal for Effective Capital Recycling and Official Development Assistance" (Tokyo: International Development Cooperation Study Group, July 1987).

25. "200 Oku Dora Shikin Kanryu Sochi-to ni Tsuite" (mimeo); and Hiroshi Okuma, "Japan in the World: The Capital Recycling Programme," *Trocaire Development Review 1988*, pp. 74-77.

26. Ministry of Foreign Affairs, *Japan's Official Development Assistance Annual Report 1989* (Tokyo: Association For Promotion of International Cooperation, 1990), p. 43.

27. A quote by the Japanese Executive Director at the ADB, in "A Trickle From Tokyo," *Asian Finance* (April 15, 1988), p. 66.

28. On President Fujioka's commitment to co-financing, see Masao Fujioka, *Ajia Kaigin Sosai Nikki: Manira e no Sato-Gaeri* (Tokyo: Toyo Keizai Shimposha, 1986); and Masao Fujioka, *Japan's International Finance--Today and Tomorrow* (Tokyo: Japan Times, Ltd., 1979).

29. See "A Trickle From Tokyo," *Asian Finance* (April 15, 1988), p. 66.

30. In terms of cumulative awards as of December 31, 1989, Japan had been awarded 20.81% of OCR, 18.93% of ADF, and 4.94% of TASF awards. For OCR and ADF projects, Japan's cumulative total was 20.18%, but has been dropping in recent years; Japan's share was 12.22% in 1988 and 6.91% in 1989. These figures include goods, related services and civil works plus consulting services. While still the leader in the first category, the United States has taken the lead position in consulting services. Figures are from Asian Development Bank Annual Reports for 1988 and 1989.

31. See Clad, "Last-Resort," p. 64.

32. James Clad, "Unhappy Returns," *Far Eastern Economic Review* (November 27, 1986), 60-63.

33. Interview, July, 1990.

34. Interview with a former staffer, June, 1990.

35. Statement by an ADB staffer, February, 1990.

36. For a trenchant criticism of Japan's attention to amounts over quality, see Alan Rix, "Japan's Foreign Aid Policy: A Capacity For Leadership?" *Pacific Affairs*, vol. 62 (Winter 1989-90), pp. 461-475.

37. Ministry of Foreign Affairs, *Japan's ODA 1988*, p. 29.

38. *Ibid.*, p. 21.

39. *Ibid.*, p. 29.

40. *Wall Street Journal*, May 23, 1988.

41. *The Asian Development Bank in the 1990S: Report of a Panel* (Manila: Asian Development Bank, 1989), p. 47.

42. For example, see Masao Fujioka, *Ajia Taiheiyo Jidai no Kinyu to Keizai* (Tokyo: Toyo Keizai Shimposha, 1990), pp. 28, 100.

43. Richard Barovick, "Asian Development Bank Charts Some New Directions," *Business America* (April 5, 1982), p. 6.

44. Information from a former Bank staffer involved in loans to the Philippines, June, 1990.

45. See Fujioka, *Ajia Taiheiyo*,p. 73.

46. See Yasutomo, *Manner of Giving*, pp. 41-55.

47. "Takeshita Announces 'International Cooperation Initiative,'" *Japan Report* (May 1988), pp. 1-2.

48. See Yasutomo, "Why Aid?" for the gradual emergence of aid as a major means of reaching the next century as a nation practicing nonmilitary statecraft in a collective diplomacy setting.

49. See Fujioka, *Ajia Kaigin*,pp. 152-68.

50. The Ministry of Foreign Affairs could not find a suitable China expert, and by the time it did dispatch an official, the Chinese membership issue was basically settled. Interviews with Ministry of Foreign Affairs officials, June and July, 1990.

51. Interview with a Ministry of Finance official, August 1989.

52. Kevin Rafferty, "Asian Development Bank: The Manila Agenda," *Institutional Investor* (April 1983), p. 168; and interview with a Ministry of Finance official, August 1989.

53. Fujioka was well-known for ignoring Japanese policy-making procedures such as "*nemawashi*" (i.e., laying the groundwork for a policy decision). He would often by-pass the Ministry of Finance, not the best method to get ministry support. On AFIC, for example, Fujioka went directly to Japanese private firms, forcing the MOF to abandon its initial hesitant and neutral stance to support its "old boy." MOF official, June 19, 1990.

54. Reported by an ADB staffer, February 1990.

55. Interview, August, 1989.

56. Interview with ADB staff member, February, 1990.

57. Figures derived from *Asian Development Bank Annual Report 1988*, pp. 197-99.

58. Kevin Rafferty, "Asian Development Bank: Giving a Boost to Privatization," *Institutional Investor* (April 1985), p. 187.

59. Observations of Bank staffers, February, 1990.

60. An ADB management official, February, 1990.

61. Interview with Ministry of Finance official, July, 1990.

62. It should be noted that Fujioka and Rogers were not the only individuals cited for their strong personalities. They were joined by other Board representatives, thus reinforcing the conclusion that personality, and not just policy differences, created a contentious atmosphere in the Bank during the mid-1980s.

63. Robert M. Orr, Jr. has extensively analyzed American and Japanese aid policies from a comparative perspective, focusing especially on systemic differences. See "The Aid Factor in U.S.-Japan Relations," *Asian Survey*, vol. XXVIII (July 1988), pp. 740-56; "Collaboration or Conflict? Foreign Aid and U.S.-Japan Relations," *Pacific Affairs*, vol. 62 (Winter 1989-90), pp. 476-89; and *The Emergence of Japan's Foreign Aid Power* (New York: Columbia University Press, 1990).

64. Wihtol, *Asian Development Bank*, p. 43.

65. *Ibid.*, p. 47.

66. Based on comments from a U.S. representative (February 1990), and from comments by U.S. Bank Governor George Folsom at the 1990 annual meeting. See Peggy Hollinger, "U.S. Hard Line Causes Split Among Industrial Countries," *Annual Meeting News* (New Delhi), May 4, 1990.

67. ADB staffer, February, 1990.

68. James Clad, "Last-Resort Lender," *Far Eastern Economic Review* (May 15, 1986), p. 64.

69. Fujioka, *Ajia Kaigin*, p. 67.

70. "Japan--Tatsuo Murayama--Governor," (mimeo), 22nd Annual Meeting, Beijing.

71. Ministry of Finance official, August, 1989.

72. Ministry of Finance official, July, 1989.

73. Jonathan Friedland, "Preparing for the Pacific Century?" *Institutional Investor* (April 1988), p. 214.

74. *Asian Wall Street Journal*, May 2, 1990.

75. Opinions of a staffer (February 1990) and a Ministry of Finance official (August, 1989).

76. Interview with ADB official, February, 1990.

77. These are the observations of an ADB official familiar with Board and Bank activities.

78. Rowley reported resentment against Australia and Canada as well as the U.S., resulting in a closing of DMC ranks behind the Bank and even Fujioka. See Anthony Rowley, "We'll Do It Our Way," *Far Eastern Economic Review* (May 14, 1987), p. 68.

16

POWER AND POLICY IN JAPAN'S FOREIGN AID

Bruce M. Koppel and Robert M. Orr, Jr.

Overview

As outlined in chapter one, the objectives of generating and bringing together the studies presented in this book were to:

1. improve conceptualization of Japan's ODA policy in the context of Japan's evolving bilateral and regional foreign economic and political policies;
2. assess how ODA policy and management have been influenced by changing relationships among Japan's international economic and political policies; and
3. evaluate how and why Japan's ODA policies vary between regions and among countries within regions.

In this chapter, we want to offer our own assessment of what the chapters have to say about these issues and then offer a perspective on the future course of Japan's ODA policies.

Conceptualizing Japan's ODA Policies

Discussions of Japan's aid often focus on the economic promotion dimensions of the program, the emphases on support for building physical infrastructure, the problems of inadequate staffing and diffuse policy management, and the strong concentration of effort in Asia. Attention is also often given to what is considered to be the lack of a clear ODA "philosophy" behind Japan's ODA policy. Conclusions follow that the policies that do exist are essentially reactive to the demands of Japanese business interests and the desires and pressures of the United States. The power in Japan's ODA is seen as hollow, i.e., there is the money, but not the vision.

The stereotype that Japan's ODA policies are simply a continuation first of Japan's domestic postwar economic recovery strategy and then later both a pillar and beneficiary of Japan's international economic strategy remains, as stereotypes often do, based on some elements of truth, some of misperception, and some of distortion.

There is little question that in the 1950s and 1960s, Japan's aid, focused principally in Asia, was one instrument for encouraging the rebuilding in some cases, and the opening in other cases, of Japan's export markets and resource import sources. There is little question that in its early phases, Japan's aid, in the guise of reparations, served important roles of stimulating and in effect subsidizing participation of Japanese trading, construction, and manufacturing companies in international economic activities.

As Japan's economy developed and as her international position as a economic power grew, foreign aid became an instrument not simply for supporting the rehabilitation of Japanese economic activities, but began to become an important instrument as well for an embryonic foreign policy that was cautiously seeking ways to express Japan's evolving international economic, political, and security aspirations and responsibilities. In the 1950s and through most of the 1960s, Japanese foreign policy stayed well under an umbrella of security provided by the United States. There could be important differences between Japan and the United States—the Vietnam War was one illustration—but by and large Japan assumed that on matters related to the fundamental international well-being of Japan, U.S. policy guidelines and security guarantees could ultimately be relied on. In this context, ODA policy was more likely to be an extension of Japan's reconstruction strategy, a strategy which included reconstructing economic relations between Japan and the rest of Asia, than the harbinger of any fundamental alternative views of international order.

The turning point for Japan generally, and for ODA policy in particular, occurred in the early 1970s, when Japan's response to the first oil shock was to revise its ODA policies as well as other fundamental instruments of international relations. These revisions had three important characteristics: (1) they explicitly extended Japanese international economic policy outside of Asia and the West;

(2) they explicitly linked international economic policy with independent international political positions; and (3) they overtly tied international economic cooperation policies to an established but continually evolving concept of comprehensive Japanese security.

The oil shock came with some proximity to the more symbolic but intensely political "Nixon shock." The "Nixon shock" is actually a reference to two U.S. decisions. The first was Nixon's decision to visit China. There was no prior consultation with Japan about this visit. This by itself would be enough to have caused some consternation in Tokyo given the concerns and interests in Japan about China. The second part was a set of decisions Nixon took regarding the U.S. economy. One of those decisions held out the prospect of an embargo on U.S. soybean exports. Soybean imports from the U.S. were important to Japan. In actuality, there was no interruption of soybean exports to Japan at that time. However, an important message had been sent, or at least, this was the Japanese interpretation: the U.S. would not hesitate to do what was in its own interest, even if that would be harmful in some way to Japan.

The two "shocks" combined to increase Japan's awareness of at least two vulnerabilities of significant consequence. First, Japan was dependent in political and security terms on the relationship with the United States. Japan understood and largely accepted this,[1] at the least as direct consequences of the occupation period, continuing insecurity on the Korean peninsula, serious concerns about instability in China, and wider concerns about the intentions of the Soviet Union in Asia.

It was not until the Nixon shock that Japan realized that she could not assume that fundamental U.S. and Japanese interests were necessarily consistent, nor could she assume that the U.S. would not put U.S. interests ahead of Japan's. One implication was that Japan saw that she would have to carry more weight in the U.S.-Japan relationship if her own interests were to be given appropriate weight. In that position, Japan and the United States were not in disagreement. What the U.S. had in mind increasingly was that Japan should share the burden of defending East Asia. What Japan had in mind, however, was what it could do, and indeed what it needed to do, to ensure that the world would be a congenial place for the expansion of her international economic activities. The allocation of ODA as a contribution to international development and stability would prove to be one way in which Japan would express its commitment to the U.S.-Japan relationship while at the same time building up interests and obligations of its own.

The second vulnerability that Japan recognized in the early 1970s was a vulnerability Japan had faced before: ultimately she could not rely on the United States to guarantee her resource security. The general problem of resource security, of course, was not new for Japan. The postwar assumption, however, was that ultimately Japan could look to the United States for help in overcoming serious threats to Japan's resource security. What Japan saw in the oil shock was that to satisfy her resource requirements, to ensure continuing access to the resources Japan increasingly needed, Japan would require a more direct, sophisticated, independent, and global form of participation in international economic and political affairs. This did not mean any systematic departures from commitment to the Western security arrangements. However, it did mean that Japan would need to consider political lines in international economic relations that were more clearly in Japan's own interest—whether or not these lines were identical with those drawn by the U.S. or other Western powers.

It also meant, and this was a major lesson for ODA policy as well as for commercial resource investment, that there were risks in concentrating on any single location of resource supply. Japan would need to cultivate access to multiple locations of critical resources, a process that would in turn, require Japan to build economic and political relations with and improved economic and political intelligence about, areas beyond her traditional focus of interest in East and Southeast Asia. At the same time, Japan recognized a need to strengthen relations with those same traditional areas of supply and support.

To do this would not only be an initiative of official policy, but would, in fact, build on a foundation of growing bilateral economic, political, and cultural contacts—especially in Asia. By 1978, Japan was already the leading bilateral donor in Asia, with most of that aid going to the Southeast Asian nations in ASEAN. In the 1980s, in reaction to increasing demands from the U.S. and other OECD members and in pursuit of objectives that were emerging from the experiences of the 1970s, Japan undertook the globalization of her ODA through a series of "doubling plans." This is a process that is still unfolding. The 1980s period had three major milestones: the international debt crisis, the Plaza accords, and political change in Eastern Europe.

The International Debt Crisis

The international debt crisis drew attention to the growing interdependence of the global economy, especially through the globalization of financial markets. Beyond that, the crisis revealed how complex North-South economic relations were becoming. For example, a more open international trading system could be significantly hampered by the inabilities of major parts of the Third World to finance their trade. On the other side, the trade surpluses of some advanced countries could not be viewed independently of the severe indebtedness and lack of access to new capital plaguing several important less developed countries.

For Japan, all this meant that ODA policies would have to be closely related to other forms of capital recycling (a point never fully understood by Japan's DAC partners) and that these in turn would not simply be matters of economics, but increasingly and explicitly, matters of international relations and politics. Of necessity, Japan had to define her role vis-a-vis the U.S. and other Western countries in reacting to the debt crisis. Japan did not disagree with the need for concerted action on broad strategies to address the debt crisis, especially strategies that involved commitments for debt restructuring. However, Japan has generally had problems with what it perceived as proposals from the United States and the World Bank group to use the debt crisis as a fulcrum for pressure on the economic policies of indebted countries.

For example, the U.S. sought to link both bilateral and multilateral ODA to agreements by recipient governments to undertake market-oriented economic policy reforms. The expectation was that a combination of budget austerity, economic growth, and new foreign capital would eventually bring countries out of their external debt traps. This linkage between aid and the domestic policy strategies of recipient countries was not consistent with Japan's ODA policy which had traditionally avoided explicit policy conditionalities. Nevertheless, Japan increasingly was challenged directly by other donors—especially the U.S.—to cease undertaking activities which they believed undermined donor conditionalities and to become an active supporter of donor coordination in favor of policy reform.

The chapters on Bangladesh, Burma, China, Indonesia, Latin America, the Philippines, and Sub-Saharan Africa demonstrate that the debt crisis has required Japan to engage in a difficult balancing act with its ODA policy between its obligations to the donor community (and through that to the West) and its own agenda of interests and objectives. On one hand, Japan was not entirely supportive of either the economic reform agenda or the use of policy conditionality by donors to obtain compliance with it. On the other side, Japan placed high value on working with other donors, especially multilateral donors, as a way to limit susceptibility to criticism about the quality of its ODA, in some cases to improve the technical basis for its ODA, and in a few cases to shield its endorsement of policy conditionality from charges of political interference by recipient countries.

The Plaza Accords

The second major milestone of the 1980s for ODA policy was the 1985 Plaza Accords which significantly realigned the major world currencies. The effect of the Plaza Accords was that the international monetary system acknowledged Japan's status as a global economic superpower. This had two important consequences. First, it significantly increased expectations of what Japan could and would do in the development assistance area. The second consequence was that it brought Japan's ODA policy in yet closer proximity to areas of friction between Japan and the United States.

It is not an exaggeration to say that the Plaza Accords were an agreement among the World's major financial powers to attempt to bring significant trade imbalances under control through adjustment of exchange rates. In particular, what the Accords sought to do was to significantly appreciate the value of trade surplus currencies (the Yen and the Deutchmark), and depreciate the value of trade deficit currencies—especially the dollar. The assumption was that this would lead to a correction in serious trade imbalances between the United States in particular, and Japan and Germany.

For Japan's ODA, the Plaza Accords set in motion new kinds of pressures for donor coordination as other donors sought to harness Japan's capital strength to their own agendas. While, as noted earlier, Japan welcomed increased donor cooperation, Japan was not entirely happy with the motivations for this kind of coordination. One strategy that emerged was Japan's attempt to gain political "credits" from donor cooperation that could be used in more contentious bilateral areas (e.g. trade and security). Japan especially had this in mind for increased ODA cooperation with the U.S. However, it soon became clear that such linkages were not feasible. In fact, conflict developed around U.S. claims that access to contracts under Japanese ODA were effectively closed to American firms. Instead of the "good feelings" from ODA cooperation infusing the trade arena, some of the issues from the trade arena infected the arena of ODA cooperation.

The Collapse of Communism in Eastern Europe

In the late 1980s, processes unfolded in Europe that were indicative of a sea change in the international environment with significant implications for Japan's ODA policies in the 1990s. Of major importance at that point were the beginnings of dramatic political changes in Eastern Europe and the then Soviet Union. From their very onset, these changes had important implications for Japan's ODA policies. One implication was that ODA and other forms of investment in Asia's socialist economies would become more feasible as the reform impulse in Europe found its way to Asia. Events in China in mid-1989 were disappointing, but the forces propelling those events along with processes of political and economic change in Laos, Vietnam, and Mongolia tended to reinforce expectations that the "transitional" socialist economies would increasingly offer interesting opportunities for both official and private capital flows.

Another implication was that Japan would be expected to play some role in financing the reconstruction of the former socialist economies of Europe. Participation in this was of special interest given the buildup to economic integration in the European Community scheduled for 1992 and the concerns Japan had about what sort of trade fortress that would turn out to be. Japanese policy-makers and corporate leaders hoped to avert some elements of the fortress by getting inside and being seen as an insider. All these prospects, in turn, raised a third implication: what was the proper basis for allocating Japan's ODA? Who should be getting Japanese ODA and what should they be using it for? As Japan considered these issues, Japan was clearly aware that concerns were growing among poorer countries that there would be significant aid diversion away from them and to Eastern Europe.

Continuing Changes in the 1990s

Two events in the early 1990s have further stimulated the rethinking of ODA policy that began in ernest in the late 1980s. One event was the breakup of the Soviet Union and the end of the Cold War. In one sense, the implication of this for ODA policy was to reinforce questions that arose in the late 1980s about the relationships of ODA to democratization processes generally and to the former socialist economies specifically. These issues were not new for Japan, but the changing international environment was bringing these issues to the forefront. Beyond that, the major implication was and is to provoke a rethinking of the relationships of ODA policy to the U.S.-

Japan relationship. While there are still serious collective security issues in Asia, the collapse of the Soviet Union and the sometimes nasty rhetoric in trade discussions between the U.S. and Japan certainly pose serious questions about which interests should be driving Japan's ODA policy.

The changes in Europe and the Soviet Union will undoubtedly have very significant longer-term implications for Japanese thinking about its international role generally and the roles of ODA policy in particular. However, it was the Gulf War that brought these issues into their sharpest focus. Once again, as it was in the early 1970s, it was the Middle East that raised basic questions about the purposes and content of Japan's ODA policy. The Gulf War generated the most serious discussion within Japan about her international role since the end of the second World War. It also set off a very serious discussion about Japan's relationships with the U.S. Increasingly, for Japan, the question would be not how to use aid to "carry her share" in the U.S. relationship or in the relationship with the West generally. This would remain important, but clearly the issues were turning in a sense back to the roots: What are Japan's international interests? What are Japan's international roles? What missions can and should ODA play to support these interests and roles?

In April, 1991, Japan announced a four-point ODA guideline that placed emphasis on recipient country performance on democratization and human rights, reduction of military expenditures, reduction of participation in arms trading, and commitment to market-oriented economic policies. Was Japan going to become more resolute in its use of ODA for purposes beyond economic issues? The 1991 White Paper on ODA has this to say.

> The Gulf crisis and the dramatic reforms in Central and Eastern Europe and the Soviet Union have led to the emergence of a national consensus in Japan that this country's aid should play a more active role in the achievement of world peace, stability, and democratization....Japanese aid has sometimes been criticized as lacking a philosophical foundation because of Japan's reluctance to impose political or economic conditions on recipients. It has also been suggested that Japan should curtail its aid to developing countries that are spending vast sums of money on weapons or are involved in the trading of arms. There have been instances in which Japan's aid activities have been influenced by such factors as democratization movements and human rights issues in recipient countries. Now a kind of national consensus has evolved as a result of such developments as the Gulf crisis and the reform process in Central and Eastern Europe and the Soviet Union. This

> consensus was reflected in the four point guidelines announced in April 1991. This does not indicate a change in Japan's basic philosophy toward aid. Although Japan intends to continue to give full weight to the cultural, historical, and social circumstances of each country in relation to the actual implementation of aid, in some cases a more resolute stance will be taken.[2]

What many of the studies in this book demonstrate is that while the specific guidelines may be relatively new, however they are actually interpreted and applied, the underlying position that Japanese ODA can be an expression of more than economic impulses and a vehicle for more than economic influence are not especially new at all. This may be surprising to those who accept conventional wisdom about Japan's ODA, but as we pointed out in the first chapter, conventional wisdom has been filtered principally through the prism of U.S.-Japan relations. The studies here have opened windows on Japan's relations with other countries and regions, and the views these provide have sometimes been quite different. This is not to deny that historically the political dimensions of Japan's ODA policy were significantly influenced by Washington. However, for example, the chapters on Burma, China, Korea, the Pacific Islands, and the Philippines all suggest that the conventional understanding was limited all along. Japan has used ODA policy as a tool to express both political support and political concern and Japan has done this quite openly. What is important to recognize, however, is that this has not been part of any rigid formula for how other countries should handle their domestic political or economic affairs as much as it has been an expression of Japan's understanding that instabilities elsewhere, especially in East and Southeast Asia, could have direct implications for Japan's economic well-being and security.

In each case where Japan has considered using ODA policy as a way of expressing political displeasure, or for that matter as a way of expressing political support, Japan has acted in reaction to several factors. These include a mix of (1) the dynamics of specific bilateral relationships and the expectations and constituencies that have evolved around those specific relationships, (2) the interests and obligations Japan feels as a member of the "West" and especially as a close ally of the United States; and (3) a concept Japan has of where she has "international" responsibility and where those responsibilities are really not hers. These points are important because they are likely to form a basis for how Japan proceeds in the 1990s.

How Japan defines and uses ODA policy to address these matters appears to fall someplace between ideological and pragmatic. Japan's ODA policy is clearly not ideological in the sense that Japan has a prescriptive view of political or economic development which it wants to impose (as seen in Japan's hesitance to use ODA to express a political position in the Philippine and Chinese cases). Neither, however, can Japan's ODA policy be accurately viewed as simply pragmatic in the sense that Japan is doing what will work without any special reference to any broader agenda (as seen in the applications of ODA policies to express political displeasure in the Korean and Burmese cases). Perhaps the best characterization for Japan's ODA policy is realistic in the sense that where Japan has achieved a more complex level of interrelation, influence, and interest, she will not necessarily be a disinterested bystander to domestic developments. Whether to intervene in some form, and whether to use ODA policy as a way to publicly express displeasure (or rewards) appears to reflect a strong sense of where doing that is within the realm of the possible, and for which there are constituencies on *both* sides who will understand and correctly interpret it.

Perhaps the strongest message, however, that comes from the cases about the question of how to conceptualize Japan's ODA is what we must introduce based on awareness of aid policy of other donors. It is that Japan's ODA policy is not so different than the aid policies of other donors—who after all differ somewhat among themselves. How Japan *manages* her ODA policy is probably where the differences are greater. The point is not inconsequential, but it has led to some stereotyped understandings of the content of Japan's ODA policy.

The Thai case study, for example, suggests that while any bilateral donor will have some problems offending nationalist sympathies in a recipient country, how Japan has managed her aid policy with Thailand appears to be at least as much a source of friction as the broad policies themselves. After all, as a general practice, few donors untie grant aid. Most donors channel their loan aid contracts to their own firms. There appear to be two important differences, especially in Asia. First, because Japan's aid management is highly centralized, the understandings and relationships among aid-professionals and recipient country policy-makers that can be developed at the country level do not appear to be present. Japan has minimal staffing in-country and private companies often monitor their own projects on behalf of the Japanese government. USAID, by comparison, maintains a significant presence in a recipient country and day-to-day familiarity with projects and policies is quite high. Evaluation is only beginning to become a serious tool both for management by Japan and project improvement by both Japan and the recipient country. A second important point, especially in Asia, is that Japan's aid amounts are large, very large. This elicits some complicated feelings in Asia about asking for and being dependent on Japan. Japan is sensitive to those feelings, even knowing that sometimes those feelings are politically manufactured.

Linkages Between ODA Policies and International Economic and Political Policies

The conventional wisdom about Japanese aid referenced earlier assumes that there is a close and deliberate coordination of policies governing trade, aid, and investment. From this perspective, aid is seen as a type of subsidy to both encourage trade and investment and at the same time, to make it less risky. Risk is reduced through market development and infrastructure provision and through the greater likelihood that recipient governments will look favorably on Japanese traders and investors in terms of policy concessions. If Japanese ODA is somehow allocated for political purposes, the Japanese policies involved are usually reactions to pressures from other donors, especially the United States. That is the conventional wisdom about the linkages between Japan's ODA policies and Japan's international economic and political policies.

The case studies suggest that while conventional wisdom is not altogether wrong, neither is it altogether correct. The strongest theme from the case studies is that there is considerable variation among trade, aid, and investment—over time and across countries and regions—and this forces us to consider what are the major factors accounting for this variation.

Outside of Asia and the Pacific, and with the exception of the Middle East, the cases suggest that while Japan's ODA has not been unconnected to trade and investment questions, Japan has been very circumspect in what it does, at what level it does it, and how it does it in terms of the application of ODA policy. In the sub-Saharan African case, for example, ODA policy is conducted with sensitivity to perceived trade problems, but that is a minor concern compared to what is clearly an overriding intent to play a role as an international humanitarian actor claiming no special expertise or insight. The Latin American case is more complicated because of much more significant Japanese investment connections, the strong American interests, and the impacts of the debt crisis on growth prospects. However, here too, Japan's aid policies appear significantly reactive to U.S. interests, certainly more than they appear to be a clear reflection of Japanese commercial interests. In the Middle East, Japan has shown her clearest example of resource diplomacy and the application of ODA policy in that context. However, even here it is important to recognize that the connection is not instrumentalist (ODA as an instrument of trade and investment policy) as much as it is an effort to create a more favorable environment for the pursuit of trade and investment policy objectives.

In the Pacific islands, Japan's economic interests have been indirect—with political, security, and in some sense historical interests playing considerably larger roles. Here one could argue for almost the reverse of the conventional wisdom and conclude that trade and investment (to the extent that they occur) are instruments of ODA policy. It is for this reason that the Pacific presents a problem of serious concern to Japan, namely the prospect of indeterminate dependence on Japanese financing. That is not necessarily a problem because of prospective levels of financing required, but rather because of another implication: indeterminate dependence can embroil Japan in difficult challenges of socioeconomic development for which it is more likely to be blamed for lack of progress than acclaimed for success.

In Asia, the issue of linkages among trade, aid, and investment is both real and complex. However, even here an instrumentalist interpretation that puts ODA at the service of trade and investment can be misleading. Cases such as China, Indonesia, Korea, and the Philippines offer a basic but important insight: Japan's ODA policy has numerous international, domestic, economic, security, and political objectives. In specific circumstances, these different objectives can be pursued in their entirety or only partially; they can be pursued concurrently or independently. The fact is that Japan's ODA policy is not irrelevant to Japan's trade and investment policies, and Japan's trade and investment policies are not irrelevant to Japan's ODA policies. However, because all these policies have multiple objectives and these multiple objectives create areas of possible overlap and areas of unlikely overlap, in most cases there will be divergences. The Chinese, Indonesian, and Philippine cases in particular illustrate how the links between ODA policy and trade and investment policy may vary because of the peculiarities of the specific case.

The variabilities here are not simply in the policies, but at least as important, in the interests of the constituencies for these policies. For example, private interests are actors in the development and application of trade, aid, and investment policies. In some cases, the private interests involved in all three policy areas will converge on matters such as the need for improved infrastructure (e.g. ports, roads, power, communications). Japan's continuing high levels of ODA to Thailand, in some sense despite Thailand's growth, is sometimes used as a contemporary example of this kind of policy link—especially given the recent high levels of Japanese private investment into

Thailand in export-oriented manufacturing. The continuing high levels of ODA to Indonesia could be cited as another example, given Japan's interests in Indonesian resources.

However, as the different interpretations offered in the chapters on ASEAN, Indonesia, and Thailand attest, it is not entirely clear how linked ODA policies actually are to Japanese trade and investment policies and practices. For example, the internal drive within Japan's ODA system to commit and obligate funds on an annual basis should not be underestimated as a force in moving funds to locations where large amounts of money can be actually spent and where there are clear Japanese interests as well. In the early 1990s, that clearly means ASEAN.

In the 1950s and 1960s, one could look at Japan's ODA policy—then principally defined as reparations—as an important lead element in the restoration of Japan's trade and investment relations, especially with Southeast Asia. By the 1970s, however, the roles of ODA policy became more diverse and consequently the relationships to trade and investment became both more complex and in some cases, less clear. This trend continued through the 1980s.

Today, for example, in the Philippines, Japan's ODA is rising while Japanese private investment is looking elsewhere—especially to Thailand, Malaysia, and prospectively, to Vietnam. One could argue that the ODA will rise for the same reason the investment may look elsewhere: concerns about instability. However, not all concerns about instability are equivalent. In the Philippine case, Japanese (and other) investors are wary of making commitments not so much because of prospects for continuing political instability as much as they are because of prospects for unpredictability in the policy environment. From the ODA perspective, instability is a problem not so much in terms of the ups and downs of Philippine politics, but because of concerns that economic deterioration could set off forces that would be problematic not only for the Philippines, but could have regional consequences. Such consequences could range from international labor migration to reduced international confidence in the ASEAN region generally. Japan's concerns about instability, particularly in ASEAN, are not narrowly mercantile in the way some visualize the trade-aid-investment linkage, but rather are better described as strategic for Japan.

Vietnam is another example. As Japan begins the resumption of aid to Vietnam, the prospective roles ODA will play appear to be quite traditional, i.e., building and rehabilitating infrastructure and laying a groundwork that would help attract large scale Japanese private investment.[3] In another sense, however, Japan's ODA to Vietnam needs to be seen in the context of Japan's continuing strong support for ASEAN and the Southeast Asia area. From that perspective, a stable and economically open Vietnam reintegrated with the rest of the region is a major political objective as much as it is a narrower investment facilitation strategy. Cases such as Bangladesh put another perspective on the trade-aid-investment linkage. Japan's aid to Bangladesh bears little correlation to any existing or prospective comparable Japanese trade and investment interests in Bangladesh. Even Japan's strategic interests, in the sense that these are clearly identified for Southeast Asia, are more difficult to locate in the Bangladesh case. In the sub-Saharan African countries, there are certainly examples of concrete Japanese trade and investment interests, but for the region as a whole, the manner in which Japan is managing her aid (through subcontracting) strongly suggests that this effort too is neither narrowly instrumental for trade and investment nor strategic in the broad political and economic sense that ASEAN or Korea are.

Indeed, the globalization of Japan's aid, especially since the mid-1980s, along with the rapid growth of Japan's international trade and investment reveals an interesting mix of conventional trade-aid-investment linkages (e.g. in the Middle East) along with what amounts to a disentanglement of ODA policy from those linkages. The interesting question in the 1990s is how Japan will utilize what amounts to the growing relative autonomy of its ODA policy.

For example, there is some evidence (e.g. from the April, 1991 guidelines) that Japan's ODA will be increasingly used to support serious initiatives in areas such as environmental protection and management, participatory development and basic human needs, democratic political development, and reduced developing country military expenditures. The rising criticisms of Japan's ODA policies coming from the Japanese private sector attest both to the disentanglement of ODA from trade and investment policies, and the perceived movement away from traditional areas of concentration (infrastructure). At the same time, however, there is some evidence (e.g. Burma and Vietnam) that Japan is prepared to strengthen the trade-aid-investment ties, through direct financing (via mixed credits) of private sector activities and the more explicit use of Japan's overall financial power to extract desired policy concessions.

Finally, there is the questions of the relationships between Japan's ODA and multilateral ODA. Several of the cases presented refer to the Japanese desire to affiliate its bilateral ODA resources with those of other donors, especially multilaterals, as a way to both gain credibility and avoid notoriety. However, as pointed out particularly in the ADB and Bangladesh cases, there are also important indications that Japan's views of appropriate relationships between trade, aid, and investment are leading to the proposition that Japanese ODA policy should be cautious about explicit and complete alliances with the agendas of the multilateral banks. One of the principal emerging lines of this argument is that Japan believes it is not illegitimate for developing countries to consider more explicit policy management of their own trade and investment situations (and for Japan's trade, aid, and investment to support this)—a position that is not consistent with multilateral lines calling for less policy involvement rather than more.

> Structural adjustments, including deregulation, no doubt have a favorable impact on economic activities. But will these adjustments by themselves have sufficient impact to generate sustainable growth? It is possible in an economy with strong potential of investment. But, in many developing countries, improvement of the investment climate through deregulation is not sufficient to cause the big wave of investment. For instance, in the Sub-Saharan countries, it would be hard to find a lot of entrepreneurs to create the anticipated wave of investment. Also, in many other countries, we find fundamentally similar situation.
>
> In case the World Bank's strategy of "from structural adjustment to sustainable growth" is not workable, what kind of additional measures will be required? These should be a measure aiming "directly" at promoting investment. In this respect, Japanese fiscal and monetary policies in the post-war era may be worthy of consideration. These were centered on preferential tax treatment and development finance institutions lending. We must, however, be cautious because the experience of one country cannot be easily applied to other countries. Modification should be made carefully taking into consideration the conditions of the specific country to be applied. It may also be necessary to implement for certain period only.
>
> However, if any other suitable policy measures cannot be found, we would recommend to reconsider the investment promotion measures adopted in Japan in the post-war era.[4]

Variations Across Regions and Countries

Variation, it turns out, is a major theme in Japan's ODA—in terms both of policy and of practice. Variation does not have to mean that there is no central guiding policy or framework, only that how central guidelines are interpreted and applied varies. To one degree or another, that much is true of any ODA donor. There are two questions, however, which arguably are more important. The first question is whether the variation is, in fact, derived from a central and coherent theme or whether, in effect, the central ODA policy is actually a rationalization of varied individual interests and policies. The second question is, whatever the relationship between ODA policy and variation in the application of policy, what mix of internal and external factors drive the variation?

The answer to the first question offered by the studies presented here is that variation in Japan's ODA policy is essentially variation around a central theme: economic cooperation offered on a request-basis to countries of strategic, economic, or humanitarian interest to Japan in order to strengthen (1) self-help abilities in those countries for industrialization and economic development, (2) economic relations between those countries and Japan, and (3) strengthening Japan's comprehensive security through reduction of international instability and ensuring access to critical resources. This theme was established in the early phases of Japan's ODA and it has remained at the core of Japan's ODA policy. Around that core, however, additional layers have developed. In some cases, e.g., Burma, Korea, and possibly China, ODA policies reflect specific characteristics of Japan's bilateral relationships with those countries at least as much as they do any transcendent principles of ODA policy. This is an important point, because in many other cases, Japan's ODA policy reflects not so much Japan's relationship with those countries, but Japan's relationship in particular with the United States. Latin America and the Philippines can be seen as examples. Finally, there is little question that there is variation which does not "violate" policy but rather reflects combinations of what specific local conditions will permit (e,g. the Pacific Islands), the limits of Japan's technical and administrative capabilities (e.g. Sub-Saharan Africa), and what can be called cautious globalization.

The question of what drives the variation has basically been answered above. The variation is driven by interests focused on ODA itself, interests focused on relationships with specific countries and regions, and interests focused in particular on Japan's relationships with the United States. The interests focused on ODA as such have been well-analyzed by Orr[5] and others and have been referenced in several of the chapters here. Clearly the interplay within the Japanese bureaucracy on ODA policy plays out against the broader background of policy-making and bureaucratic infighting in Japan, but it also plays out in effect for each country and region. However, the second game is not necessarily a perfect reproduction of the first, a point that accounts for variation. Increasingly in Southeast Asia, these differences are not only well-understood, but to some extent are a point of leverage those countries attempt to exercise on Japan. They do this, for example, through alliances with specific agencies in the Japanese ODA policy-making system. For example, it is generally recognized that MITI dominates Japan's ODA policy making in the Indonesian case, in large part because of the strength and continuity of Indonesian-Japanese business relationships. By contrast, in the Philippines, Japan's Ministry of Foreign Affairs has had the upper hand, in large part because the Philippine case has been defined within the context of the U.S.-Japan relationship. Filipinos understand this and have attempted to leverage Japan accordingly. The interests that have evolved around and are focused on relationships with specific countries have been able, in some cases, to dominate and even capture ODA policy. Burma, Indonesia, and Korea are the strongest examples of this in Asia.

The special case of Japan's sensitivity in ODA policy to the United States has been widely discussed and is in evidence in some of the chapters here. The portrayal of Japan's ODA as a surrogate for "burden sharing" on defense matters in Japan's relationships with the U.S. specifically and the OECD countries generally probably offers the major explanation for the growth in Japan's total ODA during the 1980s as well as influencing where ODA has gone (outside of Asia) or, more likely, where it has not gone. It is not, however, the total explanation. If the growth in Japan's total ODA (and the consequent pressure to disburse it) can be seen as both sources of variation as well as evidence of reactivity to the United States, it is equally important to consider the relationships between the growth of the ODA budget and the growth of Japan's defense budget in terms of domestic Japanese budget politics. It is common to hear references, for example, from people in the Economic Cooperation Bureau as well as Dietmen to the "other wheel" driving growth in Japan's ODA budget, the other wheel being defense.

The question, of course, for the 1990s, and especially in the post cold-war and post Gulf-war eras, is whether burden-sharing or Japan's defense budget will continue to prevail as primary factors in keeping Japan's ODA levels high and in influencing where ODA goes and does not go. There are important indications that both the levels and distribution of Japan's ODA are going to be more responsive to factors outside the U.S.-Japan relationship than was the case till now. This is not to say, for example, that the U.S. and Japan will go separate ways in their individual ODA programs. Exploration of areas for cooperation continue, but between two independent programs rather than between a senior and junior partner.[6]

Current ODA levels do have public support in Japan. While some (most notably former Foreign Minister Saburo Okita) argued after the Gulf War that Japan should make its Gulf contribution a permanent increment to its ODA levels, in part to raise its ODA/GNP ratio,[7] public opinion surveys have not been supportive of such steps. How ODA will be used, however, is likely to be more reflective of Japan's own interpretations of her international role and the significance to Japan of demands and opportunities presented by specific countries and regions.[8]

The major conclusion from the chapters on the variation issue are that (1) there is considerable variation in what Japan does, why, and how; (2) this variation does revolve around a central theme defining the purposes and style of Japan's aid, and (3) while Japan's ODA has gone global (in terms of allocation), to paraphrase Alan Rix, it is not yet matched, supported, or driven by a global aid policy that can account for all the variation. In the simplest terms, the variation in Japan's aid reflects the uneven and irregular interfaces between what has become a global impulse to participate in development financing and a large number of particularistic impulses reflecting the accumulation of interests and experience in specific countries and regions.

The primacy of Japan's interests in Asia, a major characteristic of Japan's ODA from the beginning, remains. Variation within Asia reflect assessments of variations in need and in absorptive capabilities. Beyond, that, the variations reflect Japanese economic and security interests, historical patterns of "burden-sharing" with the United States and other donors, and the changing politics of ODA within Japan.

This last factor requires some additional explanation. Until as recently as the mid-1980s, Japanese ODA policy was strongly influenced by powerful domestic economic interests, country-specific political, economic and cultural interests and alliances, and the routine allocative politics of the ruling LDP. On the outside, these relationships have been portrayed in caricature through the allegation of an excessively close relationship between private interests and ODA policy. In recent years, however, several more particularistic developments have occurred which enhance both the variability as well as the potential autonomy of ODA policy. With the expansion of Japanese economic interests globally, there are informal groupings of business and political interests focused around specific countries on a much larger scale than was true even 20 years ago. These private economic interests, now with access to other forms (besides ODA) of substantial financing, have taken steps to develop their own international development efforts. They have not abandoned interest in the opportunities offered by ODA, but they have also begun actively to look elsewhere. At the same time, bidding on Japanese ODA contracts has become somewhat more internationalized, a consequence of significant yen appreciation since 1985 and pressure from other major donors to open contracting competition to non-Japanese firms.

Variation therefore is a product of both international and domestic changes, changes paradoxically which have the effects both of increasing the number of new voices and possibly strengthening the autonomy of some of the old voices. Barring the passage of an ODA law and the imposition of U.S. Congress-like earmarking restrictions on Japan's ODA, it is not unreasonable to expect that ODA policy could well become more autonomous as former primary constituents (most notably the Keidanren) look elsewhere for financing they can control more directly.

A related point here has to do with the potential for future growth in the ODA budget. As referenced earlier, in the 1980s, only two parts of the Japanese budget consistently grew: defense and ODA. The deep debates that were triggered by the Gulf War raise serious questions about this linkage in the future. The disillusion that began with revelations of ODA misuse in the Philippines, unfavorable political developments in Burma and China, and concerns about the dangers of involvement in international conflict have broadened to a point where many Japanese apparently are not comfortable with an ever increasing commitment to participation in development financing, at least as it has been done in the past.[9]

As is discussed further below, Japan is now considering criteria for ODA allocation that raise potentially serious questions about existing allocations. These criteria include concerns about democratization, human rights, military exports, and military expenditures. What does this mean for Japan's ODA relationships with China, for example? What should it have meant for Japan's reactions to the military suppression of political movements in Thailand in the Spring of 1992? Japan's ODA is working more closely with non-government organizations and other voluntary developmental groups who have traditionally been very critical of Japanese aid because of its perceived close relationships with the interests of large private sector groups in Japan. In the 1980s, Japan began to work more closely with the multilateral ODA agencies and Japan has been paying close attention to the various technical discussions held under DAC sponsorship. All of this suggests that a change is underway. The change, however, will not be complete, nor rapid, nor uniform. The result will be increasing variation.

What the case studies clearly demonstrate, however, is that while there are significant continuities in the allocation of Japanese ODA, this continuity has not been complete nor rigid. Underneath the constants, variation has been present and is not new.

Something Old, Something New: The Guidelines and the ODA Charter

The future of Japan's ODA will bring forward much that already exists, but there will also be new forms, and in some cases, new content. In part, this mix reflects the evolution of Japan's ODA system. It also reflects fundamental transformations in the international system, the implications of these changes for Japan's international and regional roles, and ultimately the instrumental nature of Japan's ODA policies.

An interesting case to illustrate these changes and continuities is the story behind the issuance of the "Four Guidelines" on ODA, military expenditures, and democratization in April, 1991 and the announcement of the ODA Charter in June, 1992.[10] As noted earlier, the Gulf crisis caused significant consternation and rethinking in Japanese policy circles about Japan's international role and responsibilities. How could Japan best contribute to global peace and stability? Before the Gulf War, the assumption was that Japan could do this through its ODA and through its support of the West. The Gulf War raised serious questions about this.

After the Gulf War, discussion on the question of how Japan could best contribute to global peace and security focused on the possibilities of Japanese participation in United Nations peacekeeping operations.[11] However, the scope of this discussion soon included Japan's ODA. Specific questions were raised in the Diet about why Japanese ODA had gone to militaristic regimes, such as Iraq. The questions revealed growing frustrations within the Press, opposition parties, and some parts of the government with the perception that Japan's aid was over-emphasizing economic criteria and was paying inadequate attention to political criteria. When a Japan Socialist Party Diet member asked Prime Minister Kaifu why Japan had provided aid to Iraq, the Prime Minister offered what appeared to be a standard answer: we will study the matter. Normally, a promise to study is tantamount to dismissing the question. However, in the post-Gulf War environment, the question of the relationship between ODA and military expenditures in recipient countries was seriously examined.

After circulating drafts among concerned Ministries, the Prime Minister announced the "Four Guidelines" on April 10, 1991 in a speech to the Diet.

> The Government of Japan henceforward will pay full attention in the implementation of ODA to the following points: (1) trend in military expenditure by the recipient countries from the viewpoint that the developing countries are expected to allocate their own financial, human and other resources appropriate to their economic and social development and to make full use of such resources, (2) trend in development, production, etc. of mass destructive weapons by the recipient countries from the viewpoint of strengthening the efforts by the international community for prevention of proliferation of mass destructive weapons such as atomic weapons and missiles, (3) trend in the export and import of weapons by the recipient countries from the viewpoint of not promoting international conflicts, (4) efforts for promoting democratization and introduction of a market-oriented economy and situation on securing basic human rights and freedom by the recipient countries.[12]

There were new elements here and there were old elements. Within the donor community at large the relationships between ODA and military expenditures were under discussion, but Japan was taking some leadership by being this explicit. Moreover, Japan was challenging, at least indirectly, other donors (notably the Americans and French) to consider the relationships of their own military sales policies to issues of regional stability and economic and political development in Asia. The challenge in this form is new, but Japan's discomfort with the security dimensions of American and French aid was not new. Similarly, discussions on relationships between ODA and democratization were also underway within the DAC community, these in response to global forces that appeared to be set off by events in Eastern Europe.

The issuance of the four guidelines was welcomed by the Japanese press, but was soon followed by considerable speculation within some policy circles about if and how Japan would apply the military criteria to recipient countries such as China, India, and Pakistan. At the same time, while there were positive reactions within the governing Liberal Democratic Party to these attempts to reduce the susceptibility of Japan's ODA to embarrassing allegations, there were growing concerns that this was not enough to maintain domestic public confidence in Japan's ODA policy. While public opinion polls in Japan have shown consistent acceptance of ODA, support has grown since the late 1970s for keeping the program at its current levels while support has declined over time for expanding the program. In 1977, 43 percent of those surveyed thought Japan should expand its ODA while 33 percent thought the level at that time was adequate. By 1991, those favoring expansion were down to 35 percent while those supporting keeping the program at its current levels had risen to 44 percent.[13] This trend did not restrain Japan from its various ODA doubling plans since the late-1970s, but the trend is clearly a growing source of concern, particularly in a period when public confidence in the capabilities of the LDP has fallen. Undoubtedly, public confidence in the ODA program was challenged by a string of cases from revelations of corruption which accompanied Japan's support of Marcos to Japan's ODA policy appearing to be out of step with other donors and Western public opinion in places such as Burma, China, and Thailand.

There was also growing recognition that the "other wheel" for growth in the ODA budget, growth in the defense budget, was facing potential new restrictions. Public opposition to the PKO[14] bill along with a slowdown in the Japanese economy both imply that there may not be much room for growth in the military budget. However, if growth in that budget is restrained, the expectation is that growth in the ODA budget would also be restrained.

Two other developments put additional pressure on the ODA policy system. One was a Special Committee on Administrative Reform established earlier by the Prime Minister. The Committee was looking at what could be done to improve the administrative efficiency of Japan's ODA system. A second development was growing pressure from opposition parties in the Diet for an ODA law. Unlike American ODA, which operates in relation to a continually amended Foreign Assistance Act and which is subject to extensive Congressional oversight, Japan's ODA has been a Foreign Ministry budget item that was not bound by any fundamental legislation or legislative oversight. The ODA system was little interested in significant administrative reform, especially reform that might reconfigure relations among the major competing parties in the ODA policy system, or in subjugation to an ODA Law that would severely limit the discretion ODA policy-makers had to make allocation decisions.

To preempt the loss of relative political autonomy and improve public support, the ODA policy system saw the need to offer a more detailed statement of the principles and objectives of Japan's ODA. Work began in December, 1991. On June 29, 1992, the Cabinet announced Japan's ODA Charter. No element of the charter can be called new nor unique. What may be new for Japan, however, is how and when the charter may be used. Ministry of Foreign Affairs officials indicate that

Japan will use the charter as a basis for policy dialogue with recipient countries, in effect on the matters outlined in the "Four Guidelines." Countries will be told that in the past, Japan basically listened. Now, public pressure in Japan may require Japan to be more explicit in indicating its own views. As one official put it: "Japan can continue to be Santa Claus, but if the Japanese public says that we have to condition our aid to a country because of human rights violations in that country, we have a hard time to ignore this."[15]

These are potentially important steps. It is likely that there will be varied responses to these steps in Asia where perceived deviation from Japan's earlier proclamations that it would not interfere in domestic political matters of recipient countries will not be taken lightly by many countries. However, these steps should be seen more as new sources of variation than as a standardization of Japan's ODA policy. For example, the possibly growing responsiveness of Japanese ODA policy to Japanese public opinion, whatever that might actually mean, carries several risks as the ODA system attempts to sustain its domestic budget shares as well as its relative political insulation. On one side, it will invite more explicit comparison of Japan's ODA policies and performance to the criteria in the guidelines and charter. This could prove constraining. As one senior official put it: "we wanted to keep these criteria broad enough so that we don't lose flexibility." However, are the criteria so flexible that different domestic public and bureaucratic interests can (still) offer very different interpretations? On the other side, the policy dialogues that will come out of the charter will undoubtedly be long and difficult and will require greater understanding by both the ODA policy system and elements of the Japanese public of both diversity in the world and inconsistencies among Japan's foreign aid and other foreign policy objectives.

For example, as was pointed out in the chapters on Burma, China, Indonesia, Korea, the Philippines, Thailand, and Vietnam, Japan has been very cautious about publicly implying or confirming any direct linkages between its ODA and the domestic political characteristics of recipient countries. If Japan communicated views, this was done quietly and away from public view.[16] Will the issuance of the "Four Guidelines" and the ODA Charter bring this discussion more into the open? There is some evidence to examine since April, 1991. After the coup in Haiti, Japan suspended aid. In Indonesia, Peru, and Thailand, Japan expressed concerns about political developments and human rights abuses through diplomatic channels but did not suspend aid. In Mongolia and Cambodia, Japan has offered aid publicly in support of building democratic political institutions. What is old and what is new in the Guidelines? What may be new is an *explicit* set of criteria that are publicly stated and which may form an additional basis for evaluating ODA performance and for asserting initiative within the donor community.

The Burden That Binds

ODA is a post World War II invention. It was borne from a marriage of foreign policies based on anti-communism with acknowledged needs for supporting economic reconstruction. Initially focused on western Europe and carried out almost exclusively by the United States, ODA became an accepted policy tool for international relationships between developed countries and less developed countries. As such, it was ultimately employed by bilateral and multilateral donors of various ideological persuasions to cultivate their international support and constituencies, protect their friends and make life not easier for their enemies, and address a range of other security, developmental, and humanitarian needs. Asia was a principal beneficiary of ODA once ODA moved beyond Europe and within Asia, Japan (along with India at that time) was a prime beneficiary of ODA through the 1960s.

The impulses that yielded Japan's ODA were not dissimilar from those which characterized American and European aid. However, unlike any other donor, Japan's ODA was not born principally from a desire, however tacit, to maintain colonial links (as was arguably the case with French aid), nor to build, in effect, neo-colonial networks (as was the case with Soviet aid in Eastern Europe). Japan's ODA is the product of a recognition that Japan's own development depended on peaceful international economic relations, especially in Asia, and an acknowledgement that damages Japan had caused during the war required reparations.

Distinguishing Japan's ODA from colonial and neo-colonial intentions has not been the conventional wisdom about Japan's ODA, especially for Asia, where many continue to view it as a tool of economic hegemony. There is no disputing the relationship between Japan's ODA and Japan's economic interests. However, to conclude that the significance of Japan's ODA amounts to only that is to miss the deeper significance and distinctiveness of Japan's ODA. For example, one of the most interesting themes that emerges from the studies presented here is the evolution of Japan's concept of comprehensive security and the relationships of ODA policy to that process.

Japan's concept of comprehensive security goes beyond the military sense of security with which, by contrast, American foreign aid historically has been closely associated. It also goes beyond the narrow interpretation of economic security usually attributed to Japan's ODA, i.e., as an instrument for the interests of Japan's trading companies and construction firms. Today, Japan's understanding of comprehensive security extends to a recognition that national economic development in poorer and middle-income countries and international political stability are cornerstones of international trade, access to resources, and ultimately Japan's own well-being. Japan's search for comprehensive security as an active participant in the international economy, historically the underlying theme in Japan's relationship with the United States, increasingly has become the underlying motif for Japan's understanding of how ODA should be used as a foreign policy tool.

Some would say, and with justification, that Japan has not successfully translated this agenda into international political leadership in development assistance. The end of the Cold War, the Persian Gulf War, and the rise of economic regionalism in Europe and North America have all presented severe challenges to Japan's understanding of how to promote her comprehensive security. Japan has found it difficult to adapt rapidly to these changes in the international environment. Even in the promising instance of the new ODA charter and guidelines, it remains to be seen whether these criteria will be applied where the issues involved significantly test Japan's commitment to the guidelines (e.g. China) or where the feasibility of application is the primary attraction (e.g. Haiti).

However, whatever doubts there may be about where Japan's ODA policy is going, it is important to recognize what Japan's ODA experience has achieved. What ODA has done, first and foremost in Asia, but in recent years in the Pacific, the Middle East, Africa, and Latin America, is that it has further bound Japan to a non-military role in the international system. One could argue that Japan's trading and investment requirements would do that without ODA, and that would not be inaccurate. The ODA amounts have become small by comparison. Nevertheless, ODA—as compared to essentially private trade and investment transactions—has been the prime vehicle through which Japanese foreign policy has learned how to develop bilateral and regional relations beyond the simple promotion or defense of trade and investment interests.

Economic isolationism is not a realistic danger in contemporary Japan, at least not in the sense that American political rhetoric sometimes suggests it may be in the United States. Japan knows that its economic success and security during the past four decades and its growth and security in the future depend on continued successful participation in the international system. As the world around her has changed, however, Japan is now challenged to articulate a vision of her international role—not simply as an accumulation of economic transactions—but something more. As Japan and the international community seek to discover what that role is, it is clear that ODA has been an important thread from which the cloth of international relations for Japan has been sewn. It is likely to remain an important thread in the future.

ODA has been both an economic and political burden and in the future, it is likely to be even more of a burden. However, in ways that were anticipated (economic) and in ways that were not (cultural and political), ODA has been a burden that binds Japan not only or simply to the international system as an extension of Japan's economic system, nor as a political or economic abstraction, but to the international system as a collection of diverse interests and relationships which need constant balancing and diverse responses. Given the dramatic changes in the international political economy during the last few years, the challenges of diversity are and will continue to expand almost geometrically. In this context, the real significance of the ODA Charter and Japan's intentions to use it as a basis for policy dialogue is less the specific objectives it includes and more the recognition it represents. In the new international environment, the balancing of diverse interests will be more difficult but also will be a considerably more crucial aspect of a central long-term Japanese ODA objective, especially in Asia: the promotion of stability.

In the 1990s, the question for Japan's ODA policy—as for the ODA policies of other donors—will be whether ODA policies relate effectively to the new challenges the world presents. Indeed, for some donors, the end of the cold war has severely undermined their principal political rationale for maintaining large foreign aid programs and has exacerbated what many see as a fragementation of leadership in the foreign assistance community.[17] Depending on if Japan's ODA policies are in the vanguard of new international responses and initiatives to address North-South relations and international development, we will know whether the power and policy in Japan's foreign aid will remain hollow, as many critics now suggest, mercantile as some continue to worry, or globally responsible as others now hope. According to the evidence offered in the chapters here, the seeds are there for all three outcomes.

Endnotes

1. To say Japan largely accepted this is not to suggest there was wide consensus in Japan in support. U.S.-Japan security arrangements, in

particular, were the objects of significant criticism and a source of serious instability in the Japanese political system.

2. Ministry of Foreign Affairs. *Japan's ODA 1991* (White Paper on ODA). English summary. (Tokyo: Ministry of Foreign Affairs, 1992), pp. R48376-02, R48377-01/02.

3. "The Japanese business community, which attaches importance to human resources as well as natural resources such as coal and petroleum in Vietnam, has been calling for resumption of the aid program." *Asahi Evening News*, January 6, 1991, p. 2.

4. See The Overseas Economic Cooperation Fund, *Issues Related to the World Bank's Approach to Structural Adjustment—Proposal from a Major Partner*, OECF Occasional Paper No. 1, Tokyo: October, 1991, pp. 5-6.

5. Robert Orr, Jr., *The Emergence of Japan's Foreign Aid Power* (New York: Columbia University Press, 1991).

6. For example, the United States and Japan have held a series of aid policy consultations at the East West Center in Honolulu since 1988. In the first of these meetings, there was an attempt to find joint projects, an attempt that came principally from the United States, but to which Japan attempted to be responsive. By the fourth meeting in January, 1992 discussions were on perspectives on major problems (environment, working with NGOs, ODA and structural adjustment) and the opportunities these presented for sharing experience and in some circumstances (e.g. Cambodia) perhaps coordinating broad strategies.

7. In 1991, Japan's ODA/GNP ratio was 0.32. This ranked number 12 out of the 20 DAC donors. For comparison, the overall DAC average was 0.34. The United States ratio was 0.17, which placed it last among DAC donors.

8. For example: "Japan must make its own decisions dictated only by its long-term national interests. Japan should not give the impression that it decides only under strong U.S. pressure." Hiroyuki Kishino, *Creating a Japan-U.S. Global Partnership: Japan's Role in a Changing World*, International Institute for Global Peace (IIGP) Policy Paper 68E (Tokyo: IIGP, September 1991), p. 9.

9. See, for example, Shinsuke Horiuchi, *Points on Discussion on ODA for the Honolulu Conference*, paper prepared for Honolulu IV: ODA Management and Asia's Economic Development, Honolulu, Hawaii, East-West Center, January 14, 1992.

10. This description is based on interviews conducted by the authors with senior government officials, academics, and press people in July, 1992.

11. The so-called PKO debate continued for over a year before leading to a successful bill.

12. "On Japan's ODA in Relation to Military Expenditure and Other Matters of the Developing Countries." Unofficial Translation of the text of a speech given by Prime Minister Kaifu to the Japanese Diet on April 10, 1991.

13. Ken'ichi Imai, Yumiko Okamoto, Kazuhiko Yokota, and Akira Hirata, "Evolution of Japan's ODA," in Ippei Yamazawa and Akira Hirata, ed., *Development Cooperation Policies of Japan, United States, and Europe* (Tokyo: Institute of Developing Economies, 1992), pp. 47-48.

14. The PKO bill authorizes Japanese participation in United Nations peacekeeping operations.

15. In some quarters, the Charter is also seen as an attempt by Japan to exercise leadership among donors in relating ODA to strategies for strengthening regional and global political security.

16. See "Japan Pursues Own Diplomacy on International Human Rights," *The Nikkei Weekly* (August 1, 1992), pp. 1-2.

17. "The lack of leadership brings confusion and misunderstanding. As a result, passing development fads run rampant, undermining the effectiveness of all aid flows." John W. Mellor and William A. Masters, "The Changing Roles of Multilateral and Bilateral Foreign Assistance," in Uma Lele and Ijaz Nabi, eds., *Transitions in Development: The Role of Aid and Commercial Flows* (San Francisco: International Center for Economic Growth, 1991), p. 362.

About the Contributors

Stephen J. Anderson is a visiting researcher at Yokohama National University and on leave from the Political Science department at the University of Wisconsin-Madison. His work ranges across areas of comparative politics, political economy, and international relations. Anderson's on-going research focuses on activism in Japanese foreign policy in the Pacific Basin.

Prasert Chittiwatanapong is Associate Professor of Political Science at Thammasat University in Bangkok where he teaches Japanese politics and Japanese foreign policy. He has had visiting positions at the University of Washington, Seattle, the National Institute for Research Advancement, Tokyo, and Harvard University. He has published widely about Japanese domestic politics and Japan's relations with Southeast Asia.

Juichi Inada is Associate Professor of International Relations at Yamanashi University and a visiting fellow at the Japan Institute of International Affairs (JIIA). In 1992-93, he was a Research Associate at the Center for International Affairs of Harvard University. He has written extensively on Indochina issues.

Ichiro Inukai is Professor of Economics at the International University of Japan where he has specialized in research and teaching on economic development issues in Africa and Japan's economic cooperation with that region.

Hosup Kim is Assistant Professor of International Relations at Chung-Ang University of Korea. He has been a fellow at the Sejong Institute in Seoul and visiting researcher at Keio University. He holds a Ph.D. from the University of Michigan. He is co-author of two books in Japanese and more than twenty articles on the Japanese-Korean relationship in Korean. His current research interests are on changes in Japanese foreign policy after the cold war.

Jeff Kingston is Assistant Professor of History at the Institute of Pacific Rim studies, Temple University, Japan. For two years he worked as a research associate at the Institute of Development Studies, Yokohama National University and as a Fellow of the Japanese Society for the Promotion of Science.

Bruce M. Koppel is Vice President for Research and Education at the East-West Center in Honolulu, Hawaii and a member of the graduate faculty in sociology at the University of Hawaii. He has twice been a visiting professor at the University of the Philippines and has consulted widely for major aid donors. He is the author of numerous articles and monographs and the editor of several books on a range of development issues in the Asia-Pacific region.

Robert M. Orr, Jr., is Associate Professor of Political Science and Director of the Institute for Pacific Rim Studies at Temple University's Japan campus. He was previously Director of the Stanford Center for Japan Studies in Kyoto and has also worked for the United States Agency for International Development and as a legislative assistant in both the U.S. Congress and the Japanese Diet. He is author of *The Emergence of Japan's Foreign Aid Power* (New York: Columbia University Press, 1990), and a number of articles on Japanese domestic and international politics.

Alan Rix is Professor of Japanese Studies at the University of Queensland in Brisbane, Australia. He has been involved in the study of Japan's foreign aid program since 1975 and published the first comprehensive study of Japan's aid policy system in 1980 (*Japan's Economic Aid*, Croom Helm). He has worked as a consultant to the Australian International Development Assistance Bureau and publishes widely on Japanese foreign aid and foreign policy. His latest book is *Japan's Foreign Aid Challenge: Policy Reform and Aid Leadership*, to be published by Routledge in early 1993.

David I. Steinberg is Distinguished Professor of Korea Studies at Georgetown University. Previously he was President of the Mansfield Center for Pacific Affairs, in the Senior Foreign Service in the Agency for International Development, and a Representative of the Asia Foundation in Burma, Hong Kong, Korea, and Washington, D.C. He is the author of some forty articles and ten books and monographs, including four on Burma, the latest being *The Future of Burma: Crisis and Choice in Myanmar* (University Press of America and The Asia Society, 1990).

Akira Takahashi is Executive Director for Research at the Institute of Developing Economies in Tokyo and was previously Professor of economics at Tokyo University. He has extensive research experience in Southeast Asia, and especially in the Philippines. He has written widely on development issues in Southeast Asia and on Japan's relations with the region.

Isami Takeda is Associate Professor of International Relations at Dokkyo University in Japan and Research Associate of the Center for Asian and Pacific Studies. He is specializing on migration and refugee problems, foreign aid, and regional cooperation. His recent publications include *The Politics of Migration, Refugees, and Foreign Aid* (Tokyo)

Toru Yanagihara is Professor of Economics at Hosei University in Tokyo. He was formerly an economist at the Institute of Developing Economies. He was also a visiting scholar at University of California at Berkeley, Columbia University, and Hitotsubashi University. His research interests include open macroeconomics, debt problems, conceptual and empirical examination of structural adjustment, comparison of development policies and experiences (mostly in Asia and Latin America), and aid policy.

Dennis T. Yasutomo is Associate Professor of Government and Director of the East Asian Studies Program at Smith College. He is the author of *Japan and The Asian Development Bank* (Praeger, 1983) and *The Manner of Giving: Strategic Aid and Japanese Foreign Policy* (Lexington, 1986). Dr. Yasutomo spent the 1992-93 academic year in Tokyo as a Fulbright Scholar researching Japan's multilateral diplomacy.

Quangsheng Zhao is Chairman of the Asian Studies Committee and Interim Director of the Institute of Asian Studies at Old Dominion University, Norfolk, Virginia. He has taught or conducted research at the United States Institute of Peace, the East-West Center, Cleveland State University, University of California at Berkeley, the University of Tokyo, and Oxford University.

Index